CAPTIVATED

Piers Dudgeon knew Daphne Du Maurier and worked with her in the 1980s. When he discovered that she had put a moratorium on publication of her adolescent diaries until fifty years after her death, he was promoted to begin his researches into her background. What was the mystery that Daphne had been so keen to suppress?

He is the author of many works of non-fiction. He worked for ten years as an editor in London before starting his own company producing books with authors as diverse as John Fowles, Catherine Cookson, Peter Ackroyd, Daphne du Maurier, Shirley Conran and Ted Hughes. Subsequently, he left London for Yorkshire where he wrote a number of biographies as well as illustrated books evocative of the spirit of the place.

'Piers Dudgeon's book thrillingly investigates the cruelty and madness lurking within *Peter Pan* – and the fabrications of Hollywood's *Finding Neverland* are neatly overturned'

Daily Express

'A rattling grisly read . . . "May God blast anyone who writes a biography of me," Barrie warned and his curse was surely aimed at Dudgeon, who goes further than any other biographer . . . I defy you not to be captivated'

Frances Wilson, *Sunday Times*

'Dudgeon's portrait of Barrie – as a man who filled the vacuum of his own sexual impotence by a compulsive desire to possess the family who inspired his most famous creation, *Peter Pan* . . . will be of interest to anyone, like me, who has followed the twists of the du Maurier family history'

Justine Picardie, *Sunday Telegraph*

'Piers Dudgeon, who worked with Daphne du Maurier in the 1980s, and who has worked with such other deeply autobiographical authors as John Fowles, Ted Hughes and Catherine Cookson, has negotiated the dark back-tracks and by-ways of Barrie's chilling Neverland. Daphne du Maurier is the impressive survivor . . . He tells a terrible story without sentimentality, without sensationalism and without undue psychologising . . . What remains here would leave a bad taste in the mouth if it were not so intelligently and feelingly done'

Brian Morton, *Sunday Herald*

'*Captivated* is a riveting joy: I was literally captivated by it. Poor scintillating du Mauriers. Poor boys . . . I felt as if I was living it'

Nina Auerbach, Professor of English at Pennsylvania University and author of *Daphne du Maurier: Haunted Heiress*

'Meticulous and highly provocative . . . Dudgeon knows what he's doing and builds his case with precision and coolness . . . It was when both Daphne du Maurier and her cousin Peter Llewellyn Davies finally understood what good old Uncle Jim had been doing to them all these years, that she had her nervous breakdown and he killed himself . . . It's a gripping read that exposes the dark side to two seemingly innocent activities, writing and loving children . . . Dudgeon has exposed, in quite a magnificent way, the power and potential for abuse in both'

Scotsman

PIERS DUDGEON

Captivated

J.M. Barrie, Daphne Du Maurier and the Dark Side of Neverland

VINTAGE BOOKS
London

Published by Vintage 2009

2 4 6 8 10 9 7 5 3 1

First published in Great Britain in 2008 by Chatto & Windus

Vintage
Random House, 20 Vauxhall Bridge Road,
London SW1V 2SA

www.vintage-books.co.uk

Addresses for companies within The Random House Group Limited can be found at: www.randomhouse.co.uk/offices.htm

The Random House Group Limited Reg. No. 954009

A CIP catalogue record for this book is available from the British Library

ISBN 9780099520450

The Random House Group Limited supports The Forest Stewardship Council (FSC), the leading international forest certification organisation. All our titles that are printed on Greenpeace approved FSC certified paper carry the FSC logo. Our paper procurement policy can be found at www.rbooks.co.uk/environment

Printed in the UK by CPI Bookmarque, Croydon, CR0 4TD

Contents

Part IV: 1894–1910
Sylvia, the Lost Boys and Uncle Jim: the *Peter Pan* Inheritance

Part V: 1910–1921
Michael, Daphne and Uncle Jim: 'An Awfully Big Adventure'

Part VI: 1921–1989
Uncle Jim and Daphne: the *Rebecca* Inheritance

List of Illustrations

Second section of plates

Third section of plates

FAMILY TREE

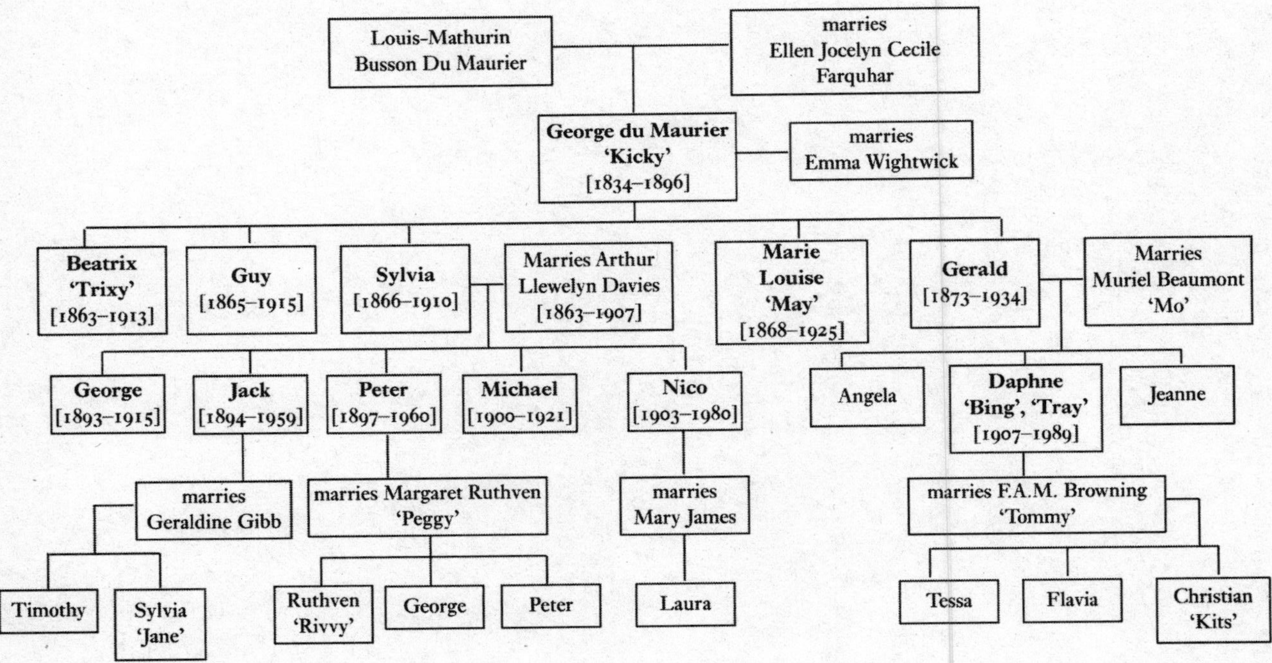

Louis-Mathurin Busson Du Maurier
marries Ellen Jocelyn Cecile Farquhar
George du Maurier 'Kicky' [1834–1896]
marries Emma Wightwick
Beatrix 'Trixy' [1863–1913]
Guy [1865–1915]
Sylvia [1866–1910]
Marries Arthur Llewelyn Davies [1863–1907]
Marie Louise 'May' [1868–1925]
Gerald [1873–1934]
Marries Muriel Beaumont 'Mo'
George [1893–1915]
Jack [1894–1959]
Peter [1897–1960]
Michael [1900–1921]
Nico [1903–1980]
Angela
Daphne 'Bing', 'Tray' [1907–1989]
Jeanne
marries Geraldine Gibb
marries Margaret Ruthven 'Peggy'
marries Mary James
marries F.A.M. Browning 'Tommy'
Timothy
Sylvia 'Jane'
Ruthven 'Rivvy'
George
Peter
Laura
Tessa
Flavia
Christian 'Kits'

Author's Note

I met Daphne du Maurier in 1987, two years before she died. We met at Kilmarth, the dower house on the Menabilly Estate, to discuss a book called *Enchanted Cornwall*, which I was to edit and co-publish, and which first led me to a close scrutiny of her autobiographical writings, her Cornish novels, and the places that had inspired them.

In 1915, D. H. Lawrence had been so inspired by Cornwall that he wrote: 'It seems as if the truth were still living here, growing like the sea holly, and love like Tristan, and old reality like King Arthur . . .' The effect of Cornwall on Daphne was similar. In her novel *Castle Dor* the Tristan myth erupts from the Cornish furze into the present day, and her communication with the spirit of place in other books is such that by the end of my research into *Enchanted Cornwall* I felt I really understood something about Daphne's imagination and empathised with it, a feeling many get from reading her novels.

Even then, however, there were intimations that her acute sense of place was not the whole story. In press clippings and documentaries she spoke of a life of pretence, of immersing herself in the make-believe of taking on the role of an imagined other.

Twenty years later I was the guest of Daphne's son, Christian Browning, this time at Ferryside, where Daphne wrote her first novel. During our conversation he let slip that before her death his mother had placed a fifty-year moratorium on publication of her adolescent diaries, which I knew to have been described by a friend of hers as 'dangerous, indiscreet and stupid'.

What, I wondered as I made my way home to Yorkshire, had Daphne been so desperate to keep under wraps until 2039?

After Daphne's death, letters which suggested she had had lesbian affairs were released. Other letters interested me more, in particular one that she wrote to Maureen Baker-Munton on 4 July, 1957, in which she revealed that she drew on real people and relationships in her novels and short stories. I was also struck by letters written to Oriel Malet over three decades, in which Daphne said she drew on fantasy persona and applied them to her own life.

In 1964 she wrote: 'When I was younger I always had to have some sort of Peg to hang things on, whether it was a character in a book developing from a real person, or a real person being pegged from a character (very muddling!).'

She claimed to have lived like that 'for most of my life'. She habitually pretended to be another person, an alter ego. Equally, she invested others with imaginary qualities irrespective of whether they actually had them. Sometimes it worked because people do often become what you want them to be; at other times, the fantasy could 'explode like bubbles and vanish, or else turn catastrophic'.

Her supposedly lesbian relationship with Gertrude Lawrence, which Daphne described as purely imaginary, was a case in point. When Gertie died she didn't miss the woman at all. She had never known her, she said, except 'in character'. The qualities that Daphne had found in Gertie were an expression of her own needs and desires, and had not truly, in an objective sense, existed. Living like this reduced love to an illusion, as Daphne realised, but she revelled in the insight, not seeing it as the sad result of her way of life.

Living like this had empowered her since her teenage years. And in 1937, at thirty, she looked into the mirror of imagination and discovered Rebecca, a whole person with no insufficiency, someone whom she had always wanted to be. 'No one got the better of Rebecca. She did what she liked, she lived as she liked.'

As she admitted to Oriel, Daphne *became* her most famous creation.

The psychoanalyst Jacques Lacan wrote that this is how we all behave. We catch sight of ourselves in the mirror and mistake an image of the whole person, in psychoanalytical terms the ideal ego, for our true self.

Whether or not this is so, Daphne did it and made a terrible mess of her personal life, but wrote some of her best novels out of the mess she created. She could never write anything unless there was a personal emotional trigger, and her adopted persona ensured that there was emotional devastation everywhere.

Eventually her fantasy life led to a nervous breakdown in 1957. Things had been under pressure since the 1940s, when she began pegging fictional characters on real people and seeking to write them out of her life by killing them off in a story.

Oriel Malet was deeply concerned. It was clear that Daphne was a victim of her imagination, but Oriel suspected more. She became convinced that something had occurred in Daphne's childhood to seal her in to this way of thinking, to cut her off from reality and to give her this dark fantastic view of life. She begged Daphne to share it with her, but Daphne refused.

Towards the end, Oriel watched with dismay as her friend's health deteriorated. She became convinced that suppression of this 'something', which had to do with Daphne's imaginative life, lay behind the mental and emotional agonies she suffered, which included a suicide attempt.

I began to look into Daphne's childhood, and came at once to J. M. Barrie, or Uncle Jim as she called him. I learned that he was part of the family even before she was born; that her father Gerald found fame in eight of Barrie's plays; that in the first play in which Barrie cast Gerald he placed him opposite Daphne's future mother in an amorous situation on stage that resulted in their marriage; that from as early as Daphne could remember he was in the habit of playing with her and her two sisters; and that he was so interested in Daphne, in particular in the special relationship that developed between her and her father, that when she was ten he wrote a play about it, which troubled her deeply, even into old age.

The more I looked, the more I saw Barrie at the very centre of Daphne's inner life. 'I grew up not wanting to be on the stage but always imagining myself to be someone else, which again links with this world of imagination which I think was Barrie's,' Daphne said in her sixties, alerting me also to a curious opaqueness of memory that I would come to recognise as endemic to Barrie's influence over children.

At fourteen she wrote her first full-length story, 'The Seekers', which revealed his method of captivating a child by telling him a story in which both he and the child figured, so consuming the child's interest with a narrative full of menace that man and child were soon alone together in a place far from the real world.

Uncle Jim must have been a part of her diaries because he was so much a part of her imagination. She wrote that the first entries showed 'no budding woman ripe for sex instruction, but someone who perhaps had been left behind on the Never Never Island in *Peter Pan*'.

Always Barrie's influence turned on the trick of reaching Neverland, 'that silent shadow-land that marches a hand's breadth from our own,' as Daphne described it. In her thirties she wrote to a friend that Barrie had told her how to get there on her own, by concentrating her mind in a particular way.

I was amazed that I had hitherto failed to pick up the many references to Barrie in Daphne's work. When I began to read Barrie's books after reading Daphne's letters, I was struck by the fact that he too had used real people, including himself, as models for his fictional characters, and that 'Tommy', who was Barrie's alter ego in his two most important novels, *Sentimental Tommy* and *Tommy and Grizel,* was the original 'voice piece' of her view that all emotion is illusory. Here was Daphne's notion that people are pegs on which we hang our emotions, that we all live a life of fantasy anyway, that our feelings for others are anything but true. I also found in Barrie the genesis of her notion about the power of texts: that a person's life can be transmuted in fiction, that the author's dream may intrude on reality, 'as a wheel may revolve for a moment after the spring breaks.'

As I was working on this, the film *Finding Neverland* was first showing in cinemas. It was loosely based on Barrie's captivation of the five Llewelyn Davies boys, the 'lost boys' of *Peter Pan*, who now took on special significance as Daphne's first cousins. I knew, of course, about the games of pirates and redskins that Uncle Jim played with them; recalled on stage in the Neverland of *Peter Pan.* But I was interested to know more about their relationship to Barrie and to Daphne, and in particular I wondered what had happened to *them* when they grew up.

Piers Dudgeon,
Yorkshire,
May 2008

'Now we are again at our wits' end, where you mortals lightly slip over into madness. Why dost thou seek community with us if thou canst not carry it through?'

Mephistopheles in *Faust* by Goethe

PART I

1945–1960

The Lost Boys and Daphne

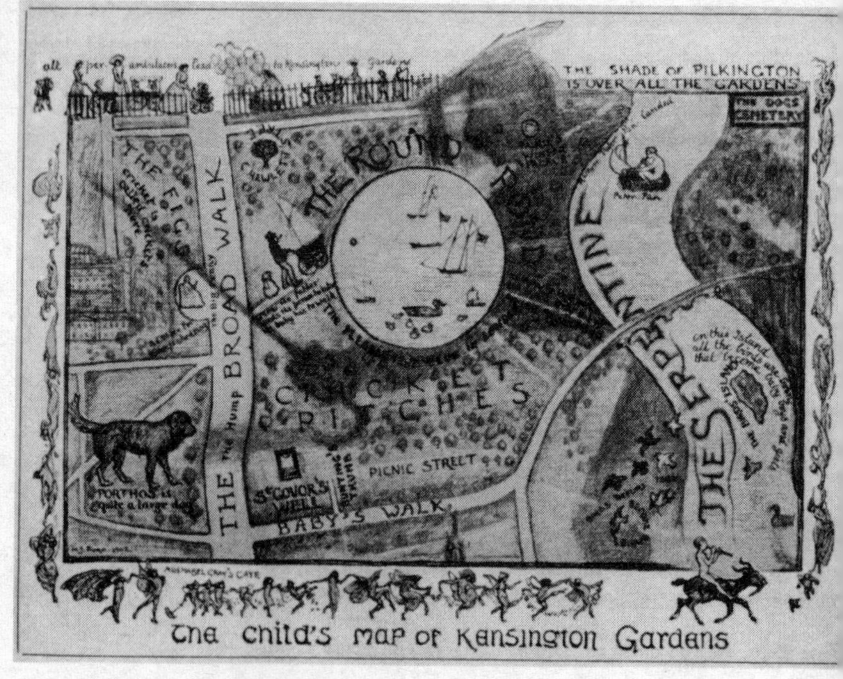

'The child's map of Kensington Gardens'

CHAPTER ONE

Peter's suicide: a case to answer

London, 1960. Tuesday, 5 April: 9 a.m. *In the restaurant of the Royal Court Hotel, Sloane Square, a melancholy man in his early sixties takes breakfast alone. Some time later he walks out of the hotel, telling no one where he is going. He is not seen again until a little before 5 p.m., when he crosses the square and enters the Underground station. He buys a ticket, moves past the little sentry box with its attendant, and turns sharp right down the steps to the platform, where, absorbed in his thoughts, he trudges up and down, up and down, staring at the ground, as if not part of this world. A train arrives, leaves, then another, but the man gives no sign that he is either about to depart or is expecting to meet someone. Then comes the rattle in the darkness and the echo of sound in the tunnel of the train he chooses. Suddenly, and with immaculate timing, he points his body towards it and hurls himself forward, just as it emerges into the light.*

The death of Peter Llewelyn Davies, 63-year-old chairman of respected book publisher Peter Davies Ltd, provoked wide press coverage and speculation, perhaps because some reporters remembered that he had been one of the 'lost boys' of *Peter Pan*, and noted that the tragedy more or less coincided with the centenary of the birth of J. M. Barrie.

There was no question that the death was suicide. An inquest opened on Friday, 8 April 1960, and concluded the following Tuesday that Peter Llewelyn Davies had taken his own life while the balance of his mind was disturbed. Cause of death was certified on Wednesday the 13th as 'multiple injuries (legs and skull). Threw himself in front of an Underground train. Killed himself.'

Peter's brother Nicholas (known as Nico) accepted the inquest's verdict: 'Peter's death – I shan't forget while I have any faculties left – it was indeed suicide,' he wrote to Andrew Birkin.* 'After hours, days? of walking up and down the platform of Sloane Square Underground station he jumped in front of the train. Terrible for the driver – terrible from most points of view.'

Geraldine (Gerrie), Peter's sister-in-law, commented: 'Peter went out after breakfast, and as far as I know, nobody knew what he did all day until five in the evening, when he jumped in front of this train. So where he spent the whole day, God alone knows . . . They'd moved out of the flat they were in then. They had stored their furniture and they had gone to the Royal Court Hotel and Peter was ill and P wasn't the right kind of wife, she couldn't cope . . . hopeless . . . He realised he was going to get worse and apparently he thought of sleeping pills and then he thought of how dreadful it would be if they pulled him round. That was apparently his reasoning, I have been told. What it really was I don't know, but I can't think of a more grim way.'[1]

'P' was Peter's wife Peggy, the Hon. Margaret Leslie Hore-Ruthven, one of four daughters of the 9th Baron Ruthven (pronounced 'Riven'). She and her twin sister Alison often dressed alike and came to be known in London society as 'A and P'. Peggy and Peter had been living on the opposite side of Sloane Square to the Underground station, at 20 Cadogan Court, before packing up their furniture and moving to the Royal Court Hotel, *en route* to Gibraltar and retirement.

Peter's childhood has been so sentimentalised as to turn it into a myth almost as famous as that of Peter Pan.

The story goes that in 1892 beautiful and enigmatic Sylvia du Maurier, the daughter of famous *Punch* magazine illustrator and bestselling author George du Maurier, married handsome young barrister Arthur Llewelyn Davies, son of a chaplain to Queen Victoria. She was 26, he 29. They settled at number 18 Craven Terrace, Lancaster Gate, on the north side of Kensington Gardens, and between 1893 and 1903 produced five sons: George, Jack, Peter, Michael and Nico.

In 1897, the year Peter was born, he was out in his pram in Kensington Gardens with his nanny, Mary Hodgson, and his elder brothers George (4) and Jack (3), when they met toast-of-the-town playwright and novelist J. M. Barrie, with his St Bernard dog.

* Andrew Birkin, writer and film-maker, carried out extensive interviews with surviving members of the family. He wrote the script for *The Lost Boys* (BBC TV, 1978) and published a book with the same title in 1979.

Mr Barrie, who lived with his pretty actress wife Mary Ansell on the south side of the Gardens, at 133 Gloucester Road, was well known in the park for his antics with this dog. Once let off its leash, the huge animal would be up on its hind legs wrestling his master. Barrie stood five feet three and a half inches (the half was terribly important to him), but seemed to grow strong in the unlikely contest, which children loved to watch. When the show came to an end he would start talking to his young audience, take one or two of them aside and captivate them with stories of fairies and make-believe woods, or do sleight-of-hand magic tricks, or pretend to hypnotise them with his eyebrows, for he had an unusual ability to elevate and lower his eyebrows separately, while gazing intently with his large, morose, staring eyes, set in a peculiarly large head, out of scale with his boyish body.

A child, who knew him then, said:

> He was a tiny man, he had a pale face and large eyes and shadows round them . . . He looked fragile, but he was strong when he wrestled with Porthos, his St Bernard dog. Mr Barrie talked a great deal about cricket, but the next moment he was telling us about fairies, as though he knew all about them. He was made of silences, but we did not find these strange, they were so much part of him . . . his silences spoke loudly.[2]

For the three Davies boys, meeting Barrie in the park became a regular event, the cheeky but imaginative George building a particular rapport with him. In Barrie's company the Gardens took on their own geography and mythology: the Figs, the Broad Walk, the Hump, the Baby Walk, St Govor's Well, the cricket pitches, the Round Pond and Serpentine were all discovered, explored, mapped, and made their secret domain, each district 'freighted' with its own stories to be recalled in bed at night, and later to be made part of a book called *The Little White Bird*,* in which Peter Pan made his first appearance. Peter Pan was supposed to have flown out of the window of his nursery to join the fairies and birds in Kensington Gardens and live with old Solomon Caw on Birds' Island on the Serpentine, a lake well known to the boys, but never the same again after Mr Barrie spoke of it:

> The Serpentine . . . is a lovely lake, and there is a drowned forest at the

* Barrie's first 'collaboration' with the boys, published in 1902.

> bottom of it. If you peer over the edge you can see the trees all growing upside down, and they say at night there are also drowned stars in it. If so, Peter Pan sees them when he is sailing across the lake in the Thrush's Nest. A small part only of the Serpentine is in the Gardens, for soon it passes beneath a bridge too far away where the island is on which all the birds are born that become baby boys and girls. No one who is human, except Peter Pan (and he is only half human) can land on the island, but you may write what you want (boy or girl, dark or fair) on a piece of paper, and then twist it into the shape of a boat and slip it into the water, and it reaches Peter Pan's island after dark.

On New Year's Eve, the last day of 1897, J. M. Barrie met the parents of the three boys at a dinner party given by society hosts Sir George and Lady Lewis, after which Sylvia and Arthur Llewelyn Davies began to see a great deal of James and Mary Barrie.

Barrie and his wife would walk the boys home from the park almost every day, Mary befriending Sylvia while Barrie continued his fun and games with the boys upstairs in the nursery. So close did the two families become that in 1899 Barrie and his wife thought nothing of showing up uninvited when the boys were on holiday with their parents in Rustington-on-Sea, which had been the Davieses' south coast holiday retreat for some five years. The boys had been thrilled to see Mr Barrie, as they called him then – it was some time before they called him 'Uncle Jim' (George would do it first). Barrie turned out to be quite the little photographer, taking pictures which had a dreamy fairy-like quality about them.

Then, in 1900, the Barries bought Black Lake Cottage, a simple house in a pretty garden across the road from a lake set in a pine forest in the shadow of the twelfth-century ruins of Waverley Abbey, at Tilford in Surrey. For the next three summers the Llewelyn Davies family joined them there.

The boys were off with Barrie every day. In the magical company of their friend, the black lake that gave the cottage its name became a South Seas lagoon, the pine wood a tropical forest where all kinds of danger lurked. With complete abandon Mr Barrie presided over games of derring-do and redskins and desert islands, heroic adventures in which he played the pirate Captain Swarthy and the boys survived his attentions and once even strung Swarthy up, while the St Bernard, Porthos, played the pirate's dog or a tiger in a papier-mâché mask.

Nothing could have been more fun or more natural. 'That strange and terrible summer', Barrie took scores of photographs, thirty-five of which were turned into a book, professionally bound. Two copies were made and entitled *The Boy Castaways of Black Lake Island, Being a record of the terrible adventures of the brothers Davies in the summer of 1901*. Peter, though only four, was named on the front cover as its author.

Many of the scenes enacted over the years at Black Lake Cottage were incorporated into *Peter Pan*, which was first staged in 1904. 'The play of Peter,' wrote Barrie in the Dedication to the first published edition, 'is streaky with you still, though none may see this save ourselves . . . As for myself, I suppose I always knew that I made Peter Pan by rubbing the five of you violently together, as savages with two sticks produce a flame.'

But in 1906, tragedy struck. The boys' father, Arthur, contracted cancer of the face and the following year, aged 44, he died a horrible death.

Barrie, by then a very rich man – within two years *Peter Pan* had grossed over half a million pounds, a fabulous amount in those days – offered to help Sylvia and the boys, and they were housed at 23 Campden Hill Square, with Barrie a frequent visitor.

Then, in 1910, tragedy struck again. Sylvia died, also from cancer, again aged only 44. And Barrie made the boys his own.

But the deaths continued. In 1915, the eldest brother, George, was killed in the First World War in France, and in 1921 Michael drowned – many believed in a suicide pact with another boy. Almost forty years later, Peter committed suicide. Jack endured depression and ill health and died shortly before Peter. By 1960 Nico, the youngest, was the only surviving brother.

When Nico first heard of Peter's death, he felt comforted that at long last Peter's 'cares were over', for he had been in a terrible state for some time. Nico wrote to Nanny Hodgson the very next day, on 6 April: 'His health – mental even more than physical I would say – had deteriorated so that he was a real melancholic: he would have lived with hardly a smile.' He suggested that 'the 1914 War ditched Peter, really.' Peter had joined up at 17 in 1914, poised between Eton and Cambridge. Barrie's official biographer, Denis Mackail,[3] wrote that on Peter's demobilisation in February 1919, 'what was left of him was for a long time little more than a ghost'.

But even in letters to Barrie from the Front, Peter comes across as unemotional, stable, composed, intelligent. According to Nico he was the 'least athletic' of the brothers, and in Nanny's eyes, 'the delicate one', but he was bright, the only scholar among the Davies boys. He emerged from the war a gentleman, reserved certainly but standing tall, with an independent streak and a very attractive self-possession, something of a loner, but quite the urbane Londoner, with plenty of friends; and, as Nico conceded, he was 'a superbly witty and funny talker – few days now go by without either Mary [Nico's wife] or I remembering some wonderfully funny remark of Peter's.'

In 1917, while back in England on leave, Peter had fallen in love with a woman much older than himself, Vera Willoughby. After the war he and Vera lived together, a unit independent of Barrie, who disapproved. Defying Uncle Jim was not the action of a man unable to cope with his own life.

Six years later, the affair over, Peter was tempted back into the fold by a plan to set him up as a publisher. Barrie organised and paid for Peter's training, first with Walter Blaikie in Edinburgh and then in London with his publisher, Hodder and Stoughton, before setting him up with an imprint of his own, Peter Davies Ltd.

Thereafter, over a period of three decades, largely through his own personality and acumen, as well as the efforts of employees including Nico, who worked for the firm as an editor, Peter made it a success, respected throughout the industry. In fact, Peter Davies Ltd still existed in the 1970s as part of Sir Sidney Bernstein's Granada Publishing Group. Does this sound like the career of a man who was 'ditched by the War'?

Another line of enquiry into the suicide is triggered by a remark made by Peter's secretary at the Queen Street, Mayfair, offices of Peter Davies Ltd.[4] She said: 'He didn't care for the suggestion that he was Peter Pan.'

Peter was seven in 1904 when *Peter Pan* first opened at the Duke of York's Theatre in London's West End. Fairies were all the rage, thanks to actor/writer Seymour Hicks's huge Christmas hit, *Bluebell in Fairyland*, in which Hicks and his actress wife, Ellaline (Ella) Terriss, starred, and which ran at the Vaudeville for some 300 performances from 1901.

Bluebell in Fairyland took London's children by storm, and the Davies boys were no exception. Barrie took them to see it and re-enacted bits of it with them in the nursery at home, taking the role of the terrifying 'Sleepy King' to overwhelming effect. It was always their number one favourite play, even after *Peter Pan* came out. When it was revived in December 1905, Barrie wrote to Ella Terriss: 'I was talking about Peter [Pan] to the little boys the other day & in the middle of my remarks one of them said "Is it true that Bluebell is coming back?" You will see us all there.'[5]

Hicks and his wife were huge celebrities to thousands of children at that time. They had long been friends of Barrie. Hicks had played opposite Barrie's wife Mary Ansell in Barrie's first play, *Walker, London*, ten years earlier, and he had been earmarked for Captain Hook in *Peter Pan*, and Ella for Wendy, but they had pulled out when Ella became pregnant.

These celebrities were a significant part of the boys' lives. In October 1903, when Ella had to call off a date with them to watch a performance of Barrie's hit play *Quality Street*, George, Jack and Peter were so fed up that Barrie had to occupy them in the theatre by paying them twopence every time the audience laughed. The play passed them by. 'They were mostly occupied in counting the laughs,' he lamented.

Living such a life, with one foot behind stage as it were, the boys were no doubt the envy of their friends at school. And one can easily imagine that Peter was ragged for having the same name as Peter Pan, and that his embarrassment deepened when it became known that the play was based on adventures he and his brothers had had with J. M. Barrie.

But why did it rankle for so long? It was in the late 1940s that Peter wrote:

> What's in a name! My God what isn't? If that perennially juvenile lead, if that boy so fatally committed to an arrestation of his development, had only been dubbed George, or Jack, or Michael, or Nicholas, what miseries would have been spared me![6]

Peter's eldest son Ruthven (known as Rivvy and in his twenty-seventh year at Peter's death) believed he had the answer:

> From the moment I was old enough I was aware that my father had been exploited by Barrie and was very bitter . . . He didn't really like him. He resented the fact that he wasn't well off and that Barrie had to support him. But when he was cut out of the will, he was livid and tremendously disappointed . . . and he started drinking heavily. My first memory of my father was with a gin bottle tipped up at his mouth. He was virtually a down-and-out by the time he died . . . My father hoped to inherit Barrie's money but at the last minute he changed his will. Our lifestyle was reasonable until then.[7]

Barrie died in 1937, and there is no doubt that Peter did have money worries, but the only recorded threat to the family's relatively comfortable lifestyle came in 1953, when there was some difficulty in paying school fees. Peter wrote to Nanny: 'We are so hard up that I can't do anything to amuse the boys in their holidays, and we have got to leave our pleasant home near Eton for something cheaper!' Peter did indeed move house, but there was no danger of bankruptcy. We know from Nico that in 1954 Peter Davies Ltd, which Peter had by that time sold for a tidy sum to a bigger publisher, William Heinemann, was in 'quite a healthy state of affairs'. What's more, Peter was kept on by Heinemann as chairman, and all the time his family was growing up and becoming less of a financial burden. Also, Cadogan Court SW3 was not an address that suggested poverty.

However, poverty is a relative term, and it is true that Peter did feel he had lost out in Barrie's will. *Peter Pan* had made Barrie fabulously wealthy, and although he cared little for money and gave much of his wealth away, there was still a net amount in the pot at his death – after £40,475 had been paid as duty – of £167,694 16s. 7d.

Out of that, Peter was left the second largest legacy – £6,000 – still a decent sum in 1937. But he had always expected that as the family publisher he would husband the artistic rights in Barrie's works after his death, and he was tricked out of them at the eleventh hour by Lady Cynthia Asquith, daughter-in-law of the Liberal Prime Minister. Barrie's secretary for the last twenty years of his life, she was a woman who looked after her own interests as a priority, and one of very few people who ever got the better of him.

Barrie had excellent relations with his doctor and had been on daily doses of heroin for some time before his death. The narcotic, originally prescribed to help him sleep, was soon being taken for the dramatic rush it gave him. Cynthia described Barrie as in 'a state of ecstasy and inspiration' while under the influence of it.

According to Nico, it was in a heroin-induced stupor that he finally yielded to Cynthia's representations that he should sign a new will, leaving her £30,000 and all the rights in his plays and books (other than *Peter Pan*, already the property of the Great Ormond Street Hospital for Sick Children). Peter had been present in the room when the fatal dose was administered at Cynthia's suggestion. 'When Uncle Jim got really ill,' Nico told Andrew Birkin, 'and was not expected to last the night, Peter made the Greatest Mistake of his Life and telephoned [Cynthia] down in Devon or Cornwall. She hired a car and motored through the night. Meanwhile, Peter, I and General Freyberg [a war hero and loyal friend of Barrie] went on watch – 8 to 12, 12 to 4, 4 to 8 am – each of us expecting to see JMB die. Cynthia arrived towards the end of Bernard Freyberg's watch . . . still alive . . . got hold of surgeon Horder and solicitor Poole with the will . . . Horder gave an injection, and sufficient energy was pumped into Uncle Jim so that he could put his name to the will that Poole laid before him.

'When Peter and I . . . were cut out from the will* we talked and thought and eventually went to consult a leading solicitor, Theodore Goddard. What did he advise? If, he said, we would get 1. Freyberg to state in Court how unconscious JMB was etc etc, and 2. Frank Thurston† to agree with the repeated manoeuvres of Cynthia [what Nico referred to as Cynthia 'crying her woes: talking of her oldest (dotty) son and her poverty etc etc etc'] then we couldn't fail – in his opinion – to win the case. We did get Bernard and Frank to say they would back us up; but then we each thought how horrid the whole thing was going to be, and we decided not to sue.'[8]

Peter's feud with Cynthia continued and was well known to the family. As fate would have it, the antagonists died within a few days of one another, Cynthia on the Thursday before Peter. But he had long given up the fight for control of the Barrie Estate, and was indeed on the point of retirement. Barrie's will had been published twenty-three years before Peter stepped under the train at Sloane Square. It would surely not, on its own, have driven him to take his life. In any case, Peter had no reason to feel that Barrie had exploited him financially. On the contrary, from 1910 Barrie generously financed Peter's upbringing, including his schooling at Eton, and he founded the publishing firm of Peter Davies Ltd for him. If Peter continued to agonise over Barrie's will, Cynthia was to blame, not Barrie, and her all too human greed was surely not enough to persuade a man like Peter to commit suicide.

Neither the legacy of the Great War nor the association with *Peter Pan* nor Cynthia's actions were sufficient alone to topple Peter into depression. Stronger by far was the shock of investigating his family background, a project which had obsessed him for fifteen years before his death. After the Second World War, Peter began to research and write a family history, making use of the thousands of letters he had inherited from Barrie, along with 'pencilled notes of conversations' with Arthur who had been unable to talk after an operation to remove his upper jaw. A six-part history, not for

* In fact, Nico inherited £3,000, as did the only other surviving brother, Jack.

† Frank Thurston, Barrie's manservant.

publication, was originally envisaged and in 1946, to extend his primary source material, Peter began consulting family friends and personal witnesses, including Nanny Hodgson.

The first part, dealing with the coming together of his father and mother, had gone well, a snapshot of late Victorian grace, charm and dignity; but, wrote Peter to Nanny, 'The entry on the scene of JMB introduces a strange and unavoidably controversial element into this compilation.'

That this was understatement was clear by December 1946, when Peter was admitting to Nanny that his work on it was 'melancholy and sad enough', and by April 1949: 'Alas, the more one learns of those sad days, the sadder the tale becomes.' So depressed did the research make him that he took to calling the history *The Morgue*, and eventually had to bring it to an early end.

One of the questions that first troubled Peter, who had with equanimity published the 'lives' of so many other people, concerned Arthur's apparent reluctance when Sylvia welcomed Barrie into their lives, and almost daily into their home when Arthur was out at work.

Peter was shocked for example to discover that his mother and father had begun to take separate holidays only a few years into their marriage.

'It was, I think, during the Easter holidays of this year [1905, when Peter was 8] that S. [Sylvia] with Jack and Michael went to Normandy with JMB and Mary B [Barrie's wife], while G [George] and I went with A [Arthur] to Kirkby. It has always seemed to me, looking back, that this arrangement can hardly have been come to without a good deal of argument and protest . . . I have no letters referring to the episode.'

On 25 November 1946, Peter wrote to Nanny: 'I am going to ask you one or two questions which you may not care to answer. If you don't want to, that's all right of course. If you find you can, I shall be grateful to you.' Beneath each of the questions he asked Nanny, Peter wrote the word 'Answer' and left a space for her to fill in her response.

There was no love lost between Barrie and Nanny Hodgson, who resented his intrusion on her territory and disliked what she regarded as his subversive way with the boys. Barrie admitted there were 'many coldnesses and even bickerings between us . . . We were rivals.'* Still fiercely loyal to

* J. M. Barrie, *The Little White Bird* (1902), in which Nanny Hodgson is lightly disguised as Nurse Irene.

her employers forty years after their deaths, and still protective towards Peter, her answers are nevertheless fair – even diplomatic. But the truth shines through.

> Q. Did JMB's entry into the scheme of things occasionally cause ill-feeling or quarrelling between father and mother?
>
> A. What was of value to the One had little or no value to the Other.

On the question of whether there was argument over Sylvia going with Barrie to France, she wrote:

> A. Any difference of opinion was *never* 'Public Property' – in the House . . . Your father was always more than willing where your mother's happiness was concerned. [On the other hand] the Barries were overwhelming (and found your Mother's help – grace – & beauty a great asset in meeting the right people etc) . . .

For the first time Peter had to entertain the possibility that Barrie had been a divisive force in his family, that he had come between his father and mother.

> Q. It is clear enough that father didn't like [Barrie], at any rate in the early stages. Would you say that father nevertheless became much fonder of him towards the end [i.e. on his deathbed], and was much comforted, in his last months, by the thought that JMB's money would be there to help mother and all of us after his death?
>
> Nanny's answer was unequivocal.
>
> A. Your father acquiesced to the inevitable with astonishing Grace and Fortitude – it would help your mother – & further than that he never desired. Nor was *able* to go. [*Her emphasis*].

Peter began to confront the picture of a wife colluding with a third party (Barrie) in the emasculation of a husband. The picture threatening to emerge was that Barrie had insinuated his way into the family against Arthur's wishes, that Sylvia had encouraged him and that, on account of his love for Sylvia, Arthur had bottled up his resentment, before, in 1906, it had found physical expression in the deadly sarcoma on his mouth and jaw.

Peter learned from other letters that 'a state of tension' existed between Sylvia and her elder sister, Beatrice, known as Trixy, who became exasperated by Sylvia's insensitivity to Arthur's feelings about her friendship with Barrie.

He began to question his own memory of his mother. What was true and what had become confused with photographs and hearsay? In desperation he found solace in the reminiscence of others of both sexes on whom Sylvia had left the indelible impression 'of something rarer than mere charm, and deeper than mere beauty'.

> Crompton Llewelyn Davies [Arthur's brother], most unemotional of men and as a rule pretty reticent, once, shortly before his death, tried to talk about her to P and me; and it was as if he spoke of a being of more than earthly loveliness. He broke down and had to stop, though not before he had brought the tears to the eyes of both his listeners. This was more than 20 years after Sylvia's death.[9]

In the summer of 1946, Peter decided to take his sons Rivvy and George to stay with his elder brother Jack, partly for a holiday, partly to get Jack's views about *The Morgue*.

Jack, who had risen to Commander in the British Navy, lived with his wife Gerrie in a cottage called Pilchard's Corner, at Port Gaverne, St Endellion, in north Cornwall. He had been the adventurous one of Sylvia's boys, athletic, devastatingly attractive and, in Nico's memory, 'a womaniser. He used to take me to such places as The Palace Theatre and thrill me to the quick at his getting glorious smiles from the chorus girls.'

Their cousin Daphne du Maurier, daughter of Sylvia's brother Gerald, had a particular fix on Jack as a result of a shared family holiday at Slyfield House, near Stoke d'Abernon in Surrey. Jack could climb nearly to the top of the great cedar tree on the lawn and she was in awe of him: 'Had I known, at the age of five, six, seven, how the Greeks felt about their Olympian gods,' she recalled, 'I would have shared their sentiments.'[10]

Jack was obviously a sensitive boy as well as athletic and good looking, perhaps more sensitive at root than any of his brothers. When he was 12 Arthur told him he had cancer. 'I remember very clearly indeed father walking me up and down the right hand (looking up the garden) path & telling me more or less what he was in for,' he told Peter. 'He drove me to tears – an easy matter! And he could talk perfectly clearly, so presumably it was at the latest before the big operation . . .'[11]

This attractive combination of adventurousness and sensitivity made Jack a favourite of Sylvia, more or less equally with No. 4 son, Michael, the most beautiful of her boys. Jack had adored his mother and, as Peter wrote, 'loved and worshipped his father', but he had a changeable and susceptible temperament, for which Nanny said Sylvia had had to 'make allowances'.

When Peter went to Pilchard's Corner to talk to him about *The Morgue*, things did not go well. 'We began squabbling in next to no time,' he wrote to Nanny.

Jack was not against the idea of the family history in principle. Indeed dialogue with Peter continued, and they found some interesting, if rather disconcerting, common ground while talking about childhood. In April 1949, Peter wrote again to Nanny, saying, 'Jack and I, while not very closely resembling each other in general, are both "*clouded over* a good deal and among those whom melancholy has marked their own." I am dimly aware of a great many "complexes" in myself, which are traceable to 1907–1910 . . .'

With Uncle Jim, the five brothers had 'lived in the boy world to the exclusion of any other', said Peter, which meant that they 'were little troubled' by the loss of both their parents. All that was remembered were the games they played, the fly fishing (their favourite pastime with Jim), the holidays in Scotland, everything a beautiful fantasy beyond which neither boy could gain access, even though by then Jack had been 16 and Peter 13.

Peter wrote to Nanny in December 1946, 'I have been a little surprised, and rather disgusted too, to find, on the evidence of old letters and the memories they recall, how little I can have felt at the time, thanks to dwelling in the selfish and separate world of childhood.'

In January 1950 Peter sent Jack the first instalment of *The Morgue*, and Jack surprised him with the strength of his feelings about it. Going straight to the heart of the matter – the Barrie–Arthur–Sylvia triangle – he wrote that

> it is to me so important that I wonder if you could mention my disagreement somewhere, as there are to be several copies. I couldn't at all agree that father did anything but most cordially dislike the bart [the boys' nickname for Barrie after he accepted a baronetcy in 1913]. I felt again & again that [their father Arthur's] remarks & letters simply blazoned the fact that he was doing all he could poor man to put up a smoke screen & leave Mother a little less

> sad & try & show her he didn't grudge the bart being hale & hearty & rich enough to take over the business. I realised of course that I might too easily be biased, so I asked Gerrie, & she agreed with me. I've no doubt at all father was thankful, but he was a proud man, & it must have been extraordinarily bitter for him. And altogether too soft and saint-like to like the little man as well . . . I'd be grateful . . . if some small sign of my disagreement could go in.[12]

As to the question of their mother's character and whether she had colluded with Barrie in a situation that had deeply wounded their father, the line Jack took was that the family had never been Sylvia's first priority anyway after Barrie arrived: 'If one of the boys was ill, it was never Sylvia who held their heads or took their temperatures – it was always Arthur who did that kind of thing.' After Uncle Jim made the boys famous, Jack wrote, 'she wore her children as other women wear pearls or fox-furs'.

Given Peter's statement that Jack was, like himself, 'clouded over' about their childhood, one has to wonder whether the forceful hand of Jack's wife Gerrie could be seen in his so certain response. When Andrew Birkin interviewed her twenty-five years later, she made a point of insisting that no one in her family had ever fallen under Barrie's influence.

Birkin asked whether she had ever watched Barrie captivate a child. 'Yes, he tried to captivate Timothy and Jane [Jack and Gerrie's children],' Gerrie replied. 'He completely failed, particularly with Jane.'

'How did he set about it? He had a rather special way, didn't he?'

'He had a rather special way, but it didn't rub off on Jane. I suppose he was trying to tell her stories, I don't know. But I do know that as far as she was concerned he cut no ice at all. I think he would go to her because she was younger and more impressionable, more likely to be captivated, but it didn't work at all.'

Again, she was absolutely insistent that '*Nothing* of Barrie's personality rubbed off on Jack at all. They were poles apart.' In her own mind Gerrie had cleansed her family of Barrie, and cleansing, she clearly felt, had been needed. It was an act which she saw as supportive of her husband.

Holed up with Jack in their isolated cottage in north Cornwall, Gerrie convinced herself that she had eradicated the 'curse' of their association with Barrie. Even their daughter, baptised Sylvia in 1924, was re-named Jane, emphatically distancing the family unit from the woman who had welcomed Barrie in. Then, in the 1970s, Gerrie introduced a competitive edge with Peggy, calling Peter's wife 'hopeless...useless, poor darling' – the implication being that she failed where Gerrie succeeded, which was why Peter and not Jack had committed suicide.

Lady Jane Barran, daughter of Peggy's prettier twin sister Alison, confirms that Peggy was 'difficult', but Gerrie was no more successful ultimately than she. For during the 1950s, in parallel with Peter, Jack descended into a deep depression. Cousin Daphne visited him at Pilchard's Corner in February 1959 and was shocked at what she found, writing to Oriel Malet* that she 'called on a cousin of mine – one of the "Peter Pan" boys, now sixty-five – and I became very depressed, at him and his brusque wife, living in a dreary little house with an east wind biting at them. I thought back to being there, when he was a midshipman and very menacing, and brought me back a balloon, and jigged me up and down, and was very gay and entertaining . . . and now he is that grousing, grey-haired man.'

Jack died the following September, seven months before Peter walked under a train. His creeping emotional and mental trauma, and parallel physical disintegration, replicated Peter's physical and mental decline almost exactly.

None of it made sense. Why should either of the brothers become so deeply depressed in later life? And what hold had Barrie over Sylvia to change her so?

It is possible that Sylvia was blinded by love for the interloper, and didn't care if she made her husband unhappy. But there is no evidence that she loved Barrie. On the contrary, all the evidence suggests that she loved Arthur deeply up to and beyond his death in 1907. They continued to conceive children long after Barrie entered the scene. Both so beautiful and in love in 1892 when they married, Sylvia and Arthur had seemed the embodiment of the romantic ideal. That both should die young had been a tragedy that went beyond their individual loss.

So, how had Barrie's intervention in their lives brought Sylvia to such self-centredness that she could persecute her husband, and turn to wearing her children 'as other women wear pearls or fox-furs'? And what was Barrie's hold over the boys that half a century later they were still 'clouded over' about what went on?

After Barrie's death in 1937, Peter commissioned Denis Mackail to write the official biography, *The Story of J.M.B.* Mackail is supposed to have written it as therapy following a nervous breakdown, not perhaps the wisest

* The writer Oriel Malet was a close friend of Daphne du Maurier and corresponded with her from 1950. She edited a collection of Daphne's letters to her – *Letters from Menabilly: Portrait of a Friendship* – in 1993.

prescription, but Mackail – a novelist and short story writer – had been an obvious choice. His mother Margaret was the daughter of Edward Burne-Jones, the Pre-Raphaelite artist and pupil of Rossetti, one of the artistic set in which Sylvia's father, George du Maurier, moved. Mackail also had the advantage of personal acquaintance with Barrie, Sylvia and the boys, even at one stage playing for Barrie's cricket team. His one problem was Lady Cynthia, who kept an eagle eye on everything he wrote, dramatically slashing whole pages with a blue pencil when it looked as if he might be damaging Barrie's reputation.

In the end, Peter declared that Mackail had made a 'searching and efficient' job of it, and his jaunty style, a response to the Asquith pressure, enabled him to get away with a great deal. Nevertheless, one reader was less than satisfied – Barrie's wife. Mary Ansell took issue over remarks that made her out to have been the daughter of a seaside landlady and, more intriguingly, over Mackail's failure to tackle head on Barrie's sexuality and his relationship with the boys. She wrote to Peter:

> J.M.'s tragedy was that he knew that as a man he was a failure and that love in its fullest sense could never be felt by him or experienced, and it was this knowledge that led to his sentimental philanderings. One could almost hear him, like Peter Pan, crowing triumphantly, but his heart was sick all the time. There was so much tragedy in his life that Mr Mackail has ignored – tragedy not to be treated humorously or lightly. Mr Mackail has a passion for the word 'little', and after a time it becomes boring. I would suggest that it should be placed on the title page and left there.[13]

Mary Ansell was suggesting that Barrie was impotent with women and that his relationship with the boys – his 'sentimental philanderings' – had been a form of compensation, an astonishingly frank allegation from someone who, according to Mackail, 'had refused to cooperate with the writing of the biography in any way, on the grounds that "Barrie would not have wished any biography to be written at all."'

Mary Ansell would have been aware of Barrie's curse – 'May God blast any one who writes a biography of me' – and had certainly known him well enough to believe that he was unlikely to conspire with God in any matter, but might yet call on powers from darker quarters.

Gossip and sexual innuendo about Barrie and the boys had been rife. A friend of Peter's had been at a literary cocktail party where ('as so often') the talk had got on to homosexuality among authors:

'Anyone in particular?' she asked.

'Well, think of Barrie!'

'Good Lord, surely not J. M. Barrie?'

'Heavens, yes! Don't you know about him and his five wards?'[14]

Nico had not been impressed by this anecdote.

> All I can say is that I, who lived with him off and on for more than 20 years: who lived alone with him in his flat for five of these years: never heard one word or saw one glimmer of anything approaching homosexuality or paedophiliacy [*sic*] – had he had either of these leanings in however slight a symptom I would have been aware. He was an innocent – which is why he could write *Peter Pan*!

Nico had been born too late to participate in the *Peter Pan* years – the play had not been made 'streaky' with the youngest of the Davies boys. He had been too young to appreciate much about Barrie's relationship with Sylvia, but at least he was not 'clouded over' like Peter and Jack, and was clear that he himself had not been interfered with by Uncle Jim.

He was, however, aware that Barrie had a special interest in two of his brothers. 'In due course, we all knew that George and Michael were "The Ones",' he wrote to Andrew Birkin, but he could not say that Uncle Jim was sexually abusing them. 'I haven't the skill – or gift, or whatever – to judge your comment about JMB being "in love" with George and Michael. Roughly, yes – I would agree: he was in love with each of them, as he was in love with my mother [Sylvia] . . . For myself, Peter and Jack at our different times different again – nearer to normal deep affection.'

It was possible for Barrie to have sexually abused George, Jack and Peter without Nico being aware of it, as he was ten years younger than George, nine years younger than Jack, and six years younger than Peter. But Nico had lived with Barrie and Michael alone for the last three years of Michael's short life, and as he was only three years younger than Michael, it has to count for something that he professed himself '200% certain there was never a desire [on the part of Uncle Jim] to kiss (other than the cheek!).' As for Barrie being homosexual, when it came to captivating children, wrote Nico, 'he had just the same success with girl children and I cannot conceive for a moment that in fact there was an important difference'.[15]

His comment that Barrie 'was an innocent – which is why he could write

Peter Pan' is interesting, because there is much to identify Barrie with Peter Pan, perhaps not least that Peter, like Barrie, according to Mary Ansell, did not know what a kiss is. But whether an innocent did write *Peter Pan*, or indeed *The Little White Bird*, the book that first introduced Peter Pan to the reading public, is not as clear as might at first seem.

It is a feature of all the so-called fictional works (plays and novels) on which our story turns that they carry a strong autobiographical content. I am not the first to claim this. One of the most interesting books about Barrie, W. A. Darlington's *J. M. Barrie*, published a year after his death, in 1938, scores because the author is of Barrie's era and knows Barrie's novels, plays and journalism inside out. Darlington was indeed a critic, but he was also the first person to point to the autobiographical nature of Barrie's work.

As for *The Little White Bird*, Barrie's own notes make it clear that David, the leading boy in the 'novel', is based on George, who was ten and had been introduced to Kensington Gardens by Barrie just as David is introduced to them by the narrator ('the Captain') in the 'fiction'. So clear is it that the whole book is autobiography that Mackail was able to write without attracting Lady Cynthia's blue pencil that there was 'a complete breakdown of any pretence that this was a novel'.

Yet, any such notion is extremely damaging to Barrie. For even convinced Barrie supporters throw their hands in the air when they read his description of the night the Captain spent with young David:

> David and I had a tremendous adventure. It was this – he passed the night with me . . . at last Mary [his mother, a dead ringer for Sylvia] consented to our having it . . .
>
> We were both so excited that, at the moment of greeting, neither of us could be apposite to the occasion in words, so we communicated our feelings by signs; as thus: David half sat down in a place where there was no chair, which is his favourite preparation for being emphatic, and is borrowed I think from the frogs, and we then made the extraordinary faces that mean, 'What a tremendous adventure!'
>
> . . . Then [soon after half-past six] I placed my hand carelessly on his shoulder, like one a trifle bored by the dull routine of putting my little boys to bed, and conducted him to the night nursery, which had lately been my private chamber. There was an extra bed in it tonight, very near my own, but differently shaped, and scarcely less conspicuous was the new mantelshelf ornament: a tumbler of milk, with a biscuit on top of it, and a chocolate riding

on the biscuit. To enter the room without seeing the tumbler at once was impossible. I had tried it several times, and David saw and promptly did his frog business, the while, with an indescribable emotion, I produced a night-light from my pocket and planted it in a saucer on the washstand.

David watched my preparations with distasteful levity, but anon made a noble amend by abruptly offering me his foot as if he had no longer use for it, and I knew by intuition that he expected me to take off his boots. I took them off with all the coolness of an old hand, and then I placed him on my knee and removed his blouse. This was a delightful experience, but I think I remained wonderfully calm until I came somewhat too suddenly to his little braces, which agitated me profoundly.

I cannot proceed in public with the disrobing of David.

Soon the night nursery was in darkness but for the glimmer from the night-light, and very still save when the door creaked as a man peered in at the little figure on the bed. However softly I opened the door, an inch at a time, his bright eyes turned to me at once, and he always made the face which means, 'What a tremendous adventure.'

'Are you never to fall asleep, David?' I always said.

'When are you coming to bed?' he always replied, very brave but in a whisper, as if he feared the bears and wolves might have him. When little boys are in bed there is nothing between them and bears and wolves but the night-light.

I returned to my chair to think, and at last he fell asleep with his face to the wall, but even then I stood many times at the door, listening.

Long after I had gone to bed a sudden silence filled the chamber, and I knew that David had awaked. I lay motionless, and, after what seemed a long time waiting, a little far-away voice said in a cautious whisper, 'Irene!'*

'You are sleeping with me tonight, you know, David,' I said.

'I didn't know,' he replied, a little troubled, but trying not to be a nuisance.

'You remember you are with me?' I asked.

After a moment's hesitation he replied, 'I nearly remember,' and presently he added very gratefully, as if to some angel who had whispered to him, 'I remember now.'

I think he had nigh fallen asleep again when he stirred and said, 'Is it going on now?'

* The name Barrie gives the nanny. In Edwardian times, it was customary for Nanny to sleep in the night nursery with her charges.

'What?'

'The adventure.'

'Yes, David.'

Perhaps this disturbed him, for by and by I had to inquire, 'You are not frightened, are you?'

'I am not frightened now,' he whispered,

'And there is nothing else that you want?'

'Is there not?' he again asked politely. 'Are you sure there's not?' he added.

'What can it be, David?'

'I don't take up very much room,' the far-away voice said.

'Why, David,' said I, sitting up; 'do you want to come into my bed?'

'Mother said I wasn't to want it unless you wanted it first,' he squeaked.

'It is what I have been wanting all the time,' said I, and then without more ado the little white figure rose and flung itself at me. For the rest of the night he lay on me and across me, and sometimes his feet were at the bottom of the bed and sometimes on the pillow, but he always retained possession of my finger, and occasionally he woke me to say that he was sleeping with me. I had not a good night. I lay thinking.

Of this little boy, who, in the midst of his play while I undressed him, had suddenly buried his head on my knee.

Of the woman who had been for him who could be sufficiently daring.

Of David's dripping little form in the bath, and how when I essayed to catch him he had slipped from my arms like a trout.

Of how I had stood by the open door listening to his sweet breathing, had stood so long that I forgot his name and called him Timothy.

Timothy is the name the Captain gives to the child he longed to have fathered, but for whatever reason could not. Timothy is called upon to effect a technique often used by Barrie – to defuse with sentimentality anything cruel, sadistic or possibly paedophiliac. At the end of the novel Barrie tells us to think of the whole experience as a wonderful expression of thwarted fatherly love. He gives David's fictional mother Mary the manuscript to read. So, in the novel, Mary is reading the novel she is in. This is Barrie staking a claim to the territory on the borders of illusion and reality that he regarded as exclusively his own. When Mary finishes reading it, he finds her 'laughing and crying, which was no surprise, for all of us would laugh and cry over a book about such an interesting subject as ourselves; but said she, "How wrong you are in thinking this book is about me and mine, it is really all about Timothy."'

The Times fell over itself to think what it was told to think: 'If a book exists which contains more knowledge and more love of children, we do not know it,' the critic wrote. And one can indeed read Barrie's story and *The Times* review in full and feel one has wandered into a production of *The Emperor's New Clothes*.* For in *The Little White Bird*, while there is evidence to suggest that Barrie was sexually aroused by little boys, he is so frank that we find ourselves thinking that if we cannot see his innocence, the problem must be ours, not his. Otherwise, how could he have got away with it?

Many a critic and biographer has come forward to claim that Barrie's love of small boys was not sexual. Andrew Birkin was so convinced of it that when Alison Lurie wrote an article in the *New York Review of Books* (6 February 1975), he is supposed to have offered $10,000 to anyone who could prove that Barrie was a paedophile. Safe money, one might say, after more than half a century, and possibly an over-reaction, as Lurie had suggested not sexual abuse but that, as the boys grew older, they had become 'embarrassed' by 'this odd little man who looked like an aged child'.

In 1989, Gerald du Maurier's biographer, James Harding wrote, 'Barrie, in the manner of Lewis Carroll and his nude photographs of little girls, was *consciously innocent*.'[16]

But how did he know that Barrie's innocence was conscious? And if he did not know, where does his desire to vindicate or protect Barrie come from?

Harding developed his theme, alluding to many of the issues that concern Barrie's accusers: 'His snapshots of the tiny lads frolicking bare-bottomed on the beach, the cowboy and Indian adventures he made up for them, the coy letters he wrote and the amateur dramatics he organised were a means to enjoy the pleasures of fatherhood with none of the pains. In Sylvia du Maurier's children he discovered an ideal outlet for the frustration which obsessed him.'

One might consider that his phrase 'consciously innocent' would not send the British judicial system into meltdown, and that a barrister may yet be found to argue against the notion that it is acceptable to use another person's family as an outlet for one's obsessive frustrations.

* Hans Christian Andersen's fairy tale in which the people of the Empire refuse to acknowledge the Emperor's nakedness in the royal parade after they have been convinced by a couple of swindlers, who have made off with the gold cloth out of which they were supposed to make his clothes, that only those with a true aesthetic sense will be able to see them.

In the end, even Harding found the scene in the night-nursery a step too far.

> One needs a tough stomach to put up with Barrie in this mood. No writer today would publish such an account without inviting accusations of paedophilia and worse.

There were many letters between Barrie and the boys when they were young. One of the few that survive was written to Michael (3) and Peter (6) in 1903:

> Dear Petermikle, i thank u 2 very much 4 your birth day presents and i have putt your portraitgrafs on mi wall and yourselves in my hart and your honey lower down. i am your friend, J.M.B.

Five years later Barrie wrote to Michael on the eve of his eighth birthday, just as he was becoming 'The One':

> I wish I could be with you and your candles. You can look upon me as one of your candles, the one that burns badly, the greasy one, that is, bent in the middle, but still, hurray, I am Michael's candle. I wish I could see you putting on the Redskin's clothes for the first time . . . I am very fond of you, but don't tell anybody.

Peter was out of the family – at the Front and living with Vera Willoughby – while the relationship between Barrie and Michael had been at its most profound. Michael's story is desperately tragic. In 1921 when he was only 20 he drowned in Sandford Pool, just outside Oxford, in the arms of his friend, Rupert Buxton. One has to wonder what, in a non-tidal pool, could lead to two fit lads drowning? A man bore witness that the pool had been glassy calm. Suicide was widely suggested. Fellow student Robert Boothby,* a homosexual and friend of both young men, stated categorically that they were not lovers, but that both had had their reasons for suicide.

Michael's reason was clear to Jack's wife, Gerrie: 'It was very bad for Michael to be so much the centre of Barrie's world.' Boothby agreed. To him and Gerrie, Michael's death was definitely suicide, and in the end Nico came round to the same view.

* Later the politician Lord Boothby.

When Peter researched *The Morgue* he found no fewer than 2,000 letters between Barrie and Michael. The intensity must have come as a shock. Peter destroyed these letters. 'They were too much,' was all he said to Nanny.

Letters to George, who earlier had been 'The One', were less plentiful, though Barrie corresponded regularly with him when George was serving at the Front during the First World War. The last he wrote is indeed extraordinary – and extraordinarily ironic and tragic, as George was killed shortly afterwards. Having informed George of the death in action of his uncle Guy (Sylvia's elder brother), he said:

> Of course I don't need this to bring home to me the danger you are always in more or less, but I do seem to be sadder today than ever, and more and more wishing you were a girl of 21 instead of a boy, so that I could say the things to you that are now always in my heart. For four years I have been waiting for you to become 21 & a little more, so that we could get closer and closer to each other, without any words needed. I don't have any little iota of desire for you to get military glory. I do not care a farthing for anything of the kind, but I have one passionate desire that we may all be together again once at least. You would not mean a featherweight more to me tho' you come back a General. I just want yourself. There may be some moments when a knowledge of all you are to me will make you a little more careful, and so I can't help going on saying these things.
>
> It was terrible that man being killed next to you, but don't be afraid to tell me such things. You see it at night I fear with painful vividness. I have lost all sense I ever had of war being glorious, it is just unspeakably monstrous to me now.
>
> Loving,
> J.M.B.

Barrie revered manly valour and encouraging George not to engage in heroics was, in the context of his peculiar vision of the world, a huge admission of how fiercely he felt for George personally. It could have been written by George's mother – or by his lover.

That is what Peter concluded, describing Uncle Jim's feelings for George as 'a dash of the paternal, a lot of the maternal, and much, too, of the lover – at this stage Sylvia's lover still imperfectly merged into the lover of her son'. Peter was 'very British' and fair as the British system of justice is fair. A man is innocent until proven guilty. Believing this brought him out, at this stage, on Barrie's side:

> Surely no soldier in France or Flanders ever had more moving words from home than those in this tragic, desperately apprehensive letter . . . taking all the circumstances into consideration, I think it must be one of the great letters of the world. Its poignancy is so dreadfully enhanced, too, by the realisation that . . . far, far the most pathetic figure in all the world was the poor little genius who wrote these words.

Peter's mature comments are not those of someone who felt tarnished or diminished by Barrie's sexual appetites. The revelation of just how intense was Barrie's love for the boys, and the discovery that Barrie had opened a rift between his parents, had made Peter, by his own admission, sad and depressed. But, while working on *The Morgue*, he had other intimations, and that is why, in 1949, he approached his cousin Daphne.

CHAPTER TWO

What is the secret?

In April 1949, Peter wrote to Nanny:

> I have some very interesting letters from my du Maurier grandfather when a young man, to his mother. They lead to the conclusion that he changed very much after marriage: and I think that my mother inherited a good deal from him.

What Sylvia had inherited from her father, George du Maurier (always known as Kicky), goes to the very heart of our story. It was for an opinion on it that Peter invited Daphne to come to see him.

Daphne and Peter, who shared this grandfather, had known one another in the old days and on occasion holidayed together. But Daphne was ten years younger than Peter and the age and gender difference meant that they had rarely if ever played together as children. Now, however, Peter identified her as having a particular insight into their grandfather. Two years earlier she had written a biographical Introduction to an omnibus edition of Kicky's novels, published by Peter's firm in association with Pilot Press. There was good reason to expect her also to have a view about Barrie. Her father Gerald, Sylvia's brother and a well-known actor-manager, owed his career in theatre to Barrie, and Barrie was as much 'Uncle Jim' to Daphne and her two sisters as he was to the five Llewelyn Davies boys.

From December 1943, Daphne had buried herself in Cornwall, living in her beloved house, Menabilly, a sixteenth-century, seventy-room pile set in magical woodland leading down through a rhododendron-strewn valley to the sea. Her publishers had long ago given up trying to extricate her from Menabilly to promote her novels. But when she received Peter's call she took it very seriously indeed. First reference to their revitalised relationship appears in a letter Nico wrote to Nanny Hodgson on 14 October 1950 in which Daphne's sisters – Jeanne (younger than Daphne by four years) and Angela (older by three) are also mentioned. 'Jeanne du Maurier has her first exhibition of pictures in London next week. Angela I see a good deal of as we publish her. Her autobiography – *Only the Sister* – comes next year. I'm correcting it now! No great literature but great fun! Daphne the really successful one is still published by Gollancz tho' she is doing an excellent preface for us for a marvellous book of Grandfather's letters . . . which we publish next Spring. Peter deals with Daphne . . .'

Reading Kicky's letters had led to a commission from Peter for Daphne to write not, in fact, a preface, but a lengthy Introduction to an edition entitled *The Young George du Maurier: A Selection of his Letters, 1860–1867*, which Peter published in 1951.

Given that George du Maurier, though famous in his day as an illustrator on *Punch* and the author of the international bestseller *Trilby* (1894), meant precious little to readers in 1951, a selection of his letters (let alone a selection restricted to seven years of his life) would seem on the face of it to be a rather risky project. Peter and Daphne did not see it as such, however, and today their decision is at last justified. For *The Young George du Maurier* represents an important source of the truth about Barrie. It is one of a series of literary clues, or stepping-stones, that Daphne saw fit to leave in her work for future generations to follow – a key piece of the jigsaw that presents a completely new picture of Kicky, Barrie and Daphne and brings new significance to the three fictional characters with which we associate them – Svengali, Peter Pan and Rebecca. Along the way, the completed jigsaw also explains why Peter Llewelyn Davies committed suicide in 1960; and why Michael died in a suicide pact in 1921; and why Peter, Jack, and Daphne herself suffered nervous breakdowns in the late 1950s.

Judith Cook, who knew Daphne in the 1960s, wrote that Daphne and Peter became 'special friends as well as cousins and he was one of the few people with whom she could happily talk for hours'.[1] This was no mere editor–author relationship, or polite huddle of first cousins. 'Daphne got to know Peter very well in his later years,' Nico confirmed in 1976.[2] They became absorbed in each other's company, she as preoccupied with the family history as he.

'We never discussed the world of today,' Daphne wrote after Peter's death, 'only the past. Always the past . . .' Their meetings initially took place in the Grill Room at the Café Royal in Regent Street, but they could never have sustained the relationship over a decade had Daphne not also had her London base.

Daphne's London apartment was on the sixth floor of Whitelands, a block at the convergence of King's Road with Cheltenham Terrace, round the corner from Peter and Peggy's flat at Cadogan Court. Daphne's second daughter Flavia described it as 'a dreary little flat with squeaky floorboards and no carpets. There were two small bedrooms, a sitting-room, a tiny kitchen and bathroom. It smelt faintly of gas and my father's eau-de-cologne.'[3] It was not the kind of place that would attract Daphne away from her beloved Menabilly, unless there was good reason. Originally the flat had been leased as the weekday base of her husband, known as Tommy, who, after demobilisation in 1947, served the Royal household.* Daphne was 'anxious to support him in his new job, [and] went up to London more frequently to attend royal functions and other social events'.

In 1949, Daphne had a play running in the West End, *September Tide*, and she was seeing a great deal of its starring actress, Gertrude Lawrence. From the early 1950s, being in London became even easier. Daphne's elder daughter Tessa flew the nest and was soon to be married, and Flavia and brother Christian (known as Kits) both took up places at boarding-school, Kits following in the footsteps of four of the Llewelyn Davies boys to Eton.

The more Peter and Daphne talked about family, the more family became the focus of Daphne's work, so that in May 1954 Peter wrote to Nanny, 'My rich and famous cousin Daphne is having lunch with me today. She has just written a novel about our naughty great-great-grandmother Mary Anne Clarke . . .'†

Later in the decade, marital problems were further reason for Daphne's presence in London, and when in July 1957 her husband collapsed and was hospitalised, 'Daphne put her own wishes aside to be with him in London, and to give him her support.' She was still writing letters from the King's Road flat in December that year, and 'trying hard to establish a new

* Daphne's husband was Lieutenant-General Sir Frederick Browning GCVQ, KBE, CB, DSO, wartime commander of Airborne Forces and Chief of Staff to Earl Mountbatten in SEAC. In 1947 he became Comptroller and Treasurer to HRH Princess Elizabeth, and from 1952 Treasurer to the Duke of Edinburgh.

† In the early nineteenth century, Mary Anne Clarke, George du Maurier's maternal grandmother, was the mistress of the Duke of York. She took the Duke to court for maintenance and struck such a splendid deal that the du Mauriers lived off the settlement into future generations. Daphne's interest in her family history is also reflected in novels such as *The Scapegoat* (1957) and *The Glass Blowers* (1963), both set in the du Maurier heartland of Sarthe in north-west France.

London routes [routine].'[4] And when Tommy handed over the reins to his successor at Buckingham Palace in the summer of 1959, returning to live full-time at Menabilly, Daphne began looking to Whitelands as an escape. She understood that Tommy needed her, but also knew she had to get away as often as possible, and fortuitously research for her biography of Branwell Brontë necessitated frequent trips to the British Museum.

So it was that Daphne was in London on and off during the entire decade, the period of Peter's descent into depression, feeding and being fed by his obsession with Barrie. She knew that Peter had fallen into a melancholia while working on the family history. Seemingly no one interviewed her or asked her why he had committed suicide. And Daphne was elusive and secretive by nature. She told no one what she and Peter had discovered.

The only person she wrote to after Peter died was Nico. In the knowledge that Nico knew nothing of deep significance about Barrie, she tried to settle his mind by suggesting that Cynthia's death had upset Peter – 'I would think Cynthia's very recent demise triggered something off in Peter's mind, almost an imp who said, "Anything you can do I can do better." Let them have it out, with Uncle Jim telling them both where he himself got off (and he had plenty of time to find that out) and then to the huge relief of Granny* (who would hate any unpleasantness) both Cynthia and Peter shake hands, everything settled at last, and Cynthia evaporates to her own clan, and Peter rushes to aunt Sylvia's arms, because really it was about time he did, having regretted them for about 50 years.'[5]

But the only imp in this story is Barrie, and Daphne's fantasy of Uncle Jim in Purgatory with Cynthia and Peter was a smokescreen for Nico's benefit. She knew well enough why Peter had taken his own life, but to speak or 'write openly about herself, or others, was against her nature'.[6] Except, that is, in her fiction.

Had Daphne indeed been interviewed in April 1960, she might for amusement have given her inquisitor a copy of *The Breaking Point*, which had been published a few months earlier. Having a sense of humour cut with satire, and no respect for people who took things at face value, she would have enjoyed doing that. Although its title begged ominously for association with Peter's dramatic demise, no one, certainly not Daphne's

* Emma du Maurier (1843–1914), Peter and Daphne's grandmother, wife of George (Kicky) du Maurier.

publisher, Victor Gollancz, or the press, had suspected that the book, a collection of short stories, might offer a key to the suicide. For the fact is that hardly anyone associated Daphne du Maurier with Peter Llewelyn Davies or Daphne du Maurier with J. M. Barrie, except in passing.

Like Barrie, Daphne used fiction to sort out her emotional life. All her novels and short stories have autobiographical triggers. I am not the first to claim this, and Daphne herself admitted it. Indeed, she depended on the autobiographical trigger to get herself going. Her stories emerged from 'something observed', but would only mature, or 'brew' as she called the process, if in the hidden places of her mind they attached to something of personal emotional significance. Daphne was no formula writer. 'Everything I write comes from some sort of emotional inner life,' she said.[7]

It was inevitable that her meetings with Peter, which struck at the heart of her emotional life, would yield telling stories. First, in 1952, three years after Daphne's association with Peter began, she published a collection called *The Apple Tree*. Her biographer Margaret Forster was struck by the new note they rang: 'These were strange, morbid stories, in which deep undercurrents of resentment and even hatred revealed far more about Daphne's inner life than any novel had ever done.'[8] All of them, wrote Daphne, 'have inner significance for problems of that time'.[9]

Her second collection, *The Breaking Point*, written after her breakdown and published shortly before Peter's suicide, is yet more transparent, a chilling reappraisal of the happy legend of Peter Pan trotted out by journalists after Peter's death. The Barrie figure, often an uncle and readily identifiable as 'Uncle Jim' (he is actually named in two stories), is presented as an interloper, a psychological controller, a perpetrator of evil. Malevolence, morbidity and psychological disturbance attend him. Evil is tangible, and invariably he wears a trilby hat. The trilby reference is not lost on those in the know, for Kicky's novel had given the soft felt hat its name.

Trilby introduced to a mass audience for the first time the notion of the unscrupulous attainment of power by one individual over another by means of hypnosis, the incredible fact that people can be made, even as they know what is going on, to do something they would not otherwise do, and be unable to remember it afterwards. The fictional musician Svengali is the agent of mind control in the novel. Trilby, an artist's model, is his victim. In Daphne's stories the trilby hat is the symbol of Svengali's hypnotic power, its appropriator the personification of pure evil.

In Daphne's story, 'Ganymede', set in Venice, the villain is an uncle who wears 'a broad-brimmed trilby' just like Svengali's. On setting eyes on him, the narrator has a premonition of disaster: 'The aroma of evil is a deadly thing. It penetrates and stifles, and somehow challenges at the same time. I was afraid.' He has every reason to be, for Uncle will change his life for ever.

In 'The Alibi', the smooth-talking trilby-wearer is middle-aged Fenton, who insinuates himself into the Kaufman family: Anna Kaufman and her young son, Johnnie. Fenton's excuse is that he is an artist, one 'Marcus Sims'. He wants to put Anna and Johnnie on canvas, wants to 'make it streaky' with them. At every point Anna falls over herself to facilitate his plan – as, in reality, Sylvia apparently helped Barrie – even offering herself to him on a plate: 'And now, Mr Sims, which would you prefer first? Come to bed, or paint Johnnie?'

Exasperated by her compliance, Fenton excuses himself from having sex with her, pleading impotence, and turns to her son Johnnie instead. Anna ties Johnnie to a chair to keep him steady, and Fenton paints his portrait. As he does so he begins to believe he has a talent and derives 'a tremendous sense of power' from capturing both Johnnie and his mother in oils. There is a nasty feeling of the occult, a sense of the Devil about Fenton. What turns Fenton on is 'the fact that the bulk of a live person . . . could be transmuted by him upon a blank canvas'. The sense of power he derives from putting them on canvas is more satisfying than sex. In the end, Fenton kills mother and son, and we discover that he wasn't impotent after all. He is caught disposing of the foetus of his child by Anna in a waste bin.

The references to Barrie putting the Llewelyn Davies family on the 'canvas' of *Peter Pan* are clear enough, but in the lingering morbidity, the callousness of the killings, and the sense that Fenton is drawing on a dark, Mephistophelean power that gives him control over others' lives, 'The Alibi' reaches into the darkest corners of Barrie's psyche.

In 'The Menace', a lighter satire, impotence is again the focus, and Barrie is actually named. The background is the world of films. The talkies are giving way to 'the feelies'. Audiences will soon be able to measure the potency of their screen idols while watching them on film. But there is a problem for Gigantic Enterprises Ltd. Their number one star, Barry (*sic*), registers only G on a scale where the high point is A. No matter how sexy his leading lady, nothing can get Barry going. His producer and the star's posse of male attendants, known as 'Barry's boys', are worried, but they don't dare 'let a psychiatrist within a hundred miles of him'. Instead, they take him on a fantastic escapade of sexual titillation and put him on a testosterone-rich diet. But Barry is not turned on and always prefers to eat porridge. Then he meets a childhood friend who shows him photographs of her grandchildren and at last there are stirrings in the undergrowth. Gee-ed up by 'a snapshot of Pinkie's second grandson in paddling drawers bending down and patting a sand-castle with a wooden spade . . .' Barry returns to the set and startles everyone by registering a Force A.

Daphne could well have been looking at the photograph to which this refers. It was once in her possession and is now in the du Maurier archive. Pinkie's second grandson in paddling drawers is straight out of an album of photographs Barrie took when he turned up at the Davieses' summer holiday retreat in Rustington-on-Sea in 1899.

In 'The Blue Lenses' again Barrie is named, as is his wife. When bandages are removed from Marda West's eyes after an operation to save her sight, the other people in the nursing home appear to have animal heads instead of their own. It's funny at first, but then Marda realises that the heads are peculiarly telling of a hidden character. A nurse, who befriended Marda while the bandages were on, and whom Marda has invited to live with her and her husband for the period of her recuperation, turns out to have a serpent's head. Her name is Nurse Ansel (*sic*). Snake-in-the-grass Ansel's friendship with Marda is revealed as a covert means to gain entry to her home in order to pursue an affair with her husband, who is a co-conspirator in the subterfuge. When he arrives in the ward, he has the head of a vulture, a feeder on death, and his name is Jim.

The power of the story is that only Marda can see the heads, only she can see the truth. The weight of this knowledge is shattering because no one believes her. Awakening to truth is the first step to breakdown when no one believes you, when only you can see.

Although she was not thinking of Jim Barrie as the culprit, Margaret Forster wrote perceptively: 'As an allegory of Daphne's state of mind this story was painfully clear – she felt betrayed, exploited and, worst of all, fooled.' It was an allegory of Peter's state of mind, too, and Daphne recognised it as potentially suicidal.

If, as this and other stories in the collection suggest, Peter's awakening to Barrie's betrayal of members of his family was the reason for his suicide, how did Barrie betray them?

'The Menace' suggests child abuse. Another story, 'No Motive', makes suicide the endgame for child abuse, after something breaks through the mental cloud that has concealed the truth for so long. But there is no reference to Barrie in 'No Motive', and sexual abuse is not a major theme of either *The Apple Tree* or *The Breaking Point*.* On the contrary, sex is sidelined. Time and again these stories suggest that spiritual ecstasy is more intense than sexual orgasm.

After reading 'Monte Verita', Daphne's publisher Victor Gollancz wrote to her: 'I don't understand the slight implication that there is something wrong with sex.' In 'The Archduchess', the life of the spirit is brought 'to such delicacy of interpretation that the coarser methods of so-called love-making are rarely used', while in 'Kiss Me Again, Stranger', physical sex is a cold business between strangers.

From the start, Daphne grasped more keenly than Peter what lay at the bottom of his well of uncertainty about his childhood, and questioned him subtly so that he might find the answers himself. 'More than once' she questioned him about Nico,[10] pointing to the fact that, unlike Peter and Jack, Nico had apparently escaped the streak of melancholy and depression which haunted the others.

Peter was soon writing to Nanny that Nico's 'subconscious doesn't seem to have been affected, for his disposition and temperament are noticeably, in my opinion, happy and sanguine and optimistic'.

Jack's wife Gerrie was in agreement: 'Nico was the odd one out. He was the complete extrovert, completely happy. Nothing has ever gone wrong for him personally. And he still bounces. He is mentally and physically utterly different to all the others.'[11]

Nico himself recognised how different he was: 'I was/am just a brother who by the grace of God is more or less normal (or at any rate think I am) . . . And of course when one – I at any rate – gets on to dreams, one is in a world of lovely non-comprehension.'[12]

So saying, ironically, Nico put the matter into its proper context: Nico, alone among the brothers, did not participate in the du Maurier world of dreams. Daphne did, always had done. Both she and her grandfather George du Maurier worked within it. They alone of all the family expressed it in their work.

As a young man, 'Kicky used to feel within himself two persons, the one serious, energetic, full of honest ambition and good purpose; the other a wastrel, reckless and careless, easily driven to the Devil.'[13]

This last phrase was not hyperbole. Kicky had a talent for hypnosis, which he described as 'a gift from the Devil'. For years it was a secret known only to the family and friends with whom he practised it. His

* 'No Motive' was in fact withdrawn from *The Apple Tree* and not published until 1980 in *The Rendezvous*.

strait-laced wife Emma Wightwick had objected to it, and he put it behind him when he married her. Kicky changed after marriage, as Peter had written to tell Nanny, adding, 'Grannie [Emma] seems to me to have been a most excellent and admirable character but comparatively ordinary.'

Emma disapproved and 'the dreamer vanished', as Daphne wrote. But the dreamer returned thirty years later to inspire three novels, including *Trilby*.

Before he died, Kicky prophesied that a girl in the family would carry his gift into the future, and it was to this that Peter alluded when writing to Nanny, 'I think that my mother [Sylvia] inherited a good deal from him.'

Certainly Sylvia knew all about her father's secret talent, but Daphne had begun to suspect that Sylvia's boys had inherited it too, to varying degrees – George and Michael definitely, Peter and Jack less so, Nico not at all.

At Eton, a boy called Roger Senhouse had been immediately struck by the aura around George and Michael, the two boys to whom Barrie was closest. The first time he saw George, 'standing naked in the shower opposite my room after my first Old Boys match . . . I shall never forget that Blake like effulgence,' he wrote to Nico after Peter's death. 'I wanted to extend the Davies family in my mind and those early memories have held an important position in my life.'[14]

Later, Senhouse became especially close to Michael, 'I have never again since Michael's death felt that those astonishing years have been equalled in intensity – the *élan vitae* in all the phases . . . I was then in touch with life forces that have since eluded me.'

It has always been assumed that this aura, this Blake-like effulgence around the Llewelyn Davies boys, was inspired by Barrie. But it was, in fact, a du Maurier secret, the very fount of Kicky's and Daphne's talent as writers, and the reason why, when Denis Mackail observed Barrie come together with Michael, aged 10, he wrote: 'He and Barrie draw closer and closer, and perhaps it isn't always Barrie who leads or steers.'

The du Maurier secret is what drew Barrie in, just as surely as it drew in Roger Senhouse. It was Barrie's intense desire to share in this secret – to possess it – that drove him to target the Llewelyn Davies boys, and extend his malign power over the whole family.

In 'The Archduchess', another of the stories in *The Breaking Point*, Daphne describes the du Maurier family secret figuratively as delivering the gift of 'eternal youth', the Romantic secret of Peter Pan, the boy who would never grow up and therefore retained his intimacy with the supernatural world. Barrie is the disenchanted interloper, maimed by his parents and programmed to maim, and he has come to steal the secret.

PART II

1789–1862

Kicky and Barrie: learning to fly

Kicky and Felix Moscheles: 'We sat into the small hours of the morning, talking of the past, present and future, a long-necked Rhine-wine bottle and two green glasses beside us . . .'

CHAPTER ONE

Du Maurier dreamers

We think of Daphne du Maurier as indelibly English. Slim, striking, and quietly commanding, with a strong confident jawline and a pronounced upper-class English accent, she was a Dame of the British Empire, and wrote novels that found their way into the folklore of England's mystical West. But, as the name suggests, the family is French; the du Mauriers came from the Sarthe region of north-west France.

No surprise, therefore, that Daphne set novels and short stories in France, or that the émigré or foreign invader is everywhere in her fiction, from *Frenchman's Creek* to *My Cousin Rachel*, from *The Progress of Julius* to *The Scapegoat,* or that she once declared that she had one foot in each country: 'If my mind and soul live in Fowey, perhaps I leave my heart behind in Paris.'

The first du Maurier to set foot in London from France was also the first du Maurier. Robert Mathurin Busson du Maurier, a charming fraudster, arrived in 1789. He was on the run from the law and had adopted the suffix 'du Maurier' in order to avoid detection, and to recommend him to the English who welcomed aristocrats escaping the French Revolution.

Robert du Maurier was an out-and-out fantasist. He fabricated not only his name, but an aristocratic lineage stretching back to the twelfth century. The original Bussons were in reality humble glass manufacturers, and 'Du Maurier' was the name of a farmhouse where Robert was born, as Daphne was the first to discover.

Robert's son, Louis, was also a dreamer. 'He invented ingenious and strange machines which because of some flaw or other failed to work.' Daphne tells us that he 'once nearly blew his family into the next world', inventing a lamp that was all set to supersede Sir Humphry Davy's, used by miners everywhere. 'He had a wizard's flair for speculation, which just missed amassing him a fortune by the proverbial hair's breadth.'[1]

Louis's saving grace was that he 'sang like an angel'. His son, Kicky, inherited this talent, as well as a certain oomph from his mother, Ellen, the daughter of Mary Anne Clarke. No one in the family had made any money until Mary Anne Clarke became part of its genetic profile. She was the original kiss-and-tell, testifying against her royal lover before the bar of the House of Commons, bringing him to disgrace and netting a huge financial settlement.

Both Mary Anne Clarke and Robert du Maurier served time in the King's Bench prison, which, according to Daphne, explained why Ellen 'fussed and worried over her children with all the singleness of purpose and forethought for their future that comes with deep-laid anxiety – the children *must* do well in the world, especially her favourite Kicky . . .'

Kicky was born on 6 March 1834. As a child he had a weak disposition: he grew slowly and was never tall. His younger brother Eugene was bigger, more athletic and far funnier than he. Kicky remained in his brother's shadow, a quiet child sitting for hours with his face in his hands, listening to his mother play the harp, but he was always happy, living as he did in a household full of love.

The du Maurier family was settled in Belgium for the earliest part of Kicky's childhood. They moved to London in 1837, when Kicky was three and a half. Here, 'my father grew very poor. He was a man of scientific tastes, and lost his money in inventions which never came to anything. So we had to wander forth again, and this time we went to Boulogne and there we lived in a beautiful house at the top of the Grande Rue', the home of Grandmama Mary Anne Clarke. In 1842, after another downturn in business, the family moved to Passy, 'a quiet village on the outskirts of Paris, facing the Bois de Boulogne'.[2]

This was Kicky's idyllic childhood time, to which he would return again and again in his dreams. One day in particular was the happiest of his entire life –

> For in an old tool shed full of tools and lumber, at the end of the garden, and half-way between an empty fowl-house and a disused stable (each an Eden itself), I found a small toy wheelbarrow – quite the most extraordinary, the most unheard-of and undreamed-of, humorously, daintily, exquisitely fascinating object I had ever come across in all my existence.
>
> I spent hours, enchanted hours, in wheeling brick-bats from the stable to

> the fowl-house, and more enchanted hours in wheeling them all back again, while genial French workmen, who were busy in and out of the house where we were to live, stopped every now and then to ask good-natured questions of the 'p'tit Anglais', and commend his knowledge of their tongue, and his remarkable skill in the management of a wheelbarrow. Well I remember wondering, with newly aroused self-consciousness, at the intensity, the poignancy, the extremity of my bliss, and looking forward with happy confidence to an endless succession of such hours in the future . . . Oh, the beautiful garden! Roses, nasturtiums, and convolvulus, wall-flowers, sweet peas, and carnations, marigolds and sunflowers, dahlias and pansies, and hollyhocks, and poppies, and Heaven knows what besides! In my fond recollection they all bloom at once, irrespective of time and season.

Here, he and two other boys would play at Alexander Dumas's *The Three Musketeers*, 'the fame of whose exploits was then filling all France', and Kicky would pretend to be Natty Bumppo in James Fenimore Cooper's frontiersman novels, rousing tales of adventure about primitive Red Indians and early pioneers of the American West, while alone he would engage in island fantasies, his first book being *Robinson Crusoe* and next favourite *The Swiss Family Robinson*.

But the real fun came in the nearby Bois de Boulogne, not at all the pristine park it is now, and in particular by a pond called the mare d'Auteuil, which was surrounded on three sides by 'a dense, wild wood . . . The very name has a magic from all the associations that gathered round it at that time.'

As a child he would fish for tadpoles and fully developed reptiles in the muddy waters, and at night, 'snoozing in my warm bed', would 'picture it to myself lying deep and cold and still under the stars, in the dark thicket, with all that weird, uncanny life seething beneath its stagnant surface'.

> Then gradually the water would sink, and the reeds, left naked, begin to move and rustle ominously, and from among their roots in the uncovered slush everything alive would make for the middle – hopping, gliding, writhing, frantically . . . Down shrank the water; and soon in the slimy bottom, yards below, huge, fat salamanders, long-lost and forgotten tadpoles as large as rats, gigantic toads, enormous flat beetles, all kinds of hairy, scaly, spiny, blear-eyed, bulbous, shapeless monsters without name, mud-coloured offspring of the mire that had been sleeping there for hundreds of years, woke up, and crawled in and out, and wallowed and interwriggled, and

> devoured each other, like the great saurians and batrachians in my *Manuel de Géologie Élémentaire*.

So, in the 1840s the highly imaginative Kicky enjoyed boyish adventures and the park and the mare d'Auteuil just like his grandsons, Sylvia's boys, who enjoyed inventive games in the early 1900s by the Black Lake, and in Kensington Gardens by the Round Pond, playground of Peter Pan. Kicky even had an Uncle Jim figure in his life in the Bois de Boulogne. Le Major Duquesnois 'took to me at once, in spite of my Englishness, and drilled me . . . and told me a new fairy tale, I verily believe, every afternoon for seven years. Scheherezade could do no more for a Sultan, and to save her own neck from a bowstring!'[3]

The park became a kind of lodestone for everything Kicky understood of beauty in later life. Here, for ever, would exist *the boy* in him to which he longed to return, and to which he did return in dreams and in his fiction, 'proving that nothing is forgotten that we and our forefathers have known, experienced and seen, but all images, like photographs, are printed on our subconscious minds forever'.[4]

His father Louis meanwhile had entered into a partnership with his brother-in-law George Clarke in London, with an idea to clear all the world's ports of seaweed. In 1851 he sent for Kicky, who had just failed the Latin paper of his baccalaureate and arrived without any qualifications at all.

Kicky worked with Louis in the Birkbeck Laboratory of University College London and hated every minute of it, except that it meant he could draw caricatures of his professor and others who worked there, who 'were hugely tickled by them at the time. Indeed, [the professor] remembers nothing else about me, except that I promised to be a very bad chemist.'

Kicky was a popular and sparky little character, with a notable ability to entertain and amuse, whatever the situation and whatever the company. In 1855, he took a train to Cambridge with a friend. They fell in with some undergraduates, among them Walter Besant,* who gave this telling account of the evening the young du Maurier passed with them:

> One day Calverley, then a fellow, stopped me in the court and invited me into his rooms after hall. 'I've got a young Frenchman,' he said. 'He's clever.

* Walter Besant was later a novelist and social reformer who stimulated the founding of the People's Palace in 1887, the famous centre for education and amusement for the poor in London's East End and now part of the University of London.

> Come and be amused.' I went. The young Frenchman spoke English as well as anybody; he told quantities of stories in a quiet irresponsible way, as if he was an outsider looking on at the world. No one went to chapel that evening. After the port, which went round with briskness for two or three hours, the young Frenchman went to the piano and began to sing in a sweet, flexible, high baritone or tenor. Presently somebody else took his place at the instrument, and he, with Calverley, and two or three dummies, performed a Royal Italian Opera in very fine style. The young Frenchman's name was George du Maurier.

Kicky's eccentric, itinerant upbringing, far from dragging him down, had benefited his personality. He was spontaneous, energetic, completely without humbug and, having been brought up in two cultures at once, had a joyous objectivity and a talent for humour ('in a quiet irresponsible way').

Then, in the summer of 1856, after a lawsuit over the miners' lamp left him high and dry financially, Louis suddenly gave up the effort of living. Refusing to see a doctor, he 'let rip', according to his son, 'with a rendering of one of Count de Ségur's drinking songs [and] left the world almost with music on his lips'.

By then, Kicky was in no doubt what he wanted to do. 'I threw up test-tubes and crucibles and went back to Paris, where I was born and brought up, and studied to become an artist in the Swiss painter M. Gleyre's studio.'

CHAPTER TWO

Peak Experience: the secret

The new way forward for art students in Paris in the 1850s was painting not from artefacts of antiquity but from human models in the ateliers of successful artists, who gave of their experience in return for a small payment.

'One day the model was male, the next female, and so on, alternating throughout the year,' Kicky wrote. 'A stove, a model-throne, stools, boxes, some fifty strongly-built low chairs with backs, a couple of score easels, and many drawing boards, completed the *mobilier*.'[1]

These were places not of tranquillity, but of undisciplined, riotous and even cruel behaviour. There are stories of new students being 'crucified' on ladders and hung out in public places, and even of one death due to an initiation by scorching over a studio stove.

Charles Gleyre's studio, at 53 rue Notre Dame des Champs, was more like the disreputable common room of some English public school:

> In those days it was somewhat a rough place, and the carefully and religiously brought up lad was much shocked at the manners and customs of the students . . . I have seen the whole atelier astride of their chairs, prancing around the model, shouting the *Marseille*, which during the Empire was a song forbidden by the police. Some wag would slip out of the room and coming back rap threateningly at the door, when the procession would stop, the song cease, and each student would at once pretend to be hard at work at the drawing or painting before him, no matter whose it was. When the man who had knocked appeared instead of the police he was received with a yell of indignation, and sometimes the strange gallop was recommenced.[2]

At Gleyre's Kicky teamed up with another English artist, Thomas

Armstrong, and a Scot, Thomas Reynolds Lamont. Armstrong gives a vivid picture of his first meeting with Kicky:

> I can revive the picture of him in my mind's eye sitting astride one of the dingy Utrecht velvet chairs with his elbows on the back, pale almost to sallowness, square shouldered and very lean with no hair on his face except a slight moustache . . . he certainly was very attractive and sympathetic and the other young fellows with whom I was living felt much as I did. We admired his coats with square shoulders and long skirts after the fashion of the day, and we admired his voice and his singing, his power of drawing portraits and caricatures from memory, his strength and skill with his fists, and above all we were attracted by his very sympathetic manner. I think this certainty of finding sympathy was one of his greatest and most abiding charms. His personality was a very engaging one and evoked confidence in those who knew him very little.[3]

The business of the fists is that Kicky liked to keep fit by boxing and had very fast hands. Daphne wrote that the strongest quality in his nature 'was his love of beauty', and that his interest in the human form was part of an intensely emotional quest to apprehend and express beauty wherever it might lie. Armstrong observed that his apprehension of beauty was never stronger than in his appreciation of music:

> Music was a powerful influence in du Maurier's life. He used to say that literature, painting and sculpture evoked no emotion which could be compared with that felt by a sensitive person on hearing a well-trained voice or a violin. In those days he spent much more time at our hired piano than he did before an easel.

Forty years later, Kicky, Lamont and Armstrong would feature in *Trilby* as Little Billee, the Laird and Taffy, 'the three musketeers of the brush' who are Trilby's friends, and music would be the ultimate expression of beauty in the story, in which Svengali, a musician, hypnotises and enslaves Trilby, a young bohemian artist's model, who has all the potentiality of a singer, but is tone deaf. In repeated practice sessions under his hypnotic power, Svengali transforms her singing voice until she sings as no human being has ever sung – but in the process he destroys her.

There is much in the novel that is redolent of Paris of the late 1850s and early '60s, in particular the place and rue Saint-André des Arts, the rue Gîtle-Coeur (the 'place St Anatole des Arts' and the 'rue du Puits d'Amour' of the novel), and their adjacent congeries of blind alleys, winding passages and narrow streets. 'Nearly every stone of that *locale* furnished the elegant record of a phase in the life of the city which Little Billee and the Laird and Taffy and Trilby loved so well and not altogether unwisely.'[4]

Among other of Kicky's Paris friends who also made an appearance in *Trilby* were James McNeill Whistler, who became Joe Sibley, 'the idle apprentice',[5] and Alexander (Alecco) Ionides, a boy Kicky describes as 'only sixteen, but six feet high, and looking ten years older than he was', the son of a wealthy Greek merchant living in London.

Alecco is introduced in the novel simply as 'the Greek' and recommended for his ability 'to smoke even stronger tobacco than Taffy'. Smoking was all the rage; many of du Maurier's illustrations of the 1850s are of young men falling into reverie in clouds of smoke. It clearly wasn't tobacco in the pipes.

After Kicky arrived in London in 1860, he and his friends would gravitate to Alecco's house to continue to enjoy certain aspects of the Paris bohemian lifestyle. Alecco was a linchpin, as Kicky recorded: 'When his Paris friends transferred their Bohemia to London, were they ever made happier and more at home than in his lordly parental abode or fed with nicer things?'[6]

In time, the Greek became a grey-bearded, millionaire city magnate. He was ever 'as genial, as jolly, and as hospitable as in the old Paris days, but he no longer colours pipes'.

Dashing, cosmopolitan Alecco Ionides was procurer to this band of artists, just as Jean-Jacques Moreau de Tours had been supplier of hashish in the form of a green paste to Le Club des Haschischins, frequented earlier by similarly euphoric Romantics: Balzac, Dumas, Gautier, de Nerval and Baudelaire.

Kicky's special interest, however, was not drugs but something else that was on tap on the left bank. It was the very art in which Svengali excelled.

The heroine of *Trilby* is an artist's model. These girls were often lovers and in a way mothers to the hopelessly disorganised artists, who lived on their dreams and not a little of the money the young women made by modelling. As Albert Vandam wrote:

> Astonishing though it may seem to those who are not familiar with the inner life of the French artists' models . . . the susceptibility of a great many of

> them to hypnotic influence, especially among the female members, is an ascertained fact. What Svengali did in such terrible earnestness and with such terrible results to poor Trilby is done out of sheer fun almost every day by the pupils at the 'Beaux Arts', at private drawing-schools, and the académies libres.

Normally, a model would pose for four hours, with ten minutes' interval between each forty minutes. However, hypnotism was all the rage in Paris at this time, and many a mischievous student artist learnt how to improve on this schedule by hypnotising these models, ensuring absolute rigidity in whatever pose was desired and for whatever length of time.

> Unfortunately many of those youngsters have that power, and a few of them exercised it to such a purpose that there was an outcry, and the authorities had to interfere. The chief culprit was a young fellow who for some considerable time had attended the lectures of the late Dr Charcot [the famous hypnotist and doctor] . . . Our amateur Charcot continued to experimentalise, and finally selected for his subject a girl of great plastic beauty, perhaps one of the most perfect specimens of the human form the world has ever seen, the well-known Élise Duval, the favourite model of M Gérôme and Benjamin Constant. Of a highly strung, nervous temperament and very playful disposition, Élise Duval showed even a greater tendency to become 'sport' for the hypnotiser, whether amateur or professional, than the majority of her sister-models, and one day, at the beginning of a séance, she was thrown into a trance which lasted for four hours, at the end of which she was awakened more dead than alive. She was suffering from a violent headache, her legs refused to carry her, every one of her limbs felt sore, and she had to be carried home and put to bed. But the hypnotisers still refused to relinquish their favourite amusement, and they got Élise Duval once more under the spell, of course with equally distressing results.[7]

Vandam puts the Duval scandal as occurring around 1880. But it is clear from the record of Felix Moscheles, who was an art student in Paris and friend of Kicky, that mesmerism was as popular in the 1850s, if not more so:

> In Paris I had had opportunities of attending some most interesting séances, in consequence of which I soon proceeded to investigate the mesmeric phenomena on my own account. Now I have not [indulged] for some thirty

years; I swore off because it was taking too much out of me; but I look back with pleasure on my earlier experiments, successes I may say, for I was fortunate enough to come across several exceptional subjects. Du Maurier was particularly interested in one of these, Virginie Marsaudon, and had a way of putting puzzling questions concerning her faculties and my mesmeric influence . . . I was not yet eighteen when I first went to Paris, to study under my cousin, the eminent painter, Henri Lehmann. At his studio I found Virginie installed as the presiding genius of the establishment, using in turn broom or tub, needle, grill or frying-pan as the occasion might require; the wide range of her powers I further extended by making a truly remarkable mesmeric subject of her . . . It needed but little to lead her on from a state of docile and genial dependence to one of unconscious mesmeric subjection, and so, a few passes shaping her course, I willed her across the boundary line that separates us from the unknown, a line which, thanks to science, is daily being extended. Madame Marsaudon was herself an incorrigible disbeliever in the phenomena of mesmerism, but as a subject her faculties were such as to surprise and convert many a scoffer.

At the séances, to which I invited my friends and a few scientific outsiders, I always courted the fullest investigation, taking it as the first duty of the mesmerist to show cause why he should not be put down as a charlatan . . . It was doubly satisfactory, then, that the good faith of subject and mesmerist could be conclusively proved.

One of these séances led to a rather amusing incident. One night I was awakened from first slumbers by a sharp ring at my bell, and when, after some parleying, I opened the door, I found myself confronted by two individuals. One I recognised as an 'inquirer' who had been brought to my rooms some time previously; the other was a lad I had not seen before. The inquirer, I ascertained, having carefully watched my *modus operandi* on the occasion of his visit, had next tried experiments of his own. In this instance he had succeeded in mesmerising a lad, but had found it impossible to recall him to his normal condition. So, securing him by a leather strap fastened round his waist, he led him through the streets of Paris to my rooms. There we both tried our powers upon him, the result being very unsatisfactory. The youth, feeling himself freed from one operator and not subjected by the other, refused allegiance to either, and, being of a pugnacious temperament, he squared up and commenced striking out at both of us. It was not without considerable difficulty that I re-mesmerised him completely, and then, having previously prepared his mind to account naturally for his presence in my rooms, I succeeded in awakening him, and all ended happily. The inquirer was duly grateful, the youth went home strapless and none the worse for the adventure, and I proceeded to do some very sound sleeping on my own account.

The practice of mesmerism had changed greatly since the eighteenth century when Franz Anton Mesmer first claimed that a universal fluid infusing both matter and spirit with its vital force could be pressed into service to medicine with the aid of magnets.

In 1831 the French Academy of Medicine had published a detailed report on five years' research into clinical experiments in hypnosis conducted at the Salpêtrière hospital in Paris, confirming that mesmerism could induce a state of semi-consciousness in which subjects became 'complete strangers to the external world' and 'new faculties: clairvoyance, intuition, internal pre-vision' were awakened.

That these practices were already held to be dangerous was clear from scientific research being undertaken long before Moscheles arrived in Paris. In 1841 Dr James Braid attended a demonstration of hypnotism in Manchester by a man named La Fontaine, a Swiss 'magnetist'.† He saw at once that what he had witnessed involved 'physiological modifications of the nervous system'. If hypnotists were intervening in the workings of the nervous system, there was the possibility, with misuse, of nervous deterioration, even nervous breakdown. Braid warned of 'nervous lassitude and innumerable other dangers', particularly if hypnosis was undertaken by 'the unscrupulous or unskilful'. Moscheles's decision to 'swear off' being hypnotised because 'it was taking too much out of me' suggests he was right.

One other danger being discussed in medical circles in the mid-nineteenth century concerned the relationship of the hypnotised subject to the hypnotiser. The former becomes subservient to the will of the latter and therefore vulnerable to exploitation. Braid reported that 'some persons are so deeply influenced that they become entirely obedient to the hypnotist'. It is interesting that Felix Moscheles slips easily into the language of domination when discussing his subject moving from 'docile and genial dependence' to a state of 'unconscious mesmeric subjection'. In Kicky's novel this is of course exactly what happens to Trilby as she falls under Svengali's power.

*

† James Braid would give Mesmer's magnetism the name hypnotism – the Greek root meaning sleep – in order to highlight the developments of the science since Mesmer's day, although hypnosis is not in fact a sleeping state.

Felix Moscheles entered Kicky's life after he left Paris and transferred to the Antwerp Academy of Fine Arts, a leading European school of painting, where he had, as he liked to point out, 'no less a person than Mr. Alma-Tadema as a fellow-student'.* Here Kicky and Felix shared a studio, and one day –

> I was drawing from a model, when suddenly the girl's head seemed to me to dwindle to the size of a walnut. I clapped my hand over my left eye. Had I been mistaken? I could see as well as ever. But when in its turn I covered my right eye, I learned what had happened. My left eye had failed me; it might be altogether lost . . . That was the most tragic event of my life. It has poisoned all my existence.[8]

For a time it was feared Kicky might lose the sight of both eyes. Wrote Daphne:

> He moved from Antwerp to the little town of Malines and for a while he felt he would never recover from the blow and even had dark thoughts of suicide. His mother, who came out to be with him, could not comfort him. For though he made light of the tragedy in public and laughed and joked about it when his friends came to Malines to see him, showing them his dark glasses and saying he was an aveugle [blind man], she knew and they suspected what the suffering must be.[9]

Kicky had suffered what would now be diagnosed as a detached retina. He had to give up any idea of becoming an artist. However, one could get from Antwerp to Malines in about an hour, and Felix became a regular visitor at weekends, delighted to discover that all was not quite as bleak in Malines as he had anticipated:

* The Dutch artist Sir Lawrence Alma-Tadema was one of the most famous artists of the late nineteenth century, his subject matter mainly classical antiquity. He looked very similar to du Maurier and had a reputation as quite a bon viveur. Years later in London, every Tuesday evening he was At Home to his friends in his magnificent studio in Grove End Road. 'I don't know how it is,' du Maurier is reported to have said one afternoon, 'but people always seem to mistake me for Tadema. Enthusiastic women come up to me at parties and say, "Oh, Mr Tadema! I really must tell you! I do so adore your pictures! The way you represent marble! Oh and the roses – and everything! Too, too wonderful!" '

'And what do you do?' he was asked.

'Always the same thing,' he said with an impish twinkle. 'I press their hands warmly and say, "Gom to me on my Chewsdays." I don't know if they do.'

> There were pretty girls about, and I need not say that, as both of us were studying art and devoting our best energies to the cult of the beautiful, we considered it our duty to take special notice of these pretty girls wherever we came across them. It is probably the conscientious performance of his duty in that direction which enabled du Maurier to evolve those ever-attractive and sympathetic types of female beauty we are all so familiar with. Nor would it have been becoming in me, who had everything to learn, to lag behind, or to show less ardour in the pursuit of my studies.

Kicky and Felix befriended a pretty 17-year-old girl called Octavia, whom they nicknamed 'Carry' and who had 'a rich crop of brown curly hair, very blue inquisitive eyes, and a figure of peculiar elasticity'. Carry was the daughter of an organist who had recently died. Her mother had set up a tobacconist's store with a small inheritance. Carry was clearly hopelessly vulnerable to the two older boys. They persuaded her to sit for them in the nude, and then hypnotised her, Kicky absorbing her and the game of mesmerism at the same time.

A mesmeric séance in Mrs L's back parlour (1858)

Before long Kicky and Felix were getting subjects off the street and hypnotising them in 'the back parlour of Mrs L.'s tobacco store'. Felix relates (and Kicky illustrates) one such session:

> There I am operating on a boy—such a stupid little Flemish boy that no amount of fluid could ever make him clever. How I came to treat him to passes

> I don't remember; probably I used him as an object-lesson to amuse Carry. All I recollect is that I gave him a key to hold, and made him believe that it was red-hot and burnt his fingers, or that it was a piece of pudding to be eaten presently, thereby making him howl and grin alternately.

Carry became besotted with the two young men* – 'not without cause,' boasted Felix; 'du Maurier could draw and I could paint; he could sing and I could mesmerise, and couldn't we just talk beautifully! We neither of us encourage hero-worship now, but then we were "bons princes", and graciously accepted Carry's homage as due to our superior merits.'

If this seems to imply that it was only Felix who hypnotised Carry, Daphne is clear on this point: 'Both Felix and Kicky practised mesmerism at that time.'[10] And Felix himself writes:

> The truth of the matter is that we shared fraternally in the enjoyment of [Carry's] good graces, he having the pull of me the greater part of the week, and only suspending operations in my favour when I came to Malines on a Saturday to Monday visit . . .
>
> There was a subtle quality in Carry, well worthy of appreciation, a faculty of charming and being charmed, of giving and taking, of free and easiness, coupled with ladylike reserve. She seemed to be born with the intuitive knowledge that there was only one life worth living, that of the Bohemian, and to be at the same time well protected by a pretty reluctance to admit as much. In fact, to give a correct idea of her I need but say her soul was steeped in the very essence of Trilbyism.

Carry was unconventional, free and easy, a disciple of truth and beauty, but transformed into the artists' plaything was enslaved and exploited by them. Her story, as Kicky confessed to his close friends, was the root of his novel, *Trilby*. He and Felix 'get Carry's soul', as Felix describes the process, just as Svengali gets Trilby's. When the two art students first hypnotised the 17-year-old, she had just lost her father. When Svengali first hypnotises Trilby, it is to relieve the pain and loneliness of losing her parents.

* The fascinating record of their time together was published immediately after Kicky's death on 6 October 1896. Entitled *In Bohemia with Du Maurier*, it was illustrated with a large number of Kicky's drawings. Felix wrote the 'few introductory words' in the month that Kicky died, which may suggest that du Maurier had not wanted it published at all, although Felix writes that his friend 'had here and there lent a helpful hand even to the correcting of the proofs'.

Years later George du Maurier was weighed down with feelings of guilt, but at the time he could not have been more turned on by the devilry of hypnotism. In one drawing he depicts Felix as Mephistopheles playing a piano, on top of which a cat is hissing at him. Kicky's caption reads: 'Felix or Mephistopheles, which?' Felix wrote that the music he was playing emanated from some sort of 'untrained inner consciousness'.

The next drawing shows a vision of Carry emerging in clouds of smoke from what looks like a cigar Felix is smoking. The caption reads: 'Inspiration papillotique', which means something like 'inspiration gift-wrapped'.

Deeper in the du Maurier archive I discovered an excerpt from an undated letter in French to Carry, which reads: 'At night George's imagination takes on the shape of an ancient hunter over which he puts on a pair of breeches so as not to hinder his movements. Decked out in this manner he goes hunting for memories in the dead forests of his mind, which are his exclusively . . . These huge forests are peopled by fantastic beings and singular trees; amongst which he meets the elegant shadows of . . .'

There the letter runs on to another sheet, which is missing. 'George' is of course Kicky, and as usual his letter is illustrated. The drawing depicts a pipe-smoking satyr carrying a bow and arrow 'on the hunt' approaching a 'cabin' made out of tree trunks and festooned with a leafy canopy. Carry has her arm around a tree trunk and is looking down upon a third figure, the artist, whose hair is standing on end, as if it were electrified, which in Kicky's cartoons means that a hypnotism is in progress.

Commenting on a drawing of Kicky in a trance on a *chaise-longue*, Felix writes, 'No wonder if he depicts himself, with fixed gaze and hair erect, sitting bolt upright on my hospital sofa, thrilled and overawed by the midnight presence of the uncanny, which I had evoked for his benefit.'

It is clear that mesmerism became more to Kicky than incidental amusement. Yet another ink drawing from this period shows him and Felix looking from the left of the picture on to a dreamscape composed of Kicky's ancestors. Hypnosis has become a visionary vehicle into his past, as it would thirty years later for the pioneer psychiatrists. In the picture Kicky is again in a trance, living in his own wholly absorbing fantasy world. Soon he would also begin to see the visionary possibilities of hypnosis in a Romantic–mystical–metaphysical sense, 'to expand his consciousness'. Nor was he alone in this.

Kicky was the complete Romantic. As a child, unlike his scientific father who 'despised all books, I . . . was enthusiastic about Byron, and used to read out "The Giaour" and "Don Juan" to my mother for hours together. I knew the shipwreck scene in "Don Juan" by heart, and recited it again and again . . . Then came Shelley, for whom my love has lasted, and then Tennyson, for whom my admiration has never wavered . . . though I now qualify him with Browning. Swinburne was a revelation to me.'

But now Romantics were alive to the scientific reality of invisible forces, and were beginning to see hypnosis as a trigger that would enable anyone to become a divine visionary like William Blake.

> What is one to make of the electrical energy vibrating through Kleist's dramas, the 'streams of magnetic fluid' coursing through Balzac's novels, the 'electrical heat' radiating from gures in E.T.A. Hoffmann's tales, and the 'magnetic chain of humanity' joining together the characters in Hawthorne's novels? And why is it that Rodolphe woos Emma Bovary by entertaining her with 'dreams, forebodings, magnetism'? Why does Charles Bovary, distraught by his wife's death, recall stories about the 'miracles of animal magnetism' and imagine that, by 'straining his will', he can resuscitate his wife? . . . The trances induced by these latter-day mesmerists represented a state in which the medium's body remained fixed on earth while his soul escaped its corporeal prison to roam through another world. No longer merely a palliative for physical ills . . . mesmerism now promised to endow man with a sixth sense that would expand his cognitive consciousness.[11]

From personal experience Kicky agreed with the French Academy of Medicine that hypnosis was a vehicle for clairvoyance and pre-vision; and also for 'a mystical feeling, half rapture, half pain . . . so sweetly profound', as he wrote to his artist friend Armstrong. He had found a way, through hypnotism, to replicate 'such as moves in sweet melodies, such as entrances in Chopin's *Etudes*, and in Schubert's *Romances*'. He discovered what a hundred years later the American psychologist Abraham H. Maslow called 'peak experiences' – non-religious, quasi-mystical and mystical experiences, sudden feelings of intense happiness and well-being, and sometimes a mystical sense of 'ultimate truth', the unity of all things.

> The experience fills the individual with wonder and awe. He feels at one with the world and is pleased with it; he or she has seen the ultimate truth or the essence of all things.[12]

That the route to this highly tuned emotional state was via neither art nor religion did not trouble Kicky, nor did it diminish art in his judgement (he had no time for religion anyway, having inherited a dislike for black-robed priests from his father and rejected God after he lost the sight of his eye). His experience of hypnosis had taken him from a 'Romantic' view of the world towards a 'modern scientific' view, which not only allowed for the existence of a supernatural 'other world', but made it the more real. It seemed to him that hypnosis awakened a sixth sense, which he described as having long been 'etiolated by disuse'.

Meanwhile, his mother Ellen was becoming concerned about his hypnotic excursions, and in his heart Kicky knew they had become an addiction. Like Felix, he sensed that they would bring him down in the end.

Fortunately, practical matters intervened. His sister Isabel wrote from London, where she was staying with a school friend, Emma Wightwick, to say that Emma's mother had heard of 'an oculist at Gräfrath, near Düsseldorf, who had cured hundreds of people near to blindness and who was said in fact to be the finest oculist in Europe. What was more, there was a school for painting in Düsseldorf itself. Why did not Kicky and her mother leave Malines and Belgium and try their luck in Germany?'

In the spring of 1859 Kicky left Felix and travelled with his mother to Düsseldorf, where he discovered that while the oculist could not restore the sight of his left eye, with care the right one would remain sound till the end of his days. His mind at once reverted to more enjoyable things. He wrote to Felix:

> Spent yesterday in Gräfrath; jolly place, lots of beauties, plenty of singing and sketching and that sort of thing, you know. Long walks in beautiful valleys, most delightful. The fact is, I'm so beastly merry since I've been here that I don't think I'm quite sane, and altogether only want your periodical visits and permission to have my fling on Saturday nights to be in heaven . . . Carry novel, of course, adjourned *sine die*; haven't got time just now—you know what a fellow I am. Just got her letter; very naïve and amusing—but don't tell her so, or else she will pose for that and spoil it.

Felix decided to drop in on Kicky on his way to Paris. 'We sat into the small hours of the morning, talking of the past, present, and future, a long-necked Rhine-wine bottle and two green glasses beside us, our hopes and aspirations rising with the cloud that curled from my ever-glowing cigar.'[13]

Both boys looked back fondly on their mutually successful psychically empowered conquests, which appear to have continued during Felix's short stay – 'Damask was another beauty whom we appreciated, perhaps all the more because we knew she was dying of consumption.'

Money meanwhile was becoming scarce. As Daphne recorded, the family 'had nothing to live upon but the annuity that Kicky's mother had inherited from Mary Anne Clarke, the original hush money from the Duke of York. His brother, Eugene, was a constant source of worry, always in debt as his father had been. And his sister Isabel, now a pretty girl of nineteen, must also be supported . . .' Kicky had hoped to be the main prop of the family. It was time for him to move on, but he knew not where, now that his ambition to be a painter had been quashed by semi-blindness. It took a visit from his friend Tom Armstrong to fix it, as Daphne recorded:

> Armstrong came to stay in the Spring of 1860 and told him frankly that he was doing no good and allowing himself to drift . . . Kicky took stock of himself. Tom was perfectly right. He was doing no good. He was living on his mother, he was selling no pictures and he was getting himself entangled with girls.

But what could he do? Armstrong told him that in London magazines were crying out for illustrators. He showed him a copy of *Punch's Almanack*, pointed out the drawings of Charles Keene and John Leech and insisted that if Kicky chose to do so he could draw as well as they. He promised he could get Kicky introductions to *Punch* and to other illustrated magazines. Several of their friends had moved from Paris to London . . .

It was true that engraving was a highly regarded medium in London at this time. Even important artists like John Millais were drawing on wood, and being well paid for it. So it was that, in May 1860, young George du Maurier borrowed £10 from his mother's annuity and set forth from Düsseldorf for London, travelling with Tom Armstrong and Isabel's friends, the Wightwicks.

On his arrival he settled at number 70 Newman Street, just north of Oxford Street in Bloomsbury, which, although he was unaware of it, was practically next door to the house in Cleveland Row where his grandfather, Robert Busson du Maurier, had lived some sixty years earlier.

He shared the premises, which doubled as a studio, with Jimmy Whistler, who was causing a few tremors in society with his picture, *At the*

Piano. Kicky quickly immersed himself in the London scene, writing to his mother:

> Tonight I am going with an old friend, Ormsby, to Munroe's, the sculptor's, where I will perhaps meet Hunt, Millais, Rossetti, Ruskin and the Deuce knows who.

The members of the original brotherhood of Pre-Raphaelites were like heroes to Kicky, but his warmest welcome meanwhile came from another quarter.

CHAPTER THREE

The boy who hated mothers

On the ninth day of the same month in 1860 that Kicky arrived in London, a boy was born in Kirriemuir in eastern Scotland. The penultimate of ten siblings, he was christened James Matthew, and known at home as Jamie.

His parents, a fundamentalist Presbyterian couple, had married nineteen years earlier. Stern, burly David Barrie was a weaver or 'warper' by trade, tiny Margaret Ogilvy (she cannot have been more than five feet tall), the daughter of a local stonemason, and six years younger.

Margaret was a member of a fiercely puritanical Protestant sect known as the Auld Lichts, 'the keenest heresy hunters' in the Presbyterian Church, according to the critic W. A. Darlington.[1] It was tradition for a Scottish wife in those days to keep her surname, which is why Jamie's mother was known as Margaret Ogilvy rather than Margaret Barrie. It was also tradition upon marriage to convert to the husband's Church, which in the case of Jamie's father was the less extreme Free Church of Scotland.

The weaving industry of Kirriemuir was a well-organised, commercial operation. It sprang in the 1760s from the development locally of a double-thickness cloth, which proved ideal for the manufacture of ladies' corsets, all the rage in the fashionable cities of Europe, and an ironic undercurrent in the Barrie house, where Margaret's fierce puritanism ran to disguising her daughters' underwear when hanging it out to dry.

Of the couple's ten children, seven were girls and three boys. Two of the girls died in infancy. Of the surviving eight children, the eldest was Alexander, known as Alick, born in 1841, a bright and hard-working boy who won a bursary to Aberdeen University from a school at Forfar, six miles away from Kirriemuir. He graduated with a first-class honours degree in Classics in 1862. Next came Mary (1843) who kept house for Alick when subsequently he started a private school – the Bothwell Academy – in Lanarkshire.

Second daughter Jane Ann was born in 1847. She grew up plain and was the austere, self-sacrificing one who dedicated her life to caring for her mother. Margaret Ogilvy, a difficult, demanding woman, outlived Jane Ann, who died an old maid at just 48.

In 1853 the Barries' second son David was born. He showed exceptional promise and much was expected of him. There was only one position higher than teacher in the mind of Margaret Ogilvy – and that was minister; nothing less would be good enough for David, who was the apple of her eye. Margaret's hopes for him turned him into something of a legend. No doubt Jamie was fed up with hearing about him.

The tenth child, Margaret, known as Maggie, was born three years after Jamie, in 1863 – she was Jamie's favourite and doted on him.

At first, the Barries lived in a two-up, two-down cottage, with one of the downstairs rooms housing a hand loom and little else. But the family never knew poverty. Local industry was healthy and David was a mover and shaker in it. By 1860 there were 1,500 hand-loom weavers in the town, and 500 more in the surrounding area. Kirriemuir weavers were producing over nine million yards of linen a year, and before long the Barries took an adjacent cottage and employed weavers on their own account.

Then, in 1867, something happened that would fix Jamie's life. His brother, David, who was being schooled a hundred miles away at Alick's Bothwell Academy, was injured in a skating accident. Wrote Barrie:*

> When he was thirteen and I was half his age the terrible news came, and I have been told the face of my mother was awful in its calmness as she set off between Death and her boy. We trooped with her down the brae to the wooden station, and I think I was envying her the journey in the mysterious wagons; I know we played around her, proud of our right to be there, but I do not recall it, I only speak from hearsay.
>
> Her ticket was taken, she had bidden us goodbye with that fighting face which I cannot see, and then my father came out of the telegraph-office and said huskily, 'He's gone!' Then we turned very quietly and went home again up the little brae. But I speak from hearsay no longer; I knew my mother for ever now . . . for many months she was very ill. I have heard that the first thing she expressed a wish to see was the christening robe, and she looked long at it and then turned her face to the wall . . .

*In his biography of his mother, *Margaret Ogilvy*, written in 1896, thirty years after the events he describes.

My mother lay in bed with the christening robe beside her, and I peeped in many times at the door and then went to the stair and sat on it and sobbed. I know not if it was that first day, or many days afterwards, that there came to me my sister, the daughter my mother loved the best [Jane Ann]; . . . This sister, who was then passing out of her 'teens, came to me with a very anxious face and wringing her hands, and she told me to go ben [in] to my mother and say to her that she still had another boy. I went ben excitedly, but the room was dark, and when I heard the door shut and no sound come from the bed I was afraid, and I stood still. I suppose I was breathing hard, or perhaps I was crying, for after a time I heard a listless voice that had never been listless before say, 'Is that you?' I think the tone hurt me, for I made no answer, and then the voice said more anxiously, 'Is that you?' again. I thought it was the dead boy she was speaking to, and I said in a little lonely voice, 'No, it's no him, it's just me . . .'

Many a time she fell asleep speaking to him, and even while she slept her lips moved and she smiled as if he had come back to her, and when she woke he might vanish so suddenly that she started up bewildered and looked about her, and then said slowly, 'My David's dead!'

Nothing Jamie could do would make her forget David. But how he tried.

After that I sat a great deal in her bed trying to make her forget him . . . and if I saw any one out of doors do something that made others laugh I immediately hastened to that dark room and did it before her. I suppose I was an odd little figure; I have been told that my anxiety to brighten her gave my face a strained look and put a tremor into the joke. I would stand on my head in the bed, my feet against the wall, and then cry excitedly, 'Are you laughing, mother?' . . . I remember once only making her laugh before witnesses. I kept a record of her laughs on a piece of paper, a stroke for each, and it was my custom to show this proudly to the doctor every morning . . .

It was doubtless [Jane Ann] who told me not to sulk when my mother lay thinking of him, but to try instead to get her to talk about him . . . At first, they say, I was often jealous, stopping her fond memories with the cry, 'Do you mind nothing about me?' but that did not last . . . He had such a cheery way of whistling, she had told me, it had always brightened her at her work to hear him whistling, and when he whistled he stood with his legs apart, and his hands in the pockets of his knickerbockers . . . I had learned his whistle . . . from boys who had been his comrades, I secretly put on a suit of his

> clothes . . . and thus disguised I slipped, unknown to the others into my mother's room . . .

After this crushing simulation, in which he surrendered to David an exclusive claim on his mother's love, and swallowed her rejection of him, 7-year-old Jamie switched the focus from himself and David, and persuaded his mother to tell him about her own childhood.

He then began to feature the child his mother had once been in sentimental made-up stories, and 'this girl in a blue dress and bonnet with white ribbons' was reborn in tales 'of desert islands and enchanted gardens, with knights on leaping chargers'.

Margaret, 'a wonder at making-believe' – and astonishingly self-centred – rose to the fantasy which became the basis of their relationship. Throughout his boyhood she would tell Jamie about old Kirriemuir and the Auld Lichts, the extreme religious sect to which she had belonged. And the stories continued in turn to pour out from Jamie, eventually to become, in his thirties, whole novels. Always there was a character in them pegged on Margaret. 'I soon grow tired of writing tales unless I can see a little girl, of whom my mother has told me, wandering confidently through the pages.'

He would bring the manuscript of a new novel from London, and sit on her bed (for Margaret was often in bed, with Jane Ann in attendance), while she looked for herself in its pages. When she found the character, she would cackle excitedly, and all would be well.

Margaret never recovered from the loss of David, and her relationship with Jamie was never a loving one in any normal sense. In 1868, a year after the accident, she sent him away to live with his brother Alexander.

Nevertheless, the fantasy world, which had bridged the gulf between himself and his mother, 'clicked' in Jamie's mind, and as a boy he went on to win the approbation of other boys in similar fashion, first as their self-appointed fantasy leader, Captain Stroke, in Jacobite games played out in a Kirriemuir den, 'the spot chosen by the ill-fated Stuart and his gallant remnant for their last desperate enterprise', and then 170 miles away at the Dumfries Academy, where at 12 years of age he was sent to school after Alick had taken a job in the town as a Schools Inspector.

Soon after he arrived at the Academy, Jamie and a boy named Stuart Gordon discovered they were both fans of Fenimore Cooper, and on the strength of it, Stuart invited Jamie to join his gang.

Stuart's father was Sheriff Clerk of Dumfries. He lived in a house with a large garden on the banks of the Nith; and here night by night the gang enacted a sort of Odyssey that was long afterwards to become the play of *Peter Pan*.

In the riverside garden, Jamie came into his own. The Odyssey may have started out as derivative of Fenimore Cooper's stories, but soon Jamie had his friends re-enacting adventures based on his own favourite book, R. M. Ballantyne's *The Coral Island*, which tells of three ship's boys – Ralph, Jack and Peterkin – wrecked on a South Sea coral island. They build their own house, make fires, gather fruits, build boats to explore neighbouring islands, and settle down to an idyllic life, until the war canoes arrive full of cannibals . . .

> We had a sufficiently mysterious cave, that had not been a cave until we named it, and here we grimly ate cocoa-nuts stoned from trees which not even Jack nor Ralph nor Peterkin would have recognised as likely to bear them. And more or less bravely we suffered for the same, the cocoa-nuts not being of the season that yielded Peterkin his lemonade. Here too we had a fire, lit as Jack used to light his, by rubbing two sticks together.[2]

It was a time of friendship, blood brotherhood, high adventure and noble action. Jamie was soon calling himself and Stuart after heroes of blood-and-thunder penny pulp magazines – Dare Devil Dick and Sixteen-String Jack. Meanwhile, *The Coral Island* 'egged me on, not merely to being wrecked every Saturday for many months in a long-suffering garden, but to my first work of fiction, a record of our adventures, the "Log-Book"'. The log book was the prototype for *The Boy Castaways*, the log he kept for Sylvia's boys nearly forty years later.

The comradeship Jamie found here was the supreme antidote to the emotional hiatus at home, and the happiest time of his life, he wrote. Jamie also enjoyed playing football and cricket, took an active part in the debating and literary societies, and at 16 got his first taste of journalism, when a fellow pupil, Wellwood 'Wedd' Anderson, the son of a Dumfries bookseller, started up a school journal, *The Clown*. But his real forte was in theatre, where he soon gained a degree of notoriety.

A local minister, who was also a member of the local School Board, publicly (and quite inexplicably) criticised Jamie's first play, *Bandelero the Bandit*, as 'grossly immoral'. Happily a critic from the *Dumfries Herald* had also been present and came to the rescue: 'Two awful villains, Gamp and Banshaw, were characters in Barrie's play . . . They were no worse, and no

George du Maurier (Kicky), as an art student in the 1850s in Paris, where he first learned about hypnotism.

George du Maurier's depiction of life with Felix Moscheles in his room at the Academy of Fine Arts, Antwerp. The following morning du Maurier wrote: 'May thy room be always as jolly, thy coffee ever so sweet … and may I never be blinder!'

The Midnight Presence of the Uncanny. George du Maurier and Felix Moscheles 'made frequent inroads into the boundless land where unknown forces dwell'. Whenever du Maurier depicts himself 'with fixed gaze and hair erect, sitting bolt upright', it is a sure sign that hypnotism is in progress. Wrote Moscheles: 'It was on one of these excursions that du Maurier was inoculated with the germs that were eventually to develop into Svengalism.'

Chère Carry,
La nuit, l'imagination de George prend le costume
d'un chapeau antique par dessus lequel il met une paire
de caleçons; affublé de la sorte, il va à la chasse aux souvenirs
dans les vastes forêts de la mémoire dont il est exclusivement
propriétaire (et à l'exclusion de tout autres propriétés) ces

Excerpt from an illustrated letter written in French by George du Maurier to Carry, who was hypnotised by both him and Moscheles.

'Moscheles, or Mephistopheles? which' du Maurier queries, as he depicts his hypnotist at the piano, and demonstrates the devilry he perceives in the psychic games they played together.

George du Maurier with his wife Emma and their daughter May, in 1874. Emma made it a condition of their marriage that he gave up hypnotism and other possibly drug-related activities.

George du Maurier in the 1880s, established in London as a successful illustrator. He drew regularly for *Punch* and illustrated novels by Elizabeth Gaskell, Thomas Hardy and Henry James.

Sketch by George du Maurier of his daughter, Sylvia, with whom he shared an exceptionally close relationship, and who was his model for the hypnotic temptress Mary, Duchess of Towers, in his novel *Peter Ibbetson*.

Henry James. After lunch on Sundays, he and George du Maurier would take a walk across Hampstead Heath to their 'bench of confidences'. Both had a strong interest in hypnosis, and both wrote novels that hinge on the erotic issues of the hypnotic relationship.

Dolly (Dorothea) Parry with her parents, the composer Hubert and his wife Maude. Dolly's teenage diaries give a vivid picture of the traditional Arthur Llewelyn Davies in love with the easy-going, Bohemian Sylvia du Maurier.

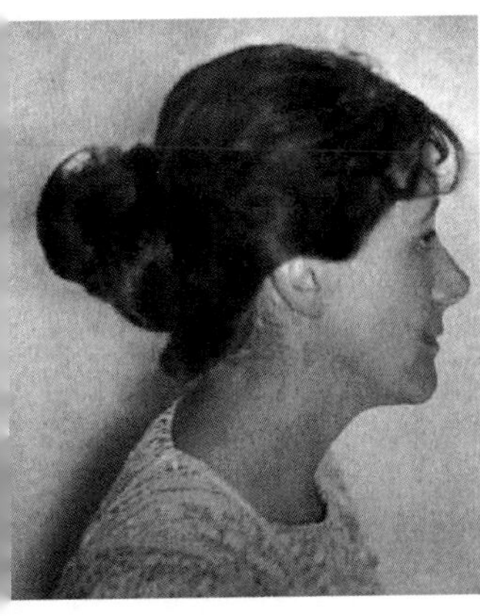

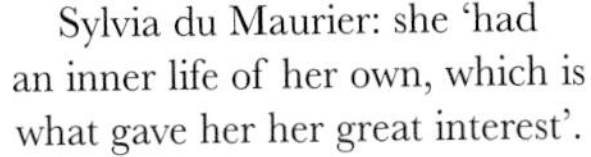

Sylvia du Maurier: she 'had an inner life of her own, which is what gave her her great interest'.

Arthur Llewelyn Davies: 'joli garçon' and 'a young warrior in an Italian picture'.

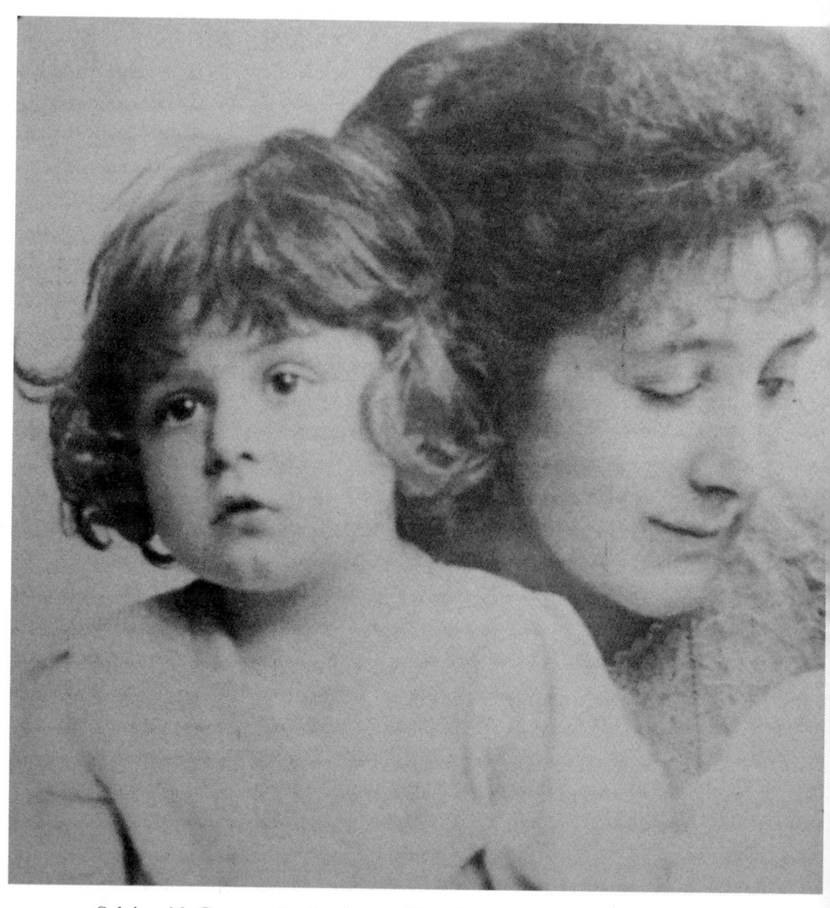

Sylvia with George, the first-born of her five sons, named after her father.

Jamie Barrie, in 1882 when a student at Edinburgh University, where Robert Galloway described him as 'exceedingly shy and diffident, and I do not remember ever to have seen him enter or leave a classroom with any companion'.

Jane Annie, who hypnotises everyone to get her own way, was named after Barrie's eldest sister, Jane Ann (*above left*), a spinster who dedicated her life to caring for their redoubtable mother, Margaret Ogilvy (*above right*). But it was the younger sister Maggie, with whom Barrie was closest, who was the medium.

(*Below*) Arthur Conan Doyle. A dedicated spiritualist, he helped with Barrie's most unusual and least successful play, *Jane Annie*, a musical about hypnosis, which Barrie undertook after reading George du Maurier's novel *Peter Ibbetson*.

Jim Barrie with his St Bernard, whose antics entertained children in Kensington Gardens. Barrie named the dog Porthos, after Peter Ibbetson's dog in George du Maurier's fiction.

(*Below*) Mary Ansell, Barrie's actress wife, who wrote 'that love in its fullest sense could never be felt by him or experienced'. She 'knew all about Jim's enthusiasms', and helped pave the way for his relationship with Sylvia.

Mary Hodgson, loyal nanny to Sylvia's five sons, in 1897, the year Barrie met the boys 'by chance' in Kensington Gardens.

better, than the average stage villain of the "penny plain and tuppence coloured" and were probably based on Deadwood Dick, Spring-Heeled Jack, a Fenimore Cooper pirate, or the cruel robbers of the Babes in the Wood.'

In one of the two other plays that evening, a comedy called *Paul Pry* by J. L. Toole, a London actor and regular player himself at the Dumfries Theatre Royal, Jamie starred as Phoebe, a girl with her hair attached to her hat. When a copy of the *Herald* article was sent to Toole in London he, 'being the kindliest gentleman in the world', as Barrie recalled, 'replied at once, and said facetiously that he hoped one of us would write a play for him some day. That amused us very much.'[3] By 1893 Toole had appeared in two of Barrie's plays in the West End of London, and another actor at the Dumfries theatre, George Shelton, played the pirate Smee in *Peter Pan*.

Jamie had discovered a real talent at 17. Letters written to a lad called Peter Irving, who had recently left the Academy and taken a job in Edinburgh, show him brimming with confidence and, though he was not regarded, nor regarded himself, as in the scholar class, he won at least one prize, for 'Excellence in English Composition'.

Then came the first downturn in his life at the Academy. His friends started talking about girls, and he found that girls were not interested in him very much, or even at all. Jamie's physical development was not so much slow as stunted. At 17 he had the tiny body of a much younger boy, with an oddly proportioned head. He had stopped growing at just over five foot, his chin was smooth and, worst of all, he was only ever picked to play female parts in the theatre. Throughout his life, he blamed his physical appearance for his lack of appeal to the opposite sex, and there is no doubt that it lowered his self-esteem yet further.

> Six feet three inches . . . If I had really grown to this it would have made a great difference in my life. I would not have bothered turning out reels of printed matter. My one aim would have been to become a favourite of the ladies which between you and me has always been my sorrowful ambition. The things I could have said to them if my legs had been longer.[4]

The girls in the Academy, according to Jamie himself, held a plebiscite to decide which boy had the sweetest smile, and he headed the poll. That they found him cute seemed to make matters worse. Had they disliked him or feared him it would be something, 'but it is crushing to be just harmless', he wrote.

Further alienation occurred during the holidays in Kirriemuir. When he went home he was turned away from the imposing new villa, Strathview, which his father's success as an administrator in the new power-loom industry had bought the family, and was billeted out instead at Pathhead Farm, on the outskirts of the town. No convincing explanation has been offered, or found, for this exile. His biographer Darlington wrote: 'Evidently because now that his home was with his brother at Dumfries, there was no bed for him at Strathview.' But after all the time away, and given his desperate need to be loved, it must have seemed like rejection.

In between fishing and walking, which became his best-loved pastimes, he did nevertheless keep up the storytelling sessions with his mother, and cottoned on to her interest in explorers, the glittering heroes of the day. Gallant tales of the search for the Northwest Passage, expeditions to the Arctic, the Antarctic, the exotic Orient and the dark continent of Africa, provided a steady stream of adventure that thrilled British society at every level throughout the nineteenth century, at once capturing the imagination and stoking the Imperialist dream. In Margaret's case, it was an absolute obsession. As for Jamie, the heroic was already a dimension of his fantasy world, and identifying with her heroes gave his tarnished self-image a shine.

> My mother liked the explorers to be alive so that she could shudder at the thought of their venturing forth again; but though she expressed a hope that they would have the sense to stay at home henceforth, she gleamed with admiration when they disappointed her. In later days I had a friend [Joseph Thomson] who was an African explorer, and she was in two minds about him; he was one of the most engrossing of mortals to her, she admired him prodigiously, pictured him at the head of his caravan, now attacked by savages, now by wild beasts, and adored him for the uneasy hours he gave her, but she was also afraid that he wanted to take me with him . . . The newspaper reports would be about the explorer, but my mother's comment was 'His mother's a proud woman this night.'

Margaret revered not only the adventurers but also those who wrote about them:

> Her delight in Carlyle was so well known that various good people would send her books that contained a page about him . . . There were times, she said, when Carlyle must have made his wife a glorious woman.

'As when?' I might inquire.

'When she keeked in at his study door and said to herself, "The whole world is ringing with his fame, and he is my man! . . ."'

All Margaret's heroes evinced the ideals that Thomas Carlyle had written about in his series of lectures, *On Heroes, Hero-Worship and the Heroic in History* (1841), the ideological backbone of the British Empire as it extended its power over a quarter of the entire globe. And of course Carlyle was Scottish, and lived in Dumfries. Jamie was soon fan enough to stalk him:

> When I was at school in Dumfries I often saw Carlyle in cloak, sombrero and staff, mooning along our country roads, a tortured mind painfully alone even to the eyes of a boy. He was visiting his brother-in-law, Dr Aitken, retired, and I always took off my cap to him. I daresay I paid this homage fifty times, but never was there any response. Once I seized a babe, who was my niece, and ran with her in my arms to a spot which I saw he was approaching; my object that in future years she would be able to say that she had once touched the great Carlyle. I did bring them within touching distance, but there my courage failed me, and the two passed each other to meet no more.[5]

Stalking came naturally to him. In London as a young journalist he stalked another hero, the poet and novelist George Meredith (who later became a friend). Indeed, his very first railway journey on arrival in the capital was to Box Hill to gaze at 'the shrine' – Meredith's house: 'There is a grassy bank . . . opposite the gate.' Barrie 'sat on the grassy bank and quivered'. Presently he saw a face at the window of a little sitting-room and knew at once whose face it was. 'Then the figure stood in the doorway, an amazing handsome man in grey clothes and a necktie. He came slowly down the path towards the gate.' It was too awful for Barrie. He ran away.

Throughout his life he was driven by hero-worship, perhaps because he felt himself to be unheroic. 'It was always terrible not to have the feelings of a hero,' he admitted in his autobiographical novel, *Sentimental Tommy*; but he seemed unable to emulate the qualities he so admired. Carlyle's 'savage sincerity – not cruel, far from that; but wild, wrestling naked with the truth of things', was hardly Jamie, any more than was the 'most gentle heart withal, full of pity and love', which Carlyle also held was part of the basic heroic material.

Later in life Barrie befriended Captain Robert Falcon Scott of Antarctic fame, and after Scott's death in 1912, his widow introduced him to his last and perhaps greatest hero: Bernard Freyberg, VC, DSO, a warrior of true courage, who adjusted well to sudden immersion in the gushing waters of Barrie's esteem. During an unusually public, oratorical phase of his life in the 1920s, he included a portrait of Freyberg in a speech he gave to the students of St Andrews University: 'There is an officer,' he said, 'who was the first of our army to land at Gallipoli. He was dropped overboard to light decoys on the shore, so as to deceive the Turks as to where the landing was to be. He pushed a craft containing these in front of him. It was a frosty night, and he was naked and painted black. Firing from the ships was going on all around. It was a two-hours' swim in pitch darkness. He did it, crawled through the scrub to listen to the talk of the enemy, who were so near that he could have shaken hands with them, lit his decoys and swam back. He seems to look on this as a gay affair. He is a V.C. now, and you would not think to look at him that he could ever have presented such a disreputable appearance. Would you?' he concluded, pointing to Freyberg sitting in the stalls.[6]

But when Scott invited Barrie along on an expedition to the South Pole, he wriggled out of it, and when yet another of his heroes Robert Louis Stevenson invited him to Vailima, the South Sea island where he lived, he exuded enthusiasm, but prevaricated and never went. He said he couldn't leave his mother. The truth was that there was a yawning gap between the heroic fantasy world in which Jamie lived with his mother and comrades-in-arms, and the real world.

Excluded, as he saw it, from the social mainstream of life at the Academy by his lack of success with girls, he adopted a new, rather bookish persona and made a friend of a frail scholarly boy called James McMillan. They went on long walks together and, while Barrie shared with him his infatuation with Carlyle, McMillan, who loved poetry and would die young, encouraged Barrie's desire to write, the inevitable consequence of the happiness he felt in 'playing so real-like in the Den', and in creative session with his mother. After McMillan, Barrie always carried a notebook in which to jot observations and thoughts to be drawn on later.

At 18, he went up to Edinburgh University to read English Literature. In the company of young adults his shyness with women conspired with a hopeless lack of a student community at the university to make him very lonely – 'The absence of facilities maimed some of us for life,' he said later, and wrote of himself in the third person as 'a man of secret sorrows, [who] found it useless to love, because, after one look at the length and breadth of him, none would listen'.[7]

Fellow undergraduate Robert Galloway recalled that he was 'exceedingly shy and diffident, and I do not remember ever to have seen him enter or leave a classroom with any companion'.[8]

Grimly, Barrie attempted to neutralise his sense of inferiority by hanging on to the heroic fantasy images of the Riverside den. In his notebook he wrote, there are 'far finer things in the world than loving a girl & getting her . . . Greatest horror – dream I am married – wake up shrieking . . . Want to stop everybody in street & ask if they've read "The Coral Island". Feel sorry for if not.'[9]

What had Margaret done to her third son? Had she made him into someone who lived exclusively in a fantasy of his own making? Where was the real Jamie? He was nowhere to be found. Jamie was an island unto himself, rejected by his mother, alienated from the world. 'To be born is to be wrecked on an island,' he once wrote.[10]

Robinson Crusoe had been his first book. He had read *The Swiss Family Robinson* too, but 'one remembers [it] as almost too satisfactory', for intuitively he knew that his island challenges would not be so easily solved as theirs. Only *The Coral Island* would do. Ballantyne's spell never left him, but as in his stalking of Carlyle and Meredith, there was a repressive streak in his adulation, later to be transformed with impish humour in the Garrick, a London gentleman's club:

> It is a few years ago and I am in a solemn London Club, which I do not much frequent because I have never been able to get the hang of clubs. I know you select a chair and cross your legs, but what do you do next? I was there to meet a learned American who had vowed that he would show me how to make a fire as Jack made it in *The Coral Island*. We adjourned to the library (where we knew we were not likely to be disturbed) and there from concealed places about his person, he produced Jack's implements, a rough bow and a rougher arrow, pointed at both ends. Then he ordered a pat of butter (the waiter must be wondering still), and, like Jack, he twisted the arrow around the string of the bow and began to saw, 'placing the end of the arrow against his chest, which was protected from its point by a chip of wood; the other point he placed against a bit of tinder. Jack had no butter, but we had no bit of tinder.' The result, however, was the same. In half a minute, my friend had made a fire, at which we lit our cigars and smoked to the memory of Ballantyne and *The Coral Island*.[11]

There was a text-book inevitability about what would become of him. Dr Eugene Bliss, an American psychiatrist who has made a study of obsessive fantasists, found that they 'all created their first "personality" early in childhood, to combat loneliness or insecurity'.[12]

Maternal rejection is a terrible thing. It can destroy a child's self-esteem. Jung wrote that a deep sense of inferiority is always balanced by unconscious compensating megalomania, the drive for power over another (and vice versa). This was the great attraction of the fantasy heroics: they always put him in charge. As Captain Stroke, Dare Devil Dick, or any of his mother's explorers – William Edward Parry, James Clark, John Ross, or the ill-fated Sir John Franklin – Jamie learned that he could be a controlling force, at least in his own world of illusion.

But it was an illusion, and the fantasy life proclaimed his emotional impotence. Denis Mackail tells us that once when Barrie was a boy he swapped jackets with a friend who was in mourning for his father, just so that he could sit down and weep, and feel what it would be like to be that sad for anyone. 'That, I tell you, is the nature of the sacket; he has a devouring desire to try on other folk's feelings,' Barrie wrote about this episode, again (as so often) in the third person.

The fact was that Jamie had lost the will to feel. This is not my analysis, it is Barrie's own admission. Maimed by his mother, he was incapable of 'even a genuine deep feeling that wasn't merely sentiment', he confided to his notebook, and as a writer he went on to question whether anybody's feelings *per se* were ever true, in the sense of altruistic, whatever they believed to the contrary.[13]

The fantasy life led to the sobriquet 'Sentimental Tommy', because sentimentality, which to true feeling is like a paper flower to a rose, is what generally passed for feeling in Barrie's fantasy world – the hollow bravado of his heroic roles and the sentiment that he liked to hang on his protagonists. To him, love was an illusion; and his fantasy relationship with Margaret was real. In the stories inspired by his sentimental relationship with his mother he could invest her with qualities he *wanted* her to have, avoiding the question of whether she did actually possess them. When invariably she would then adopt them, he came to believe that there is no true self, only what we or others want our selves to be – which finally led him to treat his whole life as if it were a fantasy he could write and rewrite, as required. This was the legacy of his loveless relationship with his mother.

*

Barrie took his degree at Edinburgh on 21 April 1882. A year later, his sister Jane Ann spotted an advertisement for a leader writer on the *Nottingham Journal* at £3 a week. Barrie applied, sending a university essay on *King Lear* as a sample of his work.

H. G. Hibbert, a sub-editor on the paper, described him as 'shy and painfully sensitive'.[14] He made no friends in Nottingham other than Thomas Gilmour, a journalist who would later be Lord Rosebery's private secretary and a flat-mate of Barrie's in London. Hibbert noted Barrie's 'immense sense of his importance', which concealed his low self-esteem, but Barrie backed it with exceptionally hard work, turning out twelve columns a week and sending articles to London magazines.

According to W. A. Darlington, the Nottingham experience gave Barrie 'the true journalist's knack of being able to turn out a readable article on anything or nothing', while his separateness from the world gave him a sometimes chilling objectivity. He took surprising standpoints on mundane topics, his increasingly cynical mind challenging the reader's routine thinking. But cynicism could descend into cruelty and some of his humour was too cocky by far, as this article, 'Pretty Boys', proved:

> Pretty boys are pretty in all circumstances, and this one would look as exquisitely delightful on the floor as when genteelly standing, in his nice little velvet suit with his sweet back to the fireplace, but think of the horror and indignation of his proud and loving mother . . . When you leave the house, the pretty boy glides like a ray of black sunshine to the door and . . . holds up his pretty mouth for a pretty kiss. If you wish to continue on visiting terms with his mother you do everything he wishes; if you are determined to remain a man whatever be the consequences, you slap his pretty cheeks very hard while the mother gazes aghast and the father looks another way, admiring your pluck and wishing he had the courage to go and do likewise. It would on the whole be a mistake to kill the child outright, because, for one thing, he may grow out of his velvet suit in time and insist on having his hair cut, and, again, the blame does not attach to him nearly so much as to his mother.

His provincial Nottingham audience did not find this amusing. Eventually, he got the sack; his last article for the *Journal* appeared on 27 October 1884. His talent was to mix satire with sentimentality and humour, but sometimes the balance didn't work, the mask slipped, and his cruel self – the side of him that announced his distorted contact with reality – peeped through.

Sentimentality was the balm that kept the lid on the truth about Barrie, and he knew it. He hated sentimentality 'as a slave may hate his master', but true feelings had not been on his agenda since he was a boy of six.

Sentimentality meant mawkishness certainly, insincerity, exaggeration, but 'far more often – he has a cruel side – [it is] satire that does not quite come off', as the writer Sir Walter Raleigh observed. At the far end of this spectrum of affectation came the gushing adoration which developed between mother and son when he became a professional writer:

> My dearly beloved Jamie my heart keeps blessing and thanking yoou [*sic*] but my love no words can say, and especially your present my head fails words for my best birthday gift. My dear beloved son God bless you and prosper you are a precious God given son to me the light of my eyes, and my darling Maggie is safe with God and you till we meet.

This is the only letter Barrie saw fit to save for posterity. It has an unnatural character, a troubled, forced intensity, as has Barrie's biography of his mother, published after her death. A peculiar feature of the purportedly eulogistic *Margaret Ogilvy* is that in it Barrie depicts his mother as arrogant, pettily snobbish, manipulative, jealously possessive, obstinate and, as W. A. Darlington concluded, 'a very tiresome old lady indeed', someone who 'accepted her daughter Jane Ann's life-long devotion and her son's adoration without a qualm'.[15]

What drew some reviewers to it originally, and convinced them of the son's great love for the mother, was Barrie's genius for sentimental engineering. Every chapter ends with a rescue operation designed to keep a place for Margaret in our hearts. But it cuts little ice today.

Why then did he persist with her, and tell the world how wonderful she was, after she rejected him? I believe it had something to do with guilt.

There are some oddities about the death of Jamie's brother David, which indicate that there was more to it than we have been told.

First, I wondered why biographers have accepted at face value Barrie's sentimental version of what happened in his mother's darkened bedroom. One has to question how so small a boy could have dressed up in the clothes of David, who was twice his age and well on the way to becoming more the size of his burly father than his minuscule mother. And the whistle. Why would Jamie need to find out what his brother's whistle was like from his friends? Wouldn't he already know?

Why was Barrie making things up about something so personal and significant? And why was he so frantically concerned about how his mother had taken the news anyway – more so than the other children? Jamie felt a very strong need to put himself in front of Margaret, after David's death, almost to plead his filial position with her. Why? And why did she resist him so?

It was never Barrie's habit to throw into question his view of things, even when an event he was describing occurred before he was born. Yet, when discussing David's death, he is at pains to distance himself from it: 'I remember very little about David . . .' 'I have been told . . .' 'I only speak from hearsay . . .' 'But I speak from hearsay . . .' – all in a matter of a few lines of *Margaret Ogilvy*. This is so out of character that it pulled me up even before I discovered some intriguing inconsistencies in reports concerning David's death.

Alick set up his private school, the Bothwell Academy, in what was then Academy Crescent, Bothwell and is now Silverwell Crescent, in 1862. The 10-year-old David was sent as a boarder there in 1863. The accepted version of David's death is the one Denis Mackail tells us:

> On the eve of his fourteenth birthday [29 January] there was a frost, and not even while skating himself, but standing watching a friend set off on the one pair of skates which they shared, he was accidentally knocked down by this boy, fell, and fractured his skull.
>
> There was little if any hope for him. His brother [Alick] telegraphed immediately to their parents, and they set off at once for the station . . . The telegraph office was there in those days, and before boarding the train David Barrie the elder thought to ask if there were any further message. A second telegram had just been received. It told him that his son was dead.[16]

This is essentially the story told in every biography of Barrie, from J. A. Hammerton's *Barrie: The Story of a Genius* in 1929, right up to Lisa Cheyney's *Life* in 2004.

However, David's death certificate tells a different story. It confirms that the boy died on 29 January 1867, at two o'clock in the morning in Academy Crescent in Bothwell, but it reveals that he had been suffering from an inflammation of the brain for *one week* before he died. Column six of the death certificate, which lists cause of death, reads: 'Inflammation of brain one week. As Cert. Bruce Goff MD.'

I noticed another oddity. According to the certificate the tragedy was reported not by Alick but by a man named William Keith, who is described as 'Guardian and occupant of house in which death occurred (present)'. William Keith had been present when David expired. Where was Alick? What could have taken the headmaster of the Academy, David's elder brother, away from Bothwell close to the beginning of the Easter term with David lying at death's door upstairs?

I then discovered that a Dutch writer and broadcaster, Hans Kuyper, had been looking into David's death too. We corresponded and met in London in 2007. I told him rather dramatically that I smelt a rat, and immediately he agreed, saying, 'It is a very smelly rat indeed – but what is the reason for all of the mystifications and what could Barrie have gained by them?'

Kuyper discovered that David's death had been reported in two newspapers: the *Hamilton Advisor* for 2 February 1867, and the *Dundee Courier and Argus* for 1 February 1867. The first announced it very simply:

> At Bothwell Academy, on the 29th ult., David Ogilvy Barrie, aged 13.

The second was very different in tone:

> At Rothesay, on the 29th ultimo., David, aged 14, second son of Mr David Barrie, manufacturer, Kirriemuir. Deceased was a very promising young lad, and is deeply regretted by a large circle of acquaintances.

According to the death certificate, the first announcement is factually correct. My guess is that it was posted by Alick. However, the second has errors in it. David did not die at Rothesay, a seaside resort on the Isle of Bute some forty miles away from Bothwell. He died in Academy Crescent, Bothwell, as the certificate shows. And he was 13, not 14.

David's age is not significant: the accident occurred on the eve of his fourteenth birthday. But the introduction of Rothesay is interesting. Could it be that the accident happened there? Kuyper went to the resort and discovered 'a sheltered little lake just to the north of Loch Fad there, called the Curling Pool'. Curling is of course a game played on ice, so it is likely that the pool is often iced over in winter. Perhaps the whole celebration – new skates, a trip to Rothesay – had something to do with it being David's fourteenth birthday on the 30th. Kuyper then spoke to Mrs Sweeten Barrie, the daughter of Alick's son, Charles, who confirmed that this was her understanding of what had happened.

On Rothesay, Kuyper met a Mrs Jess Sandeman, 'a walking encyclopaedia of the island', who remembered some Barries living there, which suggests that David may have been staying there with family. Mrs Sandeman put Kuyper in touch with one of the children of that branch of the family, a Mrs Martha Smith of Port Bannatyne, who told him a story that had come down to her 'of two brothers Barrie' holidaying there with Alick.

Suppose Jamie had travelled from Kirriemuir to Bothwell Academy with Alick and David at the end of the Christmas holiday in order to celebrate David's birthday with him, in particular to go skating with him, taking a brand new pair of birthday skates to Rothesay. Suppose Jamie had been the 'friend [who] set off on the one pair of skates which they shared', and 'accidentally' knocked David down and was the one who 'fractured his skull'.

If so, both boys might have returned the forty miles to Bothwell after the accident, and Alick might have accompanied Jamie on the hundred-mile trip home to Kirriemuir at the weekend, Saturday or Sunday, 26 or 27 January. Then the telegram had come saying that David had fallen ill, perhaps on the Sunday or the Monday, early enough to change Alick's plans to return and make arrangements for Margaret to travel with him back to Bothwell. No alarm at this stage. The second telegram, announcing his death, had arrived on Tuesday morning (David had died at 2 a.m.) while they were at the station awaiting the train.

This would fit in with the report that David was ill for a week before he died. It would explain Alick's absence from Bothwell on the day of David's death, the 29th, and why there was such a painful situation, guilt and recrimination, between Margaret and Jamie. How desperate would Jamie have been to put things right with his mother, and how difficult would Margaret have found it *ever* to forgive him.

It is of course highly speculative, but it explains the emotional dynamic between mother and son, Margaret's alienation from Jamie, and why Jamie continued, throughout his life, to make reparation. Moreover this worrying emotional dynamic between mother and son turns out to be replicated in the story of Peter Pan.

In *The Little White Bird*, the novel that preceded and set up the story for the play, *Peter Pan,* Peter, an ordinary child, flies out of the window of the nursery and goes to live on Birds' Island with Solomon Caw, becoming a 'betwixt-and-between'; part boy, part sprite. In time, however, he resolves to go home. His intention is to fly back through the nursery window, which it was understood that his mother would always keep open for him –

> But the window was closed, and there were iron bars on it, and peering inside he saw his mother sleeping peacefully with her arm round another little boy.
>
> Peter called, 'Mother! mother!' but she heard him not; in vain he beat his little limbs against the iron bars . . . What a glorious boy he had meant to be to her! Ah Peter! We who have made *the great mistake*, how differently we should all act at the second chance. But Solomon was right – there is no second chance, not for most of us. When we reach the window it is Lock-out Time. The iron bars are up for life.

For Peter, there is no second chance, no way ever to reclaim his mother's love. The desperate hammerings of his little fists on the window are Jamie's frantic attempts after David's accident to get back into his mother's love. The iron bars were, indeed, up for life.

And yes, there is a sense of Peter Pan's guilt. His mother has been crying, 'and he knew what was the great thing she cried for, and that a hug from her splendid Peter would quickly make her to smile. Oh! He felt sure of it . . .' But the 'great thing she cried for' was 'the great mistake', which Peter had made and we are never told about, so big a mistake that a hug is not going to be enough, any more than it was in Jamie's case after David's accident.

Following his dismissal from the *Nottingham Journal*, Barrie's success in London was in no small way due to Margaret: she gave him the stories that made his name, a series of articles, beginning in November 1884 with 'An Auld Licht Community', which would later be used as the basis of a novel,[17] and the tactical thinking and 'a certain grimness about not being beaten' that leaked out of the sump in the engine room of their otherwise barren relationship. In the end, Jim articulated what they both knew, that they were 'very like each other inside . . .'

> You may picture the editor in his office thinking he was behaving like a shrewd man of business, and unconscious that up in the north there was an elderly lady chuckling so much at him that she could scarcely scrape the potatoes.[18]

When he first asked her how he should net a sympathetic editor, Margaret rocked her head back on the pillows and laughed:

> 'I would find out first if he had a family, and then I would say they were the finest family in London.'
>
> 'Yes, that is just what you would do, you cunning woman! But if he has no family?'
>
> 'I would say what great men editors are!'
>
> 'He would see through you.'
>
> 'Not he!'
>
> 'You don't understand that what imposes on common folk would never hoodwink an editor.'
>
> 'That's where you are wrong. Gentle or simple, stupid or clever, the men are all alike in the hands of a woman that flatters them.'
>
> 'Ah, I'm sure there are better ways of getting round an editor than that.'
>
> 'I daresay there are,' my mother would say with conviction, 'but if you try that plan you will never need to try another.'
>
> 'How artful you are, mother – you with your soft face! Do you not think shame?'
>
> 'Pooh!' says my mother brazenly.
>
> 'I can see the reason why you are so popular with men.'
>
> 'Ay, you can see it, but they never will.'

Mother and son, unrestrained by unconditional filial love, had become co-conspirators with a cynical disrespect for the world. He had found her cynical nature, or, luxuriating in her domination of him, planted it in her. Together they rehearsed the stratagems with which Barrie would turn society to his advantage, leaving people marvelling at his genius. It was a philosophy of self-interest, justified on the altar of expediency. According to Jamie, it was Margaret who affected one response while showing another 'in her eye'. But whoever was behind it, the stratagem to dissemble came with no homily on moral virtue attached. In their book, 'finding a way' was the priority, a matter not of solving a problem, but of manipulation and control.

Margaret could not see beyond Jamie now. Their pact was Faustian, a loveless blood pact, inescapable. If he had cast her off now, she would have withered like an amputated hand.

I had no idea how desperate things had got until I came across a hand-written manuscript sheet of Mackail's official biography of Barrie. It is a remarkable document because it completely rewrites the accepted view of the Barrie home. The text is scarred by two pens, one of them certainly wielded by Lady Cynthia Asquith. A blue pen describes in two-inch letters scrawled across the page: 'KILL THIS'; the other, a more sober brown, finds its way less dramatically diagonally across the middle, from bottom left: 'Re-write this page' . Mackail's text, which was withheld from publication, paints a bleak picture.

> Jane Ann forty-six, as austere and as self-sacrificing as ever. Plain, already elderly in appearance, with no chance now to develop her mother's conceit, and morose and difficult in her scant life, for – it's no use hiding it any longer – she wasn't the only member of the family . . . to yield at last to deadly temptation. There were two [pitfalls] that lay in wait for Margaret Ogilvy's children, and only the very strongest could resist them both. Hypochondria and drink. Jane Ann, with an example and warning against one of them always under her care [i.e. Margaret, who was permanently in bed], had fought against it and had won. But only, it now seemed, by giving way to the other. Her brother [Jamie] knew, just as he knew about what was happening elsewhere, and in turn the whole unfortunate business told him what he must guard against himself. He did guard against it. Once or twice it [drink] offered him brief comfort, when one of his worlds fell to pieces, but that is the worst and frankest that can be said. It never mastered him; and though hypochondria [hung] round him all his life, he could always beat it when he chose. For he was slippery as well as courageous, even where heredity had all but got him down. But the others were weaker and more vulnerable. The stimulus of fame and position could only reach them at second hand. So they drank, & they took to their beds and refused to get up. Again it is one of those . . . biological mysteries in the union of that hand loom weaver and that stonemason's daughter. Inexplicable. Horrifying and haunting. Somehow, apparently, and whether guilty or innocent, every one of their children must pay a remorseless price.

Incapable of love, they maimed each other. There was nothing left now, but to destroy. Fed up with his sentimental turn of mind, Jamie wrote: 'If only I could write something *harmful*.'[19]

When Margaret died, Jamie deliberately avoided it, but recorded what he was told had happened as if he had been there: 'On the last day my mother insisted on rising from bed and going through the house . . . there seemed to be something that she wanted . . .' No one could guess what it was. 'They followed her through the house in some apprehension, and after she returned to bed they saw that she was becoming very weak. Once she said eagerly, "Is that you, David?"' Barrie, retelling the story that was told to him, assumes that Margaret was calling for her husband, David, but perhaps it was her dead son, for those that were attending her suddenly realise the purpose of her expedition through the house – 'what she wanted was the old christening robe', the robe she had called for to feel and hold after David died. 'It was brought to her, and she unfolded it with trembling, exultant hands, and . . . her arms went round it adoringly, and upon her face there was the ineffable mysterious glow of motherhood. Suddenly she said, "Wha's bairn's dead? Is a bairn of mine dead?" but those watching dared not speak.'[20]

David's death, and Margaret's rejection of Jamie, lie at the bottom of everything. Typically, a boy may deal with maternal rejection by withdrawing from heterosexual interaction, or becoming a bookworm, or by engaging in fantasy heroics. Barrie did all of these. But if the boy comes to hate his mother, there is the threat of a serious neurotic conflict, possibly with very dark consequences indeed.

It is not commonly known that an early title of *Peter Pan* was *The Boy Who Hated Mothers*.

CHAPTER FOUR

Nervous breakdown

When he arrived in London, in May 1860, Kicky got in touch with Alecco Ionides and his brother Luke. The Ionides family lived in Tulse Hill, Norwood, and put their immense wealth to good use, providing a meeting place, a sort of regeneration for the imagination, for some of the most gifted artists and writers of the day. They also helped some of them financially. 'My uncle Leonidas seems to have known all the literary celebrities of his time,' wrote Luke.[1] 'He used to stay with George Sand, knew Balzac and nearly all the great French authors as well as the German . . . he was a lawyer.'

At one time or another the family supported C. G. Rossetti, Edward Burne-Jones, G. F. Watts, Alphonse Legros, and Fantin-Latour, and soon Alecco would buy sixteen plates of Whistler's etchings of the lower Thames. Watts once proposed that they should give him £300 a year for life in exchange for all his works. Luke's father 'answered that he would let him have any money he wanted, so that he should not be troubled with the menace of want, but he would enter into no pact of that sort, as the time would soon come when Watts' earnings would be in thousands – a prophecy which came true.' That was the timbre of the scene, and Kicky loved it, especially the Ionides girls who typified the relaxed bohemian atmosphere of their home, which was furnished with traditional Greek artefacts and festooned with splendid embroidered materials. It was an opportunity to enjoy the life that Kicky had left behind in Europe. He describes how these dark mysterious beauties 'will sometimes take one's hands when talking to one, or put their arm around the back of the chair at dinner'. With all this 'ease and *tutoiement*', he would leave their company feeling 'very virtuous'.[2]

Kicky wrote to his mother:

> Last Sunday I went with Jimmie [Whistler] to the Greek's, such a charming house and such charming people. Seem to have quite cut out Jemmie [*sic*] there in one séance. There were about twenty people, and after dinner, being in tremendous voice and spirits I quite delighted them; Jemmie behaved me well, trotted me out to perfection – Jemmie was adored. I appeared to be idolised there, and they are very useful acquaintances.

So there were séances at Tulse Hill and also at Newman Street, where Kicky shared a studio with James Whistler. Luke Ionides recalled that 'we often had table-turning at Jimmy's, but no very important results. He had an idea that Jo* was a bit of a medium; certainly the raps were more frequent when she was at the table, but I cannot recall any message worth repeating . . .'

One of the artists Kicky met at Tulse Hill was Edward Burne-Jones, who was frequently to be found there and was at that time a pupil of Rossetti. Luke used to read to Burne-Jones from *The Arabian Nights,* in 1860 still unpublished in a complete English edition. The work captivated those artists who were focused on spiritualism, hypnotism and extending the frontiers of human consciousness.

By January 1861 Kicky shared a house with Alecco and an artist called Lionel Charles Henley (but known as Bill) whom Kicky had met in Düsseldorf. He wrote to his mother:

> Bill and I have got the house pretty much to ourselves and make uncommonly *bon menage*. He has the first floor, I the second. I have two bedrooms, one of which Alecco pays 6 bob a week for and a drawing room or studio *faut voir*. So far two luxurious armchairs and a very first rate piano, a subscription affair, which Bill is now strumming, for there is an evening at home and by and by Keene and Jimmie and co will come in . . . What splendid people these Greeks are. I never met any people like them . . . There is a great deal of goings on with these Greeks.

Felix Moscheles had been writing from Belgium, but it was some time before Kicky replied. When he did, he gave him the impression that the London scene far surpassed Malines, even Paris:

> I'm leading the merriest of lives, and only hope it will last. Living with

* Joanna, the model for Whistler's *At the Piano*, *The White Girl* and later for *Little White Girl* and *Symphony in White*.

> Henley, No. 85, Newman Street; very jolly and comfortable. Chumming with all the old Paris fellows again, all of them going ahead. Whistler is already one of the great celebrities here –
>
> Poynter* is getting on. This is a very jolly little village, and I wish you were over here.
>
> They do make such a fuss with an agreeable fellow like you or me, for instance. But I suppose Paris is just as jolly in its way. My ideas of Paris are all Bohème, quartier latin, &c, et si c'était à recommencer, ma foi je crois que je dirais 'zut.' This is a hurried and absurd letter to write to an old pal like you, but I hardly ever have time for a line—out late every night . . .

Kicky finished with an invitation he later had cause to regret, 'Jimmy Whistler and I go "tumbling" together, as Thackeray says. Would you were here to tumble with us! Enfin, mon bon, écris moi vite.' By May 1861 his old friend was in London sniffing the air, and Kicky was biting his tongue: 'Felix is a poor little posing Frenchman among a lot of heroes here. I am afraid they will not get on very well with him as the grand thing among all my fellows is the complete and utter absence of all humbug of any kind,' Kicky wrote to his mother.

Felix in fact adapted readily to the scene in London. Before long, he had a class teaching young ladies painting, no doubt hypnotising some of them. According to Kicky, Felix was bringing in 'nearly £300 a year and has himself lots of orders for cheap portraits, which he paints very quick. Whereas Jimmie, the great genius of the day . . . isn't making a sou and borrowed a shilling of me yesterday.'

From the time of Felix's arrival, Kicky began to show signs of strain. He wrote to his mother: 'I have passed a very very anxious month, but I am better now; I would give anything to go and have a fortnight's chat with you. Such a lot to pour out that I have never written . . . I am in very good health but very thin; lost an inch and a half round the neck from rage and vexation.'

As we chart Kicky's decline, it is as well to remember that Felix cut out his hypnotic 'excursions' in 1865, because it 'was taking too much out of' him. Kicky was burning the candle at both ends, too. Indeed they all were. Tom Armstrong, who invariably accompanied him to the Greeks' on a Sunday, had suffered some sort of bad trip and was fast fading from the

* Edward Poynter had also studied with George du Maurier at the Gleyre studio in Paris, and later became President of the Royal Academy.

scene, never to return: 'I am very sorry to hear of these relapses, which must be a wretched bore,' Kicky wrote to him, '– alas that ill-fated Sunday, that [illegible] devil!'

During this time, separate from his rackety encounters with the Greeks and his artist friends, Kicky had been wooing Emma Wightwick, his sister Isabel's friend in whose company he had travelled to London.*

The attraction was mutual, and it was understood that they would marry when Kicky had carved himself out a career. But finding work had been more difficult than he'd imagined it would be. In fact, he was so poor he couldn't afford the lotion he needed for his eyes, and as his letters to his mother show, he was sleeping badly.

He got his first commission from a magazine called *Once a Week*. Luke Ionides had sat for him cross-legged, dressed as a Turk, the illustration for an article entitled 'Faristan and Fatima'. *Once a Week* was 'perhaps more important than any other in furthering the new movement in drawing on wood', according to Armstrong.[3] But a series in *Punch* was Kicky's principal target. Even a year later when he was drawing for quite a range of magazines, including *Cornhill*, *London Society*, and the *Illustrated London News*, it was *Punch* he wanted.

Punch was in its heyday and known internationally for its witty take on the world. As Daphne recorded, 'People waited impatiently for the weekly *Punch* to appear as today they wait for – nothing. If you did not read *Punch* you were a Philistine, you were finished, you did not exist. And very soon those graceful drawings with "du M" in the lower left-hand corner became the best known page in the paper.'[4]

He began illustrating the magazine's 'English Society at Home' series in 1861. Perhaps it was his very Frenchness, the essential du Maurier duality, that gave him the objectivity needed to caricature the English, or maybe it was the gently satirical nature of his humour, which George Besant had noticed a decade earlier in Cambridge. Whatever it was, it worked. In September, an article published in the *Spectator* about John Tenniel and Charles Keene, two famous *Punch* illustrators, wound up with 'a very pretty compliment to me, speaking of my rapid progress & "gentlemanly feeling" and saying *Punch* will find a great acquisition in Mr du Maurier – I fancy this will do me much good.'

When he received a commission his spirits would rise tremendously, and

* Their quiet courting would be recorded years later in George du Maurier's third novel, *The Martian* (1897).

he'd be back to his old self, singing and dancing and partying, and begging Emma to save him from the dissolute life: 'I awoke with seedy eyes & weary back & parched mouth; dooced familiar sensation, yet seems quite forgotten; brought back all sorts of recollections which I hate with the whole strength of my affection for you, recollections of so many nights with Whistler & Tom A, & Tom J, & lots of fellows, years ago & even lately; & in which a great deal too much wine & smoke have been taken in, & too much wild talk let out, for happiness. So *Miss Salvation* (as T.J's friend, Watson said) you had better not lose your nose or your life in a collision.'

In December 1861, he tried to sell his Carry novel to the *Cornhill* magazine – '24 pages of closely written foolscap . . .' – and wrote to Armstrong, 'Lamont is there as the wise and facetious Jerry, you as the bullnecked & sagacious Tim; the street is Our Lady of the Bohemians. I shall idealise in the illustrations . . . make us all bigger, and develop you into strong muscularity . . . If this does succeed, I shall write lots more on the same theme and try and embody the rather peculiar opinion of our set on art itself and artists; and which I feel very strongly . . .'

A month later he took rejection on the chin: 'My MS was refused by the *Cornhill*; embêtant, mais nous y serons un jour.'* But it was not all bad news: he was already making over £400 a year, and a house in Regent's Park could be rented for £60 p.a.

There was, however, much more involved in a commitment to Emma than cash. She 'felt Paris had induced bad ways in him, which he must correct', wrote Daphne, 'and his tendency to think of himself as a Frenchman and a bohemian was something it would be better for him to forget. He must learn to become an Englishman and a respectable one at that.'

With Emma on his tail he began going to bed at twelve and getting up at eight and taking quinine, all of which 'is gradually making an improvement in my health'. As Felix saw it, Emma was weighing Kicky down, and he drew a cartoon to illustrate the point. Using their Antwerp Academy nicknames – Kicky had been *Rag*, and Felix *Bobtail*, because they had had another friend called *T A G* Sprenk† – the two friends, Rag and Bobtail, are climbing a rope. 'I am climbing with fiendish energy,' wrote Felix beneath.

* As his granddaughter Daphne commented ninety years later, 'Et comment!' The Carry novel appeared as *Trilby* in 1894.

† *Rag, Tag and Bobtail* was in fact a 1950s TV programme in Britain based on stories by Louise Cochrane about a hedgehog, a mouse and a rabbit. However, in the nineteenth century the phrase 'rag-tag and bobtail' meant 'common' or 'vulgar'.

'Rag follows, steadily ascending, weighted as he is with a treasure, a box marked "Mrs Rag, with care."'

Mrs Rag was principally concerned about Mr Rag's experimentation, the 'excursions' – the 'illusion that enervates! Feverish dream of excitement magnetic, inspired, supreme', and the 'opium-benumbing performances', which, 'in their sad wild unresting irregular flow'[5] seemed to be expressly concocted for Kicky.

Complicating his situation further, but greatly enlivening it, in 1862 a new face appeared on the scene. 'I've been fraternising most extensively with Val Prinsep,' Kicky wrote to Armstrong early that year. '[He] is such a stunning fellow – six foot 1, 23 of age, not an ounce of fat – but weighs 16 stone 6! Such a murderous looking arm of more than 14 inches! And a very jolly fellow . . . proeRaphaelite [*sic*] pupil of Watts, who lives at the [Prinseps'] parental home in Kensington, Little Holland House. I've dined there 2 or 3 times . . . Val, who is a stunner in every way, has introduced me to Burn Jones [*sic*], who is simply an angel and what a colourist . . .'*

Here, at Little Holland House, the cream of literary and artistic London convened. 'Three beautiful women – sisters – form a nucleus round which gather all that there is of swell; the nobilitee, the gentree, the litherathure, politithics and art of the counthree, by jasus! It is a nest of proeraphalites . . . where Hunt, Millais, Rossetti, Watts, Leighton, etc., Tennyson, the Brownings and Thackeray, etc. and *tutti quanti* receive dinners and incense, and cups of tea handed to them by these women almost kneeling.'

The three sisters, née Prattle, were Val's mother, Sara, and two aunts (Lady Somers and Mrs Dalrymple), famous in their day, cultural snobs all of them, but the saviour of many needy artists. There were altogether seven Prattle sisters including the pioneering photographer Julia Cameron. G. F. Watts found a taker for his proposition for patronage here. He was said to have arrived one evening in 1850 and stayed for twenty years. He did not impress Kicky much, but Val Prinsep did. 'I confess that after the first half hour, women's society bores me *pas mal*,' he wrote afterwards, 'and the jolliest part of the evening was with Val P in Charlotte Street.' Val had taken Kicky to his studio and they had read poems of Browning till 5 a.m.

Val's impressive physique exemplified the 'strong muscularity', which would pass into many of Kicky's characters in illustration and fiction.

* Valentine Prinsep trained at Gleyre's studio in Paris and exhibited many historical, classical and biblical paintings at the Royal Academy between 1862 and 1904. He was considered less successful as a classical artist than du Maurier's other friends, Poynter and Alma-Tadema.

Kicky himself said that Val measured up to 'an aesthetic ideal I had always felt'. He had already announced to Armstrong that he was going to make the male characters of 'the Carry novel' heroic in size. So, we are to think of his admiration in terms of his rapture on a visit to the Elgin Marbles: 'I *knew* that people ought to be built like that.'

The connection between Kicky and Prinsep brought the Little Holland House crew together with the Tulse Hill gang, and considerably heightened the level of consciousness-raising activity.

In July 1862 Kicky dined at Little Holland House with Millais, and in the same year, according to Luke Ionides, Dante Gabriel Rossetti first visited Tulse Hill. Rossetti's base at this time was an old Elizabethan house, 16 Cheyne Walk in Chelsea. He had a menagerie of animals, including a wombat. It was, wrote Luke Ionides, a house where 'one met all sorts of people . . .'

> One evening after dinner we went into a tent he had raised in the garden, and Bergheim, a powerful mesmerist, was asked if he could mesmerise any stranger, and as he said, 'Yes,' Rossetti sent out into the street to find two stray women, who would not mind submitting to the experiment. Both Jimmy and [his brother] Willy Whistler were there, Edward Dannreuther, the musician, and Lord Lindsay, and each one was asked to tell Bergheim what he wanted each woman to do.
>
> Jimmy Whistler suggested that one should think that she had a fleabite on her knee; and without words, from the other side of the table, Bergheim made passes and the girl proceeded to scratch her knee. I suggested that I should like one of them to come up to the table, drink a glass of claret and think it was milk, upon which she came up, drank the wine, and when asked what she was drinking said, 'Why, don't you see it's milk?'
>
> Dannreuther put them both to the severest test. When Bergheim had made passes over them, Dannreuther asked him to start one of them singing and to stop her at a certain note, then to start the other, and stop her in the same way, Dannreuther noting the note on which each had left off. Then after a few minutes' interval Bergheim restarted the first girl, and she went on exactly where she had left off, and the second girl also restarted on the note on which she had left off; a feat which Dannreuther declared was impossible to the most accomplished singers.

In the index to Alecco's book, *Ion: A Grandfather's Tale* (1927), there are five references to Bergheim, who was a famous hypnotist of the day, and all of them have been stripped out of the main body of the text, so that there is in fact no mention of him beyond the index, which suggests that they had been taken out hurriedly just prior to printing, perhaps on legal advice. One of the references directs the reader to a page otherwise wholly devoted to *Trilby*, implying that history might be missing an interesting connection to du Maurier. Clearly psychic activity among these artists was at a high. Luke describes Rossetti turning up at Whistler's while another séance was in progress, and breaking it up, saying, 'You'd better stop that, otherwise you will go mad.'

In April that year, 1862, Kicky did indeed almost go mad. He wrote to his mother that the first 'four or five days' of the 'strange illness' – after which he believed he had recovered – 'seem to have absorbed quite an age and without giving me the slightest bodily pain or weakness have inflicted on me suffering I have never dreamt of and which now I can't realise . . .'

> Don't let this alarming debut frighten you but you must know that without noticing any symptoms of disease whatever in my old carcase I have been slightly disinclined to work lately, and irritable in my temper without due cause – and figure to yourself that on Friday evening as I was sitting with my dearest and most beloved of Pems* I felt all my affection for her, you, Isabel, and my friends cease as by enchantment; yet my powers of reasoning strange to say were by no means impaired; indeed remarkably clear and active. Well, as you may fancy I went home and to bed but in such despair I cannot realise it. I awoke early to the same fearful state, feeling myself utterly lost for ever and ever, dead to all natural affection, and resolving hard to lead henceforth a life of martyrdom to duty – at length a faint glimmer suggested itself to me that perhaps some internal derangement of which I was unaware was the cause of this hideous state of mind – and catching at the straw of hope I went off to Haden's (may his name be forever blessed and his shadow never grow less!). He explained to me that my liver was altogether in a disturbed state . . .

Such a diagnosis was typical of the times. Kicky was prescribed a medicine, which appears to have done him no good at all, and he longed for some symptoms that would confirm that it was indeed a physical disease.

The attacks came in waves, so that one moment, 'I was as hard to Pem and as insensible as a flint', and the next he believed that 'the neck of the disease broke and I buried myself in my dear Pem's arms in a passion of

* Emma's nickname was Pem.

hysterical sobbing, which I can scarcely dare to think of. I had two or three relapses after, rather less violent and shorter . . . How I longed for frightful bodily pain and revelled in the notion of death.'

On doctor's orders he left Emma for Brighton in order to recuperate. On 21 April he wrote to Emma:

> You will be pleased to hear that relief has come to me at last and that today I am much better. Indeed I have been quite myself for a little while, feeling only that I have been most fearfully shaken; and of course my native facetiousness has been frightened out of me for a little while. I received your dear affectionate letter . . . I have not yet made up my mind about how long to stay . . .

But his condition was in fact far from stable. On 23 April he wrote:

> Today I am a good deal better – a sort of languid, lucid interval – yesterday was miserable.

On 26 April:

> I have had a few hours relief and then dropping down again into wretchedness. God knows when and how it will end . . . Darling, I shall remember Brighton as the place where the most unhappy hours of my life have been spent. I wonder if I shall get really well again and once more have confidence in myself and self respect and courage to struggle and work?

On the 27th:

> I have just come in from a long ride over the hills. I am constantly fluctuating between the blues and the other thing, but am beginning to acquire more command over myself rather . . .

In May he wrote to his mother Ellen, summing up the whole experience and describing it not so much as an illness as the discovery of a dark side of himself:

> It suddenly came across me that the original badness of my nature was just going to break out at last . . . temptation suddenly to break loose and to indulge in every riotous excess, drink, opium, and the most shameless

> intrigues, for I felt that come over me (as it seemed you know) that no woman in the world could resist and that when I felt downright madness reach me, as it would inevitably have done according to my theory at the time, I would kill myself and escape the asylum . . . I felt I hated Emma, you, and all those of my friends I admire the most for being so naturally and easily possessed of qualities which were denied to me, and envied you all to an extent . . . it was a downright anguish.

He had clearly suffered some sort of breakdown associated with his dabbling in psychic and possibly drug-related activities. Daphne pointed to 'his evenings at Little Holland House without Emma, the guardian angel . . . a sore temptation to what he believed to be his better nature'. Possibly she was right, although just before he fell ill he had also been on a number of excursions to 'the dear Tulse Hill people', the Greeks, who had done for Armstrong.

An especially interesting aspect of the symptoms he describes is his disdain for Emma and everyone in the 'straight' world. This feeling of superiority and contempt for those around is a cultist feature that gets the hypnotic subject coming back for more. It is also a characteristic of Trilby after she has been hypnotised regularly by Svengali. It would have broken Emma's heart to have met Kicky's entranced personality.

Emma made it clear that, if they were to be married, Kicky must give up what she saw as his bohemian activities. Of course she didn't understand that in this otherworld of imagination lay the centre from which he was living.

Kicky understood that Mrs Rag would never know this world, and on account of his love for her, Mr Rag would now bury his No. 2 self, and be 'full of honest ambition and good purpose', the person she wanted to marry and the person everyone recognised.

In December 1862 he wrote to his mother, 'Emma and I are getting married on the third of January, we are going to live on the second floor, 36 Great Russell Street,* 25 shillings a week, and I have taken a small studio in the same house, ground floor, £25 a year. It has a splendid light, all the ceiling in glass, and in time we shall be able to make it very comfortable, I have no doubt . . .'

It was a capitulation. But a capitulation that Kicky never regretted making. Nor would it be for ever.

* By June 1863 they were living at 91 Great Russell Street.

PART III

1885–1894

Kicky, Barrie and Svengali: the secret

DELICATE CONSIDERATION

Mamma. "What a din you're making Chicks! What are you playing at!"

Trixy. "O, Mamma, we're playing at railway trains. *I'm* the engine, and Guy's a first-class carriage, and Sylvia's a second-class carriage, and May's a third-class carriage, and Gerald, he's a third-class carriage, too—that is, he's really only a *truck*, you know, only you mustn't tell him so, as it would *offend* him!"

CHAPTER ONE

Impotent and ambitious

It was the Auld Lichts that first brought Barrie to London. On 8 November 1884, he sold an article with the title 'An Auld Licht Community' to Frederick Greenwood, editor of the prestigious *St James's Gazette*. Greenwood, although complimentary, cautioned him about uprooting and coming to the capital. But Barrie was already packing his box and in March 1885 he booked a one-way ticket to London, having meanwhile penned another article on spec for Greenwood, entitled 'The Rooks begin to Build'.

> Let us survey our hero as he sits awake in a corner of his railway compartment . . . He has a suspicious eye, poor gomeril, for any fellow-traveller, who is civil to him. He is gauche and inarticulate . . . Expression an uncomfortable blank . . . Ladies have decided that he is of no account, and he already knows this and has private anguish thereanent [*sic*] . . . Only asset, except a pecuniary one, is a certain grimness about not being beaten. Pecuniary asset, twelve pounds in a secret pocket which he sometimes presses, as if it were his heart . . .
>
> Having reached London for the great adventure, he was hauling his box to the left-luggage shed at St Pancras when his eyes fell upon what was to him the most warming sight in literature. It was the placard of the 'St James's Gazette' of the previous evening with printed on it in noble letters 'The Rooks begin to Build' . . . In other dazzling words, having been a minute or so in London, he had made two guineas. This may not seem a great thrill to you, but try it in his circumstances . . .
>
> Forty-five years have elapsed since this event, the romance of my life, I myself can now regard it with comparative calm, but I still hold that it was almost as if Greenwood had met me at the station.[1]

Immediately, there followed a period of intense activity lasting four years, during which time around 140 articles were accepted by Greenwood, while 'far more than twice that number had the sadder fate of rejection'; over 200 also went to other journals, with Barrie reckoning that some 800 were declined. He also wrote five books, which presented two distinct faces: 'the grave author of Thrums', who was based on his mother's tales of old Kirriemuir, examples of a regional genre made popular by Thomas Hardy,* and 'the pipe-smoking freelance journalist of Fleet Street', who appeared in the autobiographical *When a Man's Single* (1888) and *My Lady Nicotine* (1890). Otherwise, for the time being, he preferred to write his articles anonymously. 'He was a humble atom was Mr Anon,' wrote Barrie with characteristic objectivity, 'but I am glad he worked as hard.'[2]

He was not in fact humble at all. He seemed shy, but there was also the almost aggressive sense of his own importance that Hibbert, the sub-editor on the *Nottingham Journal*, had observed, and this made him a bit 'touchy', according to the comic writer, Jerome K. Jerome.

Jerome, the ex-railway clerk who found fame with *Three Men in a Boat* (1889), was writing for the novelist F. W. Robinson's monthly magazine, *Home Chimes*, which operated from a tiny office up two flights of stairs in a narrow lane off Paternoster Row in the City. Before arriving in London Barrie had written an article for Robinson entitled 'A Night in a Provincial Newspaper Office', and through the magazine he found himself in the company of a group of writers dining once a fortnight at Pagani's, a small, first-floor Italian restaurant in Great Portland Street. The group grew to include the poet Swinburne, and the rump of it later formed a club called the Vagabonds. 'We were an odd collection of about a dozen,' Jerome recalled. 'We dined together . . . at the fixed price of two shillings a head, and most of us drank Chianti at one and fourpence the half flask.'[3]

Often, however, Barrie spent his evenings alone, confronting his devils:

> I am never in my element until I reach deep water. The unfathomable sea of thought seems to buoy me up . . . I lie awake with the problems of my personality . . . My moods are as changeable as a hoary ocean. There are times when I am the best of company, when my wit sparkles and cuts. At other times I walk in the shadows . . . ruminating with the mighty dead.[4]

* The Thrums novels were *Auld Licht Idylls* (1888), *A Window in Thrums* (1889) and *The Little Minister* (1891).

His was an objective, tricksy, cynical, often funny, but sometimes deeply morose perception of the world. As Jerome commented, 'The natural solemnity of his face is a little startling to one who has come out to dine . . . It was as if he tugged the strings that work the organs of risibility, but either the strings were broken or he had forgotten to bring the organs.'[5] Revelling in a Faustian tendency to plumb the depths of his psyche, Barrie shared the purblind scholar's problem – no form with the ladies. He wrote of himself:

> If you could dig deep enough into him you would find first his Rotherschildian ambition, which is to earn a pound a day; beneath that is a desire to reach some little niche in literature; but in the marrow you find him vainly weltering to be a favourite of the ladies. All the other cravings he would toss aside for that; he is only striving hard for numbers one and two because he knows with an everlasting sinking that number three can never be for him.

Self-exposure came naturally to Barrie and won him his readers' sympathy. You never quite knew when the comedian would suddenly vanish and the darker, deeper self take over, but at least, as his biographer Darlington asserted, 'Though Barrie sometimes took an impish delight in decorating or even fantasticating his own portrait, he never falsified it.'

His problems with the ladies, Jerome knew well:

> He could easily be the most silent man I have ever met. Sometimes he would sit through the whole of a dinner without ever speaking. Then, when all but the last one or two guests had gone – or even later – he would put his hands behind his back and, bummeling up and down the room, talk for maybe an hour straight on end. Once a beautiful but nervous young lady was handed over to his care. With the *sole au gratin* Barrie broke the silence:
>
> 'Have you ever been to Egypt?'
>
> The young lady was too startled to answer immediately. It was necessary for her to collect herself. While waiting for the *entrée* she turned to him.
>
> 'No,' she answered.
>
> Barrie made no comment. He went on with his dinner. At the end of the *chicken en casserole*, curiosity overcoming her awe, she turned to him again.
>
> 'Have you?' she asked.
>
> A far-away expression came into Barrie's great deep eyes.
>
> 'No,' he answered.
>
> After that they both lapsed into silence.[6]

Barrie was most at ease in the company of children, for, if his childhood had left him in a mess, it had certainly not left him.

One of the earliest of his young conquests shared the same name as his mother. Margaret Henley was the daughter of W. E. Henley, editor of the *National (Scots) Observer*, to which Barrie contributed. Henley used a crutch and was 'a splendidly ironic, bearded man . . . When he thundered a red light came into his eye, which so entranced you that you forgot it might be a danger signal. He thundered at all of us,' Barrie explained. 'It was Kipling, I think, who presented him with a punching ball, after first writing all our names on it . . . this W.G. [Grace] of letters.'[7] Robert Louis Stevenson modelled Long John Silver on Henley. Fond as Barrie was of the father, he was besotted with the daughter. As Henley played the piano, the little girl 'fell into his lap, and sometimes danced round the instrument and under it and over me'. She called Barrie 'my friendy', but because she couldn't pronounce her R's, it sounded like 'my fwendy', which at length became 'Wendy' in *Peter Pan* (though the girl in the play was actually based on Margaret, Barrie's mother). Margaret Henley was so sweet that she became the subject of a painting by Charles Furze, but 'she died when she was about five', Barrie wrote, adding with the heartless innocence that was always there, just beneath the surface, 'one might call it a sudden idea that came to her in the middle of her romping.'

He also enjoyed the company of his brother Alick's son, Charlie, whom he wrote about as Peterkin in the *Edinburgh Evening Dispatch*. Barrie, in his role as Peterkin's uncle, reprimanded the boy for hitting him with a hammer and threatened to kick him around the room if he didn't make himself scarce. Later, the boy returned –

> He came and stood by my side, offering himself mutely for slaughter . . .
>
> 'What is the matter now?' I demanded fiercely.
>
> 'You said you would kick me round the room,' he moaned.
>
> 'Well, I won't do it,' I said, 'if you are a good boy.'
>
> 'But you said you would do it.'
>
> 'You don't mean that you want it?'
>
> 'Ay, I want it. You said you would do't.'
>
> Wondering, I arose and kicked him.
>
> 'Is that the way?' he cried in rapture.
>
> 'That's the way,' I said, returning to my chair.
>
> 'But,' he complained, 'you said you would kick me round the room.'
>
> I got up again, and made a point of kicking him round the room.

> 'Kick harder!' he shouted, and so I kicked him into the lobby.
>
> However desirous of gratifying Peterkin, I could not be always kicking him . . . and for the sake of peace I bribed quietness from him with the promise that I would kick him hard at eight o'clock . . .
>
> Most people keep their distance from me, regarding me as morose and unsociable; but Peterkin thought he had found the key to me, and was convinced I would not kick him so heartily if I did not consider him rather nice. He said that eight o'clock was longer in coming round than any other time of the day, and he frequently offered me chocolate to kick him in advance . . .
>
> He also thoroughly enjoys being tied with strings that leave their mark on him for days . . .

Friendships between adult males and children outside the family were not uncommon in late Victorian England. For example, John Millais, with what the newspapers called 'his schoolboy manner', had in the late 1870s developed a warm relationship with Beatrix Potter, when she was a little girl. Millais was one of a group of adult males, including Elizabeth Gaskell's husband and Quaker politician John Bright, who came alive in the company of young Beatrix, with her innocence, beauty and shy contemplative manner.

The fact that such Romantic relationships were inspirational presumably put parents at their ease; but there were many examples of less innocent conduct. Earlier, for instance, the critic John Ruskin had divorced amidst rumours of a suspect attraction to young girls. Ruskin's ex-wife then married Millais. Ruskin also had a bizarre relationship with the artist Kate Greenaway, who liked 'to play child' with him and indulge in baby talk. All this came in the wake of Lewis Carroll's perhaps questionable friendship with Alice Liddell* and is the historical context for Barrie's relationships with children.

Barrie also had a special friendship with Bevil Quiller-Couch – 'my favourite boy in the wide wide world,' the son of the writer and academic Arthur Quiller-Couch,† known as Q. Barrie captivated Bevil, and engaged him in adventures not unlike those he later undertook with the Llewelyn

* The inspiration for *Alice's Adventures in Wonderland* (1865) and *Through the Looking-Glass* (1871).

† Arthur Quiller Couch, three years younger than Barrie, was a novelist, critic, poet and literary journalist, and the first editor of *The Oxford Book of English Verse*. He was knighted in 1910 and took the chair of English at Cambridge University in 1912.

Davies boys. He took photographs of their adventures and made them into a book, a forerunner of *The Boy Castaways.*

Meanwhile, filling his leisure time and keeping him away from introspection and loveless lament, was village cricket. One summer's day in 1887, Barrie was walking with his friend Thomas Gilmour and a New Zealand writer, H. B. Marriott Watson,* in an old-world Surrey village called Shere. Observing a game of cricket in progress, the trio stopped to watch and, encouraged by the great age of some of the players, Barrie challenged the home team to a game. A fixture was booked.

'Barrie got us together,' recalled Jerome. 'He was a good captain. It was to have been Married v. Single, but the wife of one of the Marrieds had run away with one of the Singles a few days before. So to keep our minds off a painful subject, we called it Literature v. Journalism.'[8]

On the way down to Shere from London in the train, realising that they hadn't much hope of winning, Barrie asked his friend the explorer Joseph Thomson what the 'African' for 'Heaven help us' was. The answer came, 'Allahakbar', so the club became the Allahakbars and later the Allahakbarries. Against Shere they were all out for eleven runs, but the Allahakbarries became a famous institution, with village and country house fixtures and an annual game with the artistic community in the Worcestershire village of Broadway, where they would put up at the Lygon Arms.

At his happiest at boyish games, Barrie's widening knowledge of the world included no tangible knowledge of young women until he began to work them out on the page:

> Mr Anon, that man of secret sorrows, found it useless to love, because, after a look at the length and breadth of him, none would listen. Unable to get a hearing in person...he wrote many articles on the subject of love and the passions that purported to come from perturbed undergraduates or haughty lieutenants, by whom readers, assuming them to be of the proper dimension, were variously stirred. These young gentlemen wrote as authorities of what love should be and in the case of women was not; so that they roused many intelligent damsels to the frenzy of reply. Mr Anon had the elation of feeling that Woman listened to him at last, if only at second hand.[9]

* *Richard Savage*, Barrie's first play, was co-authored with H. B. Marriott Watson, and opened in 1891 at the Criterion. It was not a success.

The real breakthrough came when he, 'who was only able to speak to ladies when they were not there', began drawing and re-drawing and enlivening two-dimensional ladies on the pages of his fiction, and 'fiction became reality'. His maxim was: 'Without concentration you are lost; concentrate though your coat-tails be on fire' –

> He would think and think, until concentration (which is a pair of blazing eyes) seemed to draw her out of the pages to his side, and then he and she sported in a way forbidden in the tale. While he sat there with eyes riveted he had her to dinner at a restaurant, and took her up the river and called her 'little woman', and when she held up her mouth he said, tantalisingly, that she must wait until he had finished his cigar.[10]

It was on this terrifyingly sad notion, that Barrie did in fact tackle his deeply repressed sexuality and found himself a wife. Only, in reality, it was not from the pages of *his* fiction that the creature of his dreams originally arose, but from George du Maurier's.

CHAPTER TWO

Gateway to Neverland

After Kicky had married Emma in 1863, he put away 'the dreamer' and became a very successful artist. His wife had insisted that he cleaned himself up, dropped his Paris bohemian persona and became a true Englishman, as this fitted him perfectly for the position he desired on *Punch* magazine.

Witty, satirical but not maliciously so, *Punch* by the 1860s was more supportive of the Establishment than of the underdog. Successful and international, it spoke for the rising middle class and the British Empire.

Becoming so much the aspirational Englishman that he took up cricket, Kicky began to venerate and model himself on the magazine's most famous illustrator, John Leech, writing of him in *Social Pictorial Satire* (1898):

> In dress, bearing, manner, and aspect, Leech was the very type of the well-bred English gentleman and man of the world and good society; I never met anyone to beat him in that peculiar distinction of form, which, I think, has reached its highest European development in this country . . . He was John Bull himself, but John Bull refined and civilised – John Bull polite, modest, gentle – full of self-respect and self-restraint [and] by nature aristocratic; he liked the society of those who were well dressed, well bred and refined like himself, and perhaps a trifle conventional; he conformed quite spontaneously and without effort to the upper-class British ideal of his time . . .

In the autumn of 1864, while in Whitby making woodcuts for Elizabeth Gaskell's *Sylvia's Lovers*, a novel set in the Napoleonic Wars in which the Yorkshire whaling port is thinly disguised as Monkshaven, Kicky happened to bump into Leech, on holiday with his family.

The two men walked and talked and dined, and their time together appears to have raised Kicky's chances of a regular position on *Punch*.

Then, as fate would have it, Leech suddenly died, at only 46, and Kicky stepped into his shoes, first as illustrator of the *Punch Almanack*. He then took Leech's empty chair at the weekly *Punch* dinner, and with all the gravitas he could muster cut his initials on the table next to those of his late mentor. By the following July he could write to his mother: 'I am regularly on the staff of *Punch* now.'

Not quite six years had passed since that summer day in 1860 when he had borrowed £10 from his mother and left Düsseldorf for London – and he was now the perfect Englishman.

His work on the series, 'English Society at Home', caught the essence of Imperial Britain, and George du Maurier became something of a monument to the national pride of his country, which he could justifiably call *his* England. He also amused his new audience in a series called 'The Legend of Camelot', which mocked the art scene he had left behind.* So well known did Kicky become that by the time he came to illustrate Thomas Hardy's novel *The Hand of Ethelberta* for the *Cornhill* magazine in the mid-1870s, 'he and not the novelist was the more significant figure in the eyes of the reading public.'[1]

By then, five children had been born to George and Emma: Beatrice (known as Trixy), Guy, Sylvia, Marie Louise (May) and Gerald, and they too were becoming famous, illustrated by their artist father in the pages of *Punch* as the perfect upper-middle-class English family, dressed quaintly to perfection in Kate Greenaway frills, hats and pinafores. Readers followed their exploits, thinly disguised as those of 'the Brown family'. Especially popular was the family dog, Chang, a St Bernard which got its name from an eight-foot-tall Chinese giant, who had been on exhibition at the old Egyptian Hall in the British Museum in the early 1860s. The four-legged Chang sat at Kicky's feet as he worked. His fans were stricken when he died in 1883.

One cartoon springs to mind. It is set in the du Maurier garden and shows the five children in line, according to height and age, each chugging after the next, playing at railway trains. 'I'm the engine,' confides Trixy, the oldest, by way of explanation to her mother, Emma, 'and Guy's a first-class carriage, and Sylvia's a second-class carriage, and May's a third-class carriage, and Gerald, he's a third-class carriage, too – that is, he's really only a truck, you know, only you mustn't tell him so, it would offend him!'

* Besides Rossetti, William Morris and others, Oscar Wilde and Swinburne came in for a caning, the latter in a clever parody, 'A Ballad of Blunders', which gave special attention to Swinburne's taste for flagellation.

The drawing was undertaken in 1875, the year after Kicky took a long lease on a large house on the edge of Hampstead Heath, a move which confirmed that the du Mauriers had arrived. Known as New Grove House, 'the studio of his home became the centre of his world,' wrote Daphne. 'Here Kicky would blink away at his easel, smoking his innumerable black cigars, with Chang stretched at his feet beside him; his devoted wife hovered at his elbow, a couple of daughters practised at the piano, singing the French songs he had taught them, a son stood on the dais as model, and the two youngest children dressed up as black minstrels to "make Pappa laugh".'[2]

It was at New Grove House, four years later, that American writer Henry James walked through the door and greeted the entire family as he might long-lost friends, which in a way they were, for everyone who read *Punch* felt they knew the du Mauriers, 'two-dimensionally as it were'.[3]

Henry James first met Kicky at one of the 107 social engagements he had attended in the winter of 1878.* They became the greatest of friends. Henry James was nine years the younger man, but you wouldn't know it, for du Maurier was so much the smaller, slighter and more boyish figure.

Immediately they had two things in common. Both were émigrés and Henry James knew Kicky's homeland intimately, having lived in Paris from 1875 as a correspondent for the *New York Tribune*.

There was also great mutual respect. Kicky revered Henry James's stylistic purity and meticulous approach to his art.† James warmed to Kicky's sincerity and passion, as well as to his amusing repartee, and he asked him to illustrate his novel *Washington Square* (1881), despite his principled aversion to illustrated novels. Inevitably, Kicky invited Henry to meet the family he felt he knew so well.

* Henry James's novel *The American* had just been published to great acclaim and would be followed by the even more successful *Daisy Miller* (1879) and *The Portrait of a Lady* (1881). All turn on the impact of European culture on American life, which made him a popular choice among hostesses of soirées in the London of the late nineteenth century.

† Barrie would write in *The Greenwood Hat* (1930) of Henry's exactitude: 'It is worth losing a train (and sometimes you had to do that) while he rummaged for the right word . . . I remember once meeting him in the street and asking how he liked a lecture we had both lately attended. I did not specially want to know nor he to tell, and as he sought for the right words it began to rain, and by and by it was raining heavily. In this predicament he signed to a passing growler and we got in and it remained there stationary until he reached the triumphant conclusion, which was that no one could have delivered a lecture with less offence.'

By 1881, the Kicky menagerie *en famille* was quite a handful, not at all the demure English family paraded in *Punch* six years earlier. But Henry James could not have resisted them if he had tried. Here was 15-year-old Sylvia, so fiery and uncontrollable that she was nicknamed 'the blizzard', and 8-year-old Gerald, whose tomfoolery and practical joking were the fresh young shavings of Kicky's own nature, and 18-year-old Trixy, who had just 'come out', and whose beauty found a surprise response in the dedicated bachelor's breast. Also, the du Mauriers were of course a musical household – Guy (16) played piano, as did the girls. May (13) sang like a bird, and Kicky's tenor voice, not yet quite destroyed by his cigar-smoking, was a revelation as it rang out to Thackeray's 'Song of Little Billee', one of his favourites at the time.

The children insisted Henry James join in the family fun and games. No one had ever invited him to do such a thing before, and indeed he was the last person one might think would have enjoyed himself. Another friend, the writer Edmund Gosse, once described him as 'benign, indulgent but grave, and not often unbending beyond a genial chuckle.' But with the du Mauriers, he came alive.

The wholehearted welcome was the most personal of all the compliments Kicky paid Henry James, for there was a clannishness about the du Mauriers which might just as easily have been designed to freeze one out.

A talent for mockery, which served Kicky so well on *Punch*, was shared by his daughter Sylvia and youngest son, Gerald, a tremendous mimic, and later by Daphne, and by others in the family since. 'Doing someone's day' was a particular form of it, which reduced Daphne and her son Kits to fits of laughter, as they made fun of the routine activities of some poor soul who had found his way into their lives. Daphne refused to see it as cruel. 'If I mock,' she said, 'it does not mean any more than that mockery is in my nature . . . they are far from chucked.' Kicky, who hated hurting people's feelings, and for whom cruelty in any form was the worst sin, would have felt the same. It was the du Maurier way. Anyone who found it intimidating was not for them. Henry James appears to have gone along with it and probably topped it. Certainly there was no room for taking offence. The household was full of beauty and humour, and determinedly up-tempo. 'One must never be *au sérieux* about anything,' observed Charles Hoyer Millar, who married Trixy and wrote a biography of his father-in-law. 'The family in general had a rooted dislike to serious topics of any kind, at all events in the presence of each other.'[4]

This qualification – 'at all events in the presence of each other' – was significant. Serious topics were not avoided by Kicky; just kept to himself. Upon marriage to Emma, anything serious had gone the way of his hypnotic excursions and Romantic, otherworldly ideas. Habits died hard in the du Maurier family. And even two generations down the line Daphne also avoided serious topics, mocking them as 'main talks' or 'psychological politics', but in the right company she loved nothing better than discussing them.

Deep thoughts were, in fact, at the heart of what both Daphne and her grandfather were about, and from the moment Henry James stepped across the threshold of New Grove House, they were back on the agenda for Kicky after Emma's lengthy ban. A private walk became an essential part of a Sunday routine for the two men. It took them on to the Heath and into each other's innermost being.

Kicky began by telling Henry about his Parisian childhood, pointing to the trees on the Heath that grew close together like those in the Bois de Boulogne, and nodding to the Leg of Mutton pond, so like the mare d'Auteuil where he had fished and listened to the fairy tales of Le Major Duquesnois. At length, the two men would come to a secluded bench, dubbed by David Lodge in his novel *Author, Author* (2004) 'the bench of confidences'.

Henry's presence on a Sunday at New Grove House became a weekly ritual, and this bench the principal destination of their perambulations. Here the two men opened up to each other about their lives, their dreams and their disappointments, and shared their secrets.

Shortly after they met, the novelist Walter Besant invited Kicky to join a club he was setting up, to be named 'The Rabelais' after the author of *Gargantua and Pantagruel.* Its name raised certain expectations (of bawdiness, obscenity and reckless living), which were not in fact delivered, as was noted at the time. Henry Ashbee, a successful City businessman with a passion for pornography, and reputed to be Robert Louis Stevenson's model for the two sides of his most famous creation, Dr Jekyll and Mr Hyde, denounced its members as 'very slow and un-Rabelaisian', and there is a story that Thomas Hardy, a member for a time, objected to the attendance of Henry James on account of his lack of virility.

Virility was not the issue, however. The members of the Rabelais were interested in other worlds. Charles Leland was an expert in fairy lore and voodoo. Robert Louis Stevenson was the author of *The Strange Case of Dr Jekyll and Mr Hyde* (1886) which epitomised the club's psychological/

occult preoccupations. Arthur Conan Doyle, who became a member of the British Society for Psychical Research, was a dedicated spiritualist from 1916. In their company, Henry James was probably more at home than Hardy, for both his private secretary Theodora Bosanquet, and brother William, the philosopher, were members of the Psychical Society.

In many ways, the Rabelais was a celebration that Kicky's time had come. Parapsychological phenomena and the occult were becoming valid subjects for rigorous study. There was a strong feeling that the whole psychic scene would at any moment be authenticated by scientific explanation. In 1947, the poet laureate John Masefield recalled the excitement of growing up in the era:

> Men were seeking to discover what limitations there were to the personal intellect; how far it could travel from its home, the personal brain; how deeply it could influence other minds at a distance from it, or near it; what limit, if any, there might be to an intense mental sympathy. This enquiry occupied many doctors and scientists in various ways. It interested many millions of men and women. It stirred George du Maurier . . . to speculations which deeply delighted his generation.[5]

While séances challenged the Christian definition of the afterlife, scientists, such as Sir William Crookes, working on invisible forces were expected at any moment to identify and explain the force harnessed by mediums.* In 1886, Elizabeth Stuart Phelps wrote in *The Psychical Wave*:

> The force which makes a parlour table rise half way to the ceiling, with a child on top of it, or the mystery which qualifies a stranger in a back street to tell you at first sight the name of your dead, or the secret of your heart, is no longer relegated to the logic of the medium, or the oratory of the strolling charlatan. It is lifted to the desk of the scholar; and the scholar has accepted the trust. Believers in what are called spiritualistic phenomena – an army estimated at from two to ten millions in this country [North America] alone – are building from their end, and in their way, about a volume of mysterious facts which, at the other end, and from another fashion of approach, commands the attention of liberal scientific men on both sides of the Atlantic sea. The thing has overflowed the culvert of superstition; it has gone above

* Sir William Crookes, a member of the British Society for Psychical Research, invented a radiometer that led to the cathode ray tube and television.

the level of what we call a craze or a fashion. It has reached the dignity of an intellectual current.

Between 1875 and 1883, a young physiologist and future professor, Charles Richet, published a series of ground-breaking studies in hypnotic phenomena in two French journals.[6] From 1882, there appeared new scientific journals exclusively devoted to hypnotism, and all medical journals, philosophic and literary journals, as well as the daily press, carried articles about the science

Between 1881 and 1889 three volumes of stories were published by the Rabelais in members-only editions limited to 100 copies.[7] They delineate elements of the club's core interest in the psychic and supernatural, and are alive with the spirit of Kicky's formative experience of hypnosis in Europe. Central is the idea that enlightenment comes not from an authoritative source of religion, but from an altered state of consciousness, a state of trance. The stories are Romantic, revelatory, ecstatic. The narrator of one is hypnotised and sent 'into an ecstasy with his vision', which is far superior to sex. A character is 'borne away out of the window . . . carried away in an ecstasy of rapture . . . so that he took no heed when the daintiest girls in the village passed singing down the street'. Here are intense, euphoric, sometimes mystical exploits of the mind, a sixth-sense perception of the universal connectedness of things. The stories remind us of the peak experiences which were once Kicky's regular Saturday night fare.

In the 1880s Kicky was rejected for the editorial chair at *Punch*, and Henry James failed to emulate his own success with *Portrait of a Lady* (1881). Disillusioned and depressed, the two men turned for consolation to art and music and to each other on their 'bench of confidences'.

That hypnosis was a subject of their conversations is certain. We know that they discussed *Trilby*. Moreover, in 1885–6 Henry James wrote a novel concerned with hypnotism – *The Bostonians*, similar to *Trilby* in that it hinges on the erotic issues of the hypnotic relationship. In both works, an older man mesmerises a young woman (in *The Bostonians*, Selah Tarrant hypnotises his own daughter, Verena) and uses his 'psychic energy' to bring his female subject to glorious expression, and in both cases the man derives a vicarious sexual satisfaction from doing so. 'As Tarrant achieved through Verena, Svengali, the frustrated singer, obtained his dream through Trilby.'[8]

Sex had for some time been an issue for Henry James. In his thirties, he had made a decision to remain celibate. We are told that he felt disgust for the anatomical process of sex, but preferred to see his vow as a celibate dedication to the vocation of authorship.[9]

But could an aesthete who has not known passion bring it to the page? Was this perhaps the reason why the novels and plays of Henry James's middle age were not successful? Was he languishing in an emotional prison of his own making?

Kicky, as an experienced practitioner of hypnosis as an instrument of euphoria, and a loyal and admiring friend, would have had a ready-made therapeutic answer for him. Had Kicky been cooking up a personal solution for Henry James? And had the sum of his efforts been transformed into the plot line of *The Bostonians*?

Both men were thinking and writing about hypnosis at the same time. According to Henry James's notes on the outline of *Trilby* given to him by Kicky, the musician Svengali had 'no organ (save as accompanist) of his own. She [Trilby] had had the glorious voice, but no talent – he had had the sacred fire, the rare musical organisation, and had played into her and through her'.[10] The imagery speaks clearly, and in the novel Svengali derives his sexual satisfaction from hypnotising Trilby.

That Kicky was tempting Henry James to dabble in hypnosis to awaken his passions and lift his fading career is a speculation that gains credibility when one looks at a short story written by James around this time. It concerns an ailing novelist who, while sitting on a bench gazing out to sea, meets a doctor who is an ardent fan and who offers to find a cure for what is wrong with him.

A 'sense of ebbing time, of shrinking opportunity', a failing author who yearns for 'a second chance', for 'another strain of eloquence' which would prove 'the citadel of his reputation', a bench, a fan who comes to the rescue . . . There are echoes here of the relationship between Henry James and George du Maurier.

Henry James, however, came down on the side of *art* and rejected what he referred to as '*the fairy-tales of science*'. While Kicky dabbled in hypnotic fantasy games, art was the only way for Henry: the mystical, revelatory moments of trance were illusory. For true artists, doubt and the longing desire 'to know' were all that was possible in this world:

> We work in the dark – we do what we can – we give what we have. Our doubt is our passion and our passion is our work. The rest is the madness of art.[11]

By the time Henry James wrote this in 1892, Kicky was once again completely committed to living out the fairy tales of science.

In 1888–9 he had uprooted for Bayswater, letting the family's Hampstead home and taking a furnished house at 15 Bayswater Terrace, W2.* The picture is of a man who had found release from something of a straitjacket existence in Hampstead. Now that the family was growing up he was no longer obliged to keep his promise to Emma. Eldest son Guy, 25 in 1890, had, after Marlborough and Sandhurst, joined the Royal Fusiliers. Trixy (27) was married. Youngest son Gerald (17) was at Harrow, though he wouldn't be for much longer. Sylvia and May were 24 and 22 respectively, and found it easier to enjoy a social life from a base in central London.

In du Maurier terminology, the move meant new 'routes', a whole new lifestyle for Kicky. Bayswater was his coming out. The Mr Hyde side of his personality was liberated to walk the streets of foggy London. 'Du Maurier was out late most evenings,' as his biographer Leonée Ormond writes.[12]

It was on the night of 24 March 1889, while walking with Kicky down what was then Queen Street and is now Queensway, that Henry James complained he could never think of plots, and Kicky offered him the plot of *Trilby* to turn into a novel of his own. When his friend declined the offer, saying 'it was too valuable a present and that I must write the story myself', Kicky hastened home, 'when it occurred to me that it would be worthwhile trying to write, after all. So on an impulse I sat down and began to work . . .'[13]

But he did not begin writing *Trilby*. Instead he embarked on *Peter Ibbetson*. Much more clearly than *Trilby*, this first novel confirms the ascendancy of hypnotic ecstasy over physical sex. It does so in a telepathic series of peak experiences, conducted within a hypnotic excursion into the author's past, which result in an orgasm of ineffable proportions with his lover. The experiences are telepathic because Peter is in prison; he cannot enjoy physical sex with his lover.

Kicky claimed he rushed home from Henry James and wrote the entire first quarter of the story the same night. It would have been impossible to write 25,000 words of a novel in a few hours, and it is likely that Kicky 'dreamt it true', after which the words poured on to the page so fluidly that, as he said, he felt almost guilty about how easily the book had been written.

* Biographers have said that this was for only the winter months, but letters are written from there by Kicky with a handwritten address at other times of the year. It seems to have been his preferred abode at this time.

'Dreaming true' was Kicky's little secret. 'My Grandpapa George developed the ability to "visit" the past by dreaming true,' wrote Daphne. 'He would lie back and in his mind's eye become the child he once was, and he wrote about this "psychic" ability too, in *Peter Ibbetson*.'[14] Kicky had the ability to switch himself into a trance state, to access long-forgotten memories and experience the euphoric moments of his youth.

When John Masefield read *Peter Ibbetson* he immediately suspected that the hero's hypnotic excursions came from the author's personal knowledge: 'I think that du Maurier must have met some such experience . . .'[15]

Kate Greenaway, who thought she knew Kicky well, but had got to know him only after he married Emma, and therefore knew only the artist, not the dreamer, was amazed by what she saw as his hidden depths:

> I have always liked Mr du Maurier, but to think there was all this, and one didn't know it. I feel as if I had all this time been doing him an injustice – not to know.[16]

Dreaming true is a process of self-induced, hypnotic concentration and relaxation, or self-hypnosis, which, as Professor F. L. Marcuse of Washington State University describes, can be made possible on a regular basis by post-hypnotic suggestion, in the form of a trigger word:

> One technique for the induction of self-hypnosis is to give a post-hypnotic suggestion to the effect that the subject, on self-command, will go into a deep hypnotic state, but in every other respect will remain alert and in full contact with the environment.[17]

More recently, however, Dr Theodore Barber, chief psychologist at the Cushing Hospital in Framingham, Massachusetts, sampled the American population and found that 2–4 per cent of people are naturally capable of this sort of auto-hypnosis, i.e. they can slip into a trance without being hypnotically prepared with a trigger word. Barber discovered that these 'somnambules', as he called them, were all 'gifted fantasisers'. They could slip into their dream world with ease while yet coping with tasks in the real world, as if on auto-pilot. None spent less than 50 per cent of the time in a dream world, and most spent as much as 90 per cent, while often simultaneously holding down jobs. Moreover, 'the rich joys' of their hypnoid world could be 'savoured in reality'. Most had experienced sexual orgasm by means of fantasising, and eleven of the fourteen females who were asked the question had had phantom pregnancies.[18]

The first somnambule ever to be studied by the medical profession, Bertha Pappenheim, code-named Anna O, was a subject of intense interest in Switzerland just a few years before Kicky was writing. Freud's friend and mentor, Joseph Breuer, was her doctor. Anna, who could hypnotise herself, used the term 'clouds' to describe her trances, and the term 'chimney sweeping' to describe the work Breuer did on her unconscious while she was hypnotised.

Kicky was like a somnambule in that he was able to switch into this hypnotic state at will. But in *Peter Ibbetson* we sense that there has been a certain amount of preparation of Peter before he dreams true for the first time. At a party in London he is entranced by the alluring Mary, Duchess of Towers, a woman capable of 'mesmerising' people 'into feeling and intelligence'. She holds his eyes from across the room. 'It was hard to look away from her; her face drew my eyes, and through them all my heart.'

Thereafter, his auto-hypnotic ability is a matter of concentration, relaxation and an exercise of the will:

> Lie on your back with your arms above your head, your hands clasped under it and your feet crossed . . . and you must never for a moment cease thinking of where you want to be in your dream till you are asleep and you get there; and you must never forget in your dream where and what you were when awake. You must join the dream on to reality . . .You have only to will it, and think of yourself as awake, and it will come . . .

Peter practises and practises, 'as one practises a fine art', and finally it works:

> I lay straight on my back, with my feet crossed, and my hands clasped above my head in a symmetrical position; I would fix my will intently and persistently on a certain point in space and time that was within my memory . . . at the same time never losing touch of my own present identity as Peter Ibbetson, architect, Wharton Street, Pentonville; all of which is not so easy to manage as one might think, although the dream duchess had said, 'Ce n'est que le première pas qui coûte;' and finally one night, instead of dreaming the ordinary dreams . . . I had the rapture of waking up, the minute I was fairly asleep, by the avenue gate, and of seeing [myself as a child] sitting on one of the stone posts and looking up the snowy street for the major . . .

The transition was not as dramatic as one might think, and the feeling that anyone could do it was an ingredient in the novel's success. The science is that there is a spectrum of consciousness, along which brain waves, measured on an electroencephalogram, vary in frequency. Within a certain band of frequencies the brain is in a light to deep hypnotic trance.* At the 'light' end, you are daydreaming; at the 'deep' end you are hypnotised, a stranger to the real world, yet not asleep.

Kicky's psychic ability was different from the normal imaginative process only in that it fell at a point further along the spectrum – beyond light trance, at the point where deep trance becomes a fully-fledged alternative reality, complete and as realisable as a normal 'waking' day.

Marcuse, who conducted experiments with some 1,000 subjects, noted how close the daydreaming state is to the hypnotic:

> From time immemorial, people have probably brought on some form of a self-induced hypnotic state by sitting quietly beside a murmuring stream, listening to the monotonous rhythm of a chant, staring at some bright object, or possibly at their own navels.[19]

How often do we lie in bed, on the borderline of consciousness and sleep, and induce just such a state by imagining what is happening at just that minute in a place we know well? Daphne played this game, and shared it with her friend, Oriel Malet. Take, say, 'a bit of Paris, a street corner – say the Rond Point. I lie in bed and try and "see" exactly what stream of cars are passing at that moment, and the faces of the people passing by. Then I'll switch to Red Square . . . I'll think of silence, and snow falling, and suddenly a dark saloon car, and perhaps an old crossing-sweeper woman . . .'

Again: 'If I pass a place I once lived (like at Hampstead), I often do a Gondal,† where I go into it just as if it was still mine, and take my coat off, and somehow settle down, and then try to imagine the amazed surprise of the new owner coming in, and how one would behave in the Gondal just as if they were not there, and one was still in possession.'[20]

This is the method of Daphne's fiction. 'Last night I dreamt I went to

* Across the whole spectrum of consciousness, brain waves measured on an electroencephalogram vary in frequency between 1 and 30 hertz. In a light to deep hypnotic trance electrical activity from the cerebral cortex occurs in the region of 8–12 hertz, which means that you are in a relaxed, conscious state, but not asleep. At the 'light' end of the hypnotic spectrum, you are daydreaming.

† Gondal and Angria were the imaginary worlds created by the Brontë children.

Manderley again' is the opening sentence of *Rebecca*. Daphne was writing in the heat of Alexandria in Egypt. But she had the ability to dream her way back into her first trespass, as a young woman, up the twisting and turning path to Menabilly. Now, 'like all dreamers', she wrote, 'I was possessed of a sudden with supernatural powers'.

Something dreamlike touches all her fiction. In *Frenchman's Creek*, one night in midsummer, a solitary yachtsman in his dinghy leaves civilisation behind and goes exploring up the mysterious Helford River, the trees crowding thick and darkly to the water's edge. Again, it is a remembered scene, revisited in imagination, but with a spell upon Daphne it becomes 'fascinating, strange, a thing of queer excitement not fully understood'.

Concentration alerts the brain to every little item of the scene she wishes to revisit in her dream, in this case 'the shadows of the trees . . . the rustle of the leaves and the stir of a sleeping bird' – which take her deeper, calling up the dreamer's 'sixth sense', setting the creative unconscious free, entering that place in which past and present are no longer separated by time. It is *Peter Ibbetson* all over again: a matter of concentration, deep relaxation, and practice.

Suppose one night you were playing the game and instead of going to sleep, all of a sudden it did become real, you *were* there, literally in it, a little further along the spectrum of trance than you have been before. That is 'dreaming true'. And when you come to those peak experiences, entrancing moments when the world seems renewed, revealing itself in all its mystery and beauty, moments which Kicky had in real life and Peter Ibbetson has in the novel, you are not surprised to find Daphne had these experiences too.

> Suddenly I had the house to myself, and it gave me such a feeling of freedom! I took the old rug and went to the grass just above the wall and lay down, staring at those trees overhead – the mysterious ones like a Rackham picture from a fairy tale – and then sideways to the sea, with about ten ships anchored off. It was very sunny, about six o'clock, the warm aftermath of a summer's day. Then suddenly a plane, like a Comet, went high, high overhead, a tiny white arrow, no noise even, and a trail behind, and there was only sky, and the plane, and the mysterious trees, and I had a sudden feeling of absolute *bliss* – it was quite spiritual! It seemed to me that what I was seeing was Life. The Comet streak, the sky, the trees, the sea below, it all added up to a great Main Goodness. And if this was Life, so was Death, and everything was in harmony, and one ought to be grateful, all the time for every moment, instead of getting irritated and put out by the stupid things of the day.[21]

Kicky would have empathised with his granddaughter's peak experience* and recognised it too as a brief moment of clarity amidst 'the stupid things of the day'.

Daphne called the experience an 'other-world intimacy', 'the secret of the elixir of youth'.[22] It was enough to make you never want to grow up.

For Kicky that night of 24 March 1889, writing *Peter Ibbetson*, it was as though he was back again in his childhood home 'in the Rue de la Pompe, his father and mother living, his mother's sad and very beautiful sister Mary coming to visit them, leading her little boy by the hand, and they were all of them setting forth for a walk in the Bois, he, Kicky, running ahead with his small cousin. It was strange – he had only to shut his eyes, and the figures were real, as living as Emma and May.† He could smell the old scents of Passy, hear the long-dead voices, conjure the old ideals, the laughter, and the tears . . .'

But he based the alluring Duchess of Towers, Peter Ibbetson's tantric temptress, on his own daughter, Sylvia, who was no longer the fifteen-year-old 'blizzard'.

> Her thick, heavy hair was of a dark coppery brown; her complexion clear and pale, her eyebrows and eyelashes black, her eyes a dark-bluish gray. Her nose was short and sharp and rather tilted at the tip, and her red mouth large and very mobile . . . She seemed both thoughtful and mirthful at once, and genial . . . When she laughed, she showed both top and bottom teeth, which were perfect, and her eyes nearly closed, so that they could no longer be seen for the thick lashes that fringed both upper and under eyelids; at which time the expression of her face was so keenly, cruelly sweet that it went through one like a knife. And then the laugh would suddenly cease, her full lips would meet, and her eyes beam out again like two mild gray suns, benevolently humorous and kindly inquisitive, and full of interest in everything and everybody around her . . . She was much surrounded and made up to.

* In March 1970, Colin Wilson, biographer of Robert Maslow, who coined the phrase 'peak experiences', met Daphne for tea on the Menabilly Estate and talked almost exclusively about them: 'He came at one, and stayed till six, and talked and talked, very brilliant and interesting talk . . .' she wrote to Oriel Malet, and credited Wilson with giving her 'the final impetus' to write possibly her best-known psychic short story, 'Don't Look Now': 'I suddenly became inspired to begin one of the short stories I had been brewing upon. The rather nanny one about Venice – it's been on my mind for years!'

† George du Maurier's wife (Emma) and youngest daughter (May).

The fictional Peter Ibbetson uses his natural talent for drawing to become an architect. He owns a dog, a St Bernard like Chang, which he calls Porthos. Like Kicky, he has become disillusioned and depressed with his essentially soulless life, and decides to visit Paris in search of the self he had left behind as a child.

On the way to his hotel he is convinced he catches sight of Mary in a passing carriage, the first time he has seen her since the London party, where she hypnotised him. She looks at him again. Afterwards he has a dream, which at first is just like an ordinary dream, a mass of images 'distorted and exaggerated and jumbled together after the usual manner of dreams'. Then Mary appears in the dream and tells Peter to stop, for he is not 'dreaming true'. She takes him by the hand and leads him on . . .

> And I felt that this was no longer a dream, but something else – some strange thing that had happened to me, some new life that I had woken up to . . . I was conscious that my real body . . . now lay fast asleep in a small room on the fourth floor of an hôtel garni in the Rue de la Michodière . . . and yet here was my body too, just as substantial . . . With my disengaged hand I felt in my trousers pocket; there were my London latchkey, my purse, my penknife . . . I looked at my watch; it was going and marked eleven. I pinched myself, I coughed, I did all one usually does under the pressure of some immense surprise, to assure myself that I was awake; and I was, and yet here I stood.

Thereafter, Peter's dream is bound up intimately with his beautiful guide, through whose hand he feels he is 'drawing all her life into mine . . . I felt there was about me the unspeakable elation which can come to us only in our waking moments when we are at our very best . . . I was still holding the Duchess's hand, and felt the warmth of it through her glove; it stole up my arm like a magnetic current. I was in Elysium . . .

"Now you are dreaming true," she said.'

They visit the scene of Peter's childhood together – the rue de la Pompe, the house with green shutters and Mansard roofs, the memorable back garden with its beautiful roses, nasturtiums and convolvulus, the old tool shed full of tools and lumber, the magical mare d'Auteuil in the Bois de Boulogne, 'that pond of ponds, the *only* pond', which Peter (nicknamed Gogo as a child) now glimpses through a gap in a hedge.

Also returned is a long-forgotten childhood friendship with a little girl called Mimsie. Peter and Mary watch as the two children play happily together, Mimsie a sweet, but 'sick, ungainly child', full of gratitude and love that Gogo should play with her, and Gogo touchingly unaware that her little heart is so full of him that 'she would like to be Gogo's slave – she would die for Gogo . . .'

There is a boyishness about Mimsie. When we first meet her, she wears 'her thick hair cropped like a boy'. There is also an ethereal, fanciful side to her. She believes she can see 'a pair of invisible beings, "La fée Tarapatapoum" and "La Prince Charmont" always in attendance upon us . . . who watched over us and would protect us through life'.

Gogo is a keen artist. He copies woodcuts for Mimsie, one in particular from an edition of Byron, a drawing illustrating a poem called 'The Island', actually a steel engraving which represented 'two beautiful beings of either sex, walking hand in hand through a dark cavern. The man was in sailor's garb; the lady, who went barefoot and lightly clad, held a torch; and underneath was written –

> And Neuha led her Torquil by the hand,
> And waved along the vaults her flaming brand.

I spent hours copying it for her, and she preferred the copy to the original, and would have it that the two figures were excellent copies of her Prince and Fairy.'

Awakened and back in London, Peter longs to meet Mary in real life. He takes to walking in Kensington Gardens, just to 'see beautiful, well-dressed women, and hear their sweet, refined voices and happy laughter; and a longing would come into my heart more passionate than my longing for the sea and France and distant lands, and quite as unutterable'.

Later, he meets her by chance socially, tells her of his dream and is shocked to discover that she dreamed it too. Mary then tells him that she is the Mimsie of his childhood, 'the one survivor of that sweet time', and that dreaming true – which is what he has been doing – is a skill her father taught her. She shows him how to do it of his own free will, but warns him that as she is married (to an alcoholic), they never can dream true together again.

We can 'never, never dream. That will not do,' she says, for 'never never dreamland' – the world of hypnotic trance – is an environment given to rapturous sensuality.

Peter and Mary's situation changes when Peter accidentally kills his guardian, Colonel Ibbetson, after he discovers he was the architect of his father's death. Peter is sentenced to hang, but the sentence is later commuted to life. In prison his need to dream true with Mary becomes urgent. Mary disentangles herself from her husband and her 'affair' with Peter begins. Physical sex is impossible, but their union is consummated ecstatically in the mutual process of dreaming true.

The never never dreamland becomes Peter's principal reality. He is 'half crying with joy to reach the land of my true dreams again', the prison day a 'much needed daily mental rest after the tumultuous emotions of each night'. The union offers pure rapture, as Peter feels Mary's 'warm life-current mixing' with his. 'Was there ever . . . ever since the world began, such ecstasy as I feel now?'

Thus were Prince Charming and the fairy Tarapatapoum together at last.

Mary leads Peter to her childhood home in Passy, Parva sed Apta, leads him into her 'little lumber-room' and thence into rooms 'that never could have been there before', i.e. rooms she had not entered when she was an innocent child.

> 'Why have you brought me here?' I asked.
>
> She laughed and said – 'Open the door in the wall opposite.'
>
> Then she took my hand, and lo! There was a door! And she pushed, and we entered another suite of apartments that never could have been there before; there had never been room for them, nor ever could have been, in all Passy!
>
> 'Come,' she said, laughing and blushing at once; for she seemed nervous and excited and shy – 'do you remember –
>
> And Neuha led her Torquil by the hand,
> And waved along the vaults her flaming brand.
>
> – do you remember your little drawing out of The Island, in the green morocco Byron?'

These are rooms that Mimsie hadn't known. They belong to the grown-up Mary, and she is inviting Peter to explore them. The sexual symbolism is explicit, as she leads him in, 'laughing and blushing', at once 'nervous and excited and shy'. The Romantic focus – 'The Island' – is apt because Byron's South Sea coral island was an earthly paradise capable of transporting Torquil and Neuha, children of Nature, to flights of unbridled ecstasy.

A sense of the past in the present, the notion of a timeless 'other world' just out of reach, the idea that our terrestrial, mundane life is a mere front for true mystical existence – an exalted state of bliss outside time, but within our grasp – is at the heart of a myth, seeded in *Peter Ibbetson*, which captivated three generations of the du Maurier family. It is the essence of Romanticism, Daphne regarded it as 'the secret of eternal youth'.[23] Kicky had found a way into this other order of things – not just imaginatively, but a way actually to live it: by dreaming true.

'He affected us all greatly,' Daphne admitted in understatement, for she owed her success to dreaming true.

CHAPTER THREE

Purloining the key

The year 1891 was the end of the beginning for J.M. Barrie.

It saw the last of the Thrums novels[1] serialised in *Good Words* – and the start of his career as a playwright. *Richard Savage* was followed by the one-act *Ibsen's Ghost*, produced by J. L. Toole at his theatre in King William Street. On the opening night a man in the pit found it so funny that he had hysterics and had to be removed.

Published in the same year, *Peter Ibbetson* became a bestseller on both sides of the Atlantic. As John Masefield wrote, 'The effect of it upon that generation was profound. Even now, after fifty years, I can think of no book which so startled and delighted the questing mind.'

After Barrie read it, more or less everything he wrote was touched by Peter's 'other world'. He made Kicky's novel a source myth for his life.

He called Peter Pan after Peter Ibbetson, not after Peter Llewelyn Davies.* Ibbetson's *never never land*, the 'other world' forbidden because it is one of unbridled ecstasy, became the Neverland in which Barrie as Peter Pan would lose himself with the boys. And the magic of Peter Ibbetson's Bois de Boulogne and mare d'Auteuil made an easy transition to Kensington Gardens and the Round Pond. Barrie even bought a St Bernard and called him Porthos after Peter Ibbetson's dog.

In his writing, Barrie leant heavily on Ibbetson's 'Peter Pan-ish' childhood with Mimsie and the fairy Tarapatapoum, called Tippy, not Tinkerbell, in the original screenplay of *Peter Pan*. And he himself slipped into the role of Le Major Duquesnois, who lived on the edge of the park and captivated Gogo with his fairy tales, both in Kicky's novel and in reality.

* Equally, Peter Llewelyn Davies was named after Peter Ibbetson.

After *Peter Ibbetson*, Barrie lived within and wrote about the cusp between fiction and fact, between Peter's dream world and reality. This strange cross-over point became his territory. He followed Kicky into the genre of autobiographically based psycho-fiction* and dabbled in the supernatural in both novels and plays.† But he never experienced the 'other-world intimacy' that Kicky did. Without knowing the bliss of peak experience, he never could evoke it in his work. In that sense, he never did 'get' Kicky's secret, as Daphne crows in her story, 'The Archduchess', in which the fictional Markoi tries to steal the secret dream formula and she, the Archduchess, keeps it a family secret.

The first sign of change came as 1891 yielded to the New Year. Suddenly, Barrie was writing about Kicky's special area of interest, hypnosis. He called the piece *Jane Annie, or The Good Conduct Prize*. The eponymous heroine is a schoolgirl, named after Barrie's elder sister of course. She has a gimlet eye and a hypnotic power that grows as she grows. Jane Annie hypnotises fellow pupils, her family and her teacher to get what she wants, and finally she hypnotises the boy of her dreams, Jack, who had wanted nothing to do with her.

Barrie chose to write it as a musical, although, as he admitted, 'I have no ear for music. I have only once been to the opera. It was one of the great operas, magnificently done, with Melba in it . . . I still shudder at its tedium.'‡ He wrote *Jane Annie* for the D'Oyly Carte Opera Company at the Savoy Theatre.

This conflagration of oddities – Barrie writing a musical, Barrie writing a musical about hypnosis, Barrie writing a musical about hypnosis for the D'Oyly Carte – points to a gap in the story that could – just possibly – be filled by Kicky coming into Barrie's life at this time.

There is no record that they ever met, but as Denis Mackail wrote in Barrie's official biography, 'It seems likely if not certain that Kicky must have at least encountered J.M.B.' We know that the two men by this time

* *Sentimental Tommy* (1896) and *Tommy and Grizel* (1900).

† *The Little White Bird* (1902), *Peter Pan* (1904), *Dear Brutus* (1917), *A Well-Remembered Voice* (1918), *Mary Rose* (1920).

‡ Dame Nellie Melba's parents lived in Kirriemuir before leaving for Australia shortly before she was born. In the 1920s, finding himself in the same London nursing home, Barrie sent a message that he would like to meet her 'if she would promise not to sing'. She sent a message back saying that she would love to 'if I promised not to read any of my works to her. On that understanding we had a happy time.'

had many friends in common,* including Kicky's intimate friend, Henry James, and that now, according to W. A. Darlington, 'Barrie found it at times both easy and pleasant to come out of his shell.'

Certainly, Kicky's involvement would explain the otherwise inexplicable, for his obsessions were of course hypnosis and music, and he had been involved with the D'Oyly Carte Opera Company at the Savoy. Moreover, he knew what few others knew: that Arthur Sullivan had an interest in hypnosis.

Since the 1860s, Kicky had been invited to musical evenings hosted by a man called Arthur Lewis, which became the talk of the town. Lewis had a high-class drapery store, Lewis and Allenby, but his home was a centre to which artistic and theatrical London gravitated, and he was himself an artist and regular exhibitor at the Royal Academy. He was also the husband of the actress, Kate Terry, famous, but not as famous as her younger sister, Ellen.

At Lewis's, Kicky sang musical duologues and one evening someone suggested that Sullivan write something. The result was *Box and Cox,* a comic operetta based on a farce by John Maddison Morton, the libretto written by Francis Burnand, who for twenty-six years from 1880 was editor of *Punch* and another regular at Lewis's. Kicky, with his fine tenor voice, was invited to take a lead role in the operetta for charity. The first performance was at Burnand's house, but so successful was it that it found its way to the public in a performance at the Adelphi Theatre in May 1887, again with Kicky in it.† Subsequently, long after Kicky ceased his connection with it, *Box and Cox* became a staple of the D'Oyly Carte.

Also, Kicky knew that both Gilbert and Sullivan were involved with the Ionides set. Luke had been present at Arthur Lewis's when *Box and Cox* had been performed by Kicky and Sullivan's brother, but more significantly he attended a party with a clairvoyant when 'Gilbert enclosed a five-pound note which nobody else had seen, in an envelope and told the

* Thomas Hardy and George Meredith were friends of both George du Maurier and J.M. Barrie, as were Henry Irving, Beerbohm Tree, the editor W. D. Nichols, R. L. Stevenson, Alma-Tadema, J. L. Toole, W. E. Henley and the American artist Edwin Abbey. Landscape painter Alfred Parsons knew Kicky intimately and was a member of Barrie's Allahakbarries.

† Felix Moscheles writes that 'Kicky was "Box," Harold Power "Cox," and John Foster "Sergeant Bouncer." Kicky's rendering of "Hush-a-by, Bacon," was so sympathetic and tender that one's heart went out to the contents of the frying-pan, wishing them pleasant dreams.'

clairvoyant he should have it if he could tell the number on the note. The man placed the envelope against his forehead for a short time and then said: "I can see 1, 4, 3, but no further." Afterwards Gilbert said to me that those were the only three numbers of the note that he remembered himself, there having been five in all, and that gave me the impression that it was thought reading.'[2]

That Barrie was at least on the fringe of Kicky's inner circle at this time – a friend, perhaps, of Felix Moscheles who could have answered his breathless enquiries about Kicky and hypnotism – is further suggested by one or two rather telling similarities between Barrie's operetta, *Jane Annie*, and Kicky's as yet unpublished novel, *Trilby*.

The version Kicky gave to Henry James in 1889 described the work as 'the history of a servant girl'. At that stage, Trilby was not an artist's model, she was a servant girl, perhaps to disguise the fact that she was based on the real-life model, Carry. Few people apart from Henry James and Felix Moscheles knew about Carry. Was it mere coincidence, therefore, that, in Barrie's operetta, the hypnotist Jane Annie mesmerises a character called Caddie, who is a servant boy?

Meanwhile, Barrie was pursuing another strategy with links to *Peter Ibbetson*.

Knowing that he was looking for a woman to fill a role in his new play *Walker, London*, Barrie's close friend, the humorist Jerome K. Jerome, introduced him to a pretty actress called Mary Ansell. Barrie cast her in his play and began torturously to court her over the following two years, while *Walker, London* ran for an incredible 497 performances.*

So, Barrie was not only writing a play about hypnosis but actually courting a woman, for the first time. Moreover, the woman had the same name as Peter Ibbetson's tantric lover, and when Barrie eventually wrote about the affair in his autobiographical novel, *Tommy and Grizel*, he made the connection with *Peter Ibbetson* clear by having the couple make love not physically, but as Peter Ibbetson and Mary Duchess of Towers make love, 'by taking thought'.

It is possible that the whole thing began as a joke, for Jerome knew well enough Barrie's hopeless craving 'in the marrow' for the ladies. Barrie had

* *Walker, London* was a farce set on a houseboat off Tagg's Island at Moseley on Thames, which Barrie and Gilmour had hired for a month and which had already figured in *When A Man's Single*. The enigmatic title was, in fact, a telegraphic address, 'Walker', a Cockney catch-word, which you shouted if you thought you were having your leg pulled.

written about his frustration and talked openly about it with his friends. It was 'the curse of his life that he had never had a woman'.[3]

Jerome also knew about his friend's fanatical appreciation of Kicky's novel, and was instrumental not only in introducing Barrie to Mary Ansell, but also to an expert in psychic matters, who was soon advising Barrie about his new interest.

The psychic expert was the writer Arthur Conan Doyle, whose book, *The Adventures of Sherlock Holmes*, had just been published. Doyle and Barrie were Scottish, of course; both had attended Edinburgh University and both loved cricket, Doyle eventually becoming the highest-scoring batsman in the Allahakbarries. But unlike Barrie, Doyle was a member of the Rabelais and had a strong personal interest in hypnosis, and had even submitted himself to one Professor Milo de Meyer in 1891 as a candidate for hypnosis on stage.

In due course, Conan Doyle helped Barrie with the writing of *Jane Annie*, but only when, 'during the course of the libretto's preparation, Barrie suffered the first of what was to be a series of nervous breakdowns'.[4]

The cause of the first breakdown is unknown, nor has it been connected with Barrie's new obsession with matters of the mind; but it is a fact that it occurred during a period of intense interest in hypnosis on the part of both Barrie and Conan Doyle, and immediately after a visit Doyle made to Barrie at his home in Kirriemuir, during Barrie's research for *Jane Annie*.

Conan Doyle remarked in his autobiography that he couldn't understand why Barrie had decided to write about hypnosis – it seemed so alien a subject to him at that time 'unless, like Alexander, he wanted fresh worlds to conquer . . .'[5]

Doyle then agreed to meet him at the family home in Kirriemuir, presumably to instruct him. After a few days Doyle left Kirriemuir, but was called back urgently when Barrie had the first of his 'nervous breakdowns'.

Had Barrie taken his researches for *Jane Annie* a step too far? Had he attempted to emulate du Maurier's hands-on research methods, and come badly unstuck? That Barrie had sent for Doyle after his collapse, rather than calling for a doctor, suggests that their mutual interest in hypnosis was somehow implicated in his collapse.

In spite of Doyle's contributions, in the spring of 1893 *Jane Annie* was an abysmal failure,* as Barrie recalled:

* *Jane Annie* was performed once only, in 1893.

> Conan Doyle wrote some good songs, I thought . . . but mine were worthless and I had no musical sense. Also he was so good-natured that if we lost him at rehearsals he was sure to be found in a shrouded box writing a new song for some obscure member of the company . . . On the first night at the end a youthful friend came into our box, and Doyle expressed my feelings in saying to him reprovingly, 'Why didn't you cheer?' but I also sympathised with our visitor when he answered plaintively, 'I didn't like to, when no one else was doing it.'

Barrie had had his fingers burned badly with his first practical association with Peter Ibbetson's world, and in the meantime he had been finding it pretty hard going with Mary Ansell too. According to the author Marie Belloc-Lowndes in a letter to Thomas Hardy, Mary 'refused to marry Barrie many times, [but in 1894] his mother telegraphed to Mary, who came and they were married on what was supposed to be his deathbed.'

'The first time I went to Kirriemuir was when J.M. was dangerously ill,' Mary wrote to Peter Llewelyn Davies in 1941. 'His sister Maggie, whom I had previously met, sent me an urgent telegram to come, and I started for Scotland the same night. I arrived at the house the next morning and was taken at once to his room where I found two trained nurses in attendance. He was only half conscious, but managed to smile feebly as he said, "So you've got to Thrums."'

What on earth would Mary have made of Margaret Ogilvy and Kirriemuir? What emotional pressure was exerted on her to consent to marrying Barrie 'on what was supposed to be his deathbed'? One can just about imagine the scene, with the real Jane Anne managing to keep things on an even keel in the face of the dual threat of hypochondria and drink, which 'only the very strongest' in Margaret Ogilvy's family could by this time resist. Whatever and however it happened, on 9 July Barrie made a miraculous recovery and they were married in the house by Margaret Ogilvy's brother David, the minister.

After the ceremony, the couple left Kirriemuir straight away for London. Barrie avoided any practical difficulties on his wedding night by conveniently falling ill again, but once on honeymoon in Lucerne, there was no escape.

The honeymoon was a disaster. Years later, Mary told Peter Davies that her marriage was never consummated, that her husband was 'a failure as a man . . . love in its fullest sense could never be felt by him or experienced'.

To her friend Hilda Trevelyan, an actress who later played Wendy in *Peter Pan*, she confided that the honeymoon had come as 'a shock'.[6]

Barrie subsequently wrote about it in his autobiographical novel, *Tommy and Grizel*:

> Tommy trying to become a lover by taking thought, and Grizel not letting on that it could not be done in that way. She thought it was very sweet of him to try so hard; sweeter of him than if he really had loved her, though not of course quite so sweet to her. He was a boy only. She knew that, despite all he had gone through, he was still a boy. And boys cannot love. Oh, is it not cruel to ask a boy to love?
>
> . . . After some sadness to which she could not help giving way she put all vain longings aside. She folded them up and put them away like the beautiful linen, so that she might see more clearly what was left to her and how best to turn it to account . . . He was a boy who could not grow up. 'He would love me if he could.'

It seems that Barrie could not make love in the physical way, and that his attempts to make love in the *Peter Ibbetson* way – 'by taking thought' – also failed.

Still, as if announcing his continuing resolve to give Peter Ibbetson's way a chance, Barrie chose this moment to buy Porthos for Mary, who fell in love with him: 'He was a baby when I first saw him: a fat little round young thing. The dearest of all in a lovely litter of St Bernards, away there in Switzerland. My heart burnt hot for love of him.'[7]

On returning to England, Barrie dashed down to Cornwall to see his friend, Q, a man with gravitas who might restore normality and balance to Barrie's self-image. And there too, of course, was young Bevil.

Thereafter, Barrie and his wife settled at 133 Gloucester Road, on the south side of Kensington Gardens in London, just across the park from Kicky's house at 15 Bayswater Terrace.

CHAPTER FOUR

The corruption of Neverland

Kicky and Sylvia had a special relationship, and their love was bound up in the euphoria of *Peter Ibbetson*, in which father and daughter were the models for Peter and Mary.

Peter Llewelyn Davies, Sylvia's third son, treasured the copy of the novel Kicky gave to her:

> I have loved very few books in my life as much as I loved *Peter Ibbetson* when I was young, and though I don't read it with half so much pleasure now, I like to think that I got my name from it, and I cherish the copy which Grandpapa gave to S., with its charming inscription: 'To Sylvia du Maurier, from the author of her being (and of this book), George du Maurier, 1892'.

However, in 1889, the very year of the novel's conception, Sylvia had fallen in love on her own account. She met Arthur Llewlyn Davies at a dinner party given by a society hostess called Mrs Rawlinson. Among the guests were the fairy-book illustrator H. J. Ford and two writers, Andrew Lang and Anthony Hawkins. Arthur Llewelyn Davies was a young lawyer who had just been called to the Bar and was working at the chambers of Joseph Walton, QC, later Mr Justice Walton.

Ford is supposed to have led Sylvia into dinner and asked her a rather silly riddle – What did she have in common with a hinge?

'Some pretty deep thinking led to no solution of the problem,' Ford wrote to Peter Llewelyn Davies in February 1938. 'So I had to give the answer (not without a burning blush): "Because you are a thing to a door." Miss S shouted out this wantonness to the assembly, especially addressing Andrew Lang, who admitted himself still puzzled, but by the time soup was finished proclaimed that "the operation is accomplished, and if you cut open my head you will find that my brain sees it, but with pain." Arthur Davies roared and the ice was fairly broken.'

Sylvia had begun to make an impact on London society. 'In a ballroom she was always a most noticeable figure, with her crooked smile and general allure,' wrote her brother-in-law Charles Hoyer Millar. 'No portrait could ever do justice to her radiating charm and sweetness of disposition.'[1]

She was extremely popular with men, and liked men about her. She was fun, flirtatious and had her father's eye for beauty and his mocking humour, but again like the Duchess, there was a mysterious side to her – 'she seemed both thoughtful and mirthful at once'.

According to the diary of 15-year-old Dorothea Parry: 'Without being strictly speaking pretty [she had] one of the most delightful, brilliantly sparkly faces I have ever seen. Her nose turns round the corner, also turns right up. Her mouth is quite crooked. She is much too fat. Now for her virtues. Her eyes are very pretty, hazel and very mischievous. She has pretty black fluffy hair, but her expression is what gives that wonderful charm and her low voice . . . Sylvia would be able to manage any man, so it wouldn't much matter who she marries.'

Dorothea Parry, or Dolly as she was known, was the daughter of the composer Sir Hubert Parry,* who knew both the 'du Ms' and 'the LlDs' and observed a 'strange contrast' between them, regarding the du Mauriers as 'easy-going, happy, more or less Bohemian', while the Llewelyn Davieses were out of a more traditional mould. Indeed, Mary Millais, daughter of Kicky's old friend the Pre-Raphaelite painter John Millais, warned Sylvia that 'the LlDs' were 'rather formidable at first when you don't know them'.

Arthur was the second son of the Reverend John Llewelyn Davies, a Cambridge scholar, ex-President of the Cambridge Union and Honorary Chaplain to Queen Victoria. But the weight of this baggage was relieved by a progressive mix of liberalism and eccentricity.

In fact, shortly before Arthur met Sylvia in 1889, John Llewelyn Davies had been exiled from the Court and put out to pasture, expelled from his high position and moved to the tiny village of Kirkby Lonsdale, Westmorland, his crime lambasting imperialism from the pulpit when the Queen was in the congregation. 'It was regarded as a sort of banishment,' Dolly wrote to Peter half a century later, although 'Mr. Davies himself was never in the least bitter, and grew to love Kirkby and his walks over the Fells.'

* Parry is famous for his setting of William Blake's poem, *Jerusalem*, the Coronation anthem, *I was glad*, and anthems and settings for Anglican services, which remain a feature of English cathedral repertoires today.

At 'KL', as Kirkby Lonsdale became known in family letters, John Davies turned the vicarage into a hive of reform. He was a supporter of women's rights, workers' rights, and a champion of trade unionism; his sister Emily had founded Girton College in Cambridge in 1869, for 110 years a college exclusively for women.

Dolly first stayed with the Llewelyn Davieses at Kirkby in 1890, when she was 14, and wrote in her diary:

> Mrs. Llewelyn Davies was not only a perfect housewife, but a woman with a remarkable brain, and great knowledge and love of literature and poetry. She was remarkably independent in thought and I expect you know that she never went to her husband's church, and he never asked her to. As a friend rightly said, 'Creditable to both.' To me she transmuted what had hitherto appeared rather dry and difficult poems into things of interest and excitement and beauty – reading aloud so well and naturally, explaining any difficult parts or words so simply. I especially remember being thrilled by her reading after tea in the drawing-room, Matthew Arnold's 'Sohrab and Rustum'.
>
> I have often thought of her splendid life with her six sons and one daughter. At that period it was accepted as a matter of course that a daughter would help her mother. But so advanced and so unselfish was Margaret's mother, that I am sure she hardly breathed it to herself that she would have liked the feminine companionship of a daughter and her help. Margaret would attend meetings and Co-op. parties nearly every evening – and her sitting-room downstairs was swamped with pamphlets on various progressive questions of the day.

Margaret Davies was a founder member of the Women's Co-operative Guild, a pacifist, and renowned for her humanitarian and feminist views. Dolly loved the LlDs and the du Ms equally, but commented in her teenage diary: 'I can't imagine Sylvia with Margaret D at all – with [Sylvia's] love for pretty dresses, and the stage'.

Margaret's brother, Arthur, a scholar at Marlborough, had taken a First in the Classical Tripos at Cambridge University in 1884, and a law scholarship five years later at the Inner Temple. He was all set to live in Liverpool, considered an easier place to get started in the law than London; but it soon falls from mention in anyone's letters. Industrial Liverpool of the 1890s would not have appealed to a du Maurier, and the change in plan was a sure sign of who was to wear the trousers in the Davies–du Maurier family.

Dolly recognised that the young du Mauriers were a fun-loving lot. Sylvia's brother Guy sang 'delicious comic songs in a soft, low voice, and accompaniments, in the minor keys, made up by himself . . . a little dear, one of the cleverest and most delightful of human beings. He is like Sylvia and has her crooked mouth which is a great attraction.' Gerald, only three years older than Dolly, exercised his particular talent in the love-making department, moving into action to crush any possibility of Dolly fancying the much older Philip Burne-Jones (artist son of Edward, one of Kicky's Pre-Raphaelite friends) by whisking her off to 'the Urlins garden party' and exclaiming, 'I say, what is the matter with Burne-Jones, he does look seedy.'

'Gerald is a dear, dear thing,' Dolly wrote, 'so sweet to have in the house. Always happy, singing at the piano, or sitting in the garden . . . His spirits sank lower & lower as we drove to the station. He was anxious to know if I cared for Phil, whether he was coming again, and that he couldn't bear for me to like him, which I assured him I didn't. He begged me to go on the stage, as then he should not hesitate to go too, as at present he has no profession, and is trying to make up his mind what to do.'

In September 1891 Dolly's diary reads: 'Went to Phil's party at the New Gallery. We invited Arthur and Sylvia to go with us. The latter looked so pretty and was delightful. She was very wicked, and coughed and winked her eyes when Kenneth got hold of us. I gave K such a snub that he left off talking to us for a little.'

Dolly first describes Arthur in 1889, the year he and Sylvia met:

> Arthur Davies arrived – he is very handsome and nice, with a great deal of sense of humour. In the morning at breakfast, Mother said that if anyone was starving it would be quite right to steal, and I'm sure I agree with her. We then said that if one person had several bracelets and another none, it would be quite right for the poor person without the bracelets to steal some. Then we all stole each other's things – Arthur Davies stealing my beads and Mother Mrs. Rate's blue china.

In March 1890 Kicky received a letter from Arthur containing a formal proposal of marriage, to which Kicky's reply, written in March 1890, refers*:

* The following letters appear in *The Morgue*.

15, Bayswater Terrace, W.
Tuesday

My Dear Davies,
Will 9.30 do tomorrow morning?
In haste
I remain yours
G. du Maurier

Arthur's mother in Westmorland was immediately welcoming to Sylvia and wrote at far greater length and in far warmer terms.

The inevitable first visit of Sylvia to Kirkby – a distance of some 300 miles – lasted a fortnight, at the end of which she returned to the du Maurier abode in Bayswater:

15, Bayswater Terrace.
April 15th [1890]

Dearest Mrs Davies,

I feel I must just write a few lines to you, to thank you with all my heart for being so very kind and sweet to me.

The journey to Kirkby was rather painful, but the sweetness at the end of it, and the dear ones waiting to meet me, was worth going through much, much more for.

The recollection of my first visit to Kirkby will be very dear to me, and I shall never be able to thank you enough. I am very, very fond of you. I was, I think, the moment I saw you.

I had a letter from Arthur this morning, and I'm going to write to him now.

It was dreadful saying goodbye to him at Preston.

Good bye, with fond love to you all, and hoping Margaret is better.

Always affectionately yours,
Sylvia du Maurier

Mary Llewelyn Davies replied the following day:

. . . It is delightful to think that your visit to us has established an intimacy and affection which will, I hope, go on always increasing.

I have missed you so since you went away! It quite surprised me how you have got into my heart in so short a time! The little red room looks sadly desolate – no dear couple there when I look-in – not even the two chairs standing before the fire – and in the evening that corner of the sofa is empty and I don't know how the little white shawl is getting on . . .

Cold and very blowy still. Margt sends you her dear love. My little photo is better than nothing, but make haste and send us something more really like you – and eschew a head rest.

Good bye, darling. Write as often as you feel inclined. Kindest regards to yr father and mother and Mary.

Your loving

M.Ll.D

While these letters 'show very clearly the strong affection which at once developed between Sylvia and her future mother-in-law', as Peter Llewelyn Davies observed, it was Dolly in her diary who caught the developing relationship between Arthur and Sylvia.

On Saturday, 10 October 1891, Sylvia and Arthur joined Dolly on holiday at Rustington-on-Sea on the Sussex coast where the Parry family owned a holiday home:

Saturday 10th: Arthur and Sylvia arrive. Sunday 11th: Arthur spent this morning cutting down trees. We have never seen such a pair of undemonstrative lovers as Sylvia and Arthur. They hardly ever speak to each other even when in a room by themselves. Sylvia is a delightful thing . . . She is always dancing about the room. And she and I are always imitating Julia and Fred Terry.*

Monday 12th: Arthur cut down trees again . . . Sylvia and I sat down on the beach in the morning. Spent the afternoon in the music room with Sylvia, and humbugged to any extent. S being Fred Terry, and I Julia. Took Sylvia to see the Macfarlanes. We were ushered into the awful drawing room, and S nearly burst with laughing at the extraordinary furniture. The Humbug said to Flora 'What a pretty house,' and then made a face to me.

She is great friends with Father, and says he is a 'sweet man'. Arthur says he can't bear women to like men better than their own sex, it always means there is something horrid in their characters. Love was always blind!

How fascinated Dolly was by the silent, secretive, dreamy way Sylvia

* Julia Neilson and Fred Terry were famous actors of the day.

conducted her relationship with Arthur, even checking the show was for real when they went off into a room by themselves, and how different from the funny, mocking, engaging Sylvia. Her double-persona won the teenager over and had her swooning with admiration.

But what of Arthur's odd comment that he 'can't bear women to like men better than their own sex, it always means there is something horrid in their characters'? Was it a spontaneous revelation of jealous feelings because men paid Sylvia so much attention?

By 1892, doubts about the compatibility of Arthur and Sylvia were creeping into Dolly's diary, though always voiced by others, never by Dolly herself. She quotes a girl called Sue: 'Sylvia is a hundred thousand times too good for him.' Dolly's sister Gwen was also beginning to have misgivings: Arthur is 'too dull, too commonplace, and oh his voice, and above all his Merriman jokes!'

Moreover, it is clear that the du Maurier clan were lukewarm about the engagement. Letters were few and not nearly as affectionate as the Llewelyn Davies letters. Kicky was loath to let Sylvia go; Emma insisted on a two-year engagement.

Kicky found the Davieses kind, sweet people. He had nothing against them personally. But he kept them at arm's length.

When Nico sent Daphne *The Morgue* to read in 1963, three years after Peter's suicide, she felt bound to comment rather apologetically about her family's reticence. Groping for a way to explain the cool response to the infusion of 'foreign' blood, she wrote:

> I think Grandpapa and Granny would have liked to have kept their brood intact, but since they chose to marry, then son-in-laws must come into the tribe on du M terms, or keep out. The mocking critical tolerance of poor Charlie Millar [Trixy's husband], and the acceptance of Coley [Edward Coles, May's husband], suited tribal law, but your father [Arthur] was of different calibre, as were his parents, and his brothers and sister.
>
> I understand now the expression I was brought up on, 'in and out of Kirkby Lonsdale', meaning that Sylvia wore a different façade at KL from the one she wore at home, and when she came home with too much KL about her, she was presumably soon mocked out of it. In fact, I can imagine those moving letters your grandmother [Mary Llewelyn Davies] wrote to her, welcoming her as a daughter, possibly gave offence at New Grove House, if they were shown to the tribe. The attitude would be, 'Just because you are going to marry Arthur, it doesn't mean you are no longer one of us.'

But there was much more to it than that. In the late nineteenth century many Christians were hostile to the psychic arts and to the emerging science of psychology, which put Man at the centre of things and reduced the battle between God and the Devil to a conflict between the conscious and unconscious mind. The language of truth was in transition, altering with the spirit of the times.

Kicky was so anti-Christian that 'the mere sight of a clergyman's collar was liable to antagonise him'.[2] His grand-daughter Angela observed: 'All my father's family were allergic to church and the clergy.' There was simply no place for religion in Kicky's conception, no place for it in the du Maurier dream world.* He made his statement plain in *Trilby* –

> It is very wicked and most immoral to believe, or affect to believe, that the unseen, unspeakable, unthinking Immensity we're all part and parcel of, source of eternal, infinite, indestructible life and light and might, is a kind of wrathful, glorified, and self-glorifying ogre in human shape, with human passions, and most inhuman hates . . .

Equally, there was no place in the Reverend John LlD's mind for Kicky's conviction that enlightenment comes not from an authoritative source of religion, but from an altered state of consciousness, particularly as trance had links to Satanism.

It seemed like only yesterday that Kicky had been making a pen and ink drawing of Moscheles and captioning it, 'Felix or Mephistopheles, which?' Now, just as Kicky had called his secret ability 'a gift from the Devil', so in the Rabelais stories there is always a demonic dark side to what is going on.

Faustian pacts with the Devil abound, as do archetypal tricksters

* To his aversion to clerics, there was one exception, one case where personality overcame prejudice. Alfred Ainger, at one time a Canon of Bristol and Master of the Temple, was quite a character. One memorable morning, after passing du Maurier's house, Charles Hoyer Millar recalled, 'I came across the du Maurier children highly entertained by the sight of Alfred Ainger swinging round and round the bar of some railings, with his hat on the ground and his coat tails flying in the air as he revolved . . . His individuality was very strongly marked – snow white hair and a colourless face with very keen eyes, ascetic in general appearance, of delicate build and beloved of all the Hampstead old maids in particular and by everyone who knew him.'

Ainger was the source of the most famous du Maurier's cartoons – the curate's bad egg that was 'good in parts'. He was very unhappy to learn about Kicky's interest in psychic phenomena and advised him to have nothing to do with them.

'tormenting men and discomfiting them', references to the occult, to Cazotte's interviews with the mysteriously cloaked Illuminati,* to cabbalists and sorcerers who would sweep their victims to their doom. A wholehearted embrace of the Devil, the feeling that 'the Devil had come among us', a compulsion to fly away with him – 'a curious longing to sign my name' in the Devil's book – is a defining aspect of these stories, which reach back into the mists of time and seem to recognise, with a weird sort of glee –

> Part am I of that Part that once was Everything;
> Part of the Darkness, whence the Light did spring . . .

Reading them, one's mind turns to the Hellfire clubs of the eighteenth century, to Sir Francis Dashwood's notorious Monks of Medmenham Abbey, with their strange rituals and initiation rites, their members drawn from the professional classes.

Two leading members of the Rabelais were responsible, in 1886, for the most stirring evocations of the Devil ever to be put before the general public – Robert Louis Stevenson's *The Strange Case of Dr Jekyll and Mr Hyde* and Henry Irving's revival of Goethe's *Faust* at the Lyceum, both hugely successful and influential. The *New York Times* called Irving's offering 'the most daring and at the same time most admirable thing he has yet put on', which was a telling kind of acceptance.

Faust was the source myth of the Rabelais stories, and *Faust* spills over from Kicky's world into Barrie's. For Faust's little problem, and the reason for his pact with Mephistopheles, was the same as Barrie's, namely a lack of sensual experience – not only sex, but that too. In the story, Faust makes a blood pact with Mephistopheles and flies away with him through the window, like Peter Pan and the lost boys to Neverland – 'No bulky bundle must thou take. A little inflammable air will waft us, sure and speedy.' Faust's first temptation is a girl called Margaret, 'with cheeks by childhood softly rounded', who is thrilled by Faust's dark side, thrilled 'with secret horror'. Faust has sex with her and leaves her to die, along with the baby they conceive together.

Faust is at heart a Satanist text, which is for and about all those who desire to make the Devil their servant. It is why allusions to *Faust* crop up

* Jacques Cazotte was the author of *Diable amoureux* (1772), in which the hero raises the Devil.

time and again in Daphne's stories about Barrie,* and why Barrie draws on *Faust* in *Peter Pan*.

An alignment with *Faust* had other connotations, not the least of which was with alchemy, a pseudo-science reputedly dedicated to 'transmuting' base metals into gold, but widely suspected to have as its true purpose the transformation of the human psyche, which was about to become the purpose of the new science of psychology.

For Goethe, alchemy was the ultimate lore. At the end of the play Faust's soul is 'transmuted' (a word indelibly associated with the black art) within a choir of boys, where, 'in the highest, purest cell', sits Doctor Marianus, an old alchemical authority.

In 1886 Freud visited Paris and watched Jean-Martin Charcot's displays of hypnotism at the Salpêtrière Hospital,† where down-and-out patients were put into a hypnotic trance and made to 'drop on all fours and bark like dogs, or flap their arms when told they were birds, or even eat a lump of charcoal with relish when told it was chocolate'.[3] Freud saw immediately the therapeutic potential of such a hypnotic relationship.‡ He returned to Vienna and from 1867 began to hypnotise his patients and make helpful cathartic suggestions to their unconscious minds. It was the first step towards his theory of the conscious/unconscious mind, and in the design and implementation of the science of psychoanalysis.

It was left to his student, Carl Jung, to make the connections with what had gone before. Jung, born in 1875, first read *Faust* as a teenager at his mother's suggestion. His step forward came in recognising that the drama is undertaken within the mind. Mephistopheles was (as Goethe states in

* For example in 'The Alibi', 'The Little Photographer', and 'Monte Verita'.

† Charcot was not in fact trying to prove anything about hypnosis, his interest was diagnostic. Medicine was still a physical-cause-and-effect science and his purpose was to show that the sometimes bizarre physical symptoms of hysteria, a blanket term for mental distress that presents symptoms such as paralysis or phantom pregnancy, were in fact the result of mental trauma – some powerful shock in the past, or memory of it held in a part of the brain normally inaccessible to the conscious patient. He used the lectures to demonstrate the existence of this 'unconscious' part of the brain, which on stage under hypnosis could be made to produce all kinds of bizarre symptoms, including ones associated with hysteria.

‡ When Freud arrived from Vienna to study under Charcot, he realised that, if patients could be made to do these bizarre things by accessing this obviously hugely powerful 'unconscious' side of the brain, what extraordinary results might be achieved by making therapeutic suggestions to it. Freud's visit led directly to his psychoanalytical theory of the conscious/unconscious mind.

the play) one of 'the two souls' housed within – Faust's dark side, his unconscious mind.

Now, the purpose of psychology was to face Man with his unconscious mind – his Mephistopheles – and to analyse and resolve conflicts between it and his conscious mind. For Jung, embracing the Devil, something that the Church could never condone, was not Satanism, it was the first step to a balanced state of mind. He wrote that when he first read *Faust* it poured into his soul 'like a miraculous balm. "Here at last," I thought, "is someone who takes the Devil seriously."'

As for the alchemist Doctor Marianus 'in the purest, highest cell', Jung discovered, via an incredibly detailed study of its symbols, that alchemy was the original transformational science, and as such the very seat of psychoanalysis.* 'The alchemic transformation is to man's innate psychic disposition, *a reunion with the unconscious*, his inherited, instinctive make-up, which goes down into the subhuman.'

This reunification of the civilised man with the primitive was of course at the heart of Romanticism too, and the point where Kicky stood firm.

Studying the trajectory of Kicky's life, it seems that first he is a Romantic, next a Satanist, then an alchemist, and finally he has the mind of a modern psychoanalyst. In this he reflected the rapidly changing intellectual climate of his times. Kicky saw the unconscious mind as a photographic plate of suppressed memories and emotions, and hypnosis as the means to release them, as he wrote in *Peter Ibbetson*:

> Evidently our brain contains something akin both to a photographic plate and a phonographic cylinder . . . not a sight or a sound or a smell is lost; not a taste or a feeling or an emotion. Unconscious memory records them all . . . Night after night I saw reacted before me scenes not only fairly remembered, but scenes utterly forgotten, and yet as sinisterly true as the remembered ones, and all bathed in that ineffable light, the light of other days – the light that never was on sea or land, and yet the light of absolute truth . . .

A Jungian might read *Peter Ibbetson* as a fascinating psychological adventure. Once Peter is in prison, Mary has no existence outside Peter's

* Jung began this study in the 1920s, but a psychological view of alchemy was abroad before that, thanks to Herbert Silberer (1882–1922). Jung's idea of the archetypes of the collective unconscious – fundamental forms or ideas that shape or characterise our thinking – resonated with the elaborate symbolic language of alchemical texts, and provided scholars with a new way to examine alchemical material.

mind. Her role is that of his *anima*. The female genes in a man can produce a contra-sexual character known as the *anima* in dreams and fantasies ('the dream girl or dream lover'). In dreams, this character leads a man into his unconscious, exactly as Mary leads Peter into his unconscious memories, and into his libido.

Daphne read Jung in the 1950s and described the rapturous dream environment of *Peter Ibbetson* as the place where 'man found his heart's desire, or, if a psychological word is more easily understood, his *anima*'.[4]

In the early years of the twentieth century, Jung harvested many of the ideas that had previously been associated with Romanticism, the psychic arts, alchemy, the occult, Goethe's *Faust*, and the philosophy of Kant, Von Schelling, Carus and Schopenhauer, for reinterpretation in the new science. And he read George du Maurier: in *The Cambridge Companion to Jung* Claire Douglas lists du Maurier among writers who spread 'the Romantic fascination with altered states' and influenced Jung as a student.[5]

Kicky kept the Christian Llewelyn Davieses at arm's length. He did not have the objectivity of Jung, who lived until 1961 and could look back a long way and see that it is only ever the language in which we express truth that changes, not truth itself: 'Eternal truth needs a human language that alters with the spirit of the times . . . Only in a new form can eternal truth be understood anew.' Jung saw this and held no lasting hope for psychology over Romanticism, Satanism or alchemy.

But there was, in fact, a very good reason for Kicky to regret the transition of Romanticism into the science of psychology. For while psychology rescued him from Satanism by redefining the Devil as the unconscious, the new understanding of how hypnotism works offered ordinary people a handle on the Devil and the potential for misuse soared, especially in the area of child abuse.

When, from 1887, Freud began tinkering with the unconscious, he soon discovered that the process gave him powerful control over his patients. Under hypnosis the conscious, inhibiting, protective control-tower of a patient's thinking (the conscious mind) is put out of action and its function ceded to the hypnotist. Because control of a patient's unconscious passes to the hypnotist, the relationship between patient and doctor is one that involves massive trust, for in hypnosis a patient's whole interpretation of life may be changed.

What was clear to Kicky in 1893, as he finally set about writing *Trilby*, was that hypnosis was not only an agency for recapturing forgotten memory or engendering a Romantic mystical high. It would not be enough to write a story about a hypnotist called Svengali who made a beautiful but tone-deaf artist's model called Trilby sing more beautifully than the world had ever heard a girl sing. He also has to destroy her.

For, with its redefinition as a psychological tool, hypnosis was henceforth a powerful instrument of mind control.

PART IV

1894–1910

Sylvia, the Lost Boys and Uncle Jim: the *Peter Pan* inheritance

Svengali hypnotises Trilby: 'Et maintenant dors, ma mignonne!'

CHAPTER ONE

Slipping into madness

In 1894 George du Maurier's second novel, *Trilby*, was published. It appeared first as a serial illustrated by the author in *Harper's Monthly*, then in book form, and subsequently as a play, the English rights going to the actor-manager Herbert Beerbohm Tree, a friend of Kicky, for £100.

The play was so successful that Tree built a new theatre, Her Majesty's, on the proceeds. The book, which was published first in America, became the number one bestseller in 1894, and by the end of the year had sold 300,000 copies.[1] That was only the beginning. It was 1900 before a reporter in New York declared that the Trilby craze was over. It was 'probably the biggest selling novel of all time,' according to its publisher, McIlvaine at *Harper*. 'Not even Dickens had attracted such a wide and devoted audience.' It was 'the first modern bestseller',[2] the first to use a sophisticated marketing strategy. In its marketing, as well as in its embrace of modern psychology, *Trilby* was a turning point.

The narrative returns George du Maurier to the bohemian Paris of his student days, to the romantic milieu of the Left Bank, 'to happy days and happy nights . . . happy times of careless impecuniosity, and youth and hope and health and strength and freedom', and to the 'three musketeers of the brush' – the Laird, Taffy, and Little Billee.*

No 'killjoy complications of love' interfere, until one day into their lives bursts artist's model Trilby O'Ferrall. Smoking roll-up cigarettes, living for freedom, truth and beauty, and on precious little else, Trilby is the very image of bohemianism and innocence, without a sly or nasty cell in her body. Hers is an unusual beauty, subtle, hidden from the casual eye, one that Little Billee considers needs discovering by a consummate artist, until

* Little Billee is based on George du Maurier himself.

he catches sight of her foot and is overcome. It is as if the very essence of her has been revealed to him.

The episode recalled the time Jimmy Whistler drew a foot on the wall of Gleyre's studio as a symbol of the very essence of beauty, though in reality it was not the foot of a woman, but of Alecco Ionides, and his excitement was probably inspired by a pipe of opium.

But for Little Billee there is no opium; he has a strong aesthetic sense, more refined than that of either of his older artist friends. He is as sensitive to beauty as du Maurier was when in a trance. He is indeed the quintessence of Kicky's Romantic vision, which seems to draw on the ideas of his friend Henry James.

Outwardly, Little Billee's artistic sensitivity finds expression in a certain *boyishness*, which goes with 'a quickness, a keenness, a delicacy of perception in matters of form and colour, a mysterious facility and felicity of execution, a sense of all that was sweet and beautiful in nature, and a ready power of expressing it'.

To be a boy was, in the Romantic sense, irrespective of age or gender, 'the secret of eternal youth', to be liberated from 'the regular action of the world', to be a true-dreamer like Kicky himself.

When Kicky writes that Trilby 'would have made a singularly handsome boy', and 'it was a real pity she wasn't a boy, she would have made a jolly nice one', the reader realises that she and Little Billee are made for each other.

Trilby has, however, one imperfection. She is incapable of appreciating music, as the three artists discover when a German-Polish musician called Svengali arrives and plays 'some of his grandest music', which passes Trilby by. When she herself sings, she reveals a full voice, but, alas, it is excruciatingly out of tune. Rather embarrassingly, because of course she cannot hear it, Trilby is completely tone-deaf.

Svengali is fascinated by her. In threatening contrast to childlike Billee, he is a dark Satanic figure possessed of a controlling personality –

> A tall bony individual of any age between thirty and forty-five, of Jewish aspect, well-featured but sinister . . . His thick, heavy, languid, lustreless black hair fell down behind his ears to his shoulders . . . He had bold, brilliant black eyes, with long, heavy lids, a thin, sallow face, and a beard of burnt-up black, which grew almost from under his eyelids; and over it his moustache, a shade lighter, fell in two long spiral twists.

He fancies he can bring Trilby to self-expression beyond her wildest dreams. First he hypnotises her therapeutically, to cure her neuralgia. Thereafter, time and again he invades and dominates her mind, and she worships his hypnotic power over her by releasing from her lips the most heavenly music the world has ever known.

Henceforth there are two Trilbys, the one Little Billee knew, who could not sing one single note in tune and was 'an angel in paradise', and the one Svengali turns her into. He only had to say, 'Dors!' and Trilby 'became an unconscious Trilby of marble, who could produce wonderful sound . . . and love him at his bidding'.

Svengali's method is that of post-hypnotic suggestion. Trilby has been put into a deep hypnotic trance and then primed with the information that a trigger word, or indeed a sign, will return her to it, but she will remain alert and apparently normal:

> With one wave of his hand over her – with one look of his eye – with a word – Svengali could turn her into another Trilby, his Trilby – and make her do whatever he liked . . . you might have run a red-hot needle into her and she would not have felt it.

In deep hypnosis but alert to the world, Trilby holds audiences in thrall with her singing. But she is constantly in Svengali's power: it only takes a word or a sign from him to return her to deep hypnosis.* Hers is a continuing nightmare existence not because she is unhappy – dressed in sables, rouged and pearl powdered, she is, and causes, a sensation – but because her mind has been commandeered. Svengali is in occupation of the control-tower of her thinking. In religious terms, he has her soul; in occult terms, it is a case of possession; in legal terms, it is the ultimate form of psychological abuse.

Her desertion breaks Little Billee's heart. On one occasion he catches sight of her in a carriage with Svengali and she looks down at him 'with a cold stare of disdain'. As they pass he hears them both snigger – 'she with a little high-pitched flippant snigger worthy of a London barmaid.'

Trilby's whole personality and interpretation of the world has been transformed by her hypnotist.

But then Svengali dies from a heart attack, and Trilby awakes as if from

* This is the 'trigger' methodology already met in its context of dreaming true, and is perfectly feasible. I have watched Paul McKenna perform this hypnotic experiment.

a dream, unaware of what has been going on and unable to sing at all. Exhausted from years as Svengali's puppet, she dies and Little Billee, utterly destroyed, dies shortly afterwards.

The publisher's marketing department caught on to both 'Trilbyism' and 'Svengalism'.

'*Trilby* turned bohemianism into a style,' wrote Jon Savage.[3] 'It was particularly attractive to young women, who, according to Luc Sante, "derived from it the courage to call themselves artists and bachelor girls, to smoke cigarettes and drink Chianti."' Bohemianism swept Britain and America. Kicky received thousands of letters, both from women identifying with Trilby and from men lusting after her, such that the offer to Kicky of $10,000 for a signed drawing of Trilby in the nude, proposed by David Lodge in *Author, Author*, seems hardly an embellishment of the truth. John Masefield recalled: 'I well remember hats, boots, shoes, collars, toothpastes, coats, soaps, songs and dances named after Trilby . . . For many years, the Trilby hat was known to men. It persists still as a hat, but it is no longer known as the Trilby. Even the human foot is now called a foot.'[4]

Equally, the marketing men promoted 'Svengalism', appealing to the public fascination with mind control. Within a year, there appeared a parody – *Drilby Re-Versed* – in which Leopold Jordan wrote what many were thinking:

> Let this story be a warning
> It's written in that plan
> Don't introduce your sweetheart to
> A hypnotising man.

After *Trilby*, abuse would never be understood again as a term relating only to physical violence. Svengali makes licentious capital of his relationship with Trilby, and Kicky's novel promoted awareness of the sexual nature of hypnosis.

While the *Trilby* craze raged, Freud was discovering in a clinical context what Kicky had known for years, that 'sexuality works above all at the level of fantasy':[5]

> After responding quite normally to hypnosis, one of his more submissive patients suddenly awoke and threw her arms around the doctor's neck. Freud

> was 'modest enough' not to ascribe the patient's impetuous behaviour to his own 'irresistible personal attraction', and he resolved henceforth to refrain from using hypnotism Otherwise he would never be able to eliminate or at least control a 'mysterious element' operating in the rapport between his patients and himself.[6]

Partly as a result of his experience, partly because under hypnosis patients proved to be so suggestible, Freud abandoned hypnosis altogether.

The success of *Trilby* put Henry James's nose out of joint because – while the writing was wonderfully evocative of Kicky's personality – it was not, he adjudged, great art. Also, he was appalled by the marketing strategy. 'The American frenzy was naturally the loudest,' he wrote, 'and seemed to reveal monstrosities of organisation.' But he stuck by Kicky through all the consequences – including Jimmy Whistler threatening to sue him. As for Kicky, he was deeply disturbed. 'It's not just a success – it's a "boom",' he cried, and he wasn't happy about it, calling it 'freakish . . . unnatural'.

Henry James became concerned about his friend's health. 'He found himself sunk in a landslide of obsessions, of inane, incongruous letters, of interviewers, intruders, invaders . . . Kicky seemed to recoil from all the "botheration" (as he called it) in a terror of the temper of the many-headed monster.'

Was it the commercialism that precipitated his decline, which certainly dated from publication of *Trilby*, or did he suffer guilt at what he had unleashed? He had been Carry's Svengali, and now he was making a great deal of money out of it.

> Poor Carry! [wrote Felix Moscheles] Yes, she had a story. Sad. Bright. Then sad again. First she gave to Amor what was Amor's, and then to Hymen what was Hymen's. She tasted of the apple her friend the serpent had told her so much about. Then . . . she tried another; such a bad one unfortunately. It was a wonder it didn't poison her, body and soul, but it didn't. There was a moment when the Angel with the flaming sword threatened to cast her adrift, and it would have fared badly with her had not a helping hand come to save her.[7]

The helping hand had come from a young doctor, who fell in love with her and to whom she clung as to a raft in a stormy sea. Her saviour saw to it that she relinquished all contact with Moscheles and Kicky. They married, and Carry gave birth to a daughter, the only occasion that she broke her husband's rule and wrote to her Svengalis.

But then tragedy struck. Her husband developed septicaemia from a patient and died in Carry's arms. 'It was a case of self-sacrifice in the cause of science, of heroic devotion to a fellow-creature,' wrote the sentimental and insincere Moscheles. 'What can have become of Carry once more cast adrift? We never knew.'

Kicky had been close to Carry and had treated her shabbily. In August 1862 he had been visiting his mother and sister in Düsseldorf. Dropping off to see some friends in Antwerp, he had caught sight of her on a train and ignored her.

But Kicky's brain was deteriorating, and guilt about Carry cannot have been the only reason. He had seen his Romantic metaphysical vision replaced by the emerging science of psychology, with its propensity not only to free the mind, but to control it. The irony cannot have escaped him.*

There had been warnings about nervous impairment and breakdown if one indulged in hypnosis repeatedly. Kicky knew the score. Trilby had burned out in the end. In 1895, Robert Sherard interviewed Kicky and was shocked at his decline. He struck him as 'a man who has suffered greatly, haunted by some evil dream or disturbing apprehension'. The following autumn Kicky returned from holiday in Whitby and felt very ill, as Tom Armstrong recorded:

> It was found that his head, in which weakness had been discovered some time ago, was much amiss and it was supposed that he had injured it by walking too much or too far in a hilly country. He was ordered to bed for three weeks so that his head might have complete rest . . . During the last fortnight of his life I saw him twice and on the latter occasion he was talkative and apparently not much depressed although he said it was 'all over with him'. Henry James was with him when I went to his bed room . . .
>
> Soon after my last interview with him the doctors gave instructions that no more persons than were necessary should be admitted to his sick room. His breathing became difficult and he had shivering fits and, afterwards, attacks of cardiac asthma which exhausted him much . . .

* An added irony was that the marketing strategies for selling *Trilby* called on the new manipulative techniques of psychology.

On 6 October 1896, Kicky died. He was only 62. The post-mortem revealed growths in his chest on which, it was said, it would have been impossible to operate. Henry James remained unconvinced:

> They said it was matter around the heart, but it was *Trilby* that was the matter.

Before his death Kicky had taken the unusual step of making arrangements to be cremated, which was illegal at the time, or at least unaccounted for by Act of Parliament.

The pioneer of cremation was an eccentric doctor called William Price, who was a Druid. At 83, on 18 January 1884, he had cremated his five-month-old son, Iesu Grist Price (Jesus Christ Price). There ensued a court case, which Price won, a result that prepared the way for the Cremation Act of 1902. Price himself died in 1893. His body was cremated, as instructed, atop two tons of coal.

It is unknown whether Kicky had any dealings with Price, or was in sympathy with Druidism, an ancient religion which took the Devil seriously. The Anglican Canon Ainger, 'good in parts', conducted the funeral service, but the cremation took place in Woking, and was attended by Kicky's sons Guy and Gerald and sons-in-law Arthur Llewelyn Davies and Charles Hoyer Millar.

A report in the *Hampstead and Highgate Express* reassured its readers that 'there is nothing repulsive or gloomy in the aspect of the crematorium. It is well lit and the furnace is in the centre. The body or coffined corpse is pushed from a large table along a broad sheet of iron into the burning chamber.'

Hoyer Millar was less sanguine in his appraisal. 'After being admitted into the furnace-room, [we] saw – much to our horror though it was too late to go back – the swathed body lifted from the coffin and put on a steel cradle which was pushed into the furnace. At that time the process was a lengthy one; we had brought our lunch with us and stood in the damp, cold autumn weather leaning against the neighbouring fir trees. We were all too miserable, mentally and physically, to talk.' All, that is, save Gerald, who, 'unable to restrain himself, burst out with, "At all events we won't have to play rounders after lunch" ' – an allusion apparently to Kicky's love of the game, though his descendants today insist he said 'cricket'.[8]

CHAPTER TWO

Predator and victim

In 1894, as *Trilby* was published, Barrie was working on an autobiographical novel. He had intended to feature himself as an adult, but had come to the conclusion that he should start with his childhood, as Kicky had in *Peter Ibbetson*, and so one novel became two. *Sentimental Tommy* was published in 1896, and *Tommy and Grizel* in 1900.

These two novels were a world away from anything he had written before. Tommy, like Peter Ibbetson, 'passes between dreams and reality as though through tissue paper'. They are fantasies but not for the amusement of children. Introspective excursions, analytical of their author, they are autobiographical psycho-novels, a new genre created by George du Maurier at a time when introspection and analysis, and (since *Trilby*) mind control, were *the* thing.

It is of course unsafe to assume that autobiographical fiction tells the whole truth. But W. A. Darlington thought that in this case it did. 'The confessions which Barrie makes in *The Greenwood Hat* [his non-fiction autobiographical writings] agree too exactly with his description of Tommy Sandys to allow much doubt that Tommy is a projection of those traits in his own character which he most feared and disliked.'

The Tommy novels are darkly analytical of Barrie's mind, as we would expect from an author whose own personality is a constant concern.

Control is Tommy's purpose. Childhood deprivation, lack of love, a worrying absence of true feeling about anyone, and low self-esteem, result in a compensatory drive to control other people's lives.

It is psychological power he seeks, a subtle form of control that at once reveals and exploits the weaknesses of others. Finding a way to it turns Tommy on, and it is his mother, a bitter, manipulative woman, who first shows him the thrill that can be gained from the dynamics of domination versus passivity. Barrie could not have been more acutely self-analytical.

Tommy gets the children of Thrums playing his games in the imaginary Jacobite Siege of Thrums, with him as their leader. His immersion in the fantasy is compulsive, and it troubles his faithful lieutenant, Corp Shiach, 'that in his enthusiasm Tommy had more than once drawn blood from himself. "When you take it a' so real as that," Corp said uncomfortably, "I near think we should give it up."'

Not content with having his young friends in the palm of his hand, Tommy begins to manipulate the entire town, dreaming up stratagems that exploit the Presbyterian morality and thrifty Scots attitude, to line his own pockets. He sees his little world with an objectivity alarming for his age. Money is never his principal purpose. He does it for the pleasure of the thing, to rest a hand on the wheel of the fate of the citizens of Thrums.

Writing immediately after publication of *Trilby*, Barrie declares Tommy 'to be *the boy incarnate*', but this is a different sort of boy from Little Billee, the boy he had just been reading about. Wild spirits master Tommy. Innocence is not his suit. He doesn't believe people truly feel. There is no such thing as true (as in disinterested) feeling or emotion. People use their feelings to get where they want to be. Tommy exploits this deceit mercilessly to gain advantage.

It is a bitter indictment of the du Maurier dream world of feeling. Tommy's genius is that of the psychological manipulator. Getting inside people and working on them from within is his speciality. At night he lies awake, until he 'finds a way'.

However disturbing, this boy is no less an archetype than du Maurier's 'boy'. Tommy is a psychic structure of extreme antiquity, the trickster who has haunted picaresque tales, carnivals, revels and magic rites since time immemorial, an inauspicious *puer aeternus,* the very principle of discord, mischief and dissolution, who holds the fate of everyone in his hands.

In 1892, Sylvia du Maurier had married Arthur Llewelyn Davies. They moved into 18 Craven Terrace on the opposite side of Kensington Gardens to Barrie. Theirs was 'a dear little house (or Sylvia made it so), a sort of maisonette', as Dolly Parry described it. Visitors questioned how the young couple had found the money to pay for it. Arthur, besides what he could expect to earn from the law, which was little at this stage, had brought a legacy of £3,000 from his maternal Uncle Charles, but his annual budget was a mere £400, the same amount that Kicky had earned when he married Emma, nearly thirty years earlier.

Four hundred pounds, while a huge sum to the poor of Whitechapel in 1894, was not regarded as much of an income in the circles in which the du Mauriers moved, so Sylvia worked for a dressmaking business set up by her father with a theatrical costumier, Mrs Nettleship, who made clothes for Ellen Terry. Sylvia discovered a flair for design, and with her skill and taste created lovely clothes for herself and her sons, and soft furnishings for their home, often from whatever lay to hand.

From 'the hand-sewn bell-rope which pulled no bell to the hand-painted cigar-box that contained no cigars', her house was a triumph of dissemblance and inspiration –

> The floor was of a delicious green with exquisite oriental rugs; green and white, I think, was the lady's scheme of colour, something cool, you observe, to keep the sun under. The window-curtains were of some rare material and the colour of the purple clematis; they swept the floor grandly . . . The piano . . . many dainty pieces, mostly in green wood, a sofa, a corner cupboard, and a most captivating desk, which was so like its owner that it could have sat down at her and dashed off a note.[1]

It seemed that Sylvia and Arthur were blessed. They had beauty, love, promise, and an astonishingly attractive baby (for George, named after Sylvia's father, had been born in 1893).

Kicky had been pleased that Arthur was a 'joli garçon', very handsome, as handsome 'comme l'autre',[2] referring to Sylvia's sister Trixy's equally good-looking husband, Charles Hoyer Millar. 'We used to think he was a young warrior in an Italian picture,' Sir Hubert Parry once said of Arthur. Sylvia shared her artist father's obsession with physical beauty. She would never have married an ugly man. But, as the daughter of George du Maurier, she brought an extra dimension to that beauty.

People remembered the du Maurier family's appearances in *Punch*; but now, following *Peter Ibbetson* and *Trilby*, the du Mauriers were enjoying the spotlight once more, and there was a different aura about them, Sylvia in particular. People had wondered about the first novel, how true a picture it had given of Kicky. Interest was enhanced by the veil of secrecy he threw over his involvement with the psychic arts. He denied it in letters to fans, but in private he had a cultist mentality, for example writing to his close friend Tom Armstrong in French and in minuscule print (which he always used when mentioning anything sensitive) about a particular sympathiser as '*one of us*',* as if there were two camps: those who believed, and those who did not.

We know that Sylvia shared her father's special interest. Dolly had known for years that Sylvia had a secret preoccupation. In the 1940s, when Dolly was helping Peter compile *The Morgue*, she tried to guide him to it without compromising her friend's confidence. She wrote:

> Always [Sylvia's] reserve about what she cared about was very strong. She had an inner life of her own, which is what gave her her great interest.

And again:

> Sylvia couldn't talk about things she really felt to those who were not very close to her. She had an inner life of her own, & was to me always interesting.

Sylvia's inner life showed in the dreamy photographs of her, and in the undemonstrative silent moments of her courting of Arthur, as if she was away in another world. It was this that Peter was on to when he called on Daphne's help in 1949, writing that he suspected that Sylvia inherited 'a good deal' from her father that made her anything but ordinary – unlike Grannie (Emma).

Dolly's diary entry for 'Sunday, October 15th, 1892' reads:†

> Talked a good deal with sweet Sylvia, who told me a good deal about her family etc.

There then followed instructions about how to hypnotise someone:

> Place yourself before the subject with your thoughts concentrated on the effect you wish to produce, you tell him to look at you steadily and think only of sleep. Raise your hands with the palms towards him, over the crown of head and before the forehead where you keep them for one or 2 minutes, & move them slowly down to the pit of stomach, without touching subject, at a distance of one or 2 inches from body, as soon as hands reach lowest part of

* Letter to Tom Armstrong about Leslie Stephen, the academic and writer, who was a friend of Arthur's father, John Llewelyn Davies.

† In fact, there wasn't a 'Sunday, October 15th' in 1892, it would have had to be either Saturday the 15th or Sunday the 16th.

> the stroke you carry them again in a wide sweep with outspread arms over subject's head. Repeat same movements for 10 minutes.

It is possible that Kicky and Sylvia dabbled in hypnotism together; perhaps their relationship had inspired Henry James to write about the relationship between father and daughter in his 1886 novel *The Bostonians*; perhaps Kicky even hypnotised Sylvia, as in Henry James's fiction the father hypnotises the daughter.

As Kicky's life drew to a close, it became important for him to pass on his secret talent. His third novel *The Martian* was published posthumously in 1896. It took up a theme mentioned but not developed in *Peter Ibbetson*, that a 'little live spark of your own individual consciousness' can be handed down 'mildly incandescent to your remotest posterity', as he put it. It is in *The Martian* that he declared that a girl in the family would share his consciousness and would carry him into the future after his death. He appeared to be nominating Sylvia by naming his hero (as usual, a very lightly disguised version of himself) Barty Jocelyn. His successor would therefore be named Jocelyn; and Jocelyn was Sylvia's second name.

Daphne wrote about the family secret being passed down the line in her short story 'The Archduchess'. After her debriefing sessions with Peter in the 1950s, she saw, with disturbing clarity, that it was this secret that attracted Barrie as predator and marked Sylvia out as his victim. His motivation?

> He had a grudge against his parents. They had brought into the world a maimed being, and he could not forgive them for not having made him beautiful. The child who cannot forgive his parents cannot forgive the country that cradled him, and [he] grew up with the desire to lame others, even as he himself was lame.*

In the story, Daphne code-named him 'Markoi', the first syllable meaning 'spoil' or 'cause harm to', the second, 'love' (a homophone of the Japanese word *koi* means 'love', which is why koi carp are symbols of love and friendship in Japan). Barrie's own youth had been bereft of wonder, and he

* Markoi, the fictional villain of the story, was physically lame, with a twisted foot, like Mephistopheles. Lameness is the sign of the Devil in *Faust*, and is a feature of the Barrie figure in 'The Little Photographer', a story in Daphne du Maurier's *The Apple Tree* collection (1952).

had grown up full of resentment. The du Maurier secret promised the eternal youth that Barrie had been denied. The secret marked out Sylvia's sons as Barrie's victims too, for 'all princes who believe in eternal youth,' she wrote in the same story, 'offer themselves as victims.'

Barrie's invasion of the family may also have been driven by resentment of the figure he displaced. For I cannot believe that he didn't meet Kicky in the 1890s – he was too taken up with Kicky's ideas, and they had too many friends in common, for them not to have met – and, given the absence of a record of their meeting, I feel one is bound to consider the possibility that if they did meet, they did not get on.

On the surface they had much in common: both Kicky and Barrie were diminutive and boyish, and had the same dry sense of humour and lugubrious way of expressing it; both were satirical in their work, yet sentimental and whimsical. But beneath the surface no two men could have been more dissimilar. While Kicky's satire was upbeat and palpably sincere, a cynical drop of acid was the very essence of Barrie's genius. Kicky was a Romantic, he worshipped beauty. *Feeling* was what he was all about. But Barrie confessed he was incapable of 'a genuine feeling that wasn't merely sentiment', hated music, had no interest in art.

According to Barrie's biographer Denis Mackail, his insensitivity to art was the reason he 'could never, even spiritually, be one of the real or esoteric Broadway gang' – a reference to the cricket-playing artistic community in Worcestershire, where many of Kicky's friends, including Henry James, used to gather. This surely was also what estranged him from Kicky, who would have recoiled from this travesty of himself and all that he held sacred. And if that is so, what, I wondered, might Barrie have done then? Rejection was not something he found easy to take.

Henry James, with the unconscious foresight of a true artist, made the link.

> Svengali capers like a goat of poetry, and makes music like the great god Pan.

CHAPTER THREE

Philanderings in the park

Barrie began his 'sentimental philanderings' in Kensington Gardens from the time of Kicky's death, and in 1897 first engaged 4-year-old George Llewelyn Davies and his 3-year-old brother Jack, conspicuous in bright red tam-o'-shanters and rather feminine blue blouses, both hand-made by Sylvia. The Kensington Gardens nannies commandeered the Broad Walk and were happy for their charges to talk with Barrie, a famous author, sometimes accompanied by his pretty wife. The children looked forward to his every appearance.

In time, he would make the Gardens so famous in his book, *The Little White Bird*, that mothers came to expect him to captivate their children with his stories and were put out when he did not. It must have become quite difficult for him, and was perhaps partly the reason why the authorities eventually presented him with his own key, so that he could go there after lock-up time with whomever he liked. The idea came from Lord Esher, Secretary to His Majesty's Office of Works, who for some reason unrecorded took to calling Barrie 'the furry beast'.

On New Year's Eve, 1897, Barrie met the parents of the Davies' boys at a party thrown by society solicitor Sir George Lewis and his wife:

> P(eggy) Ll.D [Peter's wife] remembers J.M.B. telling her that he found himself sitting next to the most beautiful creature he had ever seen, and was overwhelmed and also intrigued by the way she put aside some of the various sweets that were handed round, and secreted them. When he asked her why, she answered that she was keeping them for Peter.[1]

Peter's own verdict on this was 'a suspect story on the face of it', and new evidence indicates that Barrie's first meeting with Sylvia was anything but chance.

Handwritten invitation lists to Lady Lewis's dinner parties and balls have recently come to light. They show that the du Mauriers had been frequent guests at her palatial home at 88 Portland Place, W1, since at least the 1870s.

Sir George and Lady Lewis had initially welcomed Kicky's fine singing voice as entertainment at their soirées. So central a part did the Lewis parties then become in the lives of Kicky and Emma that the invitation lists contain clues to the whole du Maurier story, as well as touching on many other fascinating tangential stories.

Here are actor managers J. L. Toole and Beerbohm Tree sitting next to Ellen Terry, Henry James and Oscar Wilde. Tree's wife, the distinguished actress Helen Maud Holt, was often also present. She would later work with Gerald du Maurier on Barrie's plays, and her daughter Viola, also often present, would become a close friend of Barrie as well as of Gerald and his family, especially Daphne. Among other characters who claimed my attention were Sydney Buxton, an uncle of Rupert Buxton, the boy who drowned in the arms of Michael Llewelyn Davies in 1921, and the millionaire Otto Kahn, who impinged on Daphne's life during a particularly rebellious phase – names gathering dust on paper, but triggers still to history.

The Lewis parties could be grand affairs. In June 1877, 278 invitations were sent out – there were 218 acceptances and 60 regrets. Occasionally there would be a select, high-profile evening, as in March 1885, when the Prince of Wales was principal guest, and Kicky and Emma attended with a dozen or so others. From the 1870s, Felix Moscheles is invited, no doubt initially on du Maurier's recommendation. Felix was bent on recruiting members of high society to his portraiture enterprise. Other artist friends of Kicky – James Whistler, Edward Burne-Jones and Lawrence Alma-Tadema – were also frequent guests. Guy du Maurier was entertained here with his parents in March 1890. Sylvia first appears in May 1891 with 'Llewelyn Davies', after which she is a regular guest.

As a young barrister, Arthur Llewelyn Davies received briefs from Sir George Lewis, following his marriage to Sylvia, doubtless as a result of the connection between the du Maurier family and the Lewises. It was at the Lewises', too, that Sylvia took 16-year-old Dolly Parry under her wing and made her look beautiful for her first society ball, a kindness Dolly never forgot.

The invitation lists show that the du Mauriers inhabited a completely different world from Barrie, and it is interesting that Barrie was conspicuous by his absence at other places where Kicky held sway, such as the Rabelais.

What is certain is that if you wanted to meet Sylvia Llewelyn Davies 'by chance', the best way to do it would be to find your way on to one of the Lewis party lists, which is exactly what Barrie did on 21 December 1896, just two months after Kicky's death.

He achieved this by giving the two young Lewis daughters parts in the copyright performance of his play, based on his novel, *The Little Minister*. A copyright performance was a pre-production performance of a new play, usually acted before an invited audience. In this instance a number of friends, and friends of friends, were in the cast. It would not have been difficult for Barrie to have arranged the Lewis children to be part of it.

Once Barrie had his foot in the door he took hold of the Lewises's entertainments as Kicky had done all those years before, substituting – for Kicky's vocal entertainments – revues featuring satirical skits on the guests. In the newly opened Lewis archive are programmes for events written by Barrie including *Child's Play* and *The Old Bore's Almanack*, and *The Foolies*, 'a programme of songs, recitations, imitation and dance'. It is all fairly cringe-making. For example, the author, editor and art critic Comyns Carr is one of many listed in a revue by Barrie called *Who's Here* – 'This Carr runs Peter Panhard, can travel faust or an-Dante; never tyres; one can rely on its comyns and goings.'*

Barrie became a hit. Lady Lewis would be firm in her support of him, finding him a flat during his divorce from Mary in 1909, and offering to help him with the boys after Sylvia's death. Sir George's firm of solicitors came to represent him, and a future head of it, Sir Reginald Poole, acted, according to Peter Davies, with 'extreme and coldly hostile virulence' against himself, Jack, and Nico in the matter of the boys' claims on the Barrie estate in 1937.

There is no doubt that from December 1896, the Lewises were on Jim Barrie's side, and they were powerful allies. Looking back, one might say that his friendship with the Lewises was his first and most significant step to donning Kicky's trilby and taking over his family.

Whatever the nature of the conversation between Jim and Mary Barrie and Sir George and Lady Lewis on the first occasion they met, and the

* The reference to *Faust* concerns an adaptation co-written by Carr for Beerbohm Tree.

truth about how Barrie came to recognise and meet Sylvia's boys in Kensington Gardens soon afterwards, it is likely that, two months after Kicky's death, the du Mauriers had featured in the conversation, and the groundwork was laid there.

The part that the Lewises played in Jim meeting Sylvia is certain. For when, a year later, Lady Lewis drew up a guest list for her New Year's Eve party, 1897, there was no question how one corner of it would read:

Mr. & Mrs. J.M. Barrie
Mr. & Mrs. Llewelyn Davies

The names appear in that order, next to each other in the notebook.

CHAPTER FOUR

The boy in the box

J. M. Barrie was a famous playwright and novelist. The attention he paid Sylvia on the night they met at the Lewises' will have flattered her. The story goes that he began with an allusion to *Peter Ibbetson*. He told her he had a St Bernard named Porthos after Peter's St Bernard. Sylvia responded by telling him that she had a child named after the hero of the same novel. Jim alluded to a young Peter he knew who was regularly pushed in his pram in Kensington Gardens by his nanny. Sylvia recognised Jim as the man whom her sons had told her about. Jim then spoke to Sylvia about Peterkin, testing whether she knew of his favourite character from *The Coral Island*. She didn't.

From 1898 Jim and Mary Barrie and Arthur and Sylvia Llewelyn Davies saw a great deal of one another. There scarcely was a day when Jim did not meet the boys in the park and return home with them. They would beg him to come in and he would remain with them until they went to bed.

Initially, Mary Ansell eased his acceptance by hitting it off with Sylvia. 'Mrs Barrie knew all about Jim's enthusiasms,' Mackail writes darkly. She certainly seems to have fallen in line with her husband's purpose to begin with, the two women finding common ground in an interest in interior design.

Nanny Hodgson resented Barrie's intrusion on her life with the boys. In particular, she disliked his subversive way of drawing out any waywardness in them and playing them at their own game, as no other adult would. Secretly, perhaps, she was jealous, feeling that even when they were away from him, he seemed to be more present than she. Barrie later lampooned her as the nurse, Irene, in *The Little White Bird*:

> The little nurse was ever a threatening shadow in the background. Irene, in short, did not improve with acquaintance. I found her to be high and mighty.

Barrie's 'methods' had certainly advanced since he was kicking Peterkin around the room and slapping the cheeks of the pretty boy. There was no denying his empathy with the boys, and soon Sylvia was instructing Nanny to share the children with him.

He put the fantasy light in George's eye, so we are to believe, by telling him that he had originally come across him as a missel-thrush on the sward behind the Baby's Walk in Kensington Gardens, 'a missel-thrush, attracted thither that hot day by a hose which lay on the ground sending forth a gay trickle of water'. He was lying on his back in the water, kicking up his legs. 'And gradually it all came back to him [i.e. George], with a number of other incidents that had escaped my memory . . .'

With stories like this Barrie entranced each of the boys. He also did magic tricks, having received a few simple lessons in conjuring. He had a magic egg-cup which he usually carried with him, and he 'did some astonishing things with pennies'. Suddenly, too, he was an expert in fairy lore. Another child he knew then, Pamela Maude, the daughter of the stars of *The Little Minister*, Cyril Maude and Winifred Emery, recalled his way with them, writing with delicacy in *Worlds Away* (1964):

> In the evening, when the strange morning light had begun to change, Mr Barrie held out a hand to each of us in silence, and we slipped our own into his and walked, still silently, into the beechwood. We shuffled our feet through the leaves and listened, with Mr Barrie, for sudden sound, made by birds and rabbits. One evening we saw a peapod lying in the hollow of a great tree-trunk, and we brought it to Mr Barrie. There, inside, was a tiny letter, folded inside the pod, that a fairy had written. Mr Barrie said he could read fairy writing and read it to us. We received several more, in peapods, before the end of our visit.

But George was Barrie's favourite, as he wrote in *The Little White Bird*, in which George was lightly disguised as 'David'.

> There never was a cockier boy . . . It is difficult to believe that he walks to the Kensington Gardens; he always seems to have alighted there . . . One day I had been over-friendly to another boy, and, after enduring it for some time [he] up and struck him . . . I knew its meaning at once; it was [his] first public intimation that he knew I belonged to him.
>
> Irene scolded him for striking that boy, and made him stand in disgrace at the corner of a seat in the Broad Walk. The seat at the corner of which David

> stood suffering for love of me is the one nearest to the Round Pond to persons coming from the north . . .
>
> I asked him in a low voice whether he would give me a kiss. He shook his head about six times, and I was in despair. Then the smile came, and I knew that he was teasing me only. He now nodded his head about six times.
>
> This was the prettiest of all his exploits.

For his part, George's father, with his solid Victorian image of himself as head of the family and his notion that wives should make friends with women not with men once they were married, was not impressed with the almost daily appearance of the strange little man who lived on the other side of the park. Arthur worked hard all day, looked forward to spending time with his boys in the evening, and found it irksome that he almost always found them at play with 'Uncle Jim'. But could he complain, so happy were they in his company?

Jim meanwhile worked his magic on Sylvia by praising her as the quintessence of motherliness. He would, for example, empathise with her love for her boys, and then imagine her hugging baby Peter 'with such sudden vehemence that I am sure he wondered whether you were up to anything'. So bald the innuendo, so wittily twisted, that one had to laugh, and Sylvia – used to Arthur's more prosaic style – did.

Venerating motherliness had also worked for the English artists who turned Trilby into a maternal figure as a defence against her threatening sexuality. It won her favour. We may guess what Jim's reverence for the maternal meant to Sylvia, who had given birth to three sons in four years and would soon have two more.

A genius with words, Barrie left marks of his quirky, tangential personality wherever he went, as on this sign in the garden at Black Lake Cottage: 'Persons who come to steal the fruit are requested not to walk on the flower beds.'

Even when Uncle Jim's humour was not very clever, which was just as often, it beat Arthur's 'Merriman jokes' as far as the boys were concerned. Like one night when Michael, Nico and Uncle Jim stayed at the North British Hotel in Edinburgh. Recalled Nico: 'Scene: my bedroom on, say, the third or fourth floor – Uncle Jim looking out of the window. "This reminds me, I was looking out of a hotel window once when to my horror I saw a man come falling past me – I was on the third floor like this – and as he went by I heard him saying, 'Ach michty, what a clink I'll get!' " ' It was 'Uncle Jim's slightly Scottish accent, and his slightly melancholic

Sylvia with Barrie's first favourite among her sons, George.

Barrie, 'the little photographer', took this picture of Peter on the beach at Rustington-on-Sea.

Black Lake Cottage in Surrey, where Barrie engaged the boys in games of pirates and redskins, enacting scenes which in 1904 transferred to Neverland in *Peter Pan.*

We set out to be wrecked. George, Jack and Peter at Black Lake Cottage: 'One by one as you swung monkey-wise from branch to branch in the wood of make-believe you reached the tree of knowledge,' wrote Barrie.

Uncle Jim, who analysed himself as 'that sly one, the chief figure, who draws further and further into the wood as we advance upon him'.

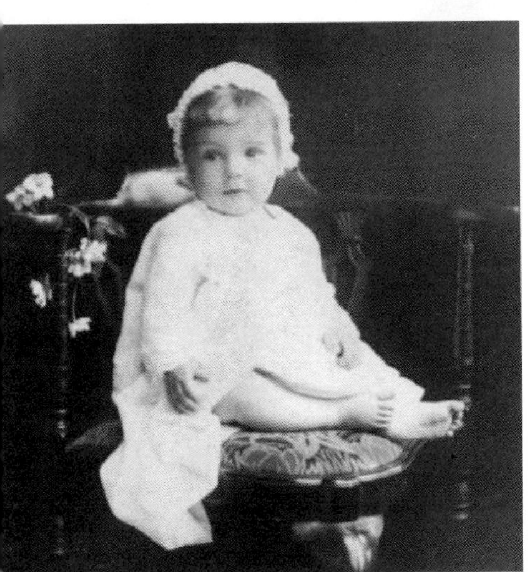

Michael was one year old during the first Black Lake holiday, 'an honorary member of the band, waving his foot to you for luck…' In his novel *The Little White Bird*, Barrie has Nanny say of the boy's captivator: 'If he takes off your socks, my pretty, may he be blasted for evermore.'

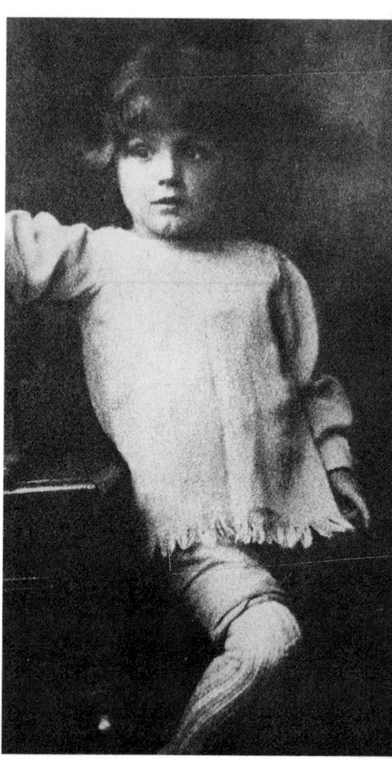

Michael Llewelyn Davies (*above*) and his eldest brother George (*right*).

'We all knew that George and Michael were "The Ones"… [Barrie] was in love with each of them.'

Jim Barrie in 1904, the year that *Peter Pan* was first staged. Its success accorded him extraordinary charisma. Thereafter, many people perceived him to live within a Peter Pan world, and some 'were rather disturbed… There was something sinister about him, rather shivery.'

Sylvia, inexpressibly sad, after Arthur died of cancer of the jaw at the age of 44.

Sylvia during her last illness. She died at the same age as her husband. '44' became the du Mauriers' unlucky number.

was there. what I wd like wd be if Jenny wd come to Mary & that the two together wd be looking after the boys & the house & helping each other. And it wd be so nice for Mary".

Sylvia's Will, which set out in her own hand who should inherit her money and who should look after her orphaned children. (*Above*) concerning the boys: 'what I wd like wd be if Jenny wd come to Mary & that the two together wd be looking after the boys & the house…' Mary was Nanny Hodgson and Jenny was her sister. (*Below*) J. M. Barrie wilfully changed 'Jenny' to his own name, 'Jimmy', in the transcription of the Will he sent to the boys' grandmother, telling her it was 'an exact copy'. In his handwriting: 'what I would like would be if Jimmy would come to Mary'. In this way, he made himself guardian of Sylvia's five sons.

for a little just as if I was there. What I would like would be if Jimmy would come to Mary, and that the two together would be looking after the boys and the house and helping each other. And it would be so nice for Mary.

The boys fly fishing, their favourite pastime with Uncle Jim.

Uncle Jim in the penthouse flat at Adelphi Terrace House, the house on the Strand to which he moved Michael and Nico in 1918, after engineering Nanny Hodgson's resignation.

(*Above left*) Daphne's father Gerald du Maurier, actor, actor-manager, and matinée idol. Barrie launched Gerald's career on the London stage and wrote parts for him in many of his plays. Whenever family problems intervened, Barrie made certain that jobs, finance and even a knighthood came Gerald's way. (*Above right*) Daphne's mother 'Mo' Beaumont fell in love with Gerald when Barrie cast her opposite him in *The Admirable Crichton*. From the start, Daphne's life was written and produced by Uncle Jim.

(*Above*) Scott of the Antarctic. He fulfilled Barrie's ideal of the heroic explorer: 'Having found the entrancing man, I was unable to leave him.' (*Right*) Lady Cynthia Asquith, secretary to Barrie and principal legatee on his death.

countenance' that did it: 'Michael and I were screaming with laughter, and his own eyes would start an ineffable twinkle.'[1]

Another favourite was Barrie's 'Mind That Post!' story:

> A relatively poorly-off couple had been married for thirty or more years in happy times together. The time came when the wife died – all solemnity and customary mourning – undertaker – put in coffin – gently carried downstairs and out through the front garden towards the hearse. Taking the coffin out of the garden it struck a post of the garden gate. This seemed to stir the dead lady as there was suddenly a knocking inside the coffin. They opened the lid – she'd 'come round' – was helped out – and they had another good year or two together. Then she died again and all as above until – as the coffin was going through the gate the husband said 'Eh, mind that post.'[2]

Much of the time, at first, Jim was just another boy, and, as Peter wrote, 'Sylvia, a strong character, couldn't help dominating him.' She would use him 'as a kind of extra nurse, extremely useful fairy-godmother, or sometimes even errand-boy,' according to Denis Mackail.

Another effective if not decisive factor in Jim's insinuation into the family was his financial leverage. 'In August 1897 JMB was 37 years old, and one of the most talked of figures in the literary world, with money already pouring in from books and plays, including the enormously successful *Little Minister*',[3] which alone earned him £80,000. And while Sylvia was very good at making do, she once said to Arthur's sister Margaret that she longed to be able to buy 'gold stays and scented bedlinen and real lace pillows' – she said it deliberately to appal Margaret, a socialist and far more self-disciplined than she, but it was nonetheless a valid pointer to part of her character.

Sylvia had been born into a privileged world, but one in which money still had to be earned. When her father died in 1896, four years into her marriage, there was the promise of a financial fillip from the massive royalties on the sales of *Trilby*, but there were other dependants with claims. Kicky had been supporting his brother Eugène and sister Isobel, and although both had died in 1890, they left children. Eugène's widow, a Frenchwoman by the name of Marie Espinasse, lived until 1917 and appears to have been wholly dependent on the du Mauriers, the dress-making business with Mrs Nettleship, for which Marie worked as well as Sylvia, having been set up to help defray that cost. Equally, if not more to the point, Kicky had left a widow. Emma lived on until 1914. Sylvia's four siblings could also be expected to share in any inheritance. Funds were also put in trust for Kicky's grandchildren.

In 1897, Arthur's career had yet to take off and he struggled to get briefs. Jim, in contrast, drew £8,000 in 1897, and £12,000 in 1898; and soon four times that annually.

The riches that Jim could give Sylvia meant motor cars and holidays abroad, hotels and no-holds-barred expenses. What's more, caring little for money made Jim free with it, particularly when he saw how Sylvia delighted in his largesse. Peter was dumbfounded when he discovered, while researching *The Morgue*, that Sylvia had taken no fewer than four maids with her to Tilford for the first Black Lake holiday with Uncle Jim. Before long, Jim would finance the entire family.

During that first holiday at Black Lake Cottage Arthur saw virtually nothing of his children, who were off playing Castaway games at the lake. There was something of a 'them and us' scenario, with Jim definitely one of the boys, and Arthur behind some sort of boring, adult protest about Jim equipping them not only with bows and arrows but with knives.

Wrote Peter, 'It is clear enough that father didn't like him . . .' When Jim made up two copies of *The Boy Castaways* into books and diplomatically gave one to Arthur, he promptly lost it on a train, 'doubtless his own way of commenting on the whole fantastic affair'. But Arthur was a gentleman and loyal to his wife. He knew that Sylvia would never upbraid Jim. As Jim wrote of Mrs Darling: 'There was something in the right-hand corner of her mouth that wanted her not to call Peter Pan names.'[3]

Jim's kinship with the boys, his financial utility and his humour endeared him to Sylvia. But it was his empathy with her inner life that captivated her. Jim saw at once that by flattering the *inner* woman he would fulfil a need in her that stiff, unimaginative Arthur could not. He recognised her need to dream.

Soon Jim began addressing Sylvia by her second name, Jocelyn, which no one else used and which marked her out as heir to the du Maurier family secret. She began signing her letters to him, 'Your Jocelyn'. And there is always a suggestion in Jim's letters that he has got something special of Sylvia. Arthur was like Mr Darling, who had all of Mrs Darling, 'except the innermost box . . . Her romantic mind was like the tiny boxes, one within the other, that come from the puzzling East, however many you discover there is always one more.'[4]

In Sylvia's 'innermost box', she was a boy. 'You are so good at boys,' Jim wrote to her, 'and this you know is the age of specialists. And you were very very nearly being a boy yourself.'

This was straight out of *Trilby*, and now, to develop her new identity, Jim wrote Sylvia into the manuscript of *Tommy and Grizel*, on which he was working: he gave Grizel, Tommy's lover, the same 'boyish' persona. 'There were times when she [Grizel] looked like a boy. Her almost gallant bearing, the poise of her head, her noble frankness, they all had something in them of a princely boy who had never known fear.' And, 'She was least able to resist Tommy when he was most a boy.'

Tommy and Grizel were 'pegged' on Jim and Sylvia. It was the first occasion that Barrie transferred a du Maurier on to the page. Grizel in both the Tommy novels had started out as Mary Ansell, but now that Mary was receding from the scene Grizel became Sylvia. He used Sylvia's 'tilted nose' to identify her, just as Kicky had in *Peter Ibbetson*. He also picked up on Sylvia's 'crooked mouth', the feature that Dolly so enjoyed, writing that Grizel's mouth 'screwed up provokingly at one side, as when she smiled', and her grey eyes, 'unusually far apart, [which] let you look straight into them and never quivered, they were such clear, gray, searching eyes, they seemed always to be asking for the truth'.

With this identification, Jim and Sylvia first became intertwined and Arthur slunk further back into his kennel, like Mr Darling after Peter Pan came on the scene.

But all was not quite as it seemed, for as we know, Tommy (Jim's 'boy'), is not like Little Billee (Kicky's 'boy'). Tommy is not pure, innocent, Romantic. He is a wolf in sheep's clothing:

> 'If they knew what I really am,' he cried, with splendid bitterness, 'how they would run from me . . . There has been nothing like it since Red Riding Hood and the wolf.'

Tommy was Grizel's Svengali, just as Jim became Sylvia's. Should we now expect Jim to hypnotise her? To change her personality and interpretation of the world so that, like Trilby, Sylvia would take on his cynical view and be a slave to his whims, until he dies and she follows him to an early grave? Jim had no intention of dying, but the rest ran pretty much to plan.

He rehearsed his captivation of Sylvia in *Tommy and Grizel*, and floated the idea that this would rewrite her fate, exploring the possibility that the fantasy might intrude on reality, 'as a wheel may revolve for a moment after the spring breaks'.

There was precedent in the annals of magic and the supernatural. Altering the state of a human psyche by 'pegging' a fictional character on a real person and rewriting his destiny is an instance of Sympathetic (or Imitative) Magic, as described in Sir James Frazer's famous study of magic and ancient religion, *The Golden Bough*. The idea is to create 'a secret sympathy' with a life and then manipulate it in the text, a more primitive instance being the moulding of an effigy of an enemy and sticking pins in it. Is it so different to the way myths, many of which were picked up in our reading, affect the way we behave?

Daphne wrote of Jim doing this as if he was an artist putting first a woman (Sylvia) and then her son (George) on canvas, saying 'that it gave him a tremendous sense of power . . . the fact that a live person, and that person a woman, could be transmuted by him on a blank canvas'.[5]

There is a suggestion that Jim came to his alchemic method after Sylvia got fed up with being treated like a child by him with his fantasy stories. Tommy winces at Grizel's ability to see through him, '"Don't you think this is all rather silly," she said, when he addressed her as the Lady Griselda, and it broke the melancholy pilgrimage of what had once been an enchanted land.' Tommy then switches with consummate ease to the more serious business.

> Ah, Grizel, what a delicious book you are, and how I wish I had written you.

Sylvia, of course, was no stranger to being featured in fiction, and in her father's drawings for *Punch*. According to Daphne, once Jim came up with the idea of putting her and her boys into his alchemical texts, Sylvia almost bullied him into it.[6]

Whether she noticed that Jim had put his customary bowler aside in favour of a trilby is not known, but he did, and if she had, they would have laughed about it together. For Jim's plan was now a conspiracy in which Sylvia was an accomplice. From this time, the new Sylvia, the Sylvia who caused Arthur heartache, began to emerge.

Henceforth, as with Trilby, there were two Sylvias – the one her husband knew, the mother of his children – and the other Sylvia, the one Jim turned her into, who left Arthur to look after her children when they were ill, who from 1902 went on expensive holidays with Jim without her husband, who handed Jim her children on a plate, and who, once the texts in which Jim transmuted them became famous, 'wore her children as other women wear pearls or fox-furs'.

So similar to Trilby – who, wearing 'sables, rouged and pearl-powdered, and her eyes blackened underneath', reached out of her carriage and looked with disdain at Little Billee standing there, relic of her boring old life.

Said Peter, years later: 'I think Sylvia's attitude to Barrie was a special and peculiar one, not very representative of her true self.'

Jim had had to ask himself how to satisfy a woman like Sylvia. He possessed neither good looks nor a passionate nature. Perhaps money would help? But Jim's creative genius knew a secret beyond such things. In his siege of the teasing beautiful Sylvia, he engaged 'a broken fellow' for her to take pity on, 'a good-natured cynic' for her to laugh at, 'a haughty boy' for her to mother, 'a grave author' and of course '*a little photographer*'.[7]

Did Jim's dreamy photographs of Sylvia fix the new persona in her mind? He took photograph after photograph of her, poking his camera at her, dancing around her like Rumpelstiltskin, while she sat on the soft earth and let him get on with it. There may have been sensuality in his actions, but physical contact, we are led to believe, once only. While her eyes were shut to the sunshine, she felt him caress her lips with his, like the touch of a butterfly wing. 'One flicker round the lips and it is done,' said Mephistopheles, who used the same ploy to seduce an angel.

But Jim was not interested in physical sex. Like his fictional creation Tommy, he was without desire, without feeling of any kind – so he said himself. He lived for the power-play dynamics of the relationship. That was his sex. His thrills came, for example, from the tension between the way the new Sylvia rose to the almost supernatural influence he seemed to exert over their lives, and the guilt and shame the old Sylvia felt about leaving Arthur and going abroad with him. Never had he 'thought to read shame' in Sylvia's 'sweet face', but it is what he wanted from her: it is what Tommy wants from Grizel.

The dynamic of psychology, which may be therapeutic or exploitative, is the dynamic of sex. Invasion and domination – the intensity of Sylvia's response and level of her transformation – were Jim's great satisfaction.

> What was it, after all, that a woman wanted? Was it mere social effect . . . a union of love and goodness . . . Did she want goodness? . . . This was the street view of her wants. Cross the threshold and you found her completely, completely cynical about the social world and its advantages. Once inside the

> house of her soul, and there was a pungent atmosphere of corrosion, an inflamed darkness of sensation, and a vivid, subtle, critical consciousness, that saw the world distorted, horrific.
>
> What then, what next? Was it sheer blind force of passion that would satisfy her now? Not this, but the subtle thrills of extreme sensation in reduction. It was an unbroken will reacting against her unbroken will in a myriad subtle thrills of reduction, the last subtle activities of analysis and breaking down, carried out in the darkness of her, while the outside form, the individual, was utterly unchanged, even sentimental in its poses.*

Tommy is the fantasist who dispenses with the illusion of truth. People are 'pegs' on which we hang our emotions. 'In love', the whole thing is a complete illusion. 'Nearly all women feel it in their hearts, though they keep it locked up till they die,' he has Grizel admit at last. 'A woman can be anything that the man who loves her would have her be,' says Tommy. We invest people with the qualities we want them to have, ignoring whether they do actually possess them.

There is deep cynicism at bottom. Bit by bit Jim broke down Sylvia's social and emotional conditioning, offering her a new kind of freedom – a freedom that set her apart from the pitiful world, not as a dreamer, but in a commanding position, gazing down from her carriage on the romantic boys and girls, whose lives were the real illusion. This was the fruit of Jim's 'tree of knowledge', at the heart of his 'wood of make-believe'.

He found resonances in Sylvia's soul. When he crossed the threshold he found her cynical about the social world in which she had been brought up. She recognised his masterfulness, the self-serving, alienating, but powerful product of the exceptional childhood that had maimed him.

How fascinated Sylvia must have been by this mocking, dangerous game, the new reductionist science of psychoanalysis; it was knowledge that raised her above the masses. Here was the New Woman that Arthur would never understand.

She was too captivated to see that Jim's philosophy was the death-knell of her father's philosophy in *Trilby*, that it was a cruel game which, from his position outside the matrix of human emotion, he could not fail to win,

* D. H. Lawrence, *Women in Love*. For the connection between Barrie's seduction of Sylvia and Loerke's of Gudrun in Lawrence's novel, see Part VI: Chapter One, and Appendix.

that it was only about him *finding a way*. She did not see that he cared nothing for the Sylvia whom Arthur loved, that for Jim *that* Sylvia never existed. Or, maybe she saw it all; really did see that Jim was right.

In November 1902, in a letter to his father at Kirkby Lonsdale, Arthur wrote: 'Sylvia is at present on a trip to Paris with her friends the Barries . . . The party is completed by another novelist, Mason,* and they seem to be living in great splendour and enjoying themselves very much.' The letter makes pathetic reading. He went on: 'I don't know what your arrangements are for Christmas, nor if you are likely to have the vicarage very full. I should like to come, if possible, bringing one boy or perhaps two. It is just possible that Sylvia may be induced to come too, but that is not likely . . .'

When Jim had the Sylvia he wanted, where he wanted her, the world was all that his fancy painted it and he moved seamlessly into the second stage of his strategy – 'ever since relentlessly pursued' – which, he revealed, is 'to burrow under her influence with the boy [George], expose her to him in all her vagaries, take him utterly from her and make him mine'.[8]

To effect this he moved from *Tommy and Grizel* to his next alchemic text, *The Little White Bird*, in which, as Jacqueline Rose observed:

> The narrator is trying to steal the child, to get at the mother and replace the father. His involvement with the child is, therefore, anything but innocent. In fact it can be traced back to an unconsummated sexual desire for which [George] is the substitute and replacement. This is not an analysis of the book, the motives and the past history are all given by the narrator himself . . . [which is what has made] this book such a biographical landmine in relation to Barrie himself.[9]

Rose might have added that the mother (Sylvia, known in the book as 'Mary') is far from blameless; as the Captain (Jim himself) says, she was 'culpably obtuse to my sinister design'.

One would have thought that Arthur, upon reading Barrie's book, would have thrown him out of the house. But he did not. Instead, he wrote to his father: 'Barrie's new book, The Little White Bird, is largely taken up with

* A. E. W. Mason, remembered best for his 'heroic' novel *The Four Feathers*, published that year, 1902. For a single term from 1906 Mason was also a Liberal Member of Parliament and he had been an intimate of Barrie since 1898. The letter is available in full on Andrew Birkin's website jmbarrie.co.uk.

Kensington Gardens and our and similar children. There is a whole chapter devoted to Peter.'

This is so unexpected and inexplicable that one wonders whether Arthur was given the same text to read. The oddest thing is that there is no mention of Arthur's son Peter in the book. The only Peter who has 'a whole chapter devoted' to him is Peter Pan. Peter Davies comments on this in *The Morgue*, 'I have always regarded [the book] as being much more about George than me. I can't say I like it . . .'

How Sylvia and Jim must have laughed at their own bare-faced cheek. Tommy's triumph over Grizel so intoxicated him that, in the novel, he has to scream at intervals: 'We're here, I tell you, we're here!' And she gasped with realisation at what had been going on:

> 'I believe – I think – you are masterful . . . I was afraid you were masterful! . . . Now I know why I would not kiss your hand, now I know why I would not say I liked you. I was afraid of you, I—'
>
> 'Were you?' His eyes began to sparkle, and something very like rapture was pushing the indignation from his face. 'Oh, Grizel, have I a power over you?'
>
> 'No, you have not,' she cried passionately. 'I was just frightened that you might have. Oh, oh, I know you now!'
>
> 'To think o't, to think o't!' he crowed.

To crow is a favourite expression of Jim's, first when writing of himself as Tommy, then as Peter Pan, who 'crows like a rooster when he sees how clever he has been'. Said Mary Ansell, who had witnessed her husband make Sylvia and the boys his own:

> One could almost hear him, like Peter Pan, crowing triumphantly, but his heart was sick all the time.

CHAPTER FIVE

Flying Uncle Jim to Neverland

What did the boys think about Uncle Jim coming between their parents? Daphne suggests[1] that there *was* an awareness that something was not quite right, that deep down they were disturbed to see their mother acknowledge Jim as the family's new leader, but that as time wore on they settled into the new arrangement. 'He was, after all, a relation, an uncle', an accustomed figure, and by then they, too, were on a fantasy trip of their own with Jim, who was leading them to the tree of knowledge.

In 1902 Barrie moved with his wife to a house at the corner of Leinster Terrace, close to where Kicky had lived and facing the Bayswater Road. Porthos had died at the end of 1901 – he barely survived the first Black Lake holiday as the pirate Swarthy's dog or tiger in a papier-mâché mask. To Mary Ansell his death spelled the beginning of the end of her marriage. He was replaced in 1903 by a black and white Newfoundland, Luath, who would be 'pegged' as Nana in *Peter Pan* (no living thing in the inner circle escaped pegging).

It was unthinkable that Mary should live without a dog, in Jim's company. A dog, she wrote politely, was 'a most admirable accompaniment to a husband. He supplies those darling little ways, so dear to a woman's heart, and so necessary to her well-being, that come tripping along so gracefully before marriage, but by the end of the first year have tripped away – less gracefully – into oblivion . . .'

As Jim's life revolved more and more around Sylvia and the boys, he froze Mary with his silences, which did not 'speak loudly' to her, as they had done to Pamela Maude. Then Porthos and later Luath were her salvation. 'To quote an instance,' she wrote. 'Those silent meals. Haven't most of us experienced them? When the mind of your man is elsewhere, lord knows where, but nowhere in your direction. Just when the silence is becoming unbearable, your dog steps in and attracts your attention. He lays his head on your knee, or he presses your hand, as it is in the act of conveying a succulent morsel to your mouth. "Merely asking for food," you interrupt. Quite true. But to be asked for anything is a relief.'[2]

Leinster Corner, as Mary named the house, was close to the Lancaster Gate entrance to Kensington Gardens, a mile or so from where the Davieses now lived in Kensington Park Gardens, and just yards from young George's school in Orme Square.

In 1902 George turned nine. George was 'the One' and the proximity of the school and Sylvia's hard-earned trust in him gave Jim unprecedented access, and he entered into exclusive sessions with George, dedicated to the production of *Peter Pan* (1904).

> [Peter] escaped from being a human when he was seven days old; he escaped by the window . . . standing on the ledge he could see trees far away, which were doubtless the Kensington Gardens, and the moment he saw them he entirely forgot that he was now a little boy in a nightgown, and away he flew, right over the houses to the Gardens.[3]

George, it appears, had a moment or two's doubt that such a thing could have happened, or at least that it was a common occurrence for babies to fly away to the park. He told Uncle Jim he was certain that he had never tried to escape. So, Jim told him to concentrate hard:

> I told him to think back hard, pressing his hands to his temples, and when he had done this hard, and even harder, he distinctly remembered a youthful desire to return to the tree-tops, and with that memory came others, as that he had lain in bed planning to escape as soon as his mother was asleep, and how she had once caught him half-way up the chimney. All children could have such recollections if they would press their hands hard to their temples, for, having been birds before they were human, they are naturally a little wild during the first few weeks, and very itchy at the shoulders, where their wings used to be . . .
>
> I ought to mention that the following is our way with a story. First I tell it to him, and then he tells it to me, the understanding being that it is quite a different story; and then I retell it with his additions, and so we go on until no one could say whether it is more his story or mine. In this story of Peter Pan, for instance, the bald narrative and most of the moral reflections are mine, though not all, for this boy can be a stern moralist; but the interesting

> bits about the ways and customs of babies in the bird-stage are mostly reminiscences of [his], recalled by pressing his hands to his temples and thinking hard.

Jim's relationship with George was clearly creative, but was it ever really about writing a play? In his Dedication to the first published text of *Peter Pan*, in 1928, Jim discusses the Castaway games at Black Lake Cottage as the play's inspiration. He writes:

> They do seem to be emerging out of our island, don't they, the little people of the play . . .

This immediately struck me as odd, as there was no island in the Black Lake. What can Jim have meant? To what island was he referring?

The image of an island was of course pervasive in Jim's life. You could say he had an island fixation. The first book he read was *Robinson Crusoe*. *The Coral Island* became a symbol of his alienation from the rest of the world in his youth. All the fantasies he indulged in with his mother initially concerned 'desert islands and enchanted gardens', and Tommy's reading matter 'is about desert islands; he calls them wrecked islands . . . and sees that unless his greed for islands is quenched he is forever lost'.

Then there is Birds' Island in *The Little White Bird*, and, after *Peter Pan*, islands are significant in Jim's plays *The Admirable Crichton* and *Mary Rose*. He also made sure that islands figured prominently in the boys' lives, by taking them on holiday to Eilean Shona on the west coast of Scotland, to the Outer Hebrides, and Amhuinnsuidh on the Isle of Harris. But this mention of the little people emerging from 'our island' did not refer specifically to any of these. So, what did Jim mean?

The Dedication to *Peter Pan* is addressed personally to the Llewelyn Davies boys. He jogs their memories of adventures on Black Lake, in the pine-tree forest, etc. It is all very *entre nous*, with phrases such as, 'We are not going to give away all our secrets' and 'None may see this save ourselves'. Uncle Jim was writing to George, Jack, Peter and Michael on a personal level. The boys knew what 'our island' meant, and it was so significant that it had to remain their secret.

Then I recalled something about Barrie and islands in Margaret Forster's biography of Daphne. In a (1940) letter to a friend, Garth Lean, Daphne let slip that Uncle Jim had shown her how to release herself from the material world with its illusory claims, how to lapse out and live in another world, from another centre by concentrating on the image of an island just surfacing from the sea . . .

> Ever since J. M. Barrie had inspired her with the notion, her mind centred on an island, the island of her dreams . . .
>
> She drew a picture of it for Garth, with the sun behind the island and a boat sailing towards it . . .

Immediately I connected this with the island often employed by actors in theatre workshops to encourage improvisation. I have played the island game myself. You lie on the ground, relax deeply and concentrate your mind on an island while a narrator in a gentle voice paints a picture of it in increasing detail in your mind. The notion of the island resurfacing from the sea is a good approach, because its gradual appearance aids concentration. Bit by bit you get a closer view of the island, of its landscape, its natural vegetation. And eventually of course 'the little people' of the island emerge, and soon you might have the rudiments of a play. But you also have a perfect light, hypnotic environment. Brain activity passes effortlessly into that band of consciousness known as hypnotic trance.

Uncle Jim asked George to concentrate hard and at the same time to relax, because that is how you enter a state of hypnotic trance.

> Hypnosis is a process involving a hypnotist and a subject who agrees to be hypnotised. Being hypnotised is usually characterised by (a) intense concentration, (b) extreme relaxation, and (c) high suggestibility.[4]

Psychologists accept 'that there is a significant correlation between being imaginative and being responsive to hypnosis . . . that those who are fantasy-prone are also likely to make excellent hypnotic subjects'. Also, 'vivid imagery enhances suggestibility', and 'the greatest predictor of hypnotic responsiveness is what a person believes about hypnosis'.

Freud observed that children, unconscious of a hypnotist or controller's 'motivation, anxieties, wishes and possible conflict, are particularly susceptible and vulnerable'. It is difficult to imagine a more susceptible set of subjects than the children of the imaginative du Maurier family.

What Sylvia believed about hypnosis was what had been passed down to her by her father, and the island game would surely have been acceptable to her, for an island lay at the centre of the du Maurier myth. In *Peter Ibbetson* the steel engraving that triggers the flights of unbridled ecstasy of

Peter and Mary is an image of an island where, as Byron describes, the Songstress teaches the stranger boy 'Passion's desolating joy', where 'all our dreams of better life above close in one eternal gush of Love', where the object of love is 'in years a child . . . the infant of an infant world, as pure as Nature – lovely, warm and premature' . . . whose 'heart was tamed to that voluptuous state at once Elysian and effeminate'.

Jim was concocting a hypnotic environment of sensuousness within which to woo his young collaborators, who, like Peter Ibbetson and Mary in the novel, progressed to it after leaving their fairy games behind. The island was the entry point to their 'never never dreamland' – the world of hypnotic trance – an environment given up to rapturous sensuality, the 'other world' that comes into existence only when we are made conscious of it under hypnosis.

Just as Mary drew a picture of the island for Peter Ibbetson, so Peter Pan would lift 'the film that obscures' it for Wendy, and Daphne would draw it for Garth, flirtatiously, with the sun behind it and a boat sailing towards it. As Barrie explained in *Peter and Wendy* –

> The Neverland is always more or less an island, with astonishing splashes of colour here and there, and coral reefs and rakish-looking craft in the offing, and savages and lonely lairs, and gnomes who are mostly tailors, and caves through which a river runs, and princes with six elder brothers, and a hut fast going to decay, and one very small old lady with a hooked nose . . .[5]

The environment Uncle Jim created for the boys was custom-made to initiate a hypnotic procedure which, in psychologist Nicholas Spanos's words, is designed to 'influence behaviour indirectly by altering subjects' motivations, expectations and interpretations'.[6]

Dr Spanos dislikes talk of hypnosis as a state of trance, accepts the idea that it is a function of concentration and relaxation, but prefers to see it as arising out of a cognitive-social context in which the roles of hypnotist and subject are constantly reinforced. This describes perfectly what was going on between Uncle Jim and the boys.

There is a control figure (Jim) and a subject (George). Each is aware of his role and prepared to reinforce the other by his performance. Suggestions are made to the subject by the control figure – 'First I tell it to him . . .' The subject then responds to the suggestions – 'then he tells it to me . . .' This is exactly the context Spanos has in mind. Indeed, George's fantasy that in the pre-natal stage children are birds is just the kind of symbolic material to stream from the first stage in a Jungian analysis, where a subject is encouraged to identify with his personal infantilism.

The question is in what ways the boys' minds were affected by these sessions, and you only have to look at the nihilistic and morbid ideas in Jim's novels and plays for the answer. But in none of the works is there quite the morbidity that is present in the character of Peter Pan.

The reason for Peter's mother's rejection of him – the 'great thing she cried for' – was 'the great mistake' which Peter had made and we are never told about, but is so big a mistake that a hug is not going to be enough to put it right. I have suggested that Peter's mistake is associated with death.

Death had been 'a thing' for Jim ever since the death of his brother, David. He hid with his sister Maggie under the table on which David's coffin had been set, and thereafter was aware that there was something unusual about his relationship with Maggie. She never believed ill of Jim. When they were together, he became the man she wanted him to be.

In *Tommy and Grizel* it is suggested that he mesmerised Maggie (she is Elspeth in the novel) and thereby 'maimed her . . . There's no life for her now except what you mak'; she canna see beyond you.' Denis Mackail indicated that this was a fair picture of their relationship.

In May 1892, Maggie became engaged to the Reverend James Winter. Shortly before the wedding he was flung from a horse and killed. Maggie responded to this death as Margaret had done to David's. She took to her bed and stayed there. The guests she had invited to her wedding attended her fiancé's funeral instead.

Jim had given Winter the horse.

Death stalks Tommy in the fiction as it did Jim in his life. At one stage he dreams of 'a very noble young man, and his white dead face stared at the sky from the bottom of a deep pool'. In the dream the young man's lover came to the edge of the pool 'and peered down at his staring eyes and laughed'. In the story, the dream breaks through into reality. Tommy finds a boy in precisely this condition. The scene is darkly suggestive of what would befall Michael twenty years later.

Death continued to be a theme in the build-up to *Peter Pan*, and Jim went further to invest his character with an association with death. While walking with Jim one day in Kensington Gardens, George pointed to two stones with 'W St M' and '13a PP 1841' inscribed on them. They indicated the boundary line for the parish of Westminster St Mary's and the parish of Paddington, but Jim told him they were gravestones for two children (Walter Stephen Matthews and Phoebe Phelps) who had fallen out of their prams and died. Peter Pan had his work cut out burying dead children after lock-out in the Gardens and would dance on their graves, playing on his pipes, to make them laugh as they began their journey in the afterlife.

Then, shortly after the first run of *Peter Pan* in 1904 came the clearest expression of Jim's obsession with death. A new Act III was written in which Peter is brought to the brink of death, marooned on a rock in a lagoon.

The stage directions, always an integral part of the significance of a Barrie play, suggest a new hypnotic island focus for George, but this time the island does not rise out of the sea, it disappears beneath the waters, which rise up until they are 'lapping over the rock . . . and Peter knows that it will soon be submerged'.

> *Pale rays of light mingle with the moving clouds, and from the coral grottoes is to be heard a sound, at once the most musical and the most melancholy in the Neverland, the mermaids calling to the moon to rise. Peter is afraid at last, and a tremor runs through him, like a shudder passing over the lagoon; but on the lagoon one shudder follows another till there are hundreds of them, and he feels just the one. Next moment he is standing erect on the rock again . . .* PETER *(with the smile on his face and a drum beating in his breast as if he were a real boy at last).*
>
> 'To die will be an awfully big adventure.'

George was accredited with the famous line. It came out of one of his sessions with Jim in which death was the focus.

From 1905, 'to be a real boy' was to pass over to the other side – destiny, of course, of Michael, who was four in the year the play opened and fast becoming of interest to Jim.

The first outsider to notice how morbid shadows of the dream had begun to cleave to Sylvia and the boys was Dolly Parry, who had by this time herself married an Arthur, a diplomat and later a Liberal and then Labour Member of Parliament, eventually to become a Labour Lord – 1st Baron Ponsonby of Shulbrede, a beautiful twelfth-century Augustine priory.

It was to this thoroughly English home-county jewel that Sylvia brought Jim, Peter and Michael one afternoon in the summer of 1903. Dolly, now mother of two-year-old Elizabeth, known as 'Girly', was expecting them for tea. The party arrived in Jim's motor car (they had come from Black Lake Cottage, which lies a few miles to the north). It was a sunny afternoon at the end of a week of incessant rain. The idyllic picture was captured in Dolly's diary –

> Jim Barry [*sic*] with a child clinging to each hand at once went & sat in the dining room chimney corner & looked so characteristic & like one of his own books. Elizabeth petrified at all the company sat refusing to eat her tea. Sylvia beautiful & satisfying – loving the house & appealing to 'Jimmy' [Barrie] about it . . . It was very charming to see Girly give her hand to Jimmy & with Michael on one side & her on the other they walked down the garden path into the field – his devotion & genius-like understanding of children is beautiful & touching beyond words – as he has none himself.

This is the Barrie legend. The children, captivated, absent from the adult world, holding hands with the quiet and gentle Uncle Jim. One can imagine nothing but beauty and goodness coming of it.

But a dark side was immediately apparent. For Dolly also reported that Sylvia had 'a sort of morbidness about her'. Later she interpreted this as 'a sort of premonition'.

She also recalled that when she began to say something critical about Jim in the presence of 3-year-old Michael, 'I remember [Sylvia] saying "Ssh" when I burst out with [it] . . . looking at Michael [in case he heard], and I felt quite ashamed'. Dolly referred to this as Sylvia's 'apprehensive imagination'.

Intensity, apprehension, morbidity attended Sylvia's attachment to Jim even in 1903. Michael's attachment to Jim a decade hence was haunted by similar doubts, and – given the dark, cynical view of life he was feeding them – I am not surprised. Yet, as Grizel follows Tommy in the novel, so they still would follow him, because somehow they knew they must.

Jacqueline Rose concluded, without any reference to the hypnotic environment in which Barrie went to work on the boys, that his guilt lay in 'a form of investment in the child . . . not so much something which could be enacted [i.e. sex] as something which cannot be spoken. The sexual act which underpins *Peter Pan* . . . is an act in which the child is used (and abused) . . .'[7]

The 'investment' of hypnotist and subject in the process of hypnosis is indeed enormous: 'the whole personality of both patient and doctor is called into play . . . It often happens,' wrote Jung, 'that the patient is exactly the right plaster for the doctor's sore spot.'[8] That George was the right plaster for Jim's sore spot there is no doubt.

But George was a child in the subject seat, and the enduring tragedy is that it is in the very nature of hypnosis that from within a controller can make deep and lasting changes to his subject. Professor Marcuse warned: 'The inexperienced hypnotist . . . may forget to take out suggestions which he has given . . . It is wise and a standard procedure among experienced hypnotists to remove whatever suggestions have been given.'[9] On one occasion a student of his was hypnotised by a friend who suggested that he was drowning. Scared at what he had done, he awakened the subject without removing the suggestion. The subject continued to experience the breathing difficulties of a drowning man until Marcuse was called in, re-hypnotised the subject, removed the suggestion, and brought him out of it.

It is readily seen that when the suggestion implanted is a nihilistic or morbid philosophy, not immediately visible in behavioural change – no obvious suffocating, no symptoms of drowning – there is no urgency to return the subject to his status quo.

Uncle Jim did not 'release' the boys, or Daphne. A piece of him – a 'little live spark of individual consciousness' – lodged in a corner of their minds until the end.

Can we now begin to understand why Peter said that 'Jack and I while not very closely resembling each other in general, are both "*clouded over* a good deal and among those whom melancholy has marked their own." '?

For George, who had been in thrall to Jim since he was a child of 8 or 9, the effect was devastating. At 20, the once bright, imaginative, cocky little boy had, according to a friend of his, Norma Douglas Henry, 'almost what the Germans called Weltschmerz – a sadness of the world . . . but never said anything unkind about Barrie'.[10]

He could not. So mesmerised was he, he would not have been able to see through the cloud. This terrible image of George resonates with Dolly's description of the 'morbidness' of Sylvia while under Jim's influence. It was how Daphne showed that her fictional Archduchess, with whom she identified, 'had been hypnotised . . . Because her eyes had all the grief in the world.'

CHAPTER SIX

Peter Pan, a demon boy

Peter Pan opened at the Duke of York's Theatre on 27 December 1904, the day after Boxing Day, having been postponed due to difficulties with the flying equipment. Three days later Sir William Nicholson, who designed the costumes, reported: 'It is a huge success – biggest bookings they've ever known.'

Judging by early fan letters, there was more of an interest in Wendy than Peter, with a number of 6- to 9-year-olds wanting to marry her. The part of Wendy was taken by Mary Ansell's friend Hilda Trevelyan and the consensus was that she 'acted the best'. Kenneth Morrisson pleaded: 'Please write and tell me whether your love for Peter Pan (Miss Paulene Chase) is real, I should so love to know.'

Mark Twain described the play as 'a great and refining and uplifting benefaction to this sordid and money-mad age'. To the *Daily Telegraph* the play was 'so pure, so natural, so touching that it brought the audience to the writer's feet and held it captive there'. Bernard Shaw's judgement, however, was that it was an 'artificial freak . . . foisted on the children by the grown-ups', and Anthony Hope* was reduced, by its sentimental treatment of children, to pleading, 'Oh, for an hour of Herod.'†

The American impresário, Charles Frohman, who was Jim's partner in most of his successful work, was happy about the sentimentality, and no doubt euphoric about what almost certainly stuck in Anthony Hope's craw: a scene at the end called 'The Beautiful Mothers', in which Wendy auditions applicants for the position of 'mother' for each of the lost boys,

* Author of *The Prisoner of Zenda* (1894).

† The reference is to a famously heavy play about the Massacre of the Innocents by Stephen Philips, performed four years earlier at Her Majesty's Theatre.

submitting them to a series of mawkish and very silly tests to decide their suitability.*

The fact that here was a demon boy who not only has no love in him, but steals children from their beds in the night, changes sides in a fight, and kills without conscience, was ignored. It was not in the nature of the production that anyone should notice.

The play underwent constant revision from the moment of its first rehearsal. Captain Hook was almost nowhere to be seen initially. It was only after Gerald du Maurier, who played both Mr Darling and Hook, made such a good job of the pirate that Hook assumed a large presence on stage, eventually to command a whole Act of his own. But that of course meant that when Peter defeated him, the demon boy was taken to be a terrific goody.

The original audience, which was almost entirely adult, saw what they wanted, perhaps needed, to see. Then the children took over, and its pantomimic quality shone through.

Lost was any interest in why the author should have chosen the name Pan, after the goat-foot god of Greek myth, who was abandoned by his mother as a child and appeared to Faust with his pipes and Dionysian maenads – 'the Wild-folk', who 'know what no man else doth guess'. Pan is also of course the origin of the European Pied Piper myth, in which all the children of Hamelin are stolen from their homes and led into the mountain. It would be some time before biographers dug out of Jim's original notes for the play that Peter was marked out as 'a demon boy, villain of the story'.

After the first production, Jim set about restoring the balance to his original vision. The Mothers scene disappeared. Neverland, which had only been mentioned twice in the first performance, was made ever more a supernatural environment, with magical islands, mermaid lagoons and heavenly moments.

And by 1911, in the novel *Peter and Wendy,* Peter's true character was revealed in his conceit and cockiness, characteristics that shock Wendy, and in his 'greed' and 'cunning' and 'slyness' – all words used to describe the manner of his persuading the children to fly away with him. Peter's

* It is possible that Jim meant this to allude to 'the Mothers' in *Faust*, of whom Mephistopheles speaks in awe. For Goethe, mothers are the creative force that weaves the Ideas, Forms and Archetypes into the human mind. But, as in *Jane Annie*, when Barrie attends to serious ideas he generally prescribes a high dose of saccharine to sweeten the pill.

anarchic character is much clearer in the novel than on stage. This played havoc with audience perceptions, as W. A. Darlington, who witnessed this personally, observed: 'The differences between book and play disconcerted the many sentimentalists who had by this time lost all sense of proportion, regarded the play as a kind of holy writ, and visited it in much the same frame of mind as if its performance were a religious ritual.'

The image of Peter in people's minds was not Barrie's at all, which was probably just as well. Audiences were happy. Aiding this process of appropriation was the fact that no script was published until 1928. In January 1907, the *Bookman* observed: 'Mr Barrie has often been asked to write a short narrative or libretto of his immortal child's play and has as often refused. This encouraged others to perpetuate a myth that was never Barrie's in the first place.' As Jacqueline Rose wrote: 'While Barrie hesitated, others moved in, with pictures and images from the play, or mementoes or biographies of Peter Pan.'

Still trying to redress the balance, Jim criticised a statue of Peter, which he had commissioned from Sir George Frampton for Kensington Gardens and which was erected overnight to appear on May Day 1912, by saying: 'It doesn't show the Devil in Peter.'

Nobody associated Peter with the Devil. Nor is it clear how Frampton was supposed to capture this demon boy, since Uncle Jim gave him photographs of the beautiful, angelic, naked Michael to go on. He wrote to Sylvia: 'Frampton was very taken with Mick's pictures & I had to leave them with him,' but, no doubt to Michael's relief, 'he prefers the Peter clothes to a nude child . . .'

Everyone took Peter out of Barrie's hands, even the sculptor.

Meanwhile, within the Llewelyn Davies household, Arthur had a plan to take his boys out of Jim's hands. He moved his family to a large suburban house, Egerton House, in Berkhamsted, preferring to commute to London each day if it meant that he could be rid of Jim.

Dolly described her first visit to the house in her diary:

> Took E. [Elizabeth, her daughter] to Berkhamsted with me to stop with Sylvia & Arthur. They have a beautiful large Elizabethan house in a street – the outlook is dreary, but nothing could be more perfect than the inside especially for so large a family. Huge nurseries & schoolroom with mullioned windows that occupy whole sides of the room – then odd long shaped bedrooms with beams & slanting floors – & all so charmingly done as Sylvia

> only can do things with harmonious chintzes & linens & lovely bits of Chippendale furniture – the whole thing is very ideal – a perfect & very cheap school next door where the 3 elder boys go, returning to meals – a kindergarten for Michael. Arthur D. came down in the evening looking handsome & severe. Poor little Girly very much distressed at my leaving her for a minute & is very quiet & subdued . . . I like to see [Sylvia] at luncheon seated at the head of her long table in the beautiful Hall with its huge windows & immense sixteen century chimneypiece & serving food to the 4 beautiful boys who all have perfect manners & are most agreeable companions – especially George.

But there was to be no escaping Jim. He went down to Berkhamsted 'quite a hundred times over the next three years'.[1]

In 1905, Jim brought the entire production of *Peter Pan* to Berkhamsted just so that Michael could see it, a clear sign that Michael was fast becoming 'The One'.

'We took the play to his nursery,' Jim wrote, 'far away in the country, an array of vehicles almost as glorious as a travelling circus; the leading parts were played by the youngest children in the London company, and No. 4, aged five, looked on solemnly at the performance from his bed and never smiled once.'

The following spring Jim invited Sylvia to Dives in Normandy. She travelled with Michael. That summer the family split again, Sylvia and Michael going to Black Lake Cottage alone.

With the boys outside London, Jim had time on his hands, and now, just as he was enjoying unprecedented public adulation, there began another extraordinary episode.

In 1905 A. E. W. Mason, a dedicated bachelor and firm friend of Jim's, introduced him to Captain Robert Falcon Scott. They took to one another 'instantaneously', according to Mackail – 'something more than a response on both sides. Here, for Jim, was the bravest and manliest sailor in the world. There, from Scott, was such instant admiration – spurred on by all the tricks and all the spells – that he was captured and appropriated at once.'

Jim describes their first meeting in an Introduction to *The Personal Journals of Captain R. F. Scott, RN, CVO, on his Journey to the South Pole*, which he edited after the explorer's death in 1912.

> On the night when my friendship with Scott began he was but lately home from his first adventure into the Antarctic, and I well remember how, having found the entrancing man, I was unable to leave him. In vain he escorted me through the streets of London to my home, for when he had said good-night I then escorted him to his, and so it went on I know not for how long through the small hours. Our talk was largely a comparison of the life of action (which he pooh-poohed) with the loathly life of those who sit at home (which I scorned); but I also remember that he assured me he was of Scots extraction . . . According to [family traditions] his great-great-grandfather was the Scott of Brownhead whose estates were sequestered after the '45 . . .

Scott's widely publicised first expedition to the Antarctic had coincided with the three Black Lake holidays. Reports of his heroic exploits had added spice to the games of Jim and the boys, and now Jim began to court him (there is no better word).

That Scott's family might have links with the Jacobite Rebellion excited him tremendously – the '45 characterised the boys' games in *Sentimental Tommy* and this connection made Scott 'one of the gang'. Jim accorded Scott a Tommy-style fantasy childhood, as befits a member of the Thrums elite:

> He enters history aged six, blue-eyed, long-haired, inexpressibly slight and in velveteen, being held out at arm's length by a servant and dripping horribly, like a half-drowned kitten . . .

Jim's cameo continues in a cringingly embarrassing vein of hero worship; Scott seems to have met this adulation a little uncertainly, with shyness and reticence, though it was not the first occasion he had excited such interest in another man.

Clements Markham, President of the Royal Geographical Society, had selected Scott to captain an expedition to the South Pole in 1901. Scott was then an undistinguished officer of average ability, and this would be his first command. David Crane[2] argues that what appealed to Markham, who was a homosexual, were Scott's arctic good looks and charm. The explorer Apsley Cherry-Garrard told him that there was not a crevasse that he would not happily fall through with Scott: 'I know Scott intimately . . . I am sure that you will come to know him and believe in him as I do, and none the less because he is sometimes difficult.' Cherry-Garrard added that he never knew a man who cried so easily as Scott.

Barrie wanted immediately to show him to his friends:

> I remember the first time [Scott] dined with me, when a number of men had come to meet him, he arrived some two hours late. He had dressed to come out, then fallen into one of his reveries, forgotten all about the engagement, dined by himself and gone early to bed. Just as he was falling asleep he remembered where he should be, arose hastily and joined us as speedily as possible . . .[3]

Already Jim had his hero down as a dreamer. He confessed himself 'intoxicated' by Scott's two-volume record of his first Antarctic expedition, *Voyage of the Discovery*, which he 'fell on [and] raced through' before flying with his new friend to a rehearsal of *Peter Pan*, which left Scott 'exhilarated and impressed'. He next took him to Black Lake Cottage, and mounted an accelerated re-run of the Castaway games, which, he told him, had been designed to teach 'by example lessons in fortitude and manly endurance'. From this time his letters to Scott were signed, 'Your loving . . . J. M. Barrie'. Soon he would invite Scott into the inner sanctum, his 'family' – Sylvia and the boys.

In September 1906, Scott mentioned a vacant place for a boy at Osborne Naval College. Jim pursued the project with gusto, recommending Jack Llewelyn Davies for his heroic qualities, as 'a fine, intelligent, quick boy with the open fearless face that attracts at first sight'.

In London the unheroic writer and the handsome explorer were inseparable, as this undated letter from Jim to Scott suggests –

> Sunday. Welcome home. Want to see you much. This chill will probably keep me in the house [Leinster Corner] some days. The maid has instructions to admit you at any hour, day or night, and the sooner the better. So do come.

Buoyed up by Jim's interest in him and by the image of intrepid Polar explorer, which at every opportunity Jim projected back on to him, Scott decided to mount another expedition to the South Pole. Jim was quick to reply – 'I chuckle with joy to hear all the hankerings are coming back to you. I feel you have *got* to go back again . . .'

In the six years between their first meeting and the second expedition, there was a marked change in Scott's personality. In 1905 he had been 'a man of ambition without direction, of aspirations without vision, of will without conscience, of charm without kindness, of character without centre',[4] but by 1911 he had become completely steeped in the heroic myth, with a clear view of himself as hero. He changed into a man who was self-confident, self-important, petulant, and possessed of a sense of the significance of 'the explorer' as the custodian of the British heroic vision, one who needed to suffer and show courage and discipline and duty and endurance, and who would therefore eschew the 'modern' technology of exploration* because it was, in effect, 'cheating'. Scott had become a fantasist, and his expedition was a tragic disaster.†

Where can this dangerous fantasy persona have come from, if not from Jim, the hero-manqué, the greatest fantasy streamer of them all, whose reverence for the heroic ideal was driven by a psychosis, and who, from the moment he met the explorer, melted before Scott's charm and good looks?

In Scott, Uncle Jim found the very flesh and blood model of his fantasy hero, and Scott played Jim's game, even to the point of joining him with Michael and Nico after lock-out in Kensington Gardens for what Jim referred to as 'our Antarctic exploits'. These involved a race with Jim's team to reach the Pole 'in advance of our friend Captain Scott and cut our initials on it'. Wrote Jim years afterwards: '[It was] a strange foreshadowing of what was really to happen.'

So lost a fantasist was Scott after six years in Barrie's company that he insisted on man-haulage in place of dogs, because, he wrote, 'In my mind no journey ever made with dogs can approach the height of that fine conception which is realised when a party of men go forth to face hardships, dangers, and difficulties with their own unaided efforts . . . Surely in this case the conquest is more nobly and splendidly won.'

Scott translated Jim's fantasy into reality. When Scott invited Jim to join his expedition, Jim wrote: 'Your invitation is really the only one I have had for years that I should much like to accept. I can't. I mustn't, I have been doing practically nothing for so long, [etc. . .] I know it means missing the thing I need most – to get into a new life for a bit . . . Altho', mind you, I would still rather let everything else go hang and enrol for the Antarctic . . . I want to know what it is really like to be alive. I should probably double up the first day. So they say, but in my heart I beg to inform you I am not so sure . . .'

* Pioneered by Peary and Nansen.

† Scott left in 1911 and was beaten to the South Pole by the Norwegian, Roald Amundsen, the following year. Scott and his colleagues, Wilson and Burrows, died a terrible death just eleven miles from safety, and famously Captain Oates trudged to his frozen grave with the immortal words, 'I am just going outside and may be some time.'

*

In the spring of 1906 the sarcoma presented for the first time in Arthur Llewelyn Davies's mouth. He had an exploratory operation at a London nursing home, writing to his sister Margaret on 26 May that 'there are no grounds for anxiety'.

Subsequently, when the cancer was diagnosed, he underwent a second operation to remove half his upper jaw and the roof of his mouth. Afterwards, outside his room, Sylvia fell on her brother Gerald's shoulder and wept: 'They've spoiled my darling's face.'

Thereafter, Barrie stood sentinel over Arthur in his decline, playing, as Peter Llewelyn Davies put it, 'the leading part in the grand manner'. While Arthur scribbled notes of what he was thinking about – his sons, 'S's blue dress', Porthgwarra,* etc. – Jim made notes for a prospective work – 'The 1,000 Nightingales: A hero who is dying. "Poor devil, he'll be dead in six months."'

And Sylvia? Dolly wrote to Peter that during Arthur's illness Sylvia 'developed the most courageous and remarkable character; she suffered intensely, because her power of feeling and her love was so strong, and in connection with your dear splendid Father's illness I had some agonizing, unforgettable moments with her. But she was very controlled and reticent – and minded so much [her sister-in-law] poor Margaret's outpourings and desire to help her. She felt much too much to talk about it in that way.'

How could Sylvia discuss her deepest feelings with anyone? How could she still the tensions and recriminations inside? This was assuredly Arthur's most difficult and courageous time, when, for the sake of his family, he had to bury his feelings too. He, Sylvia and 'Jimmy', as Arthur began to refer to him, made 'as odd a variation of the ménage à trois as ever there was', as Peter had to admit. Before the end, Arthur 'surrendered utterly'.

'Arthur's surrender' is Peter's phrase, but 'Barrie's triumph' would seem more appropriate, when Arthur asked Margaret to bring him the one surviving copy of *The Boy Castaways.*

On top of that, they gave him the just published *Peter Pan in Kensington Gardens*, the Peter Pan material from *The Little White Bird*. One can only guess what Arthur made of Barrie's Dedication:

> To Arthur & Sylvia Llewellyn Davies and their boys – My Boys

* The place in Cornwall where Arthur and Sylvia spent their honeymoon.

Dolly visited Arthur in the nursing home and wrote with perfect balance in her diary for 14 June:

> It was very sad but they are both so remarkable. He looked very altered but with his usual determination insists upon speaking in spite of having no roof or teeth, both of which he will have later* – in spite of this I understood nearly everything he said. He tried to smile & made a remark as I left about my being beautiful in his old dry chaffy way . . . But to see Sylvia tending this poor maimed creature was something I shall never forget. She seemed a living emblem of love, tenderness & sorrow – stroking his hair & his hand & looking unutterable love at him & so beautiful – it seems to have completed her. She broke down a little outside & we talked about it, but she is brave – it was wonderful to see her . . .

Two weeks later, Dolly returned.

> Wed. 27th Up to London. Went to see Arthur Davies. It seems sadder than ever & I hate his not being able to use one eye. Sylvia looks better & is more cheerful . . . Little Barrie was of course there, lurking in the background!

It is possible that Dolly voiced her concerns, for Barrie's follow-up letter to her visit reads as if she had expressed disquiet to Sylvia, or asked for some sort of explanation:

> Oct 10, 1906
>
> Dear Mrs Ponsonby,
>
> Dr Rendel and the local doctor are attending Arthur mainly to do certain necessary things that any medical man can do. They have not and never have had in any way this case in their charge, that is [surgeon] Mr Roughton's, from whom they have their instructions. He is in touch with Sir Frederick Treves [also a surgeon . . . who said] that everything that could be done for a human being was being done.
>
> Yours sincerely,
> J. M. Barrie

* He was to have an artificial jaw fitted, which was not a success.

As Treves was the surgeon who treated and supported the Elephant Man, Dolly might have been reassured. Meanwhile, Sylvia wrote to Michael (now 6), 'Mr Barrie is our fairy prince, much the best fairy prince that was ever born because he is real.'

Arthur was worried about paying for the education of his eldest two boys, who were 13 and 12 in 1906. George sat the Eton scholarship while Arthur lay ill, and failed it, whereupon a friend of Arthur's from Cambridge, Hugh Macnaghten, a housemaster at Eton, offered financial assistance to get him a place as an Oppidan. Sylvia wrote to Dolly in May 1907, 'I am so grateful to Hugh for his love and generosity.'

At this stage there were no references to financial support from Jim. He was not mentioned in Sylvia's letter, though that may have been because she sensed Dolly's antipathy towards him. Sylvia had learned to handle people's inability to understand Jim's influence over her. Jim certainly steered matters regarding Jack's future. He recommended him to Scott for Osborne Naval College, and by 11 April 1907 Jack had passed his second exam for the College and was lined up to leave home.

According to both Peter and Nico,[5] Jack, alone of the brothers, represented a threat to Uncle Jim. Sylvia was especially close to Jack, and Jack resented Jim's assumption of the role of father after Arthur's death. Entering him for the Navy effectively removed him from the family for months at a time, often when his brothers were home from school. Jack was the only one of the boys who did not go to Eton, and he hated the Navy.

CHAPTER SEVEN

Sylvia's Will

Arthur died on 18 April 1907.

Years later, Daphne recalled with discomfort, 'I am rather shaken that the du Ms kept themselves out of the picture when Arthur was ill and dying.' To quote Edmund Burke, 'All that is necessary for the triumph of evil is that good men do nothing.'

Jim immediately contacted Dr Rendel and asked him to prepare 'a sleeping draft' for Sylvia. Two weeks later she wrote to Dolly:

> Dear darling Dolly,
>
> I think of you so often & I know how you love Arthur and me & that helps me in my sorrow – you will love me always won't you – and help me to live through these long years. How shall I do it I wonder – it seems to me impossible. We were so utterly and altogether happy & that happiness is the most precious thing on earth. We were not going to part. I must be terribly brave now & I know our boys will help me. They only keep me alive & I shall live for them and as always what Arthur wd most like in them. How he loved us all & he has been taken from us . . . just now I am full of deadly pain & sorrow & I often wonder I am alive . . . I think of him almost always now as he was before the tragic illness & God gave him the finest face in the world.

It is a touching letter, which surely confirms the depth of Sylvia's love for Arthur. Perhaps it marked a turning-point.

She also wrote:

> The five boys are loving & thoughtful & I always sleep with my George now – & it comforts me more than I can say to touch him & I feel Arthur must

> know. He will live again in them I feel & that must be my dear comfort until I go to him at last. We longed to grow old together – oh my dear friend it is all so utterly impossible to understand.

Shortly after Arthur's death Sylvia made notes for a will. She named Florence Gay, a family friend, to look after her children, along with Nanny Hodgson ('I hope she will stay with them always'), and she called upon Arthur's sister Margaret, upon Barrie, and upon her own sisters and brothers (in that order) to give advice. But she ended the document, 'Of one thing I am certain – that J. M. Barrie (the best friend in the whole world) will always be ready to advise out of his love for . . .'

She never finished the sentence. Was it 'me'? Was it 'George'? Or 'the boys'? Maybe she desisted because 'love' was not something Jim did, and in the wake of Arthur's death she realised that, after all, she rather needed love. Jim's influence was not so readily disposed of, however.

From June to September 1907, after which George was due to go to Eton, Jim took the family on holiday to Dhivach Lodge on the banks of Loch Ness. Various of his friends – including Captain Scott – were invited. This was followed by a trip to Ramsgate, where Sylvia's mother, Emma, lived. Then came the move back to London from Berkhamsted, to a three-storey townhouse at 23 Campden Hill Square. 'No doubt the cash was partly put up or guaranteed by JMB,' wrote Peter.

Late in 1907, word reached Jim that Scott was seeing a woman, a young sculptor called Kathleen Bruce. He heard it first from Mason. Not only was Scott seeing a woman, he had married her. That Jim was furious is understatement. Scott had been so worried about his reaction that he had not dared approach him.

Kathleen advised Scott by letter, 'Please write quite by return of post . . . As nice a letter as ever you can think of.' Eventually Scott invited Jim to be godfather to their son, whom they planned to name Peter, after Peter Pan. But Scott knew that this would not be enough. He had rejected Jim. Wounds like that did not heal. Four years later, even as he lay in Antarctica – 'in a desperate state, feet frozen etc, no fuel, a long way from food' – knowing he was about to die, Scott wrote to Jim, 'It hurt me grievously when you partially withdrew your friendship or seemed so to do – I want to tell you I never gave you cause,' and ended his note by pleading: 'Give my memory back the friendship which you suspended – I never met a man in my life whom I admired and loved more than you but I never could show you how much your friendship meant to me, as you had much to give and I nothing.'

Dolly noted a stiffening of Barrie's attitude during this period, an ever keener focus on the boys, and a hardening of resolve. On 12 August 1908, she wrote in her diary:

> Mr Barrie arrived in the evening . . . We talked a great deal of Sylvia's boys & it is extraordinary to see how they fill his life & supply all his human interest.

Dolly remarked on his talkativeness and on his trenchant opinions. But something about him also triggered a wariness in her.

> JMB does alarm me. I feel he absolutely sees right through one & just how stupid I am – but I hope also he sees my good intentions.

Jim was reasserting his control. At Christmas 1908 he organised an extravagant holiday for Sylvia and the boys at the Grand Hotel in the fashionable Alpine resort of Caux. Mary Ansell was to come too, and Gilbert Cannan, a recent graduate of Cambridge and would-be author and actor, who was at that time reading for the Bar and had been pulled in to be secretary to a campaign Jim had agreed to undertake to abolish the Censor.

Cannan had been Kathleen Bruce's boyfriend before she took up with Scott. Now he was working with Mary Ansell on the Censor business out of Black Lake Cottage, and discovering consolation in her arms.

Jim did not know about Cannan's affair with his wife. Sylvia did know, and wanted to promote it. Diana Farr wrote in her biography of Cannan[1] that 'Sylvia encouraged and abetted Cannan's affair with Mary Barrie, making it easy for them to see each other unknown to Barrie.' Denis Mackail suggested that Sylvia saw how the situation could play into her hands. With Mary out of the way, Barrie could make her financially secure in the wake of Arthur's death. Mackail wrote: 'Temptation here, as well as elsewhere. The money again.' All of which suggests a Sylvia rather different from the one who had written to Dolly a year earlier.

Even the boys were aware that something was not quite right. 'Why is Mr Cannan always with Mrs Barrie?' Jack asked. Why, he might as well have been asking, was Mummy always with Uncle Jim? As Mackail put it: 'One sees who Sylvia's chief companion would be.'

In the end it was the gardener at Black Lake Cottage who spilled the beans, telling Jim that his wife had observed Mrs Barrie committing adultery. Jim sent a telegram to Mary telling her to remain in London. His expectation was that she would toe the line and stop seeing Cannan.

Cannan was attractive and twenty years Mary's junior. Her marriage had been over before it started. She told Jim that she wanted to marry Cannan, and she asked for a divorce.

Barrie was adamant he did not want a divorce and instructed Sir George Lewis to offer Mary a financial settlement – 'virtually on her own terms'.

Friends were appalled at his treatment of her. Maurice Hewlett wrote to her blaming Jim's behaviour on advice from Lewis, whom he described as 'a loathsome Jew'. Mary stuck to her guns. She would not be bought. She wanted out, whatever the financial consequences. Barrie could cut her off, if he wished.

The divorce hearing on 13 October 1909 was a bitter business. Mary wrote to H. G. Wells that Jim 'came out badly in court. 3 lies'. First, that Mary had said the affair with Cannan was the only one she had had; it was not, nor had she said that it was. Second, that Black Lake Cottage was his property, when it had been Mary's money that bought it in 1900, not Jim's. Third, that he had lived happily with his wife.

Mary got her divorce, and Jim agreed a settlement. Eventually they made friends again and he left her money in his will. Mary had won. Most unusual. One wonders what she knew.

Jim had moved out of Leinster Corner and into Mason's flat in Stratton Street. Subsequently, Lady Lewis came to his rescue with a flat at 3 Adelphi Terrace House, just off the Strand, on a bend of the Thames affording a view of no less than seven bridges. 'Granville Barker went with me to see the flat,' Jim wrote to her, 'and we both thought it amazing what you have got done in the time.' He slept there for the first time on 20 November 1909: 'I am in and it is all so comfortable and beautiful & all owing to you.' What she had done for him, he said, he would never forget.

By 13 May 1910, in far better fettle, he wrote to Lady Lewis, describing the awesome feeling of looking out through the high expansive windows of the apartment across the Thames:

> I feel I am writing on board the good ship Adelphi, 1200 tons. The wind is

> blowing so hard. The skipper has lashed himself to the wheel. Down in the terrace a bicycle has just been blown across the street. Mr Shaw* has just made a gallant attempt to reach the pillar box. His beard is well in front of him. I feel I ought to open my portal and fling him a life-buoy. See if he does not have a column about this in tomorrow's *Times*.

Even as the party had returned from Caux, it was clear that there was something wrong with Sylvia and by February 1909 she was looking 'very ill and thin, though lovely'.[2]

There is much about Sylvia's death that bears an uncanny resemblance to Arthur's – including, of course, its tragic consequences for the boys. Like Arthur's, Sylvia's death certificate read cancer, though the shenanigans that surrounded her last few days seemed to throw doubt even on this – 'I have always been under the impression that mother died of cancer. Surely this is the truth?' Peter asked Nanny, seemingly bemused at the absence of a proper diagnosis or post-mortem.

The location chosen by Jim for the final scene of Sylvia's life was Ashton Farm, a remote holding near Countisbury in the Oare valley on Exmoor – Lorna Doone country, beautiful, dramatic and hopelessly inaccessible.

The suggestion in *The Morgue* is that Sylvia hadn't been told of the fatal diagnosis based on an X-ray, which Nanny had seen but which, she said, 'conveyed nothing'. Dr Rendel was again on the case. He and a specialist had apparently decided against an operation because the tumour was too near the heart. Sylvia, in spite of feeling some pain, did not realise that she was terminally ill until almost the end. She was told nothing by anyone. She caught wind that something was up, however, and suggested a holiday on Exmoor assuming that, if she were badly ill, Jim and the doctors would not have allowed her to travel.

The notion of a trip to Exmoor at such a time was absurd. Sylvia, a very sick woman, would be far away from specialist treatment or a top hospital or nursing home. Nevertheless, the whole family set out together, travelling five hours by rail and not far short of an hour by road across the moor. Once again, Barrie stage-managed the proceedings as if they were in a West End play that would run and run. Sylvia was the tragic star, of course, and Dr Rendel the attendant medic.

An alarmed Emma du Maurier, at 67 years of age, pursued them. She expressed horror at the isolation of the house and its distance from doctors

* George Bernard Shaw.

and told Jim to get Dr Rendel to send for Spicer, a specialist. Sylvia's nurse – Nurse Loosemore – squabbled with Nanny Hodgson. The boys meanwhile took off, fishing for trout every day in the Doone Valley, or, as Peter recalled, 'made expeditions to Lynton and ate huge teas with bilberry jam and Devonshire cream, or on idle days watched the buzzards circling slowly, high above the valley of the Lynn – while, in fact, we went our boyish ways – Sylvia weakened rapidly, and I think she never again left her room.'

Sylvia died on 26 August 1910, a Friday. Dr Rendel, Jim, Nurse Loosemore and Emma du Maurier were the only ones present at the end. Cause of death was described at the time as increasing obstruction to breathing, and finally its complete prevention. The death certificate, certified by A. H. Spicer MB, states that cause of death was a malignant tumour in the posterior mediastinum (the thoracic cavity that contains the heart), 'involving left lung Trachea and Oesophagus'.

There was, however, no post-mortem. The death was registered two days later by Arthur's brother, Crompton, in Barnstaple, an oddly speedy business, and arranged presumably at some expense, as the 28th was a Sunday.

Initially, Michael and Nico stayed with Nanny, who 'was not consulted about matters. You yourselves,' she wrote to Peter, meaning George, Jack and Peter, 'requested packing done and disappeared – re-appearing in a day or two with JMB . . . Have no recollection of Jack returning.'

Barrie took the boys to London for Sylvia's funeral, but only George and Peter returned with him. Presumably Jack had gone back to college.

On the day his mother died, Jack was informed by Jim that Sylvia had agreed on her deathbed to marry him. Said Jack: 'I was taken into a room where [Jim] was alone and he told me, which angered me even then, that Mother had promised to marry him and wore his ring. Even then I thought if it was true it must be because she knew she was dying.'[3]

That Jim did this is either a mark of utter insensitivity or it was a lie and intended to introduce the idea that henceforth he would act as father to the boys. To Jack, the thought of Jim marrying his mother 'was intolerable, even monstrous', wrote Peter, who doubted that Sylvia had ever agreed to it. Years later, Nico reiterated that 'Jack, who worshipped our father and mother, could not stand the thought of this little man thinking he could take father's place.'

Having packed off the uncooperative Jack, Jim arranged to be alone with the other boys in the area of the River Oare for some length of time, thereby avoiding contact with anyone who might intervene by offering a helping hand with his new 'family'.

We know this from a letter dated 10 September and sent from the rectory at Brendon, Lynton, close to Ashton Farm, to Lady Lewis, who had offered refuge:

> Thank you very much for your kind letter. Sylvia died very peacefully. At no time can it be said she had pain. She gradually became feeble physically tho' in no other way. Her boys were constantly around her, and she preserved to her last smile the secret of keeping them happy.
>
> I am alone with them here. At the end of next week the older ones go back to their schools, and we shall return to London for that. I don't know anything more at present.
>
> Thank you very much for saying I could go to you. I think I had better not go anywhere at present.
>
> Always yours, J. M. Barrie

Thus, casually and with minimum fuss, did Barrie make the boys his own.

He returned with them to Campden Hill Square, where they were reunited with Nanny. Jim stayed with them for some time, anxious to keep his hand on the tiller. A new notebook, dated 22 October 1910, registers his address as 23 Campden Hill Square. Mackail writes that this was 'his home far more than the flat, at present'. And Nico: 'As often as not he was there.'

The house was an all-male domicile, except of course for Nanny, who was especially important to the two youngest, Michael and Nico. 'She was the person in our lives,' said Nico later, an interesting turn of phrase. 'She was the mother.'[4]

The atmosphere seems to have been rather like that of a public school common-room; a large room on the first floor was known as 'the school-room'. It was a form of society already familiar to the boys. Jim loved it. He was exultant at the very notion of the institution of the English public school, Eton in particular: 'I am like a dog looking up to its owner, wondering what that noble face means,' he wrote of the English public-school boy, lifting Little Billee's wonder-love line for Trilby straight from Kicky's text. He now had four such noble faces that could own him. Number 23 Campden Hill Square was an apparently safe environment.

But, as anyone who went to public school in England in the twentieth century knows, one that could conceal a multitude of sins.

The boys rallied: 'We were selfish little creatures,' admitted Nico, like Peter rather embarrassed in later years that they had accepted the transition so easily. Nico noted that henceforth there was an emphasis on games – 'He was always egging us on to play this or that.' Principal joy and the focus of life for the boys was a long table which could be converted into a three-quarter-sized billiard table, and was also used to play ping-pong. Nico recalled as typical a game Jim bought called ARBOCU, 'a mixture of ARchery, BOwls, and CUrling . . .', but it was just as likely that Jim would be found 'bowling at one of them between two chairs'.[5] Then there were the regular holidays to Scotland and the fly fishing. The boys' fishing rods became like sacred things to them, instruments of an activity of high concentration and relaxation, something in which George in particular was well practised.

The ease with which Jim was permitted to slip into this new role and take complete control of the boys is extraordinary. Did other members of the family turn a blind eye? Was there no 'summit' between the Davieses and the du Mauriers? Emma, now 69, wrote: 'I am too old to be really any use to them. He [Jim] is unattached* and his one wish is to look after them in the way Sylvia would have wanted.' Sylvia's brother Gerald was 'thick' with Jim in the West End, acting in his plays. Arthur's sister, Margaret, who had shown herself willing to help during Arthur's illness, couldn't have taken on five boys.

As for Dolly, Jim took special care to put her and her husband, who was in a position of some power, at ease about the arrangement. On 23 February 1911, we find him in chatty form with Dolly and Arthur Ponsonby over lunch at his London flat.

As on their earlier meeting after Arthur's death, Dolly felt a little intimidated – 'He always a little frightens me because his insight is so acute,' she confided to her diary. Jim talked again of politics and of 'the boys & their characters & of how George, though at Eton, was still a strong Liberal. He says they write one another long letters on politics. The little ones too, he says, are violent Radicals & at one moment would hardly consent to a Tory entering the house.'

Dolly found this a bit hard to take – she knew these boys, after all – and asked Jim what they really understood about it. Barrie 'explained so

* As if 'unattached' was a point in his favour.

charmingly & simply his method – "I tell them that the dirty little raggamuffins are as good as they, & why shouldn't they have the same advantages." – or words to that effect.'

After lunch, Arthur Ponsonby excused himself and Jim took Dolly and her two children, Elizabeth and Matthew, to Campden Hill Square for tea, to satisfy her that all was in order there. She saw Michael and Nico, the other three being at school and college, and then 'Margaret* came in & was rather depressed & unnatural.'

When later they went upstairs to the children's room, rather than a political discussion, a more 'characteristic conversation took place', as Dolly's diary records: 'Nicholas remarked as Elizabeth and Matthew were putting on their gloves, "I like Matthew's gloves best." Michael says, "I don't like kid gloves," looking at Elizabeth's. I say, "They are not kid gloves, they are doe-skin." Michael says, "I like suede." Margaret says, "Surely Michael, you prefer no gloves at all."'

Realising that a wrap-scene was required, Uncle Jim told the children how he had himself flown on stage on the set of *Peter Pan*, and that when word got out that he was going to fly 'all rushed round to the front to see him – & JMB had the iron curtain let down as promptly'. Everyone laughed. *Peter Pan* always did the trick.

In spite of Dolly's and Margaret's misgivings, no one challenged Jim's abduction of the boys. He had no legal right to them. Their mother had not asked him to be their guardian. Years later, Dolly raised this with Peter, who replied in February 1946:

> You are of course perfectly right about our being spirited away, as children, from my mother's and father's friends. It would not be easy to say to what extent, if any, the process was deliberate, and to what extent inevitable in the peculiar circumstances; the whole business, as I look back on it, was almost unbelievably queer and pathetic and ludicrous and even macabre in a kind of way – and I dare say comic too from certain points of view. But at all events it was a bad thing, among some things that were good, for the children concerned; and I can well imagine what the thoughts of old friends of Arthur's and Sylvia's must have been.
>
> I myself am only now, in middle age, after thirty years or more, beginning to uncoil myself from the various complexes (I suppose the word is) 'all that' twisted me up . . .

* So, at least their aunt Margaret was a presence in the boys' lives.

Jim had a friend called Charles Turley Smith who wrote books about schoolboys. He loved 'Chay' and his books so much that he used to give them to every boy he knew. Turley Smith was always 'somewhere between the lines' in the pages of Jim's life.[6] He lived in Cornwall, but still managed to be a regular member of the Allahakbarries, and as 'Chay Turley' was written into later editions of the *Peter Pan* play.

A sequence of letters from Jim to Turley Smith express Jim's thanks for gifts of hand-picked spring flowers. The first reads: 'Many thanks for the bluebells and a squeeze of the hand for every one you plucked.' Later, Jim wrote: 'We are as close in love I think as two old friends can be.'

Jim liked to keep him informed about the boy-world he now inhabited with Arthur and Sylvia's sons:

> I have been visiting at Campden Hill for a longish time owing to one thing and another . . . I have been teaching Michael to bicycle, running up and down the quieter thoroughfares of Campden Hill and feeling what it must be like at the end of a marathon race. Have also taken him to a garden in St John's Wood where an expert teaches fly fishing on a lawn. I saw a little of the Eton and Harrow match, but Harrow were so slovenly in the field it was poor sport . . . Peter is bowling very promisingly also. We are going for seven weeks or so beginning of August to Scourie in the west of Sutherland. 630 miles rail, then a drive 44 miles. The nearest small town is farther than from here to Paris in time. Nothing to do but fish, which however is what they want . . .[7]

But Barrie did not yet feel entirely secure. And all of a sudden – at some point in March 1911 – a document was found, headed 'Sylvia's Will'. It was seven pages, written in Sylvia's hand as she lay dying in Ashton. It detailed, with unmistakable clarity, who was to inherit her money and effects, and, most important, whom she wanted to look after the boys.

The relevant part of it is the second paragraph.

> What I would like wd be if Jenny wd come to Mary & that the two together would be looking after the boys & the house & helping each other. And it would be so nice for Mary.

'Mary' was Mary Hodgson – Nanny. 'Jenny' was Nanny's sister.

In an extraordinary manoeuvre Jim copied the whole thing out with one alteration: he changed 'Jenny' to 'Jimmy', and then sent his version to the boys' grandmother Emma du Maurier, as head of the du Maurier family, with a note:

> The above is an exact copy, including the words 'Sylvia's Will', of paper found by me at 23 Campden Hill Square.

Andrew Birkin was aware of it, but writes on the jmbarrie.co.uk web site, that Barrie substituted his name for Jenny's 'no doubt inadvertently'. There is of course the logical possibility that he honestly mistook the word 'Jenny' for 'Jimmy' and – delighted that he had proof of Sylvia's desire for him to take control of the boys – rushed off a copy and sent it to Emma. Unfortunately for Barrie, the original and his copy still exist. There is no mistaking 'Jenny' for 'Jimmy'. That Jim made the alteration exposes him utterly.

What's more, Sylvia had written that the arrangements she was making in the will would be 'so nice for Mary', i.e. for Mary Hodgson. Barrie knew better than anyone that his presence at Campden Hill Square would not be nice for Nanny Hodgson, not nice at all. He and Nanny never got on. What *would* have been nice for Nanny Hodgson was what Sylvia intended, namely that her sister Jenny had come to live in and that they looked after the boys together.

The alteration of Sylvia's Will shows that Barrie's strategy was predatory. But for him, in his lifetime, it did the trick. It salved Emma du Maurier's conscience and gave him free rein with the boys.

Dolly meanwhile kept on the case. On 1 July she arrived at Adelphi Terrace. Jim, still anxious to reassure the Ponsonbys, disarmed her by 'confiding' in her about the second Will, which pre-empted her finding out about it and defused any curiosity about following it up.

> I went to see JMB in his flat where we had a nice talk about the boys & Sylvia & he told me how they had found Sylvia's will 2 months ago, & except for 2 things he said he had done all she wished before seeing it. He said – there were 3 large sheets* well written in a clear firm hand & with no hint of emotion.

So, the Will had been found by the boys among Sylvia's things at

* These are, in fact, seven large sheets in Sylvia's hand, and five in Barrie's copy.

Campden Hill Square. Not by Jim, by the boys. *That* was why he had had to act on its discovery, and make the false copy of it and send it to Emma. Had he found the Will and not bothered with it, had he put it on the fire, it would certainly not have altered anything. He already had the house, the boys, the wherewithal. But when the boys found it he had to act, because they were bound to mention it to someone in the family. So, he altered Sylvia's Will to suggest that she wanted him to be their guardian.

Revealing its existence to Dolly made him seem open-handed to her, when in fact, as his fraudulent transcription shows, he was being quite the opposite.

He needn't have worried. No one in the family much cared.

PART V

1910–1921

Michael, Daphne and Uncle Jim: 'An Awfully Big Adventure'

"TO DIE WILL BE AN AWFULLY BIG ADVENTURE?"

CHAPTER ONE

Looking for Michael

Michael was 10 when Sylvia died. His time had come. Ten was the age at which George had been Uncle Jim's favourite and is the time when a boy is at his most beautiful, if he is to be beautiful at all, the beauty special because it is ephemeral. Michael was the most beautiful of the brothers, the image of his mother, and dangerously vulnerable to Uncle Jim. Denis Mackail was there in 1910. He knew both the child and the man:

> An orphan at ten. Not wax for Barrie – not by any means – but you can steer or lead little boys of ten in a way that you don't do afterwards. The spell is still irresistible when it chooses, and here is the boy – quick, sensitive, attractive, and gifted – who is to be everything else that the magician most admires. There is no cloud between them. From Barrie, as yet, Michael has no secrets. You can call him the favourite, if you like – indeed there are plenty of moments when it is impossible to call him anything else – but his brothers are the last to resent this. He and Barrie draw closer and closer, and perhaps it isn't always Barrie who leads or steers. He has given his heart to Michael . . . and has transferred an enormous part of his ambition. Is it dangerous? No answer. One mustn't say so . . .

We don't know how Mackail got this passage past Cynthia Asquith's censoring pencil, but we do know that Geraldine Gibb, soon to become the wife of Michael's brother Jack, thought the relationship between Michael and Uncle Jim 'unhealthy. Everybody else did too . . . It was very bad for Michael to be so much the centre of Barrie's world.'[1]

Michael had attracted Uncle Jim from the start. The fourth of the brothers, born in 1900, he was a year old during the first holiday at Black Lake, where 'he was merely an honorary member of the band, waving his foot to you for luck when you set off with bow and arrow to shoot his dinner for him'. But later, it was he who first saw Tinkerbell. 'It was one evening when we climbed the wood carrying No. 4 to show him what the trail was like by twilight. As our lanterns twinkled among the leaves No. 4 saw a twinkle stand still for a moment and he waved his foot gaily to it, thus creating Tink.'[2]

In *The Little White Bird*, Michael's foot makes as significant an appearance as Trilby's in the du Maurier novel. The Captain (Jim) mocks Nanny Irene (Nanny Hodgson) for keeping the child away from him, and an arrangement is made for him to see the child alone. Nanny begs to be allowed to stay, but the boy's mother has already acquiesced and Nanny is dismissed. As she takes a tearful farewell, she says to her charge: 'And if he takes off your socks, my pretty, may he be blasted for evermore.'

The taking off of a baby's sock, the ultimate transgression, gives the Captain something to aim for, and Jim, as omnipotent author, dares us to see it as a metaphor for abuse.

The innocence in the boy's eyes shames the Captain into seeing himself as he really is. 'In them I saw my true self. They opened for me that peddler's pack of which I have made so much ado, and I found that it was weighted less with pretty little sad love-tokens than with ignoble thoughts and deeds and an unguided life.' The peddler, the trickster of tradition, is the sidekick of the Devil, which is why he must ever move on. The Captain looks dejectedly at the boy, 'because I feared he would not have me in his service'.

But then the child smiles, and is at once a lost boy. 'I felt myself a fine fellow . . . never before had I come into such close contact with a child; the most I had ever done was, when they were held up to me, to shut my eyes and kiss a vacuum . . . and yet we managed it between us quite easily. His body instinctively assumed a certain position as I touched him, which compelled my arms to fall into place, and the thing was done . . . I discovered that he wanted me to take off his sock!'

The first boy actually to be born into Jim's Peter-Pan boy cult, Michael never found it easy. In 1912, when he was 12, Daphne recalled overhearing a conversation between Nanny Hodgson and her own nanny: '"Michael has bad nightmares. He dreams of ghosts coming through the window." At night I would stare at the window and understand.' But Michael's nightmares were severe:

> There was a horror looking for him in his childhood. Waking dreams we called them, and they lured him out of bed in the night. It was always the same nameless enemy he was seeking, and he stole about in various parts of the house in search of it, probing fiercely for it in cupboards, or standing at the top of the stairs pouring out invective and shouting challenges to it to come up. I have known the small white figure defend the stair-head thus for an hour, blazing rather than afraid, concentrated on some dreadful matter in which, tragically, none could aid him. I stood or sat by him, like a man in an adjoining world, waiting till he returned to me, for I had been advised, warned, that I must not wake him abruptly. Gradually I soothed him back to bed, and though my presence there in the morning told him, in the light language we then adopted, that he had been 'at it again' he could remember nothing of who the enemy was. It had something to do with the number 7 . . .[3]

The following year Michael was sent to Eton as a boarder. Jim wrote to Turley Smith and thanked him 'for the affection that made you know how sad I would be about Michael gone to school. He is very lonely there at present, and I am foolishly taken up about it. It rather broke me up seeing him crying and trying to whistle at the same time.'[4]

Michael disliked Eton from the start, and Jim found the separation so difficult he took to creeping around the playing fields of the school, a ghostly presence through the mist, 'so that he may at least see me nigh though we cannot touch'.

George, meanwhile, who had joined the Army on the eve of the Great War was still very much in the frame. In September 1914, Jim was in New York with Gilmour and Mason when he received news of George's summons to Sheerness in Kent for training. Staying mostly 'in hiding' to avoid being chased by reporters, Barrie wrote marvelling at the American cult of celebrity, but was obviously enjoying life – 'Last night I had a Gin Whizz with a Long Tom in it. I slept well. Mason had two and slept better.' Shortly afterwards, Peter joined George at Sheerness, where both young men awaited orders from the Front.

Now that Michael was away for extended periods at school – Nico was never a favoured one – Jim began to take a serious interest in his godson Peter Scott, who was three when Jim wrote him this letter:

My dear Peter,

Hallo I am so glad too get your ripping letter it is a lovly let ter the reaso
N I have not wrote [strike through] writ [strike] rot before is because I have
been in Switserla
Nd with Ni
Kolas and Mi
Kal and them
Uther boys . . .
It is time u sawed Pete
R Pan I am
Too ring youre
Mother up
About it tomo
Rrow. He is br
Ave he can fly

I am
Yure lovin
G
Godfather

Ure fotogrfs is grand they is on my
Bookshelf

Peter Scott made frequent visits to Adelphi House over the following years, and his mother Kathleen was happy to leave him alone with Jim. Peter remembered 'long silences'.

Soon Jim began actively negotiating with Kathleen to become the boy's guardian in the event of her death. 'No one could love Peter more than I do,' he wrote to her. Kathleen resisted being cast as 'another Sylvia' and called on the support of Lord Knutsford. Soon all three were writing letters, Knutsford asking the most pertinent question – 'What sort of life do you want for Peter and could Sir J B or my family the better give this?'

Kathleen eventually had the guts to turn down Barrie's offer. But the seriousness of his intent, or more likely the willingness of one of Barrie's many friends in Fleet Street to participate in his dark sense of humour, was revealed in a note she received at this time:

> The News Editor of the 'Daily Chronicle' presents his compliments to Lady Scott and would be obliged if she would confirm or deny a report which has been forwarded to the News Editor this afternoon that she was married to Sir J. M. Barrie six weeks ago . . .

At Christmas 1914, just as George was arriving at the front line in France and his brother, the other Peter, was poised to join him, Peter Scott was Uncle Jim's guest in a box at a performance of *Peter Pan*, where he enjoyed himself tearing up the programme and throwing the pieces on people's heads.

Between 1915 and his death the following year, George's letters to Uncle Jim show the ghastly realities of trench warfare on the Somme – liquid mud up to the knees, the stench of rotting corpses beneath the feet, and the agony of frozen and frostbitten extremities – but Jim's remarkable talent for 'finding a way' served to lighten the young man's spirits. 'Boxes and boxes' of goods from Fortnum & Mason, dispatched on Jim's orders, somehow found their way through.

In March 1915 the 9th Infantry Brigade, 3rd Division, prepared for an attack 'with the object of straightening out the line' at Saint-Eloi. George told a comrade that he had a premonition he would be killed. He was sitting on a bank along with the rest of his Company being addressed by his Colonel when he was shot through the head. He died almost immediately.

That same night, Nico and Nanny were awakened by a loud knocking on the door of 23 Campden Hill Square. (Michael was away at Eton.) The knocking was Uncle Jim. Nico sat up in bed listening as a 'Banshee wail' filled the house. Jim mounted the stairs, came into his room, and sat on his bed in silence.

George had been the leader, and in the wider family the sadness was augmented by the death in battle that same year of Sylvia's brother, Guy du Maurier. Naturally the boys were deeply affected by the losses but for Michael there was the additional dimension that George's death increased the intensity of Uncle Jim's attentions. Explained Nico years later –

> George being dead – we all knew Michael was The One. If George hadn't been killed, who knows? Probably Michael would always have been Number One.[5]

For Michael, now 15, life with Uncle Jim became a game of chess, 'the game of trying to know each other without asking questions'. Jim's moves took the boy from dependence on him to a position of domination over him. Just as Sylvia had initially relied on Jim as 'a kind of extra nurse, extremely useful fairy-godmother, or sometimes even errand-boy', and Jim had used this platform of dependence to dominate her from within, with his alchemic text rituals, now he created a similar sort of relationship with Michael:

> When Uncle Jim was strongly attracted by people, he wanted at once to own them and to be dominated by them whichever their sex. There's no denying that he did increasingly 'own' Sylvia and her boys. Later, I think, he achieved something of the same *peculiar equilibrium* with George, and much more with Michael.[6]

Since the death of Sylvia, Jim had enjoyed being 'the one needed' in his relationship with Michael. And now he puffed up Michael's self-esteem by involving him closely in his work.

> No. 4 jumps from being astride my shoulders fishing, I knee-deep in the stream, to becoming, while still a schoolboy, the sternest of my literary critics. Anything he shook his head over I abandoned, and conceivably the world has thus been deprived of a masterpiece . . . Sometimes, however, No. 4 liked my efforts, and I walked in the azure that day when he returned Dear Brutus* to me with the comment 'Not so bad.'[7]

Macnaghten, his tutor at Eton, said that Michael was the brightest boy he had ever taught, even that he was a poet of genius. It is true that Michael became editor of the *Eton College Chronicle* and wrote many a leader article, also that his friend Roger Senhouse thought him a genius and tried unsuccessfully 'to keep some sort of pace with Michael'. Michael was certainly out on his own in one sense, a loner, 'very reserved – not a seeker after popularity', as another friend, Clive Burt, put it. But no evidence of genius comes down to us – some passable journalism and two poems, fairly average for a boy of 20, a bit pretentious.

George had won the Essay Prize at Eton, Peter was the scholar, yet always it is Michael, Uncle Jim's protégé, who is the genius. Perhaps Macnaghten, who was keenly aware of Michael's sensitivity to the tragedy

* First performed in 1917, starring Gerald du Maurier.

of his parents' death, talked his talents up. This may not ultimately have been to the boy's advantage, any more than Jim using him as an editorial adviser. Encouraging Michael to exercise control over his work meant that the boy became immersed in Jim's ideas, which shaped the relationship between them beneath the surface, allowing Jim to get 'inside' him just as he had done with Sylvia.

Besides the annual production of *Peter Pan*, with its developing ideas about the supernatural and death, three plays in particular set the tone of the relationship. The first, Barrie's play of 1917, *Dear Brutus*, takes up Henry James's idea, aired in 'The Middle Years', of a second chance. It dramatises what happens when a group of characters, all of whom yearn for a second chance in life, enter an enchanted wood on Midsummer Eve, and one by one go back in time to reshape their lives. Characters pass from one world into a parallel reality, in this case not the world of the dead, but a dream world. As in all three plays the main relationship is that of a father and his child.

The second, *A Well-Remembered Voice* (1918), was inspired by George's death. A group of people gather for a séance for a young victim of the Great War, but when the young man crosses over from the spirit world, it is only to his father that he appears. The returning soldier is recognisably George, his voice 'as boyish as ever'. The father to whom he returns is recognisably Jim. They meet in Jim's study at Adelphi Terrace and talk eerily about the battlefield, and the lightest of veils that separates the living from the dead. As in *Peter Pan*, we are led to appreciate 'what a little thing' death is.

The third play that shaped the Michael years, *Mary Rose* (1920), is also about the supernatural and the morbid. It tells of a mother who disappears on a magical Hebridean island and returns to her son as a ghost. Again there is a crossing over between life and death, and with special significance this time, because it is an idea that had its origin in Jim's belief, first expressed in *The Little White Bird*, that the only ghosts are 'dead young mothers, returned to see how their children fare', the implication being that no other inducement is great enough to bring back the departed.

Supernatural currents, born out of George du Maurier's work, drove Jim's work and made a little god of Michael, celebrating his aura, the 'Blake like effulgence' that Roger Senhouse noticed also about George.

But there was also a morbid streak about Jim's captivation of Michael, both in the plays, which he discussed with Michael, and in the way he dealt with Sylvia's death. We know that after Sylvia died Barrie made a point of writing a letter to her on each anniversary of her death, bringing her up to date with the progress of the boys.

Nanny became increasingly concerned, and when Nico went as a boarder to Eton in 1916 she offered her resignation. Jim saw immediately that that would not do. In spite of her disapproval of him, Nanny Hodgson had been a silent witness, hidebound by her loyalties. Jim needed her discretion, rooted in her continuing loyalty to Sylvia and Arthur, which a new nanny would not have. Jim did all in his power to persuade her to stay. Reluctantly, she agreed.

He then set about securing a position that was not beholden to this woman, who had been a thorn in his side for as long as he had known her. He moved from his flat on the third floor of Adelphi Terrace House (fifth if you looked at it from the Embankment side) to a larger studio apartment on the top floor of the same building. No expense was spared in its redesign by Edwin Lutyens. A large study room ran the length of it to huge casement windows looking out over the Thames, making it even more like the Captain's bridge than the flat below. The walls were mahogany panelled. Large brown wooden book-shelves were installed. The overall impression was one of brownness. Immediately to the right on entry was a large inglenook fireplace, into which Jim, at just over five feet, could wander without bending, and tuck himself away on a hard settle to read in the light of a log fire. The floor of the room was covered with matting, and later by rugs chosen by Michael. In one corner stood a polished iron stove, where Jim brewed tea when his manservant, Thurston, was not in attendance.

'Somehow the apartment seems just like him,' wrote a visitor.* Dark, bookish, imposing, hard, it would not be out of place in the opening scene of *Faust* as the 'high-vaulted, narrow Gothic chamber' where we first see the scholar sitting restless at his desk.

Jim's plan was to dispense with Nanny and move Michael and Nico in there with him.

On 4 September 1917, Jack, who had served the war in the Royal Navy, married Geraldine Gibb after a year-long engagement. Peter was still away at war and already in a relationship with Vera Willoughby, a love affair which would keep him out of the family until 1921.

Jim, without consulting Nanny, arranged for Jack and his new wife to take over the running of 23 Campden Hill Square.

When the young couple arrived, Nanny, unprepared and deeply offended by the assault on her authority, turned her back and refused to

* Charlie Chaplin.

speak to Gerrie, who was to take her place. Jack was furious. Nico and Michael, however, wouldn't have a word said against Nanny. Tensions were high between the two factions, but when Jim was there he appeared completely oblivious.

Doggedly, and not a little courageously, Nanny continued to ignore Gerrie, and would not give in to Jim by resigning her position.

Then one night Nanny pushed a note under the door of Jack's bedroom. It read –

> Things have been going on in this room of which your father would not have approved.

It is not known what Jack made of it, but the response within the family was shameful. Gerrie later recalled that Edward Coles, husband of May du Maurier, and therefore Michael's uncle, read Nanny's note and quipped: 'She probably heard the bed squeaking.'

Why did no one do anything? 'Because they were intimidated,' admitted Gerrie to Andrew Birkin in 1975. 'All the other relations said they were intimidated.'

Certainly Jim could be intimidating. Dolly Ponsonby was afraid of him; Denis Mackail recalled that he would meet your conversation with an expression 'horribly like a sneer'. There was something dark about him. Norma Douglas Henry, a friend of both George and Jack, had this to say:

> I think one or two people were rather disturbed about Barrie, though of course it was never talked about openly. There was something sinister about him, rather shivery.[8]

Brave Nanny stood alone against Uncle Jim. But she could not win. She issued an ultimatum to Gerrie to leave Campden Hill Square. Gerrie and Jack retreated to a Knightsbridge hotel, where Gerrie suffered a miscarriage. Nanny broke down, never fully to recover.

Peter, at war in Flanders, wrote to her, 'It seems to me from what I've heard which is very little – that things are happening otherwise than they might have happened had I been at home; Nico would be heart-broken if you were to go – Michael too, I think. But I know so little – I wish you'd write.'

But it was too late. Nanny had resigned. She refused compensation of £1,000, made up of £500 left to her by Sylvia and £500 put up by Jim. By Easter 1918, Michael and Nico were installed at Adelphi Terrace House. Campden Hill Square was closed down.

*

The ability Jim had developed to disturb and intimidate was the result of his success, but also of the nature of the material on which his success was built, and his own increasingly morbid, possessive personality.

To the Tommies (his various fantasy personae) in his armament at the time of his possession of Sylvia – the broken fellow, the good-natured cynic, the haughty boy, the grave author – he had added 'the Establishment figure' and 'the Demon Boy'.

Both were controlling. Both made one feel what Dolly had felt when they had met after Arthur Davies's death that 'he absolutely sees right through one & just how stupid I am'. But they won him many admirers too.

Jim's contacts during the war went high in the military. He had a close trusted friend in General Freyberg, VC, DSO, and was once given a privileged personal 'view' of the front line, conducted with utmost security. This explains how he knew within a few hours that George had been killed. He also dined with prime ministers, and found himself in the humbling position of being offered a knighthood, and then in the chastening position, after turning it down, of settling on a baronetcy instead – a little irony here, for this was an inherited title, and there was no chance of a natural-born son. By 1917, this Tommy was interviewing Lady Cynthia Asquith, daughter-in-law of the recent Prime Minister, now Leader of the Liberal Party, to become his secretary. He was part of the Establishment, rich and successful, and this was intimidating enough. But even more intimidating was the 'other' Jim, the supernatural Jim, the Demon Boy who purported to live in a Peter Pan world and was so untouchable that he could, in the most casual way, announce his part in the demise of Michael's parents:

> In the house of Mr and Mrs Darling . . . there never was a simpler happier family until the coming of Peter Pan.
>
> Peter had seen many tragedies, but he had forgotten them all . . . 'I forget [people] after I kill them.'[9]

Jim published these lines less than twelve months after Sylvia died, around the time he forged her Will. He identified himself with Peter in *Peter and Wendy*, but wrote about him as if he was describing someone else.

Theatre-goers lapped up his supernatural plays, but never quite understood why, as Denis Mackail recalled of the thousands who flocked to *Mary Rose*:

> For 399 performances . . . audiences wept, sniffed, swallowed and choked, without ever being able to explain what had reduced them to this state. Being human, some of them still sought for a meaning, but it was never vouchsafed. For nobody knew it. The players certainly didn't, and the author had told everything by this time and had nothing more to say.

He had transmuted himself into a Demon Boy by means of his alchemic texts, and everyone played the game – 'between two worlds' – as cricket writer Neville Cardus showed in his classic account of staying at the Adelphi Terrace flat, described by Nico as 'vividly true'.[10]

> This week-end at Barrie's flat will make so strange a story that I must assure the reader that in telling it I have made no exaggeration and have carefully overhauled my memory. Maybe I suffered from delusions; I do not deny the possibility; the point is that if delusions did seize me they were so potent as to become inextricable from fact.

After ascending in a lift to the penthouse suite, Cardus was met at the door by his host.

> After Barrie had greeted me he showed me my bedroom and a shiver went down my spine when he told me, unnecessarily as I still think, that it had been 'Michael's' room.

Michael had drowned four years before. Cardus surrendered his baggage to Barrie's manservant, Thurston, and was shown into the long study room.

> Thurston had a ghostly face; he was from a Barrie play – so was Barrie, and the flat, and everything in it; the enormous cavern of a fireplace, the wooden settle and old tongs and bellows, and the sense the place gave you that the walls might be walked through if you had been given the secret. Barrie trudged the room smoking a pipe; on the desk lay another pipe already charged, ready for immediate service; he coughed as he trudged and smoked, a cruel cough that provoked a feeling of physical pain in my chest; and his splutterings and gaspings and talk struggled on one from the other. At last he came to sit facing me in front of the smouldering logs, and for a while the silence was broken by groans only to be heard in our two imaginations – the groans of men separated for ever by a chasm of shyness and uneasiness. Until midnight we lingered on. He offered me no refreshment. Thurston apparently

went home to sleep each night. Or perhaps he merely dematerialised.

Throughout Cardus' stay, people appeared as if out of nowhere and disappeared, so that he too began to feel he was a character in a Barrie play. At one stage he came upon a woman who was the spitting image of Margaret Ogilvy. By that time he was ready to believe that he had indeed come face to face with Jim's mother, dead these thirty years. But it turned out to be Barrie's younger sister Maggie, who invited Cardus to a '*conversazzione*' in her boudoir, and surprised him with the news that she had been in communication with his own mother 'on the other side'.

> And that my mother and she had loved one another at once, and that my mother was proud of me and that they, the two of them, would watch over and take care of me. I was naturally ready to perspire with apprehension. Was I to be mothered or Wendy'd in this flat in the tree – I mean chimney tops?

This is extraordinary information. Scottish Presbyterian Maggie Barrie is now, under her brother's influence, a medium! The story shows beyond any doubt how far the Barries had flown on George du Maurier's coat-tails.

In such a context as this, is it not credible that what had been 'going on' with Michael in Barrie's bedroom at Campden Hill Square, and what Nanny Hodgson had tried to report, was not sex, as May's husband quipped, but a psychic ritual of some sort, hypnosis or perhaps a séance? It makes more sense for another reason. Would Nanny have stood by for so long had Jim and Michael been having sex? I think not.

When finally Cardus's long weekend came to an end, it was with a sense of relief that he made his goodbyes.

> Thurston led me to Barrie . . . he was in bed in a bandbox of a room, bare and uncomfortable – what little I could see of it through thick tobacco smoke, for his pipe was in full furnace as he lay there, frail in pyjamas, like a pygmy with one of those big pantomime heads. He hoped I had enjoyed my stay and would come again; the flat was open to me at any time: I had only to give him short notice. Thurston carried my suitcase down the lift cage. He got me a taxi. In my highly emotional condition – feeling I had emerged from another dimension, and only just emerged – I forgot to tip him. I called on Barrie at the flat once or twice after this experience; but never stayed the night. I prefer my Barrie plays on the stage in front of me, where I can see what they are doing; I don't like them taking place behind my back in the night.

CHAPTER TWO

Daphne's initiation

Principal among Jim's contacts within the wider du Maurier family, and vital to the success of his strategy since Sylvia's death, was Gerald du Maurier, Sylvia's brother, the youngest of George's children.

Born in 1873, Gerald was a spoilt, irresponsible, irrepressible youth when Jim first met him around 1900–01 – great fun, but cheeky and a show-off. Hopelessly unacademic at Harrow, he was nevertheless a social success and a natural actor. He made his first appearance on stage in *An Old Jew*, a comedy by Sydney Grundy, in January 1894, and thereafter he had a small part in every play produced at the Garrick, until he toured with Mrs Patrick Campbell's company. 'I have taught a clown to play Pelleas,'* Mrs Pat is supposed to have exclaimed.

Eight years older than Gerald, Mrs Pat gave him what he needed: discipline. And took him into her bed. When in November 1901 she let him go and went off to New York, she became his destroyer too – a goddess indeed. It was then, when Gerald returned deflated to his mother, that Jim stepped in and was only too pleased to take him on. Jim loved Gerald's boyish good looks and 'gay, happy-go-lucky' flair. Nico said that Jim 'thought Gerald irresistible'; and for Jim, Gerald was 'the only manly actor on the stage'.

For a week in the summer of 1902, Gerald joined the Barries and the Llewelyn Davieses on the second of the Black Lake holidays. In November of the same year Jim made Gerald an offer of a part in his new play, *The Admirable Crichton*. This play not only made Gerald's name in the theatre, it wrote him into an amorous situation with an actress called Muriel ('Mo') Beaumont and, as ever with Jim, shadows of the dream clung to the reality. In the script, Jim sent his fictional characters to a coral island to fall in love

* *Pelléas et Mélisande*, a play by Maurice Maeterlinck.

– which the real Gerald and Mo promptly did. Daphne was, of course, born of this fantasy union; in effect, she was written and produced by Uncle Jim.

The relation of writer to actor is susceptible to the 'peculiar equilibrium' that Jim sought to establish with people to whom he was attracted, wanting at once 'to own them and be dominated by them', as Peter Davies put it. The playwright's fantasies are fed into the actor; the actor then makes them his own. Thereafter, the playwright controls the actor's very identity from within. This was the rapport Jim developed with Gerald. 'The author and actor must go hand in hand to make a success of a play,' Jim wrote in 1931 – and he was a very hands-on playwright indeed, attending rehearsals and discussing Gerald's parts in depth.

But perhaps because Gerald was resistant to closeness with Barrie, or thought he should be, Gerald always kept a gap between them. Gerald had an abhorrence of homosexuals. Possibly he was himself a repressed homosexual. Given his way, he would have rid the West End theatre of homosexuals. Intimacy between men was not something he was going to be so unmanly as to admit.

He put himself across as a ladies' man, shamelessly boasting to his young daughter Daphne about his liaisons with beautiful actresses. But when Daphne questioned him about boys 'making friends with other boys' at Harrow, he responded abruptly, as if she had touched a nerve. Also, rather surprisingly for a ladies' man, on stage he had what Daphne described as an 'oddly hostile' attitude to women. 'He seldom kissed women, unless it was on the back of the neck or the top of the head, and then he would generally slap them on the face afterwards, and say, "you old funny, with your ugly mug".'[1]

The friendship between Gerald and Jim was a perilous intimacy. As Mackail commented:

> They thought they saw through each other, and then again they weren't at all sure that they weren't being seen through themselves. There was often a kind of jealousy, too, when each found himself wanting the other's more special and peculiar gifts – though of course as well as his own . . .

There was, however, no question who was in control. 'Barrie understood Gerald much more than Gerald understood Barrie,' Daphne said with utter conviction in 1973.[2]

Whatever was going on deep down, they came together brilliantly on stage:

> Gerald's best performances took place most especially in the plays of J.M. Barrie. He was made for these parts, as no one else can ever hope to be. He brought a delicate, pristine quality into his interpretation of those characters so peculiarly and lovably original: a note from the woods and the wild places – something wistful, something gay, a faun-like carelessness, a happy-go-lucky shrug of the shoulder.[3]

The earliest roles Jim created for him pointed a finger at Gerald's empty soul. In *The Admirable Crichton* he cast him as the Hon. Ernest Woolley, an outwardly impressive upper-class Englishman, who is two-dimensional, ignorant of deeper issues. In Jim's stage directions he is 'light-natured', 'endearingly selfish', 'too busy over nothing to think of anyone but himself, happy to be the person he is (whom he regards as ideal), a bachelor (but not of arts) and a favourite of the ladies, a man who dresses in excellent taste but with a dash of humour that saves him from the dandiacal'. He was Gerald in and out of costume. Daphne's abiding memory of her father was 'wearing silk pyjamas from Beale and Inman of Bond Street, topped by a very old cardigan full of holes that once belonged to his mother'.

After *The Admirable Crichton* came Jim's *Little Mary* (1903), in which Gerald played the lead, the weak-minded son of the Earl of Carlton. Casting *Peter Pan* in 1904, Jim was bound to think of Gerald for the ineffectual Mr Darling.

But then along came Captain Hook, a 'dark and sinister' man, based on the pirate Swarthy, who famously made Peter Davies walk the plank into the Black Lake. Hook was the menacing side of Jim, deemed 'by those in the know', as the playwright put it, 'to be autobiographical'. Gerald wanted Hook. Jim was not so sure, but finally agreed that he should play *both* Mr Darling and Hook, and, to ease the fit, made the pirate a product of 'a famous public school', whose traditions 'still clung to him like garments'.

The actor in Gerald responded by at last welcoming the dark spirit of Jim 'inside him', his own two-dimensional self gaining a terrifying substance. 'When Hook first paced the quarterdeck,' wrote Daphne, 'children were carried screaming from the stalls.' On another occasion she marvelled at Jim's possession of her father in the role, writing: 'Alas! James Hook, that dark, unhappy man, what pains were endured in his begetting' – so similar to her comment about Sylvia's boys, whose 'possession will remain a memorial to them for all time'.

This was the secret of Jim and Gerald's success on the London stage. So empathic did the relationship between writer and actor become that, as

Mackail put it, Gerald made Jim's plays 'even more like Barrie plays than they were already, though he hated, or thought he hated, everything fanciful and whimsical, and swore by whisky and cold beef and golf'.

The relationship reached a turning-point with Jim's hit play *What Every Woman Knows*, which began its long run in 1908. Jim gave the two leading parts characters (and a situation) which reflected their own: he 'pegged' them on himself and Gerald. Again, Barrie was meddling with alchemic texts.

A controlling character, Maggie Wylie (Jim), writes speeches for susceptible railway porter John Shand (Gerald), which get him elected as a Member of Parliament. Shand is nothing without Wylie, who, unknown to Shand, not only guides his career but loves him. The question is: will Shand (Gerald) return the love of Wylie (Jim), or succumb to the young aristocratic beauty Sybil? (In real life the hopelessly unfaithful Gerald would undoubtedly have chosen Sybil.)

Gerald wrote to his mother after the first night: 'It's all over and we're none of us sorry. It was a highly strung, nervous business, and no good to one's internal arrangements.'

After *What Every Woman Knows* Gerald made an attempt to go his own way. As Mackail wrote, 'there was a long and complete break'. He did not act in a Barrie play for another seven years.

Rejection for Jim again. It was not in his nature to forgive, but he needed Gerald. Arthur Llewelyn Davies had died in 1907. Jim was getting ever closer to the boys. He needed to keep Gerald sweet, needed him on side.

Out of the blue, the theatre manager Frank Curzon offered Gerald an actor-management deal, whereby he would be paid £3,000 a year and receive 25 per cent of any profits. It was an excellent deal, but there was a downside. Gerald could be wiped out if a play failed, for as his eldest daughter Angela said,[4] the du Ms 'were hardly well-to-do people' at the time. Gerald wrote to his mother: 'It's rather a knotty problem,' and he wondered if he could count on Barrie letting him have a play 'later on'.

It is probable that Jim backed Gerald in the venture with Curzon. More than that, it is likely that he put the idea to Curzon in the first place. Jim was rich. The deal was struck as Sylvia died. Could Jim now count on Gerald's tacit approval when he took the boys for his own? Events showed that he could.

I believe that Jim's bankrolling of Gerald was the material foundation of the control he held over him. According to Mackail, there were 'plenty of reasons for mutual gratitude, but plenty, undoubtedly for rankling resentment as well'. Whenever the du Mauriers suffered tragedy, which was often during Jim's tenure, Gerald's star rose. And Gerald never resisted.

Jim had Gerald where he wanted him, so for the whole of Daphne's childhood, even when Gerald was not acting in a Barrie play, Uncle Jim was a fixture. Margaret Forster wrote:

> Barrie was 'Uncle Jim' to the du Maurier girls just as he was to the Llewelyn Davies boys . . . He and Gerald were great friends and he was in the habit of coming home with Gerald to play with the girls in the nursery. Daphne not only liked Uncle Jim but identified totally with his creation of fantasy lives. His imaginary islands and woods, which featured so heavily in the stories he told the children, were real places to her.[5]

Daphne claimed him as 'part of our family life'. To Angela, he was 'almost as a relative', and *Peter Pan* 'practically our birthright. Barrie used to visit us in our nursery and we used to act it for him by the hour. Daphne always bagged Peter, and I was Wendy and Mrs Darling and several of the pirates, Jeanne was Michael and I rather think Eliza. It was quite easy to act all the parts in turn, and we flew from chair to chair and swam as mermaids on the floor, completely without any fear or shyness that Barrie might be sitting on the fender watching us. Daddy, at such times, was probably Hook.'

Evidence of Jim's influence on Daphne's imagination filters through as early as 1911: 'An incident – strangely relevant – comes to mind,' Daphne wrote. Her first governess, Miss Torrance had just arrived. 'She asked me if I could write. I turned to her and said, "Yes, I have written a book."

' "What is it called?"

' "It's called John, in the Wood of the World."

'It was not true, of course. I could barely turn pot-hooks into capitals let alone form sentences to write a book. So why say it? Showing off, no doubt. But what on earth made me choose such a title?'

As early as four, Daphne was making her way through Jim's 'wood of make-believe' in which the du Maurier children swung one by one 'monkey-wise from branch to branch' and 'reached the tree of knowledge', as Jim put it.

In her autobiographical fantasy, *The Parasites* (1949), written nearly forty years later, Daphne, as Celia Delaney ('One of the three people in the novel I know myself to have been'), looks back at the passing of the children's make-believe way of looking at things then:

> Celia shut the door of the children's bedroom behind her. It is true, she said to herself, what we were saying this afternoon; they are different from what we used to be. Our world was one of fantasy. Theirs is reality. They don't pretend. An armchair is always an armchair, to the modern child, never a ship, never a desert island. The patterns on the wall are patterns; not characters whose faces change at dusk. Games like draughts, or ludo, are games of skill and chance; even as bridge and poker are to an adult. Draughts to us were soldiers, ruthless and malignant; and the crowned king on the back line a puffed-up potentate, jumping with horrible power, backwards and forwards, from square to square . . .

As a child, Daphne was always going to be interested in fairies. It was an interest both matured and complicated by being in and around the theatre, the great fantasy generator powered by Gerald and Jim. At six she was furious with a maid who fabricated a fairy ring on the ground and pretended it was real, while 'I knew the light that danced about on the stage [representing Tinkerbell in *Peter Pan*] was really shone by the theatre men.' Angela, three years older, could not countenance such deception, but Daphne understood that these things had to be done for ordinary children. She rather liked the idea of being on the side that manipulated the imaginations of the people she could see sitting there in the front row, because she, a du Maurier, knew when something supernatural was real:

> I have more memories of hanging about backstage as a small child than I have of actually seeing Gerald perform. The scene all set for the next performance was tidy and neat, like an empty room, and then behind the backcloth, out of sight, the moveable set for the next act, which might be a garden, or another room, and somehow this was fascinating, the pretence flowers, the pretence trees, or perhaps a street of houses on a backcloth, and it was like being let into a secret that only the people behind the footlights shared. These others, who sat in front, did not know! In today's language, they were being conned! I enjoyed this.[6]

Daphne's favourite fairy tale was *The Snow Queen*, which tells of a wicked hobgoblin. He is the trickster of myth, who makes a looking-glass which has the power to make everything good or beautiful that is reflected in it almost shrink to nothing, while everything worthless and bad is exaggerated and made worse than ever. The wicked demon laughs till his sides shake when young Kay gets a splinter of the glass in his eye. Only when Kay bursts into tears, and weeps so that the splinter swims out of his eye, does he recognise little Gerda again, and see that he has been away in a different world, a world distorted and distinct from reality.

If Jim was the imaginative guru, Gerald was the lighter, more theatrical influence. A terrific father at this stage, he saw something ridiculous in every sort of situation and had his children in stitches pulling faces behind people's backs. On family holidays, Daphne recalled, he would arrive on the station platform ahead of time, and 'as soon as he caught sight of his daughters, he would act a part, bending suddenly, his hand to his heart, coughing and groaning as one in the last stages of a malignant disease, feigning conversation with an unknown old lady whose back was mercifully turned, and who did not perceive the maniac who gibed at her with trembling finger and incredible grimace.'[7]

To settle disputes between the girls, he might hold an imaginary court, with himself as judge and the girls doubling as plaintiffs, witnesses and jurors, until everybody was having such fun that the original argument was forgotten. Angela, Daphne and Jeanne were their father's captive audience.

Soon, the girls were caught up in the spirit of Jim's Castaway games. Wielding a piece of wood for a sword, Daphne was determined to 'be a boy', using his mantra and emulating her Llewelyn Davies cousins, whom she held in awe, while at night she lay awake like Michael, expecting ghosts to come in through the window.

In *Myself When Young*, her autobiographical fragment, Daphne describes all three du Maurier girls enacting male heroes from history and the novels they were reading. Although Gerald bothered little about their education, said Daphne, 'he encouraged us to read historical novels, and bought us all Alexander Dumas and Harrison Ainsworth and Walter Scott, and then, of course, we pretended to be the various characters in the novels, and sometimes Gerald joined in . . . he was a tremendous feeder of the imagination . . . the actor in him . . .'

In the enactments of *Peter Pan*, Daphne pushed herself forward, leading her sisters in fantasy games: 'I was never myself in those days,' she wrote, 'I was whatever character that I was reading or interested in at the time.'

There were boyish team games also, as there had been for their cousins:

> Gerald taught us to play cricket, and without boasting, I think he taught us rather well! We played with a Harrow Yard ball – the kind they use at the

> school – and he even put up nets to make the practice seem more real. Then he encouraged our imagination to run riot, and we became in turn the members of the Eton and Harrow elevens, all with different personalities! . . .The only one to raise a mild objection was our mother, who said the wear and tear on our pitch spoilt the lawn which I've no doubt it did. But it was even worse in winter because then we played Rugger. Oh, yes, we did! And the dog Brutus joined in, and used to make off with the ball . . .[8]

This world of fantasy play, particularly the enactment of male swash-buckling roles such as Hawkins and d'Artagnan, was seen by Margaret Forster as indicative of a deeply laid male persona in Daphne, but I think the directive and precedent came from Jim's boy-cult. From his earliest contact with Barrie, Gerald was reiterating the Master's mantra – 'be a boy and never grow up'. In 1900, he wrote to his mother, 'Give my love to Sylvia and the boys, and tell 'em it's not worth growing up.' And in 1902, after the Black Lake holiday: 'Thank Sylvia for her dear words of wisdom, and tell the boys to stay young while they can.' Now, a decade on, he was making his daughters do boyish things.

Gerald fell in line with Jim's boy-cult in all that he encouraged his girls to do, and Daphne threw herself into the activities admired by both Jim and Gerald. That it was a pattern imposed from outside, by Jim, one that Gerald acquiesced in but deep down suspected was not best for his middle daughter, was made clear in a touching lament which he wrote for Daphne when she was 10:

> My very slender one
> So brave of heart, but delicate of will,
> So careful not to wound, never kill,
> My tender one –
> Who seems to live in Kingdoms of her own
> In realms of joy
> Where heroes young and old
> In climates hot and cold
> Do deeds of daring and much fame
> And she knows she could do the same
> If only she'd been born a boy.
> And sometimes in the silence of the night
> I wake and think perhaps my darling's right

And that she should have been,
And, if I'd had my way,
She would have been, a boy.

My very slender one
So feminine and fair, so fresh and sweet,
So full of fun and womanly deceit.
My tender one
Who seems to dream her life away alone.
A dainty girl
But always well attired
And loves to be admired
Wherever she may be, and wants
To be the being who enchants
Because she has been born a girl,
And sometimes in the turmoil of the day
I pause, and think my darling may
Be one of those who will
For good or ill
Remain a girl for ever and be still
A girl.

Daphne suffered many years of heartache sorting out the confusion of gender and imagination in 'being a boy', the concept at the centre of Barrie's boy-cult.

For Daphne's grandfather, Kicky, boyishness was the quintessence of the Romantic ideal, Little Billee's artistic sensitivity. It went with 'a quickness, a keenness, a delicacy of perception in matters of form and colour, a mysterious facility and felicity of execution, a sense of all that was sweet and beautiful in nature, and a ready power of expressing it'. Boy was 'the secret of eternal youth', irrespective of age or gender (both Trilby and Mary, Duchess of Towers are boyish). It was liberation from 'the regular action of the world', an ability to be a true-dreamer and to possess a psychic 'sixth sense'.

Barrie traded on Trilby's boyishness in his seduction of Sylvia, writing to her that Sylvia herself was 'very very nearly being a boy'. And of course Tommy was 'a boy', and there were times 'when Grizel looked like a boy'. And Peter Pan was a '*demon* boy', having, like Jim himself, made 'the great mistake'. George and Michael were literally boys, and they had that special aura endemic to du Maurier boyishness. Now Daphne, as 'the being who enchants', was a more natural boy (in Kicky's sense) even than Sylvia, but as Gerald's poem shows, he doesn't understand what this means. Gerald gets stuck in the gender politics and makes his daughter long to be masculine.

Boy is what Uncle Jim, physically and emotionally impotent, was after, and would never know. In his pursuit of it, he brought many of the du Mauriers to destruction. Here, in Daphne's early immersion in his boy-cult we have a glimpse of the emergence of a masculine self-image that would be with her for decades hence – a real desire *to be a boy*, which would in the years following be encouraged ten-fold in the 'special relationship' (as Angela described it) with her father, again under the tutelage of Uncle Jim.

Only in 1954, in the company of Peter Davies, having begun to 'chimney sweep' her mind of Jim and Gerald, did Daphne realise that she could be a boy in her grandfather's sense without ceding her femininity, that boy meant what Kicky had meant it to mean in *Trilby* – her fantasy side, her creative side, the part of her that was a dreamer.

Earlier she had devastated her own daughter, when Flavia reached puberty, by telling her that now she was 'no longer really boyish, but just a boring old girl.'[9] Once she saw Jim's boy-cult for what it was, she was able to write to Flavia that being 'madly boyish . . . has a lot to do with my writing'.

Between 1907 and 1915 many of the du Mauriers died or were killed: Arthur, 1907; Sylvia, 1910; Trixy, 1913; Emma, 1914; George and Guy, 1915. Of Kicky's children only Gerald and May remained. Gerald was now head of the family, and as after Sylvia's death, family tragedy marked a rise in his fortunes.

In 1915 Viola Tree, daughter of the actor producer, Sir Herbert Beerbohm Tree,* and one of Jim's regular cast, took Gerald to view a spectacular house, Cannon Hall on Hampstead Heath. It was close to his boyhood home, New Grove House.

* There is a line of continuity from Kicky through Jim, Gerald and Daphne drawn by the Trees. Beerbohm Tree produced Kicky's *Trilby* on stage and backed Jim's application for membership of the Garrick, which was also Gerald's club. Tree's wife, the distinguished actress Helen Maud Holt, worked with Gerald on Jim's plays, *What Every Woman Knows* (1908) and *Shall We Join the Ladies?* (1921). Their daughter Viola was friends with Jim, and with Gerald, and his family, especially Daphne. The film director Carol Reed, who fell in love with Daphne, was an illegitimate son of Tree.

Nineteen huge windows looked across a hard terrace and broad sweeping lawns. There were, in addition, two Queen Anne cottages in the grounds. Inside the main house, a huge staircase swept through three floors. Daphne was fascinated by the paintings that Gerald bought to decorate the massive walls: 'sad King Charles in profile came on the right-hand wall as one started to climb the stairs, and above him I remember, stretching the whole width of the wall, was a great battle scene, which would be enacted by us children again and again.'[10]

In the same year as Cannon Hall was purchased, Gerald accepted the lead role in *A Kiss for Cinderella*, the first role written for him by Jim for six years. It was no coincidence that with Gerald back on Jim's team, Gerald's lifestyle soared. He even took delivery of a Rolls-Royce. 'Largesse was distributed liberally and without hesitation,' Daphne recalled. There were many servants, holidays abroad (Algiers, Cannes, Monte Carlo, a villa in Italy) and stunning parties. Sundays, Gerald's one day off, were extra special, as Angela wrote –

> If it was summer people came to lunch who afterwards would stay on to play tennis, remaining to tea and often to supper. If it was winter the lunch would be more serious perhaps, followed by a nap and sometimes people to supper followed by bridge or bezique.
>
> The summer was by far the greatest fun. . . the Shakespeare border a riot of colour . . . tennis with John Drinkwater and the 'Bunny' Austins . . . Irene Ravensdale, Mary Newcomb, Madeleine Seymour . . . names, names that mean nowt to me. Tennis would be played for hours, with new Slazengers for every set (one of Daddy's many extravagances), and the silent grey-alpaca-clad maids brought terrific spreads of cakes and cucumber sandwiches and iced coffee and tea, to the terrace.
>
> They were wonderful Sundays; I loved them, Daphne couldn't bear them . . . Cannon Hall Sundays were frankly anathema to her.[11]

Daphne didn't like the loud, gushing, theatrical world that now enveloped them, not because she was shy, although she appeared to be, but because these actor friends, with a few exceptions such as Gladys Cooper and Viola Tree, were artificial.

Angela was gregarious, and destined to 'come out' as a débutante. Daphne was an introvert, withdrawn, highly imaginative. 'Daphne was always pretty and became quite lovely at ten . . .' wrote Angela. 'Luckily I never realised I was so plain.' Yet it was Angela who fancied she could make a career in the theatre as an actress; she would play Wendy to Gladys Cooper's Peter Pan in 1923-4 and to Dorothy Dickson's Peter in 1924-5, although not inappropriately for the less imaginative sister her flying harness broke and she crashed to the stage, hurting herself badly.

Meanwhile, Jim and Gerald were preparing something special for Daphne. They had been working together on the script of a new play, *Dear Brutus*. The key act (Act II) reveals Gerald in a magic wood as Will Dearth. The script challenges the value of Dearth's love for his wife and offers him instead a highly questionable relationship with a fantasy daughter. At the end of the act, this fantasy daughter is cruelly written out as a 'might-have-been',* a figment of his imagination.

Early in the play, the daughter is terrified that people will want to take her Daddy away from her, because 'things that are too beautiful can't last'. In her Daddy's arms she wonders whether she is 'sometimes stranger than other people's daughters'. She can't countenance the image of her Daddy wandering about the world without her. She thinks 'Men need daughters.' Her father agrees that 'Daughters are the thing', because 'by the time a son is ten you can't even take him on your knee'. The best time in a father's life is the year before his daughter 'puts her hair up', when a girl turns 18. The girl counters that there is one time better, 'The year she does put up her hair.' She then puts her hair up and asks him, 'What do you think? Will I do?' Dearth's eyes fall on the young woman 'that is to be', with 'the change in his voice falling clammy on her', as Jim's stage direction reads. Smitten, Dearth speaks 'with an odd tremor', and his daughter manhandles him, 'bumping into him and round him and over him', saying he will be sick of her with her hair up before he has done with her. Then she teases and tantalises him with the thought of one day being in love with a boy.

Absent is a father's natural love for his daughter. Instead, their dialogue has a quasi-erotic ring. Daddy is controlling; he has taught her all she knows, as a master teaches his dog how to catch a biscuit in its mouth. He even takes credit for her beauty: 'I wore out the point of my little finger over that dimple.'† The daughter's independence threatens to cheat her

* Jim despised 'might-have-beens'. In his memoir, *The Greenwood Hat*, he writes: 'Sadder far than any word was the tragic story told in the phrase "I Might Have Been" . . . It implies fault on your part; and what so bitter in this vale of tears as the consciousness that you suffer for your own error, your own blindness . . .'

† Daphne's dimple on her chin was a childhood feature.

father of something that is by rights his. Daddy holds ultimate power over her.

But as the child recedes from his imagination, he leaves her in the wood on her own, and she cries:

> Daddy, come back; I don't want to be a might-have-been.

As the curtain fell, Daphne ran from her seat in tears. None of Barrie's alchemical texts had ever had so immediate a reaction.

'First nights played a big part in our life,' Angela recalled, 'not only Daddy's but those of our many friends.' So, when 10-year-old Daphne attended the first night of *Dear Brutus*, there was nothing unusual or stressful about the event. Yet, when she recognised herself and her relationship with Gerald and watched his cruel disposal of her, 'I had to be led sobbing from the box.'

There is no doubt that Gerald's special relationship with Daphne was the focus of the play. Sixty years later she could still exclaim, in an interview with BBC Radio: 'I was his daughter. It absolutely finished me!'

Why did Jim do this to Daphne, and, more to the point, why did Gerald let him? Jim and Gerald must have discussed the play at great length. But Act II takes Gerald's relationship with Daphne into very dubious territory. It is the equivalent of Jim's bed scene with George (as 'David') in *The Little White Bird*, except that this plot involves two men, a writer and an actor, and their victim is a girl.

It was a feature of Gerald's particular style of acting that he was unusually susceptible to Jim's notion of alchemic texts. Daphne called her father the founder of 'the naturalistic school'. Gerald *became* his stage characters, and often brought them home with him, which made him vulnerable to the influence of the man who wrote his lines.

Suddenly, the slapstick father-figure who had been Gerald was joined by a new Gerald, who began sharing tales of his sexual conquests with his young daughters. Naturally, the girls joined in: 'Who's the latest in the stable, and what's the form this week?' Daphne remembered jeering, without a thought for her mother. It became known as 'the stable game', admitted Angela, and it 'could only be played amongst children who had Gerald as a father . . . Sometimes the conversation would be strangely bawdy.' If Mo heard what was going on, she would stamp her stick on the floor of the room above.

This 'unorthodox game' had a deep effect on Daphne, distorting her values and warping her sense of humour, so she wrote in *Gerald* (1934), her biography of her father. But the game was only a part of what was going on.

In time, Gerald and Daphne followed to the letter the suggestively incestuous relationship prescribed for them by Jim in *Dear Brutus*. Neighbour and family friend Bunny Austin told journalist and biographer Michael Thornton: '[Gerald] couldn't keep his hands off her. It was quite embarrassing at times.' Thornton claims that Daphne told him in 1965: 'We crossed the line, and I allowed it.'[12] But in a rare extract from her diaries, written at the time, Daphne admits only that she engaged in 'a sort of incest' with her father, her feelings 'tragic' because they never were fulfilled.

However far it went in fact rather than fantasy, the point is that her 'Daddy complex', as Daphne came to refer to it, the main destructive drive in her life and work, was conceived in her by Uncle Jim – *Dear Brutus* the catalyst, her father the instrument of Jim's power over her.

One immediate effect was the impact that it had on Daphne's relationship with her mother. 'I could never feel quite sure of [my mother],' she wrote, 'sensing some sort of disapproval in her attitude towards me. Could it be that...she resented the ever-growing bond between D and myself?'

So significant to Daphne was this alienation from her mother that she considered that it encouraged her more intimate relationships with women. In January 1948, in a letter to Ellen Doubleday, one of the three great female loves of her life, Daphne considered that her desire to be with Ellen was an attempt to recover the mother love which had been a casualty of her relationship with her father.

One might argue that Uncle Jim cannot be held responsible, that Gerald would have seduced Daphne even without his encouragement, but there was no suggestion of incest prior to *Dear Brutus*, while after the play Gerald's intense relationship with his daughter proceeded in parallel with Jim's with Michael, already a recognisable pattern in the Barrie boy-cult.

Moreover we have seen how Jim held Gerald in his power and how Jim used his novels and plays as instruments of power first over Sylvia and George, and more recently over Michael. Literary alchemy was his métier and method, his fantasy works drawing on real lives, his imagination in reality transforming them.

Dear Brutus worked its dark magic on Gerald and Daphne, as her reaction to it at the first night suggested it would. Everything was bound up with the imagination. All the du Mauriers captivated by Jim lived their lives within his imagination, losing their souls to him thereby. For Daphne alone the Faustian payload was her success as a writer.

Incest is, as would be expected, given the importance of the real-life emotional trigger in Daphne's fiction, a persistent theme. The saddest, most explicit reference is in her novella, 'A Borderline Case',[13] where the daughter has sexual intercourse with the father. But perhaps the most troubling occurs in *The Scapegoat* (1957), a novel in which, as Daphne wrote to a friend, she was trying to assuage 'the sins of the family'. In an effort 'to give myself a penance to fit the crime', the daughter fetches 'a small leather dog-whip with a knotted end', slips off her nightgown and lashes herself across her back and shoulders – 'There was no feint about it.' She then asks her father to do it for her. The daughter is thereafter in control of the father. She teases and tantalises him, raising his desire to impossible heights. Daphne was the victim, the scapegoat of the title.

The dynamic of her relationship with Gerald is most clearly laid bare in another novel, *The Progress of Julius* (1933). I am not the first to point this out. Daphne's biographer Margaret Forster concedes: 'What makes [*Julius*] startling is its clear autobiographical content.'

Julius, a French émigré in London, rages to possess his daughter Gabriel, who reminds him of his dead father (as Daphne reminded Gerald of Kicky).

> It seemed to Julius Levy that the discovery of Gabriel was the most exciting thing that had ever come to him in life. It was stimulating, it was crude; because she was unknown to him though part of him the realisation of her was like a sudden secret adventure, tremendously personal to them both, intimate in the same absorbing fashion as a disease is intimate, belonging to no one else in heaven and earth, egotistical and supremely self-obsessing.

When Julius sees his 15-year-old daughter playing her grandfather's flute he is overcome 'by an odd taste in his mouth, and a sensation in mind and body that was shameful and unclean'. He cannot resist asking her, 'Do you like me?' Her evasive reply enrages him. Yet Julius and Gabriel never have sex. They have an 'adventure' together, which is 'secret', 'tremendously personal', until Julius drowns her.

The secret is something passed down from the grandfather to the granddaughter. In the novel it is the ability to play the flute, a neat side reference to Pan pipes perhaps, but clearly the du Maurier secret is the reference: 'You play the flute like my father would have played it if he'd sold his soul to Satan,' says Julius (the father) to Gabriel (the daughter). We are to believe that Daphne inherited a similar secret from Gerald's father, Kicky.

> To Julius with his eyes shut it was like the song that Père had sung to him as a child and the whisper that led to the secret city, but this was another whisper and another city, this was not the enchanted land beyond the white clouds, so melancholy, so beautiful, forever unattainable land of promise unfulfilled – for there was a sudden swoop and a turn and a plunge into the bowels of the secret earth, heart beating, wings battered and scorched, and this new discovered city was one that opened and gave itself up to him – there were eyes that welcomed and hands that beckoned, all mingled in extravagant confusion of colour and scent and ecstasy.
>
> 'Do you like that, Papa?' said Gabriel.

The incest is bound up in the inheritance of the family secret. And this is how it was for Gerald and Daphne in their secret city.

In taking Cannon Hall, Gerald had returned to the scenes of his own childhood. All around were places that held memories of Kicky and Peter Ibbetson. Daphne – aged 10 and at her most impressionable – became imbued with it all. And Gerald was happy to be swept up by the intensity with which his favourite daughter rose to the seduction.

> Daddy would take me up to New Grove House where he had lived as a boy. 'There's the studio,' he'd say. 'That's where Papa drew every day . . . And there behind the wall is the small garden. You've seen the picture he drew of us, pretending to be trains, with Aunt Trixy leading, and myself the baby at the end.' Later he had written three novels, of which the first, *Peter Ibbetson*, was to exert a great influence on my life.

Time and again Daphne would relive the walk on the Heath, which Kicky had so often undertaken with Gerald as a boy. She enjoyed doing what Gerald had done, sitting in the crook of a tree where he had sat, walking along the walk that had reminded Kicky of Passy, of the trees in the Bois de Boulogne, of the mare d'Auteuil, of his childhood, which of course was Peter Ibbetson's childhood too. 'Here was a new perspective,' she wrote. 'His past was my past too . . .'

She read *Peter Ibbetson*, learned about dreaming true, was encouraged by Jim to play the island game like Peter Ibbetson and Mary, and, at length, was given to believe that she might have inherited Kicky's secret ability to dream true and realise the 'sixth sense', which had been the source of Peter's ecstasy in the novel.

Daphne found it 'haunting, queer' to know that Kicky's past was her own past, and it didn't take much to believe that she was the one in the family to inherit his secret ability, his 'gift from the Devil'. Originally, it was thought that this was Sylvia's inheritance, on account of Sylvia being given the name Jocelyn, which tied her to Barty Jocelyn, the hero of Kicky's novel *The Martian*, where he discussed who would 'carry him' into the future. In her Introduction to *The Martian* written in 1947, Daphne played with the suggestion that Sylvia's younger sister May was the model for Marty, the legatee in the novel. But no-one was less like Marty than Aunt May. Marty 'with her boyish ways, her striped skirt, her fisherman's cap on the back of her head, and her passion for making up stories about shipwrecks' was Daphne, and it was Daphne who in the 1920s was photographed with the fisherman's cap on the back of her head, and who wrote all about boats and shipwrecks in her first novel, *The Loving Spirit*.

Here was serious fantasy material for Uncle Jim to conjure with. Here too were all the ingredients of a classic steering strategy, which, according to forensic psychologist Dr Keith Ashcroft, 'characteristically involves destabilising a victim and getting them to accept the controller's novel, often warped version of reality'.

Make your victim feel vulnerable by exploiting a relationship which means a lot to her (Daphne's relationship with Gerald). Follow this with her removal to an environment which favours her immersion in the story you want her to believe and which will empower her (the move to Cannon Hall, centre of the Ibbetson/du Maurier myth). Separate the victim from someone close who may not approve of the controller, in this case Mo, who was a conventional wife and did not approve of plays about her children that made them cry, or any other sort of suspicious investment in Daphne by Jim. Whether or not this steering strategy was actually contrived, these things occurred and the environment was set for Daphne's initiation.

While there is a humiliating taboo on incest in the eyes of the world, in a fantasy or cult it can be empowering. With a cool and remote air and mask of indifference, like Trilby, and like Sylvia, Daphne was definitely empowered by the du Maurier myth. She became cynical about the real world. School friends of Jeanne complained that she was 'haughty and rather fierce'. Meeting her for the first time, adults felt 'summed-up and judged, and definitely discarded', an attitude encouraged by Jim, who himself held ordinary people with 'a cold stare of disdain'. Daphne admitted at the time: 'I only think of myself and pity anyone who likes me',[14] but secretly she felt, like Gabriel in *The Progress of Julius*, 'scornful of the pitiful world . . . apart, taller than before . . . someone who lived with dreams, and beauty and enchantment, who conquered by silence, who dwelt in a secret city'.

*

From 1920 to 1922, between the ages of 13 and 15 Daphne pretended to be Eric Avon. There was something a little odd about Eric, and yet he was strangely familiar. Looking back on her childhood, Daphne described him as a man of action and adventure, but 'there were no psychological depths to Eric Avon. He just shone at everything.' Eric is Gerald, or rather Jim's vision of Gerald, the empty hero, outwardly impressive, ever ignorant of deeper issues, a role which he often played for the Master on stage.

This fantasy persona had such an impact on Daphne that 'Eric remained in my unconscious to emerge in later years – though in quite a different guise – as the narrator of the five novels I was to write in the first person singular, masculine gender* . . . each of my five characters depended, for reassurance, on a male friend older than himself.'

In modern culture, in the film *Star Wars*, Luke Skywalker is an example of Eric, the hero who must be guided by the older, wiser Obi-Wan Kenobi, in order to confront and overcome the dark side in Darth Vader. When Daphne played Eric, she was identifying with her father, and at the same time engaging in a fantasy expression of Gerald's relationship with Jim.

As Professor Auerbach notes,[15] not only do all Daphne's novels in which there is a male narrator proclaim this 'paradigm of intimacy', as she calls it, between two men – the weak narrator (the Gerald figure with whom the author identifies) 'bound to an elusive male leader' (the Jim figure) – but this duo always make a girl (the Daphne figure) their victim. Auerbach did not identify Barrie as the elusive male leader, but darkly she points out the inimical nature of the paradigm, in which the 'incest' and Daphne's mythic initiation did indeed subsist.

* *I'll Never Be Young Again*, *My Cousin Rachel*, *The Scapegoat*, *The Flight of the Falcon*, and *The House on the Strand*.

A good example of the relationship is in her second novel *I'll Never Be Young Again* (1932), where Jake's power over Dick is Jim's over Gerald in reality. Daphne wrote in the first person as Dick describing the older, wiser, invasive Jake:

> He had an intuition of my every mood. He joined in with them as though he were part of myself. Even my thoughts were not hidden from him. We were bound henceforth as comrades and I loved him and he understood.

Dick (who, like Gerald, lives in the shadow of his famous father) moves from a close friendship with Jake (the Jim figure) to a sadistic love affair with a girl called Hesta (the Daphne figure).

In her biography of Daphne, Margaret Forster observes the special intimacy of Dick and Jake and describes Gerald and Jim's relationship almost too perfectly.

> There is an implicit though never realised homosexual relationship between them.

CHAPTER THREE

Michael's suicide

By 1918, Michael was bursting to break free and live his own life apart from Jim. He had shown talent as a painter at school, and expressed a desire after leaving Eton to follow his grandfather's example and go to Paris to study art. But Uncle Jim's plan for him was Oxford, and Michael's idea was not even given consideration.

In August 1918, Jim took Michael and Nico on holiday in Scotland, and his letter to Elizabeth, the estranged wife of E. V. Lucas* tells of Michael's despondency:

> All the highlands of Scotland are denuded of their young men [due to the war], there are scarcely any tourists, and we have this big hotel to ourselves – indeed we seem to be almost the only people in Glengarry. I had to knit my teeth to come away at all and it is uphill work to make the days pass. Michael feels the dreariness and the sadness of it too and we flounder about my lochs and streams with an effort. I am out with them all day, carrying the coats . . . I'll try to stay in Scotland four weeks, but we may make tracks south before then . . . Now I'm off to read *War and Peace*.

On 17 January 1919, after passing the entrance examination, Michael went up to Oxford for the first time. Jim wrote again to Elizabeth:

> Michael went off today to Oxford and Christchurch full of suppressed excitement. He has a very nice panelled sitting-room, with furniture that would make you shiver. He hopes to be able to put in pieces from Campden Hill in place of it.

* A long-term friend of Barrie, one of the inner circle. According to R. G. G. Price's *A History of Punch*, 'his polished and gentlemanly essayist's persona concealed a cynical club-man – very bitter about men and politics – [with] the finest pornographic library in London.'

At Christ Church Michael was considered 'very reserved', artistically gifted, impressionable. Robert Boothby described him as 'very sensitive and emotional, but he concealed both to a large extent'. Lucas noted his alienation from the world, calling him 'an elvish spectator', something of an analyst of the pitiful world like Barrie, and yet no one spoke of Michael as cynical. On the contrary, Nico remarked on his genuine consideration for others. It seems that, unlike Uncle Jim, Michael was capable of disinterested love and compassion.

Among the few close friends he made was Rupert Buxton, who did not come up until the following year. Rupert Buxton was the youngest son of Sir Thomas Fowell Victor Buxton, the 4th Baronet Buxton, who had died in 1919. In April 1920 Rupert Buxton wrote to his mother that he and Michael had had a working holiday in Surrey, though precious little work had been done. On the last two days they had walked from Chichester to Beachy Head along the South Downs, managing thirty-five miles a day.

> I have never known such a walk for views – southward over the hills to the sea and northward over the whole expanse of Sussex & Surrey on a narrow grassy plain with steep sides covered with primroses, violets, cowslips & wood anemones. A most inspiring place to walk on. I can well understand the enthusiasm of Belloc & Kipling for the 'great hills of the south country' and the patriotism that they breed.

Buxton had been head boy at Harrow. But on 4 December 1918, he had found his way into the pages of *The Times* in a most mysterious set of circumstances. A letter, unsigned and unstamped, had been left for him at his house at Harrow. It read:

> You will be well advised to walk up Peterborough-hill alone at 10 minutes past 7 on Sunday night. Your help is needed.

Peterborough-hill lay only a few yards from Buxton's house. He sent a note to his housemaster, Archer Vassall, enclosing the letter and informing him that he was keeping the appointment. He had then disappeared. Vassall and another master had watched the road for some time, but nothing was seen of the boy. The police were called in after he failed to appear on the last train from London.

The following day, a Monday, another letter, in the same hand as the first, was, according to *The Times,* received at Buxton's home, 'stating that he was safe, but that his brains were needed. The letter concluded – "Ill if he refuses, well if he agrees."'

The next anyone heard was from Buxton himself. A telegram from Newcastle, signed 'Rupert', was received by his school and by his father stating that he would shortly be returning to London.

On 9 January 1919, a second, shorter article appeared in the same newspaper, following a statement about his earlier disappearance made by Buxton's father to the effect that 'his son had, in the doctor's opinion, been suffering from overstrain resulting in some measure from preparing for a scholarship examination at Oxford . . . He is already much better and it is confidently expected that a short period of rest will completely restore his health.' There then followed a quote from the headmaster, the Reverend Lionel Ford, about the qualities Buxton had exercised as head boy at Harrow, in particular his 'high-mindedness, loyalty, tact, and consideration for others'.

This was no idle puff. Buxton was an unusual and enlightened boy, and, like Michael, a poet. As head boy, he never beat other boys: this was unheard of in any English public school at the time. He also had a social conscience and even as a schoolboy faced up to the inequalities and prejudices of the world, going out of his way to make friends with 'strange out-of-the-way people such as pavement artists and street hawkers', as one Harrovian put it, and going into London for days at a time on philanthropic quests, one of which may have been connected to his mysterious disappearance in December 1918. He was sensitive to anything or anyone at all artificial, and was a lover of nature. All of this he combined with an outsize ego. Buxton was quite a handful even at 18, and some of his qualities were clearly shared by Michael.

It was Boothby who said of Michael that 'he had a profound effect on virtually everyone who came into contact with him', and a colleague at Harrow said of Buxton, 'Humble people always thought him a kind of saint as soon as they looked at him.'

However, according to Boothby, 'Buxton was dark, gloomy, saturnine, with an almost suicidal streak in him. I remember Michael asked me, "Why don't you like my being friends with Rupert Buxton?" And I said "The answer to that is – I have a feeling of doom about him."'

Boothby's insight into Buxton would be entirely consistent with the character of one so young and inexperienced emotionally taking on the sins of the world. Boothby made it clear that it was never a homosexual relationship between Rupert and Michael, and he would have known. But there is no shadow of a doubt that they became close, and I wonder whether it was Michael's gloom that was fed to Rupert. What Boothby is telling us is that something was going on and that it was melancholy and abnormal. Boothby also had an insight into Jim and Michael:

> It was an unhealthy relationship. I don't mean homosexual, I mean in a mental sense. It was morbid, and it went beyond the bounds of ordinary affection . . . I thought there was something twisted about [Jim].

Boothby had often visited Michael at Barrie's Adelphi Terrace flat, and on one occasion recoiled from the scene as if it were the lair of the Devil:

> There was a morbid atmosphere about it. I remember going there one day and it almost overwhelmed me, and I was glad to get away. We were going back to Oxford in Michael's car, and I said, 'It's a relief to get away from that flat,' and he said, 'Yes, it is.'

One is aware above all of the unnatural nature of Jim's relationship with Michael, and that Jim was obsessed with death.

Around this time Roger Senhouse introduced Michael to friends of his in the Bloomsbury Group. Here there was similar concern. He never seemed to relax at parties at Garsington Manor, and Dora Carrington wrote to Lytton Strachey of Michael's moodiness –

> Perhaps that is just the gloom of finding Barrie one's keeper for life.

Rupert Buxton decided to sort the situation out. He invited Barrie to dinner, alone, just the two of them. That must have taken some guts, and was characteristic of the young man. There is a rather sickening letter from Jim to Buxton's mother: 'Rupert treated me quite differently from any other of my various boys' friends. They were always polite and edged away from me, as of a different generation, but he took for granted that Michael's friend should be mine also . . . I daresay the two of them chuckled over it [the dinner], for they could both be very gay. They were either wildly gay or very serious as they walked together to Sandford [where they drowned].'

If Buxton had planned a sociable evening, wouldn't Michael have been included? More likely Buxton invited Barrie to dinner alone because he wanted to say things to him that would have upset Michael. Michael was drawing away from Jim, but Jim was hanging on. Buxton wanted Michael to get away. There the critical tensions lay. But Jim was in control. As with Sylvia, as with George, he threatened to be Michael's keeper for life.

In August 1920 Barrie took a house on Eilean Shona, a small island off the coast of Argyll. Michael arrived with Nico and some friends, among them Senhouse, but notably not Buxton.

The process of rejection had begun. Rejection of Barrie always went hand in hand with danger. Barrie wrote of Michael, in 'Neil and Tintinnabulum', that he had begun receding 'farther from my ken down the road which hurries him from me . . . he no longer needs me as he did, and he will go on needing me less'. Of the boys and young men on Eilean Shona, he wrote to Cynthia Asquith, who was by now his secretary:

> We are a very Etonian household and there is endless shop talked, during which I am expected to be merely a ladler out of food. If I speak to one he shudders politely then edges away.

In 1975 this was reprinted in an article by Alison Lurie,[1] which infuriated Nico, for Lurie went on to say that the boys, 'one by one, as they grew older, began to find his [Barrie's] games and jokes embarrassing, and to resent his presence in the household – an embarrassment and resentment complicated by the knowledge that this odd little man who looked like an aged child was paying the tradesmen's bills and their fees at Eton and Oxford'.

Of course, Barrie's hold over the boys was more than his generosity with expenses. His morbid streak, and its roots in a neurosis and death fixation, was being fed to Michael as if through an umbilical cord. And it was true. Michael *was* trying to get away, and Barrie knew he was: 'The new life is building seven walls around him. Are such of his moves in the game as I can follow merely an expert's kindness to an indifferent player?'[2]

Michael wrote two poems on Eilean Shona. One, 'The Island of Sleep', tells of the opportunity so remote and time-lost a place afforded to hear 'in murmurs of a woodland stream Arcadian incantations of resurgent Pan'. The word 'incantations' is nearly illegible, but the rest of it is clear. Pan, the Greek god, ran with Dionysus, the god of ecstasy, on the mountains of Arcadia. 'Yet will not touch again thy perfumed shore . . . to tread the foot-prints of old deities, So thou do not send echoes to remind of those sweet pipes, and charm him from his kind.'

Michael is saying goodbye to the Barrie boy-cult. And he pictures it as linked to some sort of ancient religion – 'foot-prints of old deities', pagan deities, a Satanic reference. Islands and Satanic references run through the writings of both Jim and Kicky.

The other poem is the more literary of the two –

Throned on a cliff serene Man saw the sun
hold a red torch above the farthest seas,
and the fierce island pinnacles put on
in his defence their sombre panoplies;
Foremost the white mists eddied, trailed and spun
like seekers, emulous to clasp his knees,
till all the beauty of the scene seemed one,
led by the secret whispers of the breeze.

The sun's torch suddenly flashed upon his face
and died; and he sat content in subject night
and dreamed of an old dead foe that had sought and found him;
a beast stirred boldly in his resting place;
And the cold came; Man rose to his master-height,
shivered, and turned away; but the mists were round him.

Nico recalled Michael showing him this poem, just after he'd written it, 'and my saying words to the effect that I liked it but I hadn't a clue what it was all about! Which I remember rather disappointed him as he thought it was "so simple". I've never tried to think who was his "old dead foe", just taken it to be imaginary.'[3]

The old dead foe – I am led to believe – is 'the same nameless enemy', a Mephistophelean spirit, that pursued Michael in his nightmares as a boy. The 'seekers' are what in *Tommy and Grizel* Barrie himself calls 'little gods', but in truth they are devils because they enjoy the cruel games he plays with Grizel's heart, and when Tommy is about to offer poor Grizel marriage, 'He heard the voices of his little gods screaming to him to draw back.'

> Did I never tell you of my little gods? I so often emerged triumphant from my troubles, and so undeservedly, that I thought I was especially looked after by certain tricky spirits in return for the entertainment I gave them. My little gods I called them, and we had quite a bowing acquaintance. But you see, at the critical moment they flew away laughing.

Tommy's little gods, the dissolute trickster people of his imagination, do not always help him; they make him as 'miserable as the damned' when he does the right thing by Grizel, which suggests that he is less in control than he seems.

Voices in the head are an occupational hazard of one who lives with multiple personalities and cannot distinguish what is real from what is unreal.

Barrie was convinced that he was attended by a malignant devil, as in 1922 he explained to an audience of uncomprehending students at St Andrews University. He read them Michael's poem, but without naming Michael:

> Spirits must sometimes walk St Andrews. I do not mean the ghosts of queens or prelates, but one that keeps step, as soft as snow, with some poor student. He sometimes catches sight of it. That is why his fellows can never quite touch him, their best beloved; he half knows something of which they know nothing – the secret that is hidden in the face of the Mona Lisa. As I see him, life is so beautiful to him that its proportions are monstrous. Perhaps his childhood may have been overful of gladness; they don't like that. If the seekers were kind he is the one for whom the flags of his college would fly one day. But the seeker I am thinking of is unfriendly, and so our student is 'the lad that will never be old'. He often gaily forgets, and thinks he has slain his foe by daring him, like him who, dreading water, was always the first to leap into it. One can see him serene, astride a Scotch cliff, singing to the sun the farewell thanks of a boy . . . If there is any of you here so rare that the seekers have taken an ill-will to him, as to the boy who wrote those lines, I ask you to be careful.

This was the nightmare world – the Satanic dark side of J. M. Barrie – from which Michael was endeavouring to escape when he walked with Rupert Buxton to Sandford that day in April 1921.

A push-and-pull series of escape attempts led up to it. On 9 September 1920, Michael wrote to Robert Dundas, Tutor and Senior Censor of Christ Church:

> Your emotions will not, I know, be violently stirred, when I say I am not going up to Oxford again . . . I feel very much the young fool; but wish to be obstinate into the bargain, even if the first step I take for myself be into the deepest of deep ditches . . . I do incidentally intend to quit education for some trade.

Six days later he wrote again to Dundas, asking whether after all he could return to Oxford: 'I dislike always bringing up the whole question of my existence before you. Would you come to lunch here, say, Friday?' Then: 'I'm sorry to be a bother; but should I possibly be allowed to creep into the House again in October, into some obscure corner?'

On 28 September he sent a telegram to Dundas –

> Have become moral and ask leave to return to work but is this possible as have opened no book this vacation. Query collections await verdict meanwhile starting to read.

In the Easter 1921 vac he went with Rupert Buxton on a reading trip to Corfe Castle in Dorset, staying at a little inn by the sea. Jim appeared and left with Michael for London.

Thursday, 19 May was a warm summer's day during Eights Week. Edward Marjoribanks, a fellow undergraduate of Christ Church, saw Buxton and Michael around noon. Michael said he was going to have a swim in Sandford Pool in the afternoon, and would not be able to watch the Eights. Buxton did not say anything. The two young men left the city shortly after two o'clock.

> The pool under Sandford lasher, just behind the lock, is a very good place to drown yourself in.

So wrote Jerome K. Jerome in *Three Men in a Boat* in 1889. Other fatalities have been recorded there. On one occasion a Christ Church student was drowned while attempting to 'shoot the lashers' (the weir) in a boat. John Beckly, a son of the lock keeper, was drowned while taking fish from a trap 'on the big lasher'.

Sandford Pool, an idyllic spot a few miles south from Oxford on the way to Radley, lies on a stretch of water which is these days out of bounds to the inquisitive tourist, but can be reached by walking across the fields. Entry upon the weir or lasher that separates two pools is prevented by high fencing, but the pools, high and low, are open enough, and quite beautiful and tranquil in spring and summer.

The view of the jury at the Coroner's Inquest was that Michael was accidentally drowned while bathing, and that Rupert lost his life trying to rescue him.

However, the jury did not visit the site, and the Dean of Christ Church was not only called to serve on the jury, but was appointed foreman of it. This is not just bad form, it is irregular, because a verdict of accidental death rather than one of suicide was clearly in the interest of the College.

Additionally, the state of mind of the two dead boys was never a matter of analysis at the inquest. Yet the potential for suicide is high in two young men as idealistic, mentally rigorous, poetically romantic and as doom-laden as Rupert and Michael.

The verdict states that one boy was trying to rescue the other, which suggests that the one needing to be rescued was in difficulties, which implies accidental death. But, as Peter wrote to Dolly on 1 June 1921: 'As a matter of fact, though the coroner chose to express a definite opinion, there was not the slightest evidence as to which of them was trying to help the other.' No evidence was given at the inquest of any rescue attempt. An eyewitness told of hearing one shout, which could as easily have been a shout of triumph as of panic. What the witnesses actually saw was two men holding each other, not struggling, quite still in the water, before they disappeared.

Much was made of Michael's ineptitude as a swimmer. But Marjoribanks gave evidence that while 'Mr Davies could not swim very well . . . It was his pride, however, to swim about twenty yards.' And again, as Peter Davies, a sensible man who visited the site, as I did, wrote to Dolly: 'The place is too calm, and the distance from bank to bank too small, for the question of swimming capacity to enter into it at all.'

The two eyewitnesses, Charles Henry Beecham, engineer's assistant at the Sandford Paper Mills, and his assistant Matthew Gaskell, testified that the pool was 'as still as a mill-pond'.

Beecham said that when he went up to the weir with Gaskell to regulate the water for the mill, he was standing on the Oxford side of the weir when he heard a shout. He looked and saw two men as it were standing together in the pool, their heads above water. Assuming that the shout had been for assistance –

> I immediately ran across the bridge to get the lifebelt, and Gaskell followed. Gaskell held the line while I threw the belt, but the men had already disappeared.
>
> *What did you do then?*
>
> I left Gaskell at the weir and ran to Radley College boathouse for assistance. Some of the Radley students were bathing, but some of them came back with me and others brought a boat.

> *How far is the boathouse from the pool?*
>
> About a ten minutes' run there and back. It would take about ten minutes to bring a boat up.

When Beecham got back to the weir he pointed out the spot where he saw the men go down, and then returned to the mill to telephone information to the County Police. Gaskell gave corroborative evidence and, answering a juror, said it took less than a minute from the time he heard the shout to get the lifebelt. A juror asked whether the witness could say whether the men were clinging to each other as though one was trying to help the other?

> Their heads were close together.

In other words, he couldn't say that.

> *You could not see anything else?*
>
> They appeared as though they were just standing in the water with their heads above the surface.

Said another juror:

> *Was there anything to suggest that one was supporting the other?*
>
> One might have been, but I could not say.

Thomas Frederick Carter, of 34 Nelson Street, Oxford, employed by the Thames Conservancy, then said he was in the depot at Osney when, just before five o'clock, he received a call to go to Sandford Pool. The superintendent sent him to drag the pool for two undergraduates who had been reported drowned. With two other assistants, he continued dragging operations, but up to dark neither of the bodies had been recovered. At seven o'clock the next morning dragging was recommenced. One body was recovered shortly after two o'clock about thirty yards from the weir, in about twenty feet of water.

> As I was hauling the body up I noticed something drop off when within about 8 ft from the surface. At first I thought it was a limb of a tree, but have now come to the conclusion that it must have been one body dropping from the other.

One body was taken to the hotel while they dragged for the other, which was recovered an hour later. Asked the Coroner –

Where?

At the same spot I found the first.

Which body was first recovered?

I do not know the gentleman's name, but he would be about 6 ft 2 in.

The Dean of Christ Church asked the witness –

Are there any notices at Sandford drawing attention to the depth and extreme danger? –

Yes, at both gates.

So anyone going to bathe must have seen them?

They should have seen them quite plainly.

Asked a juror –

Did you form the impression that the bodies were clasped?

Yes, that was my impression.

And you thought they became separated when you were drawing them up?

Yes.

Said the Dean of Christ Church –

I suppose as you were pulling them up the weight suddenly became lighter?

Yes.

The Dean – as he gave the jury's verdict – was overcome with emotion.

On the evening of 19 May Jim was at home alone in the Adelphi, writing his daily letter to Michael, saying that he hoped he would be able to come down for the opening performance of his new play, *Shall We Join the Ladies?* which starred Gerald as Dolphin, a butler. At eleven o'clock, with the intention of posting the letter, he walked out of the flat and took the lift to the ground floor. As he opened the gate of the lift and moved into the hallway, he was approached by a stranger who raised his hat, said he was from a newspaper and asked if Sir James could oblige him with a few words on the incident. Jim asked what he was talking about. It was in this way that he learned of Michael's drowning.

He turned and went back into the lift. In a daze he telephoned Gerald and Peter first, and then his secretary Cynthia Asquith, who recalled that he spoke 'in a voice she hardly recognised'.

When Cynthia arrived at the flat Gerald and Peter were already there. They tried to persuade Jim to go to bed, but he would not. Eventually they left for their own beds, and when Cynthia arrived the following morning, Jim had still not slept. He had been pacing up and down the length of the study floor all night long.

Nico was playing cricket at Eton while Michael drowned, and in the evening sang at a Musical Society concert. He was told of his brother's death by his tutor after lights out, at around ten o'clock, but had gone to sleep not really believing it. The full import hit him when Peter arrived at his bedside the following morning and his housemaster Macnaghten,* made it worse by coming in, kneeling by his bed and holding both their hands.

Peter then drove Nico to Slough for breakfast and on to Jim's flat. Recalled Nico: 'Uncle Jim's immediate reaction on seeing me was "Oh – take him away!" Strangely I don't remember feeling hurt at this.'

Nico was given the responsibility of telling Nanny, who was working as a midwife at Queen Charlotte's Hospital.

He was excused from the funeral and went to stay at Cannon Hall with the du Mauriers. In the 1970s, in an interview with Andrew Birkin, he said:

> I've always had something of a hunch that Michael's drowning was suicide – he was in a way the 'type' i.e. exceptionally clever, with varying moods.

Drowning in a pool had resonances with the original myth, in which the boys were immersed: Peter Ibbetson's suicide attempt, his 'one fixed idea – that of self-destruction' after the death of Mary, Duchess of Towers, when he filled his pockets with stones and made ready to throw himself into the mare d'Auteuil, but desisted when Mary's ghost appeared to him. It was also an idea force-fed by Jim, as author, into Tommy's weirdly predictive dream of 'a very noble young man, his white dead face staring at the sky from the bottom of a deep pool'.†

* Himself a suicide in later years.

† The dream occurs in *Tommy and Grizel*. When Tommy awakes he finds that a boy really is drowning.

Equally, of course, drowning identified Michael with Peter Pan, who stayed on the magical island as the waters of the lagoon rose, knowing 'that it will soon be submerged', standing erect with a smile on his face and a drum beating in his breast, knowing that 'To die will be an awfully big adventure.'

The lagoon was a hypnotic focus for the boys; 'to be a real boy' was to pass over to the other side by drowning.

There is a programmed inevitability about Michael's death, and the programmer is Uncle Jim. The significance of it cannot have been lost on Daphne although she, the self-styled biographer of the du Mauriers, omitted ever to mention the great family tragedy of Michael's death in any of her three biographies of the family.*

The du Maurier secrecy about 'matters au sérieux', which had been Kicky's and concerned the psychic arts, and was then given to Barrie's invasion and destruction of the family, was compulsive. But, as ever, Daphne could not keep it out of her fiction.

When she began to unravel the mystery of her life in the late 1950s in *The Breaking Point*, the collection that reveals how she and Peter 'awakened' to the predatory nature of Jim's possession of the family, Michael's death rose to the surface in 'The Pool', which makes devastating reading.

Daphne takes a central image of Barrie's, the lagoon in *Peter Pan*, an image of Neverland, where acceptance – the closing in of the waters – means another kind of seeing, another kind of hearing, and just as the lilies fold so does the soul submerge and new knowledge flow from 'the secret world'. But then she shows it disintegrating before our eyes. For this story, like Michael's suicide, is one of disillusionment. The pool becomes what it was in reality for Michael. As Daphne's heroine, Deborah, sleepwalks into it, 'the lilies held her. . . up to her armpits and her chin', exactly as Michael and Rupert were held up in Sandford Pool, appearing as though they were standing in the water with their heads above the surface, before they gave themselves to death –

> The triumph was that she was not afraid, was filled with such wild acceptance . . . She ran into the pool. Her living feet felt the mud and the broken sticks and all the tangle of old weeds, and the water was up to her armpits and her chin. The lilies held her. The rain blinded her . . .

* Daphne du Maurier, *Gerald: A Portrait* (1934), *The du Mauriers* (1937), and *Myself When Young* (1977).

> 'Take me too,' cried the child. 'Don't leave me behind!' In her heart was a savage disenchantment. They had broken their promise, they had left her in the world. The pool that claimed her now was not the pool of secrecy, but dank, dark, brackish water choked with scum.

Daphne told her children that the story was written to mark Flavia's loss of 'boyishness' when she reached puberty, and there are plenty of references to this in the text. The implication is that, now she is no longer a boy, Deborah will no longer be allowed through the gate and into her 'secret world' in the pool, her Neverland. Likewise, Michael, who has grown out of Jim, who has left the young man a deranged and damaged soul, 'will not touch again Pan's perfumed shore'.

According to Peter, Uncle Jim bore Michael's death 'somehow, with wonderful composure, and physically at least with better success than could have been expected'. He wrote this to Dolly Ponsonby. Denis Mackail took a different view: 'He never got over it. It altered and darkened everything for the rest of his life.' Jim himself wrote in a letter to Dundas a year after the tragedy: 'What happened was in a way the end of me.'

Peter was aware that it wasn't long before Jim was making notes for a story based on the tragedy. To be entitled *Water* or *The Silent Pool* or *The 19th*, it told of a dream he had of Michael returning from the dead, the boy unaware that he had been drowned until 'the fatal 19th' approached again and he realised the inevitability of his death being repeated and walked with Uncle Jim, holding his hand, into Sandford Pool – 'He said goodbye to me and went into it and sank just as before . . .' Chillingly, Jim then added a note –

> Must be clear tht [*sic*] there is nothing suicidal about it.

PART VI

1921–1989

Uncle Jim and Daphne: the *Rebecca* inheritance

'A most beautiful person . . . dressed in skeleton leaves'

CHAPTER ONE

Rebecca, a demon boy

The shock waves of Michael's death eddied beyond his immediate family. There was genuine sadness within the Bloomsbury set. Lytton Strachey wrote to Ottoline Morrell, 'I am sure if Michael had lived he would have been one of the most remarkable of his generation.'[1] The effect on Roger Senhouse was devastating. D. H. Lawrence wrote –

> My dear Mary, we had your note after your second trip to England. No, I hadn't heard of the boy's drowning. What was he doing to get drowned? J. M. Barrie has a fatal touch for those he loves. They die.[2]

'Mary' was Mary Cannan (née Ansell), Barrie's ex-wife. She met Lawrence in 1914 when living with her new husband Gilbert Cannan in a cottage in Buckinghamshire a mile away from where Lawrence was living with Frieda Weekley. The two couples invited each other over to dinner, got to know one another, and in 1914 celebrated Christmas together. Lawrence described them in unusually flattering terms: 'Gilbert and Mary Cannan are here. I rather love them. There is real Good – power for Good – in Gilbert.' Lawrence also corresponded with Barrie directly during this period, though sadly their letters are lost. And they had a meeting in London in 1915, probably arranged by Mary.*

As all this was going on Lawrence was writing *Women in Love*. A month before he wrote to Mary about Michael's death, he had written to Cynthia Asquith, telling her that he had arranged for her to receive a copy of *Women in Love*, and adding in a postscript: 'Tell J.M. [Barrie] what I think of him.'

* Harry T. Moore, *The Priest of Love: A Life of D. H. Lawrence* (1980). It is generally supposed that Lawrence came to Barrie via Lady Cynthia Asquith, who became his 'patroness', but Lawrence had a hot line to Barrie through Mary Ansell long before Asquith became Barrie's secretary.

It is fair to assume that what Lawrence thought of Barrie had been influenced by what Mary had told him. Mary refused to speak to any biographer, but she seems to have revealed much to Lawrence, including ideas which were incorporated into *Women in Love*.*

The du Maurier family was, meanwhile, in uproar. There were rumours about Jim's relationships with the boys. Gerald was struggling with a situation in which neither emotion nor reason could justify his head-in-the-sand collusion.

There were discussions about what should go on Michael's tombstone. Jim suggested including 'adopted son of J. M. Barrie'. According to Nico, 'Uncle Gerald flew into a rage and said no Barrie should be mentioned etc.'

Tod, Daphne's faithful governess, chose this moment to hand in her notice and take up a position with the children of Sultan Prince Abdul Madjid in Constantinople.

But, in the end, the family closed ranks and, as usual in times of stress there was a fillip for Gerald: he was honoured with a knighthood. No one could quite work out why. Even Mo was baffled. But one didn't have to look far for a sponsor.

By now, Jim was very well connected within the Establishment. But, aware that 'the greatest power is the one that is subtle and adjusts itself', he kept his head down. In the theatre he made a tactical withdrawal. *Peter Pan* continued each year and some revivals were staged, but there was no new play until almost the end of his life. However, in 1922, the year after Michael's suicide, there were discussions about a film of *Peter Pan*. Jim met Charlie Chaplin, dined with him at the Garrick and invited him back to the Adelphi Terrace apartment.

Chaplin, an observant and sassy young man of thirty-two, whose best films were yet to come, described Jim as 'a small man, with a dark moustache and a deeply marked, sad face, with heavily shadowed eyes; but I detect lines of humour lurking around his mouth. Cynical? Not exactly . . .'

He recognised that he was dealing with a clever operator and was immediately on the defensive:

> Barrie tells me that he is looking for someone to play Peter Pan and says he wants me to play it. He bowls me over completely. To think that I was avoiding and afraid to meet such a man! But I am afraid to discuss it with him

* See Appendix (p. 293 below) on D. H. Lawrence, Mary Ansell, and *Women in Love*.

> seriously, am on my guard because he may decide that I know nothing about it and change his mind. Just imagine. Barrie has asked me to play Peter Pan! It is too big and grand to risk spoiling it by some chance witless observation, so I change the subject and let this opportunity pass. I have failed completely in my first skirmish with Barrie.

Gerald appeared at Jim's apartment after dinner. Around three in the morning he walked Chaplin back to his hotel and felt the need to mention 'that Barrie is not himself since his nephew was drowned, that he has aged considerably'.[3]

In the same year, in a small windswept town in the far north-east of Britain, Jim made a confession. In his 1922 speech to undergraduates of St Andrews University, who had elected him Rector, he acknowledged a 'darker and more sinister' side of himself; saying he had not always been master of it, he admitted it had pushed him in a direction that 'every instinct of self-preservation told him was dangerous'.[4]

This stirring of conscience would have been lost to the North Sea winds had it not been published as a book with the title, *Courage*. Perhaps it had taken courage, but not as much as it had taken Michael. Jim described his occupation as 'playing hide and seek with angels', and himself as of Lucifer's descent:

> It is M'Connachie who has brought me to this pass. M'Connachie, I should explain, as I have undertaken to open the innermost doors, is the name I give to the unruly half of myself: the writing half . . . he is the fanciful half . . . he prefers to fly around on one wing. I should not mind him doing that, but he drags me with him.

He pleads for our sympathy, at once penitent and victim, a variation on the sentimental line he had taken so often in his work:

> I might have done things worth while if it had not been for M'Connachie, and my first piece of advice to you at any rate shall be sound: don't copy me. Beware of M'Connachie. When I look in a mirror now it is his face I see. I speak with his voice . . . You will all have your M'Connachies luring you off the high road. Unless you are constantly on the watch, you will find that he has slowly pushed you out of yourself and taken your place. He has rather done for me.

M'Connachie gets the blame, just as Tommy and Peter Pan and all of Barrie's personae were blamed, because, as Tommy himself once cried, with bitter conceit, 'If they knew what I really am, how they would run from me.'

In 1928, Jim completed the rehabilitation of his conscience by donating the copyright in *Peter Pan* to Great Ormond Street Hospital. He made the gift 'for the very best reasons', according to Nico, 'but also for the not-quite-so-good reason that he hoped everyone would say what a splendid thing to have done'.

Following the tragedy of 19 May 1921, Daphne wrote a story, calling it 'The Seekers' after Uncle Jim's little gods, one of whom, being malicious, had done for Michael, 'the lad that will never be old'.

But in Michael's poem about Eilean Shona seekers appear to have the power to make 'all the beauty of the scene seem one'. Daphne's story peters out before we meet her seekers, but what we have suggests that she identified more with Michael's seekers than Uncle Jim's malignant ones at this time.

'The Seekers' was her first serious piece of writing. It tells of a boy called Maurice, a thinly disguised Michael Davies. She wrote to Tod that it was about 'a boy who is searching for happiness, at least not exactly happiness, but that something that is somewhere, you know. You feel it and you miss it and it beckons and you can't reach it . . . I don't think anyone can find it on this earth.'

Uncle Jim is central to the plot and known as Tommy Strange, 'the man with the pipe',* who 'never grew up properly. He was only a very cocky little boy . . . [who] loved people to like him . . . he almost strutted up the drive towards the house thinking desperately how to show off in some way . . . No-one could quite understand Tommy. I don't think he did himself.'

Maurice's mother Sylvia, 'dark, with Maurice's eyes' and 'an adorable smile of her own', is fêted by many men, none of whom she cares for. Daphne even caught the little bit of cruelty in Sylvia's humour: Maurice's mother does not laugh at the circus, but at Nurse when she slips on some orange peel. Naturally, Tommy has an 'affair' with this Sylvia look-alike and loves her 'as much as it was possible for him to love anything but himself'.

* Jim sucked on a pipe constantly.

Maurice first meets Tommy when he gets lost in Regent Street and is picked up by 'depressive Mr Tibbs', a grocer who takes him to meet Tommy, who, we learn, 'likes young gentlemen'.

Tommy lives in a block of flats overlooking the river (recognisably Jim's flat in Adelphi Terrace House). He opens the door to Maurice looking 'rather tired'. He offers the boy tea and after asking his name and where he lives, and why he has not asked a policeman the way home, he fixes him with his eyes and says darkly:

> 'You are a lonely traveller in Mexico who has lost his way in a terrific storm. You have come to me for shelter and do not know I am a brigand who will take your life.'

And so their hypnotic adventure begins; it was 'one of the most thrilling games Maurice had ever played'.

The story confirms that Daphne's imagination at the age of 14 was inspired by Jim, that she was *au fait* with his flat at Adelphi, with his penchant for boys, with his captivating stories, and with his supernatural take on life.

But the effect of the 'indelible bond' between Jim and her father cut deeper. She makes this clear in her fictional exposé, *The Progress of Julius*, where, as Margaret Forster noted, what Daphne crossed out in the original manuscript, a series of school exercise books, is more suggestive even than what appears in the published novel. She draws on a family holiday to Algiers in 1922.

Sexuality oozes with 'the heat and sweat of humanity, the scorching, dusty, amber, Alger smell'. Her father's favourite music was 'the music thumped on drums in the native quarter of Alger and danced to by little naked prostitutes of twelve years old'. Daphne was 15, Gerald 49. In the novel, Gabriel is 15, Julius 50.

> 'We have fun, don't we?' She took hold of his hand and crumpled up his fingers, squeezing them against each other so that his signet ring cut his skin and he cried out.
>
> 'I like your hands,' she said, 'they're the best things about you,' and then she dropped them and moved away, humming a tune.
>
> 'There you are,' he said. 'That's what I meant. Are you a child or do you do it on purpose?'
>
> 'I don't know what the devil you're talking about,' she said.

'You're a bloody liar,' he said.

They were silent for about five minutes. It was getting dark. He could scarcely see her face. The fire burst in the grate and shot up in a quiver of flame, lighting them to one another. 'I'm sorry,' he said abruptly. 'I don't want you to be angry.' She crossed over and pinched the back of his neck.

'I'm not angry.'

'Is it that you're a child and happy like that?' he said.

'I expect so.'

'You'll tell me, won't you, when you begin to feel things? You'll come to me?'

'You'll know without me telling you,' she said.

Back in Cannon Hall, Daphne's life was intense and unrelenting. Angela was dispatched to boarding-school, Jeanne attended day school locally; Daphne alone was taught by a governess at home. Her life was so confined that she forged a special friendship with one of the maids to find out about the ordinary world outside. She wrote to Tod, whom she missed terribly as a confidante: 'When I hear a foxtrot I go mad for want of dancing.'

In the summer of 1921, while lying on a beach in Thurlestone in Devon on another family holiday, her cousin Geoffrey Millar, Trixy's son, and at 36, twenty-two years older than Daphne, caught her eye.

> My heart missed a beat. I smiled back . . . I knew instinctively that we shared a secret . . . When we all lay out on the lawn like corpses to catch the sun, rugs over our knees, Geoffrey would come and lie beside me, and feel for my hand under the rug and hold it. Nothing, in a life of seventy years, has ever surpassed that first awakening of an instinct within myself. The touch of that hand on mine. And the instinctive knowledge that nobody must know.

Geoffrey, an actor, was fun, devastatingly attractive, and a philanderer. Daphne, of course, was forbidden fruit. When Geoffrey stayed at Cannon Hall, Daphne would come down to the drawing-room after the others had gone to bed and let him kiss her.

Kissing Geoffrey is 'exciting, and it's fun creeping down late in my pyjamas,' she wrote in her diary.

> The strange thing is it's so like kissing D. There is hardly any difference between them . . .

Daphne du Maurier, as a small child, with 'hypnotic eyes'.

George du Maurier's illustration of the artists' model Trilby, originally modelled on Carry, the girl he hypnotised and loved when he was young.

Daphne looking like Trilby (*below left*) and (*below*) dressed as Marty, who would inherit the du Maurier secret. Acting out her fantasies, Daphne found her way naturally into the 'other order of things', believing that enlightenment comes from an altered state of consciousness, a state of trance. This was what drew Barrie in.

THE FIVE LLEWELYN DAVIES BROTHERS AND THE THREE DU MAURIER SISTERS:

George (*right*), the first of the boys to be captivated by Barrie, developed 'almost what the Germans called *Weltschmerz* – a sadness of the world'. Killed in France in 1915, he had with him a copy of *The Little White Bird*, Barrie's novel in which George himself featured alongside Peter Pan.

Jack (*below left*), wary of Barrie's influence, descended into depression and died in his early sixties.

Peter (*below right*), whose mind, like Jack's, was 'clouded over a good deal' about the Barrie years, committed suicide months after Jack died.

(*Left*) Michael, who could not break free from Barrie, drowned in what appeared to be a suicide pact, aged 20.
(*Below*) Nico, mentally and physically different from the others, and the youngest, was the least influenced by Barrie. 'Of course when one – I at any rate – gets on to dreams, one is in a world of lovely non-comprehension.'

The du Maurier sisters: Angela (older than Daphne by three years) and Jeanne (younger by four) and Daphne with their mother. It was Daphne who was captivated by Barrie and liked to lose herself 'in that silent shadow-land that marches a hand's breadth from our own'. She became close to her cousin Peter in the 1950s, suffered a nervous breakdown, and later herself attempted suicide.

Michael and Nico with Uncle Jim, on Eilean Shona on the west coast of Scotland, the summer before Michael died.

Michael on the river at Oxford, with friends. Robert Boothby is holding the pole.

Sandford Pool, where Michael drowned. Said Peter: 'The place is too calm, and the distance from bank to bank too small, for the question of swimming capacity to enter into it at all.'

Barrie, still impish in 1920, before Michael's death.

Barrie inconsolable a year later. He is wearing the trilby hat which – in Daphne's stories – is the symbol of Svengali's hypnotic power, its appropriator the personification of evil.

Barrie, 1930, looking out over the Thames from the top floor of Adelphi Terrace House, as it were from the Captain's bridge.

Daphne with Gerald in 1925, when she was 18. She referred to her relationship with him as her 'Daddy complex'. Gerald's interference in her childhood had a strange affinity with Barrie's interference in the lives of George and Michael as boys.

Daphne rowing from Fowey to Ferryside in Bodinnick. 'Here was the freedom I desired, long sought-for, not yet known.'

'Tommy' Browning, Major in the Grenadier Guards.

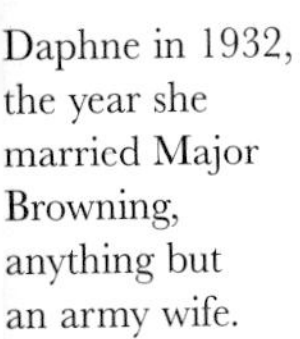

Daphne in 1932, the year she married Major Browning, anything but an army wife.

Daphne dreaming in the 'writing hut' at Menabilly. The locals believed 'she would call up the spirits and get them to write her books. She was always in a trance, they used to say.'

Daphne in 1948, in the Aldwych Theatre with Gertrude Lawrence, discussing her play *September Tide*, in which Gertie starred.

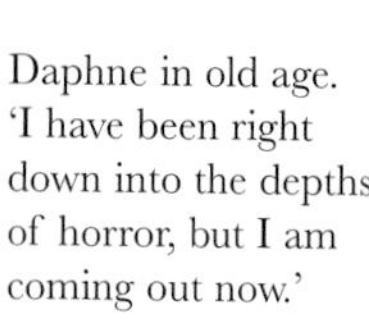

Daphne in old age. 'I have been right down into the depths of horror, but I am coming out now.'

What sort of kissing with her father was like kissing as illicit as this?

> Perhaps this family is the same as the Borgias. D is Pope Alexander, Geoffrey is Cesare, and I am Lucretia. A sort of incest.

Lucretia married at 13; Cesare was her brother and Pope Alexander her father. Incest indeed! But whatever she felt about Geoffrey, all the while it was her father, not Geoffrey, who was on her mind, as she discovered when given an anaesthetic by a dentist to remove wisdom teeth. Coming round, Daphne heard 'someone groaning, "Daddy, Daddy!" through a mist and it was myself emerging from the darkness'.

> So it was not the Borgia brother but the Borgia father that the unconscious self demanded.

Daphne's 'Daddy complex' was at the centre of everything, and she used this 'affair', maintained for at least six years, to tantalise her father mercilessly, just as Gabriel tantalises her father in *Julius*. She deliberately made him suspicious that something was going on with Geoffrey, enjoying the power it gave her over him. Gerald became wildly irritable.

What 'the secret city' was making of Daphne's personality was clarified again in 1925 when she was sent away from home for the first time to a finishing school at Camposena outside Paris. It was run by Fernande Yvon, 'thirty-ish, slanting green eyes, [with] a manner that seemed a blend of sarcasm and veiled amusement' (an easy mix with the du Maurier personality). Showing off her knowledge of what it took to be a master of manipulation, Daphne invaded Ferdie's inner sanctum to the consternation of the in-group girls already there. She picked up Ferdie's dropped handkerchief, 'anointed' it with perfume and returned it to her. Ferdie, a lesbian, knew how to respond and took Daphne, still legally a minor, to a health resort at La Bourboule where she was to take a 'cure', and where, Daphne claimed, she loved Ferdie 'in every conceivable way'.

And yet her poetry had shown another side. She wrote about beauty, and the 'warm, maternal' love which had eluded her, thanks to Gerald and Jim and their 'indelible bond'. Here was the unrealised light of Daphne's imagination, her true inheritance, her grandfather's sense of beauty, the secret that Uncle Jim could never understand.

On returning from Camposena she took off with Jeanne to a farm in

Cumberland, near Derwentwater, and found fulfilment of a different sort – in nature.

> Mountains, woods, valleys, farms – earlier holidays in the South of France could not compare with this, my first experience of rugged scenery, of running water coursing through the hills down to the lake.

They walked. One of their excursions was to Wordsworth's Dove Cottage. Daphne felt blissfully free from the pressure of the 'secret city'. 'This was all so different from the world that I knew – a real awakening – a feeling for the countryside as opposed to the city, primitive, elemental, a desire for roots in the soil,' she wrote in her diary. And yet, even here, thoughts of Jim were never far away. She noted that the lakes were 'Mysterious, often shrouded in mist, and with little islands upon them like the island in *Mary Rose.*'

It is possible that following the furore over Michael's death Daphne's meetings with Uncle Jim had become clandestine. Gerald was still seeing Jim, but it is unlikely that Mo actively encouraged Jim's relationship with Daphne to continue. An unsigned letter to her in the summer of 1926 alludes to a secret rendezvous in Richmond Park, miles out of the way for Hampstead-based Daphne, but a favourite meeting-place during Jim's courting of Mary Ansell. Daphne was now 19. The letter reveals her through the writer's eyes, a most original and attractive young woman, chic, self-possessed, shrewd, but full of life; amusing, and with an elusive, beguiling nature all her own.

The mysterious correspondent, a man with 'a certain twisting smile', returned home with a bunch of bluebells – Jim's favourite flowers – which she had picked for him. At once he had 'shot' into a trance, from which he declared he never wanted to wake up. He advised her to remain young rather than become old and wise. Daphne had shown him her diaries, which he described as 'dangerous, indiscreet and stupid'.

Later, she wrote a poem with more clues to the writer's identity. His business was

> Fashioning for children nursery rhymes
> Or listening to a sentimental waltz.

The references hint at Sentimental Tommy himself. Indeed, at the moment of their meeting Jim had been engaged in putting the finishing touches to his contribution to Cynthia Asquith's *The Flying Carpet* (1926), an anthology of prose and verse for children.

This meeting prompted an inquisition at Cannon Hall. Daphne said that they 'had played halma, talked and read'. Subsequently she wrote a second poem called 'Richmond Hill'. The day had left her with a memory of:

> Crushed ferns amidst a haze of blue –
> The sun, egg sandwiches – and you.

The meeting inspired her. She went on holiday to Brittany with Ferdie and returned with three stories under her belt – but they were desperately cynical.

Since reaching puberty, Daphne had entered into a relationship with a man twenty-two years her senior, which she had used to 'juice up' a highly questionable relationship with her father. She had become self-centred and manipulative, and initiated a relationship with a French woman, also much older. The stories she was writing at this time reflected the turmoil going on inside. Was there perhaps the fear in the family of another Michael situation? No one could let that happen.

On 13 September 1926, Daphne found herself in Bodinnick in Cornwall, with her mother, Angela and Jeanne, viewing a romantic old boathouse later named Ferryside, a short pull across the river from Fowey, the river lapping against its outer walls, the granite cliff-face an integral part of one wall within.

Daphne's 'condition' was the reason for its purchase. In a 1973 BBC Radio interview, her sister Angela said:

> We came down to Cornwall because Daphne was very delicate in those days and we were told that she should have a place in the country to live in always.

Nothing could be further from the picture that we have been given of Daphne at this time – the strong, even manipulative and cynical young woman in control of her life. The emotional reality was that she was vulnerable, even 'delicate'. The family was concerned, and no temporary solution would do. She must live in the country – away from the secret city – 'always'. Her strange life was taking its toll.

Cornwall was the best prescription possible. Once released from Cannon Hall, her spirits soared.

> Here was the freedom I desired, long sought-for, not yet known. Freedom to write, to walk, to wander, freedom to climb hills, to pull a boat, to be alone. One feature of my excitement was the feeling that it could not be mere chance that brought us to the ferry. It seemed so right.[5]

Fowey was of course home to Jim's great friend Q, Sir Arthur Quiller Couch. Cornish to the core, Q had held the chair of English at Cambridge University since 1912. Daphne was soon taking tea with him, not in Cornwall, but in his rooms at Jesus College. No one from the du Maurier family accompanied her. Why should they? They did not know Q. The meeting confirmed Jim's awareness of the Ferryside arrangement, if not his initiation of it. Q's daughter Foy, sister of Bevil (another casualty of the First War), became Daphne's best friend.

Gerald, meanwhile, remained distinctly uninvolved and was never very happy visiting Ferryside. From this period, his star was on the wane. There were money difficulties, discontent, disenchantment, regret, and at length some inexplicable depressive symptoms of the sort that invariably affected those whose fate Jim commandeered.

Daphne's relationship with her father, still strangely in step with Michael's with Jim, entered a new phase. When first Angela and then Daphne began to show an interest in boys, Gerald became incensed. In her memoir Angela recalled having to put boys off from taking her home, for fear that Gerald would be there:

> Daddy's face was to be seen peering through the landing curtains on the rare occasions one had been 'seen home'. And my goodness! The catechisms.
>
> 'Who brought you home? Who is he?'
>
> '. . . . .'
>
> 'Did he kiss you?'
>
> . . . Having His Daughters Kissed was the last straw to poor Daddy . . .

In 1929, as the guest of Edgar Wallace, in whose plays Gerald was acting, Daphne was introduced to Carol Reed,* the illegitimate son of Sir Herbert Tree, at the Palace Hotel, Caux, the resort where Jim and Sylvia, with Gilbert Cannan and Mary Ansell, had holidayed with the boys after Arthur's death.

* Carol Reed would become a film director – *Our Man in Havana*, *A Kid for Two Farthings*, *The Agony and the Ecstasy*, etc. Daphne's son Kits assisted on the first.

Daphne was 22. Reed was Daphne's first serious boyfriend. Gerald was deeply jealous. In an effort to thwart the affair, he arranged for Daphne to join a three-week cruise to the Norwegian fjords with the millionaire Otto Kahn on his private yacht, the *Albion*. It was not a good idea. At one stage Daphne had to escape the clutches of her host by stripping off and diving into the sea.

Aware that Daphne was slipping away (as Jim had prophesied in *Dear Brutus* she would), Gerald began to look with clearer eyes at what had befallen Arthur and Sylvia. There was anger and bitterness in his cry: 'Why should a fellow like Arthur be taken who never said an unkind word in his life, and what possible good can it be to anyone in the world for darling Sylvia to break her heart?' Daphne's response revealed a chillier allegiance: 'Gerald would not acknowledge that Arthur and Sylvia were spared many things [by their early deaths] – the war, and fear for their sons, and the reaction of a weary country; that had they lived longer they must have suffered greatly, for they would not have belonged, they would have been out of place in a hurried, fevered world.'[6]

In Daphne's eyes, Gerald's questioning made him an apostate to the 'secret city', and she could not countenance her father's betrayal. In her 1934 biography, she berated him for being blind to 'the real treasures of life that lay within his grasp'. She criticised the shallowness of his art, while over-praising Jim. Most would consider her assessment of Jim's plays not just exaggerated but partisan. None, except *Peter Pan*, has endured. But nowhere was her subjugation to Jim more sadly expressed than in her praise for 'the upbringing and the security' he gave the boys.

Here was the true neurotic basis of Daphne's 'Daddy-complex', an emotional conflict caused by Gerald's disenchantment with Uncle Jim and Daphne's love, deep down, for her father. Evidence of it is everywhere in her fiction.

Now that Gerald was awakening to Jim, and his favourite daughter was fading from his life, he began drinking heavily, waking up 'gloomy, spiritless, flat', suffering 'black fits' of depression. He 'kept breaking down and crying'. Gerald was beginning to see beyond the web in which he had been caught, to see the lie that he had lived. Terrible anxieties rushed in and he suffered repeated attacks of what he called 'the horrors . . . He put his hands over his eyes and [would] stand and tremble and hold on to Mo or one of his children . . . until the terror, fear and loneliness were gone.' We will see Daphne suffer in the same way in the 1950s after her own 'awakening'.

Without Cornwall, Daphne would surely have been lost. When she first stayed at Ferryside she seized every opportunity to explore, and no adventure was more exciting than the day she set out with Angela to find Menabilly, whose roofs she had espied from afar –

> It was an afternoon in late autumn I first tried to find the house. October, November, the month escapes me. But in the West Country autumn can make herself a witch, and place a spell upon the walker. The trees were golden brown, the hydrangeas had massive heads still blue and untouched by flecks of wistful grey, and I would set forth at three in the afternoon with foolish notions of August still in my head . . .We came to the lodge at Four Turnings, as we had been told, and opened the creaking iron gates with the flash courage and appearance of bluff common to the trespasser. . .We slunk away down the drive . . . We did not talk . . . That was the first effect the woods had on us.
>
> The drive twisted and turned in a way that I described many years afterwards, when sitting at a desk in Alexandria . . . The woods were sleeping now, but who, I wondered, had ridden through them once? What hoof beats had sounded and then died away? What carriage wheels had rolled and vanished? Doublet and hose. Boot and jerkin. Patch and powder. . .[7]

This is vintage du Maurier experience. Kicky used his imaginative powers to explore the deeply rooted memories of his own mind; Daphne is after the unconscious memory of place. All around she saw clues to the past, 'footprints in the sand', 'imprints of the suffering and the joy'. She believed in this 'shadow-world that marches a hand's breadth from our own'[8] to the point of keeping the aged, fading wallpaper on her bedroom wall when finally she moved into Menabilly in 1943.

> Who can affirm or deny that the houses which have sheltered us as children, or as adults, and our predecessors too, do not have embedded in their walls, one with the dust and cobwebs, one with the overlay of fresh wallpaper and paint, the imprint of what-has-been.[9]

For Kicky (and for Jung), to know your past was to know yourself. But for Daphne, to sense the past in a place was to know something mysterious about life, a nameless truth that Kicky experienced euphorically in his peak experiences, and that had something to do with the limitation of human perception and the great possibility of what lay beyond.

Daphne's sense of the past in the present is what many readers love about her novels. It carries with it a great beauty and none of the morbidity of Uncle Jim's attempts at lifting the veil between life and death in plays such as *Peter Pan* and *Mary Rose*.

Barrie's art was neurosis-driven. He could not free himself from his obsession with death, and he ensured that Daphne would suffer similar agonies, by teaming up with Gerald and by his part in inflicting her 'Daddy complex' on her. That was the piece of Jim that lodged in her mind until the end. And ironically, that piece so aggravated her that it often produced the energy needed to get her writing.

This is shown in her first novel, *The Loving Spirit*, written in Ferryside in 1929. It is a long way from being the best example of Daphne's imagination at work, but it is interesting because it is immature and transparent.

Scholars say that it owes a lot to the Brontës. The title is from a poem by Emily Brontë, and in 1931 the novel would be marketed by its publisher, Heinemann, as Brontë-esque. More importantly, it is about Fowey (called Plyn in the fiction). Daphne came across a derelict schooner, the *Jane Slade*, on the mud flats as she was walking by Pont Creek. She discovered the tomb of the real Jane Slade in nearby Lanteglos churchyard. And the Slade family, still living in Fowey, gave her a big box of letters crumpled and yellowed with age.

Daphne's imaginative sixth sense was always stirred by place:

> One night when *The Loving Spirit* was in embryo, scarcely born in thought, I walked up to Castle Point. The moon was high in the sky, and there was no sound but the moan of the still water lapping the rocks beyond the harbour. It seemed to me that I was standing on the cliffs years hence with a grown-up son. I was a ghost, long dead, existing only in his thoughts. And from that I passed on to thinking about my unborn book. My thoughts were of a past and future no longer separated in time, and I knew it must be the story of four generations.[10]

In the novel she has Janet Coombe, the fictional Jane Slade, do the same – her heroine leans against the old ruins at the mouth of the Fowey river, closes her eyes and breaks through into that other-world where past, present and future are one. As in Daphne's 'dream', her heroine is 'a ghost long dead' and confronts the figure of a man she recognises as her (as yet unborn) grown-up son. And so the generational saga begins.

But it is a terrible cheat. The scene is a take from Jim's play, *Mary Rose*, where a long-dead mother appears to her grown-up son. Daphne was young, a mere 22. She was writing her first novel. We should not be surprised that both her dreams and her novel are influenced by Jim.

In the mid-1950s, when Daphne became aware of how far Uncle Jim had got 'inside' her, she took to calling herself 'Tray' instead of her usual family nickname, 'Bing'. Tray is the name of the dog in *Trilby* who loves and looks up to Little Billee (Kicky) 'with sapient, affectionate eyes' and sings to his tune, but is 'a barytone [*sic*] dog by nature, with portentous, warlike chest-notes of the jingo order'.

Daphne sang her grandfather's tune, but, as a member of Jim's boy-cult, she sang it 'barytone'. Her dreams were as adulterated by Uncle Jim as Michael's had been.

Yet there was an active ingredient in her writing that was down to Jim, a live spark that provided the essential dynamic between Janet Coombe and her son. The grown-up boy who appears beside Janet assumes the spiritual blindness and 'black fits' of depression of the author's own father, and she reasserts her loyalty to him with an alternative vision to his, one of eternity, beauty and peace. As I said, her Daddy complex is everywhere in the fiction.

The Loving Spirit was published in February 1931. Denis Mackail was aware of Uncle Jim's high regard for Daphne – 'Clever Daphne, we salute you,' he wrote, 'and Barrie saluted you too.' The novel was successful enough for her publishers to enter into a contract for two more – *I'll Never Be Young Again* and *The Progress of Julius*. Readers and reviewers were astonished that these two novels were so different from *The Loving Spirit*. Daphne's first novel drew on the du Maurier secret; the next two were caught up with Daphne's relationship with her father and Uncle Jim, and with Jim's relationship with Gerald.

I'll Never Be Young Again was finished before *The Loving Spirit* was published. *Julius* was completed at the end of September 1931. One can imagine an eyebrow being raised at Adelphi Terrace House, and we know that Jim's friend Q chose this moment to take Daphne aside and speak to her 'about a code of living, and a standard, and that marriage and children meant more in life than all the novels and successes ever written'. Daphne decided on a big change, and included the decisive moment in her novel. At the end of *The Progress of Julius*, Gabriel announces that she is 'going to be someone else. Gabriel will go forever . . . I can't tell you what it's made me feel – all young again, and unspoilt, and as though I didn't know things.'

This was Daphne performing an alchemic ritual on herself, a tactic learned from Uncle Jim. She was effectively writing the manipulative 'Gabriel' out of her life. In October 1931 (a month after she finished *Julius*) a 35-year-old Major in the Grenadier Guards, Frederick Browning, sailed upriver towards Ferryside in a 20-foot cruiser named *Yggdrasil*. He and Daphne eventually met, fell in love, married in July, and honeymooned in Frenchman's Creek.

Daphne herself said it was 'a queer stroke of fate' that she had been 'picked' by a man who embodied precisely the kind of integrity Q had been expounding. Angela wrote, 'Fate or a good fairy played into their hands.' Yggdrasil is of course the enchanted ash in Norse mythology. The word means 'the tree of fate'. But there is more.

The family legend goes that Frederick Browning read *The Loving Spirit*, and so liked it that he came to see the place where it was set, hoping he might meet its author. When I first heard this twenty years ago, long before I knew about Jim, I wondered that a matter-of-fact, macho soldier like Browning should have enjoyed such a romantic novel so much that he decided to track down its author 300 miles away.

Later I discovered that there were, in fact, connections between the Brownings and the du Mauriers, which centred round the Garrick, a club to which Gerald and Jim belonged. And Daphne's suitor had two nicknames. One was 'Boy', the other 'Tommy'.

Was it all romantic happenstance, or was the puppeteer working overtime? What is certain is that the 'delicate' Daphne was now – with Romantic Tommy's intervention – someone else's responsibility. There is no record of Jim's reaction to the news of their engagement. Gerald is supposed to have broken down and cried.

Daphne and Tommy married three months after their first meeting. There was no question of it having been a shotgun wedding. Tommy, true to Q's principles, had awed Daphne with a polite refusal to sleep with her before marriage.

But Daphne was unsuited to the role of army wife, and Tommy soon began to aggravate her 'Daddy complex', emerging as something of a father-figure. He was ten years older than Daphne and expected her to minister to him, as Gerald had always expected Mo to do. Also, like Gerald, he was emotionally fragile and would take to bed with a collection of tatty, well-loved teddy bears.

Then, of course, their first child, Tessa, was not a boy. Later Tessa wrote:

> [My father] had very exacting standards of discipline and was well known for them. He expected his wife to conform, take an interest in the other officers' wives, as well as that of his soldiers' wives. Daphne was totally out of her depth. It was not her scene at all. She became pregnant and immediately decided that this was to be the boy that she longed for. When I was born her disappointment was intense.

So programmed was Daphne in Jim's boy-cult that she could not countenance mothering a girl. 'Daphne had wanted six little boys,' wrote Angela (one more than Jim). Her second child was another girl, Flavia, and when finally her boy did arrive, in 1940 – Kits – he alone of the children was allowed into her writing room, and Daphne was ecstatic.

In 1934, Gerald died. In the same year Daphne wrote and published her biography of him. She then left Tommy and Tessa in London in one of the Cannon Hall cottages and went to Cornwall to write *Jamaica Inn*, in which her 'muddled troubles' with her father and Jim drive the melodrama.

Orphan Mary Yellan falls prey to her adopted father, drunken Joss Merlyn, keeper of Jamaica Inn, who feels 'they ought to have made you [Mary] a boy'. Mary discovers Joss's secret, that he is bound into a secret society with an evil, elusive leader, Francis Davey, the Satanist Vicar of Altarnun ('Altar none'). Their business is the wrecking of ships off the north Cornwall coast. Conspiracy and secrecy pervade the text, as does the threat of violence and sexual abuse. Joss bends Mary's wrist (reminiscent of the father–daughter sadism in *Julius* and *The Scapegoat*) and tells her that he can 'have her' any time he pleases. At the end of the novel, Mary determines to follow Joss's brother, in effect her adopted uncle. She follows him like a hypnotic, not by choice but 'because I must'. His name – one might have guessed it – is 'Jem'.

The novel, later filmed by Alfred Hitchcock, was published in 1936, as Tommy took command of the 2nd Battalion Grenadier Guards in Alexandria. Daphne sailed to join him with Tessa and her nanny, Margaret, and on arrival loathed everything about Egypt, especially the official duties expected of the commanding officer's wife. Instead, she got on with a biography of her family, *The Du Mauriers*.

On 16 January 1937, Daphne took a boat back to England.

Daphne may have fled Egypt because she was pregnant and wanted to escape the oppressive atmosphere of life in Alexandria. But there is an additional reason: Uncle Jim was very unwell. He had been in ill health since the previous October. It had started with pains in the back, but he seemed to become smaller and more and more fragile as the days went by. Denis Mackail wrote of Barrie's 'Deep, deep depression in the solitude of the flat. And pains and sleeplessness, and the feeling that the doctors knew what was wrong with him, and wouldn't tell him because they were afraid.'

In February 1937 he was advised that 'the symptoms were chiefly psychological' and was treated 'with some electrical apparatus'. Moments of relief would be followed by others when 'he was just a scared, baffled and tormented mass of nerves'. Not until he was prescribed heroin did he get any relief.

Daphne's boat docked at Tilbury, but instead of disembarking she offloaded Margaret and Tessa (aged three and a half) and continued alone to Plymouth, thence to Ferryside. She stayed there until March, when Jim began to show signs of recovery and was well enough to receive visitors. In April he lunched with Stanley Baldwin, the Prime Minister.

On 1 April Daphne checked into a short-let apartment at Queen Anne Mansions, Queen Anne's Gate, less than a mile from Adelphi Terrace House, and to her surprise, because she wasn't yet due, gave birth to Flavia the following day. Thereafter, she remained in London until July.

Daphne was at a crossroads. The du Mauriers were planning a move. Mo and Jeanne were going to live at Ferryside, which would no longer be available to Daphne alone. Daphne's Cornwall was slipping away from her, and she was never going to escape from being an army wife, an itinerant appendage of Tommy Browning.

There is no record of her appointments in London, but it is inconceivable that she did not consult with the newly revived Uncle Jim, still well enough in May and early June, according to Mackail, to dine out and be 'in wonderful form, gay, competitively and successfully funny', though just as often deeply depressed. On 9 May he turned seventy-seven and the BBC broadcast a revival of *Dear Brutus*.

It was then that the idea of *Rebecca* was conceived, 'a sinister tale about a woman who marries a widower... Psychological and rather macabre,' as Daphne wrote to her publisher, now Victor Gollancz. The novel would be set not at Ferryside in Fowey, the Cornwall of *A Loving Spirit*, but at magical Menabilly, the house she had come upon beyond the Lodge at Four Turnings and which had been part of her dreams ever since. No one could take Cornwall from her imagination.

On 19 June, Jim died.

His funeral took place in Kirriemuir, and a memorial service was held in

St Paul's on the 30th by the Archbishop of Canterbury, who commented shrewdly:

> Though he saw the ultimate problems of human life with all the clearness of his vivid imagination, he attempted no solution of them, sometimes even seeming to resent while he could not resist their intrusion.

Resentment was the key.

When Daphne returned to Africa the following month, she left alone with Tommy, who had come to England on leave. Henceforth, *Rebecca* took precedence over everything, as Tessa reported:

> In July of that year [Flavia and I] were both left with our nanny in the charge of our paternal grandmother, whom we came to love dearly. Daphne and Boy returned to the terrible heat of Egypt.

Back in Alexandria, Daphne couldn't write and she couldn't sleep. She complained that she did not have the 'psychic energy'. She was prescribed Medinol, a sleeping pill, which calmed her. She managed 15,000 words of the novel and then threw them away. Was she upset by the separation from her little girls? Flavia was only three months old when Daphne left her. But when she returned to England in December, Daphne elected to go to Ferryside alone to finish her novel rather than spend Christmas with her children. Perhaps her writer's block had more to do with the loss of Jim. In any event it was Menabilly that eventually facilitated the writing of *Rebecca*. Dreaming true, Ibbetson-style, she fixed her mind not on an island but on a house:

> Last night I dreamt I went to Manderley again. It seemed to me I stood by the iron gate leading to the drive, and for a while I could not enter, for the way was barred to me. There was a padlock and a chain upon the gate. I called in my dream to the lodge-keeper, and had no answer, and peering closer through the rusted spokes of the gate I saw that the lodge was uninhabited.
>
> No smoke came from the chimney, and the little lattice windows gaped forlorn. Then, like all dreamers, I was possessed of a sudden with supernatural powers and passed like a spirit through the barrier before me. The drive wound away in front of me, twisting and turning as it had always done, but as I advanced I was aware that a change had come upon it . . .

The images are no longer those of the author's memory of Menabilly. The drive is '*not* the drive that we had known'. Nature has overwhelmed it, a nightmare of 'stealthy, insidious' growth, encroaching upon the drive with 'long, tenacious fingers'. The woods have triumphed, she sees 'the squat oaks and tortured elms . . . along with monster shrubs and plants, none of which I remembered'. This thread of a path led, surely, not to the house at all 'but to a labyrinth, some choked wilderness', journeying as it were down into the subhuman, through the dreamer's unconscious mind.

But then suddenly she emerges into a clearing, 'and I stood, my heart thumping in my breast, the strange prick of tears behind my eyes' –

> There was Manderley, our Manderley, secretive and silent as it had always been, the grey stone shining in the moonlight of my dream, the mullioned windows reflecting the green lawns and the terrace. Time could not wreck the perfect symmetry of those walls, nor the site itself, a jewel in the hollow of a hand.

Maxim de Winter's first wife, Rebecca, has been drowned, apparently in a yachting accident, her body never reclaimed from the holed boat at the bottom of the sea off the coast below Manderley. Maxim, handsome, commanding, with a strong military bearing, has married again. Quiet, self-effacing, vulnerable, the second Mrs de Winter is never named but identified by Daphne with her own dull, socially inept side as an army wife. Alfred Hitchcock always addressed the character as 'Daphne de Winter' on the set of the film.

Mrs de Winter is met by Rebecca's demonic acolyte, the mesmeric housekeeper, Mrs Danvers, who still worships her dead mistress, and now sets about mentally overpowering her replacement, who she can see is unfit to fill Rebecca's shoes. Rebecca's intimidating spirit pervades the house.

Daphne said that Rebecca sprang from an image she had of a beautiful, exotic brunette called Jan Ricardo, with whom her husband had had a brief affair before they were married, her long sloping handwriting on letters found in Tommy's desk indicating the dominant personality that Daphne thought Ricardo must have been.

But jealousy of Tommy's old flame, whom Daphne never knew, was not going to drive the writing of this novel. Mrs Danvers tells us what did, when she lets slip that Rebecca had the 'spirit of a boy . . . She ought to have been a boy, I often told her that . . . No one got the better of Rebecca.

She did what she liked, she lived as she liked.' Maxim couldn't possess her, and killed her when she proved his inadequacy.

In the finest scene of the novel, Mrs Danvers tempts the second Mrs de Winter into throwing herself from the window of Rebecca's bedroom, looking out through a sea mist over 'the little clearing where the satyr [Pan] plays his pipes . . .'

Rebecca's spirit is the supernatural 'spirit of a boy', untouchable, none other than Jim's demon boy. And finally we realise Daphne's purpose in writing *Rebecca*. She is writing Jim's demon boy into her life.

Mrs de Winter has a dream. She is writing letters in the morning room of Manderley. She looks down at what she has written and notices that it is not her handwriting. She gets up, looks at herself in the mirror, and it is not her face that stares back at her: 'The eyes narrowed and smiled. The lips parted. The face in the glass stared back at me and laughed.' Maxim brushes her hair, but it isn't hers. It is Rebecca's 'cloud of dark hair'.

The transmutation of Mrs de Winter is complete. 'I so identified with Rebecca that my own dull self did not exist.' And Daphne's single-minded purpose in writing the novel was also complete. She told her friend Oriel Malet that in writing it she had once and for all eliminated the doe-like Mrs de Winter side of her own character – 'I've never been her since.' *Rebecca* was Daphne's first alchemic text, her *Tommy*, her *Peter Pan*.

She took from the writing of *Rebecca* 'a power thing', which was exhilarating and altered her life completely. Imbued with Rebecca's spirit, instead of remaining the itinerant wife of an army major, she became one of the world's most popular novelists, and had an affair with a married man, Henry 'Christopher' Puxley, which led him 'to drink himself to the brink of insanity while his wife lost her youth because of it'.[11]

She then wrote *Frenchman's Creek* (1941), based on the affair, setting the most romantic part of it in a creek off the Helford River, where Daphne and Tommy had spent their honeymoon – ultimate treachery perhaps.

In 1943 followed *Hungry Hill*, a thinly disguised fictional history of Puxley's family, with Christopher, charming, attractive, but weak and inadequate, a mixture of lost alcoholic 'Wild Johnnie' and his lovably treacherous brother Henry.

Thereafter, still driven by 'the demon boy' in her, Daphne engaged in two affairs with women, Ellen Doubleday and Gertrude Lawrence.

Throughout this period, from *Rebecca* to the start of her awakening in 1950–51, her relationships had little to do with reality, they were 'pure Gondal'.[12] She dwelt in a fantasy world in which she treated real people as mere 'pegs' onto whom she hung her emotions. Only later, in 1955, could she accept that 'Pegs, poor dears, have their emotions also.'[13]

That Rebecca appeared on Daphne's fantasy palette in the very year that Jim bowed out is at least appropriate. The persona was conceived when she was in England during the last months of Jim's life. It was the little spark of himself that retained control. The demon boy was, until after her breakdown in 1958, part of Daphne's self-image. He had been written into her life.

In December 1943, with the huge royalties from *Rebecca*, Daphne took a long lease on Menabilly. This was her new persona's crowning achievement and immediately proved its value to the imagination in a new novel, *The King's General* (1946), which celebrated Daphne's possession of her 'house of secrets' by exhuming an episode in its history – the discovery, during building works in 1824, of a skeleton of a young man seated on a stool, a Cavalier of the Civil War, walled up in a sealed room. The cavalier was an Eric Avon/Gerald character, walled up in the house that was a symbol of Daphne's unconscious.

Menabilly was all to Daphne that she hoped. It became the only place where her creative self could operate freely. At Menabilly there was always a book brewing in her mind. Flavia recalls that she would spend all morning in her writing hut with its view of the sea, 'and in the afternoon she would be free for an hour or so to go for a long walk. Wrapped up against the chill wind we would set off across the fields, armed with stout sticks to feel more boyish', and invariably they would talk 'about a character in the book she was writing, about how she would start thinking like that person and pretend to be them . . . And I would tell her of the strange dreams I had.'[14]

The Menabilly woods were home to other eccentrics too. Here a certain Captain Vandeleur lived in his hut, 'painted green to camouflage it during the War'. Further afield, two old ladies lived in 'a witch's cottage, half-submerged by undergrowth . . . overtaken by time and forgotten', as Oriel Malet wrote. These were strange neighbours, glimpsed but occasionally, perfectly in keeping with the imaginative world Daphne, and the children, now occupied.

Tommy was demobbed in 1947, and took up a position as Comptroller and Treasurer to Princess Elizabeth. For the next twenty years he led a dual existence between London during the week and Menabilly at weekends. It was not ideal. When he grew unhappy, disconsolate and demoralised Daphne changed his nickname from Tommy to 'Moper'.

It was clear to Daphne that Browning could no longer lay claim to the title of Tommy. Their marriage had proved Jim's principle that people are pegs on which we hang our emotions. Browning never was Tommy; she could see that now.

At weekends, when he was at home, this was obvious. Flavia gives us the picture:

> If [my father] was in a jolly frame of mind he would hold forth on politics, local events and his boats . . .Kits and I would stay mute, in case picked on. Bing, if she was brewing a story, would sit at her end of the table, picking at her food and staring into space, a vacant look on her face. My father would suddenly pounce and ask her a question: 'Well, what do you think, Duck?' (They called each other Duck.) She would drag herself back to the present: 'Well, I can hardly say, Duck,' she would reply, a faint smile on her face. My father would look down the table at her and thunder, 'Woman, you live in a dream!' which indeed she did . . .[15]

In the same year as Tommy returned, a lawsuit citing Daphne and alleging plagiarism in *Rebecca* came to court in America. One Edwina L. Macdonald sued over a story she had published in October 1924 in *Heall's International Magazine*, under the title 'I Planned to Murder My Husband', which was then written as a novel, *Blind Windows*. Daphne had not heard of the woman or her work, but she had to take the witness stand in New York, and suddenly her Rebecca persona was to be put to a real test.

She was to be the star witness. It should have been Rebecca's greatest performance. The plan was to travel with Flavia and Kits on the liner *Queen Mary* and stay at Barberrys, the home of Ellen Doubleday, wife of Daphne's American publisher. Ellen appeared one morning in the stateroom. Flavia recalled 'a slim elegant woman, her arms filled with white flowers for Bing', who was 'closely followed by a steward bearing a basket of splendidly wrapped gifts for us all. We were quite taken aback.'[16]

Daphne was 'made speechless' by the 'Rebecca qualities' she perceived in Ellen, the well-heeled daughter-in-law of the founder of Doubleday, at that time the largest publisher in the English-speaking world. Ellen was sophisticated, at ease with people and the power she held over them. Later Daphne came to admire her maternal qualities just as much, marvelling that this career woman could also be a caring mother of four and a comforting wife to her husband Nelson Doubleday, head of the family firm, a hard drinker and beset by neuritis. But, in particular, she loved the way Ellen comforted and advised her each day when she came back from court. Without Ellen, she would have been lost.

Daphne's problem in court was insoluble. She was asked to expound on the genesis of *Rebecca*. How could she? She could not even explain to herself how she had come to write it. Her silence was fused into the nature of the secret world of imagination in which she lived – although she did not see it like that.

She wrote to Maureen Baker-Munton that she couldn't bring herself to make public that she had written the novel out of feelings of jealousy over Tommy's affair with Jan Ricardo, and that the fear of this becoming known had sent her 'nearly off my rocker'.

But jealousy is not an issue in the novel. *Rebecca* is about *possession.* Rebecca possesses Manderley and then she possesses Mrs de Winter. And possession was Jim Barrie's scene, not Jan Ricardo's. The brief fling between Tommy and Ricardo had been before Tommy had even met Daphne. Moreover, Ricardo was now dead. She had married another man in 1937 and died during the war, having thrown herself under a train, an event that occurred (with its own tragic coincidence) after *Rebecca* was published. At the time of the plagiarism case Ricardo was not around to protest, and Tommy couldn't have cared less what Daphne said in New York. So, why was she so concerned not to make the Ricardo affair public? Was it that her jealousy would make her appear petty or silly? Possibly. But was this enough to bring on a nervous breakdown? For that is what happened. Daphne had a serious breakdown after the case.

Daphne's problem in court was not Ricardo, but that of most victims of possession when they are told to name their controller: they cannot see that they are being controlled. None of Jim's victims ever had anything bad to say about him. Nor do victims of possession in the many cases that come before the courts today.

For example, in 2005 Robert Hendy-Freegard commandeered the lives of eight people by persuading them that their safety was under threat by the IRA, duping some of them into thinking he was recruiting them to MI5, subjecting them to a series of bizarre rituals and relieving them of a million pounds (he is now serving a life sentence). His victims described being controlled as being in 'a prison cell that followed you around and *you couldn't leave*'.

Freegard was described in the press as having 'kept a Svengali-like hold' over his victims, all of whom were intelligent people, among them a lawyer, a psychologist, a company director, a civil servant, and three students. They were completely bound up in his fantasy world, but in the real world were on auto-pilot, unable to see what was going on. A friend of one victim said, 'It was impossible to talk to her sensibly.'

After Freegard's conviction, they were able to accept that they had been manipulated, but it took special counselling to bring them to it, and their awakening was a delicate process. Had they been summoned as witnesses to court beforehand – as in effect Daphne was being summoned before her awakening – they would have been quite unable to give evidence against Freegard, and might have manufactured an alternative 'Ricardo' explanation for what had been going on, fully believing the story themselves. Lawyers pushing them into a corner might have opened the floodgates to anxiety, and quite possibly to breakdown.

In the *Rebecca* case the judge was asking Daphne to look into areas into which a skilled psychoanalyst might have been reluctant to take her. It was, Daphne wrote, one of two occasions when 'the fear of reality' broke in.* Confusion and paranoia ensued. Daphne broke down, and that is when, as she put it, 'I turned bang to Ellen.'

She turned to Ellen, the mother of four, as if to her own mother – the mother she had never had. Ellen released 'a subconscious thwarted longing to have sat on Mummy's lap'. Daphne even believed herself possessed by the spirit of a miscarried child of Ellen. Sending her a manuscript for publication became 'like a child thrusting a bunch of daisies into its mother's hand'.

Ten years later she explained that her relationships with Ellen, and with Ferdie and Gertrude Lawrence, were 'all part of a nervous breakdown going on *inside myself* [her emphasis], partly to do with my muddled troubles, and writing, and a fear of facing reality'.[17]

Jim had a hand in all of it: Daphne's 'muddled troubles' with Gerald; the 'writing' of Rebecca into her; the 'fear of facing reality' from the 'prison cell' of fantasy to which he had consigned her: 'I wasn't just fighting a foolish case for plagiarism,' she wrote from to Ellen, 'I was fighting all the evil that has ever been.'

Central to Daphne's affair with Ellen was Eric Avon, Daphne's teenage alter ego. Her feelings for Ellen released 'a boy of eighteen all over again

* Letter from Daphne du Maurier to Maureen Baker-Munton, 4 July 1957. The other occasion was in 1957 when she wrote to her husband, Tommy, confessing her affairs.

with nervous hands and a beating heart, incurably romantic and wanting to throw a cloak before his lady's feet'. Wrote Margaret Forster:

> A boy, not a girl, the boy she explained she had 'locked up in a box' long ago when she had accepted that, since she was outwardly a girl, she must face facts and live as a girl.[18]

But this 'boy' was not a lesbian, as this suggests; '. . . by God and by Christ,' Daphne wrote later to Ellen, 'if anyone should call that sort of love by that unattractive word that begins with "L", I'd tear their guts out.' Her desire to play 'boy' was a return to the fantasy boy released in her by Jim and suppressed since childhood – she even cast Ellen in the role of Mary Stuart as her foil. Sex was not the point. Unable to face reality, either in or out of court, she ceded control once more to Jim. It was the inevitable character of the breakdown, because at bottom the breakdown was due to Jim. She was, as later she acknowledged, short-circuiting, reverting to her childhood fantasy world. Just as Daphne reverted when under pressure in New York, so George on the fields of the Somme was reading *The Little White Bird*, the story of his captivation. One wonders what fantasy reversion eased Michael into Sandford Pool, and tipped Peter into nothingness at Sloane Square tube station.

Ellen handled Daphne's breakdown with exquisite poise, above and beyond the call of duty as her publisher (though she did end up with the American copyright of *Rebecca*). Nor did she blanch when Daphne wrote her into a play, *September Tide*.

Ellen had been dreading a lesbian plot. Had she known Daphne better she would have expected what she got: not quite incest, but 'love within the family', between a young artist, Evan, and his mother-in-law, Stella. Evan was pegged on Daphne; Stella on Ellen. Daphne as playwright then conspired to make Stella fall in love with Evan, as Jim had conspired to match Gerald and Daphne in *Dear Brutus*. But the casting of the play changed everything.

Noël Coward came to dinner at Barberrys, made a great fuss of Flavia and Kits, 'showing us tricks of throwing nuts into the air and catching them in our mouths', and introduced Daphne to Gertrude Lawrence. Gertie had form with Daphne's father, Gerald. She had been one of his 'stable'. They had starred together in *Behold, We Live* by John Van Druten at the St James's Theatre in 1932.

There was never any question from the moment Daphne met Gertie that she would play Stella. 'Suddenly I was overwhelmed with an obsessional passion for the last of Daddy's actress loves,' Daphne wrote to Maureen Baker-Munton. At the heart of everything Daphne wrote, and everyone she loved, was her relationship with her father, disfigured by the 'paradigm of intimacy' with Jim.

Her next step was to put her feelings in a novel and try to effect a relationship with Gertie. She set about writing *The Parasites* (1949) about a theatrical family called Delaney. Weak, possessive Pappy Delaney was Gerald. His children, Niall, Maria and Celia, were to be 'the three people I know myself to have been'. Daphne 'who turned to Ferdie, and later to Ellen and Gertrude' cast herself as Niall (the boy on stage) and had him fall in love with Maria (the actress on stage).[19] The alchemic reaction worked. Gertie and Daphne made love over a weekend in Florida.[20] Thus Daphne's affair with Gertie was predicted in her fiction, just as her intimacy with her father had been sealed in *Dear Brutus*. She was again operating in main-stream Barrie-inspired mind control territory.

From *Rebecca* on, she used her fiction to 're-write' the lives of herself and the people she used as pegs, to exercise her will upon relationships, and eventually to rid herself of unwanted influences. All of this came directly from Uncle Jim.

Now was the time that Peter Llewelyn Davies came back into her life, and Daphne began putting her life in order. Her tenth novel, *My Cousin Rachel*, written shortly after her foray with Gertie in Florida, was the alchemic vehicle selected for the purpose.

Daphne explained all in a letter to her friend Maureen Baker-Munton: 'Gertrude and Ellen merged to make the single figure of Rachel . . . In the book I killed both.' Later, she reiterated in a letter to Oriel Malet that she was writing her two female lovers out of her life by killing Rachel off. 'It was only by making [Rachel] die that I was able to rid myself of it [my obsession]. For writers, the only way we can do it, is to write them out.'

Coming upon Daphne at Menabilly at this time, one could be forgiven for thinking one had stepped into a world more supernatural even than Barrie's flat on the Strand. Daphne revelled in her reputation locally for being something of a psychic. She joked to Oriel that the locals believed her to have 'a little Hut somewhere in the woods, where she would call up the spirits and get them to write her books. She was always in a trance they used to say.' She was laughing at the locals, but the truth was that she did have a hut where she wrote her books, and she did believe that 'a writer is a kind of medium', and was perfectly serious about her alchemic use of texts.

Her friend of twenty years, the explorer Clara Vyvyan, went on holiday with her, and marvelled at her ability to sit in a trance on some mountainside in Europe and return hours later 'in a mood of mountain ecstasy'. At Menabilly, in the summer of '58, she slept out for nights on end beneath the stars and on one occasion (not for the first or last time) experienced a sensation of breaking through into the order of things that lies beneath the everyday world.

My Cousin Rachel was published in 1951, and in the following year Daphne's meetings with Peter yielded her first short story collection, *The Apple Tree*. The opening story, a novella called 'Monte Verita', is, as she wrote to Maureen, 'about myself and Tommy'. Here, for the first time Daphne takes the blame for the tensions in her marriage, but there are other concerns. The story cuts right into the fabric of the fantasy world in which she had been living since she was a child.

Tommy (Victor, a mountaineer in the story) loses sight of Daphne (Anna), with whom he is helplessly in love, while climbing Monte Verita, a mountain in an unspecified European country. Anna has been taken in by a cult of boys lodged in an ancient monastery on the mountainside. Under their guidance she appears to find her Nirvana and experiences a mystical sense of ultimate truth, an insight into the essence of all things. Her husband, Victor, is convinced that she has been 'hypnotised and is speaking under suggestion'. He descends the mountain on his own, and has a nervous breakdown.

The third character in the story is the narrator, who tells us what happened when he went up the mountain to try and trace Anna. He hears the cult members chanting; it is 'unearthly, terrifying, yet beautiful in a way impossible to bear'. He is then surprised by the cult of boys and thrown into a cell, where he is haunted by the mocking laughter of one boy in particular, referred to as 'that damned boy'. He is overcome by the boy, indeed by a whole host of boys, and knowing he is no match for them he gives himself up to death at their hands. 'I expected the laughter again, mocking and youthful, and the sudden seizing of my body with their hands, and the savage thrusting of me through the slit window to darkness and to death.' He closes his eyes and waits, braced for horror. Then, amazingly, he feels 'the boy touch my lips . . . [and] it was as if the peace of God came upon me, quiet and strong, and, with the touch of hands, took from me all anxiety and fear'.

The cult of Monte Verita is unmistakably Barrie's boy-cult, where being a boy heightens awareness, and never growing up is the path to immortality. It is also a reference to *Faust*,* Goethe's play in which Faust is himself 'transmuted' into a boy and admitted into the 'choir of blessed youths', as part of his rehabilitation and transformation after his soul has been rescued by the angels. In the first draft of the story Anna was transformed into a boy, but Daphne's publisher Victor Gollancz refused to accept what he saw as a trans-sexual transformation and Daphne did not enlighten him.

Following his initiation the narrator is convinced that, like Anna, he has found his Nirvana, as Daphne too had felt. But it will be bad for him, as all of a sudden, we see it was for Anna. When she and the narrator meet, she throws back her cowl and reveals the truth. 'You see, it isn't Paradise . . .' she says.

The narrator reels in horror.

> It was as though all feeling had been frozen. My heart was cold. One side of Anna's face was eaten quite away, ravaged, terrible. The disease had come upon her brow, her cheek, her throat, blotching, searing her skin. The eyes that I loved were blackened, sunk deep into the sockets.

The whole ghastly vision is a sick recollection of the vision of hell that had been Sylvia's on seeing her beloved Arthur's face, ravaged by cancer.

As *The Apple Tree* appeared in the bookshops, on 6 September 1952, Daphne was shocked to learn that Gertrude Lawrence had died suddenly of cancer.

Just fourteen months after she pegged Rachel on Gertie in *My Cousin Rachel*, with the express purpose of killing her off and thus writing Gertie out of her life, the actress had died for real, at only 54. 'My God,' Daphne wrote to Oriel, 'you have to be jolly careful when you bring [pegs] into practical living issues.'

Daphne claimed that it took four years to get over Gertie's death, not because she missed her, but because she was shocked to discover that Gertie, after she died, meant nothing to her at all. In truth, Daphne cared

* The *Faust* reference is detailed and incontrovertible, although the original notion of a pagan choir probably occurred to Daphne on a trip through the Valley of the Rhone, where she and her friend Clara Vyvyan witnessed a primitive service in a church in the mountains. The holiday is described in Vyvyan's book *Down the Rhone on Foot* (1955).

less for losing Gertrude than for the gap her death left in her fantasy life. 'I was quite bouleversée by the death; *not* because how sad, a friend had died, but how bottomless – a Peg had vanished! A fabric that one had built had disintegrated!'

Their affair had been a fiction inscribed by her imagination on the fabric of her life. It was, she said, 'pure Gondal', purely imaginary. Recording her feelings about this woman whom she had 'known' intimately but only ever 'in character', Daphne began to realise that in allowing not only 'a character in a book to develop from a real person [but also] a real person being pegged from a character', she was living in an unenviable realm totally divorced from reality.

'Tray goes through many more inner experiences than you have perhaps credited her with,' she wrote to Oriel in October 1956, 'and when you say, as you have in the past, how beaming my life must be, you have perhaps not realised the rather fantastic inner world I have so often dwelt in . . .'

More incredible still, the whole episode parallels *Behold, We Live*, the play in which Gerald had starred with Gertrude in 1932. Gerald (Gordon Evers) doesn't want to upset Gertrude (Sarah Casenove) by telling her that he is terminally ill. In their last farewell, an emotional scene, the audience knows that they will never see one another again, but Sarah (Gertie) is unaware. Charles Laughton said it was the most effective scene he had ever witnessed in the theatre. And it was exactly the one played out in America the last time Gertie and Daphne met – but this time the roles were reversed. The reality was, if you like, a mirror image of the fantasy. Gertie knew she had cancer when she said her last heartfelt goodbye to Daphne from her bed at two o'clock one morning in Florida, but she withheld the information so as not to upset her. Daphne remembered her last words: 'Go from me, and don't look back, like a person walking in their sleep.' She used them in 'Kiss Me Again, Stranger', another story in *The Apple Tree*.

CHAPTER TWO

Breakdown and suicide

In 1954 Daphne began experiencing physical symptoms of another breakdown. Margaret Forster wrote simply: 'Daphne felt strange and could not account for it . . .'

From her stories, and her decision to put her life in order, we know that Daphne's awakening had begun, but there was a long way to go before she could look outside the 'prison cell'. Her discussions with Peter Davies had made her conscious of her predicament. She had a modicum of objectivity and had begun to see that her fantasy life was impinging on the real world to the detriment of her marriage and possibly other facets of her life.

Now, fired by events, she embarked on a lengthy period of soul-searching, surrounding herself with books about psychology and ancient religion. In the process, she discovered Jung and was drawn to his division of the psyche into the No. 1 conscious self and the No. 2 unconscious, creative self, which gave her a modern way to understand 'boy'. It was at this time that she wrote to Flavia that being 'madly boyish . . . has a lot to do with my writing'. Her boy-self was her No. 2, her creative unconscious. That was henceforth how she thought about it. She made it her purpose to follow Jung and find a new balance between her two selves. Naturally, she turned to writing to effect this balance.

The idea for *The Scapegoat* came to her in 1955 while on holiday in the du Maurier homeland of Sarthe, in north-west France. Its title implies Daphne's status as victim, 'scapegoat of the family's sins'. The author's two selves are the Englishman John (No. 1 self) and his physical double and dark side, the Frenchman Jean (No. 2). As she later wrote to Maureen: 'The two sides of that man's nature [John/Jean] had to fuse together to give birth to a third, well-balanced.' The novel, filmed with Alec Guinness, is a telling analysis of where her thinking had brought her only a few years now before Peter committed suicide.

However, Daphne's good intentions were thrown out of the window when, in July 1957, Tommy became ill. The diagnosis of Lord Evans, under whose care he fell, was that he had suffered a nervous breakdown, that there was an underlying psychological problem which manifested itself in his excessive drinking, leading to liver damage, arterial dysfunction, 'personality deterioration' and collapse. Evans realised that Tommy's troubled relationship with Daphne lay at the bottom of it. He told Daphne that she could be as useful as the pills he could give her husband. Meanwhile, to complicate the issue, Tommy confessed to having been leading a double life in London with a mistress.*

Daphne was knocked back by the revelations of Tommy's infidelity. Biographers have implied that this led to her most serious nervous breakdown in 1957–8. But Daphne had been unfaithful to her husband on and off for sixteen years, possibly with both female and male lovers. She had insisted on separate bedrooms at Menabilly, and mocked him when he demurred. Would she have had a breakdown because he had conducted an affair with seemly solicitude a long way from home?

Nagging at the back of Daphne's mind was the feeling that Tommy's illness fitted into what she referred to as 'a strange chain of events'. After *My Cousin Rachel*, which predicted Gertrude's death, Gertrude had died suddenly. Now, after 'Monte Verita', in which she had Tommy (as Victor) suffer a breakdown, Tommy really was having a breakdown. And there had been other more mundane coincidences. When she wrote about a character catching German measles in *The Scapegoat*, she herself contracted the disease within the month. When she wrote about a pregnant woman having

* Daphne was told who Tommy's mistress was, and made a point of meeting her, but by chance I discovered that Tommy's London lifestyle had been a good deal more racy than even Daphne learned. In the early 1950s Barbara Taylor Bradford was a young journalist in Fleet Street and a firm friend of a lady from Kentucky called Jeannie Gilbert, who had been very close to Tommy Browning.

'When I met Jeannie she was already working at the Savoy. At some point while promoting Diners Club she met this man, Lieutenant-General Sir Frederick Browning, who was very taken with her. He must have been a director of the Savoy Group because he got Jeannie the job of PR of the Savoy, Claridges and the Berkeley. She was widely regarded as the best press officer the Savoy Group ever had . . . And she was very pretty. There was a picture of Browning always in her house, with him in that uniform. He was living in London and she saw a lot of him.'

Tommy had indeed been a director of the Savoy, and Jeannie had helped keep him away from that dreary little flat in Whitelands, with its squeaky floorboards and faint smell of gas and eau-de-cologne. 'Now, whether or not they had intercourse I don't know,' Barbara concluded. 'I wasn't under the bed. But she always said to me that that is how she got the job.'

to have a blood transfusion in the novel, her daughter Tessa gave birth to a son who had to have two transfusions.

Immediately after Tommy's collapse, on 4 July 1957, Daphne wrote a letter to Maureen Baker-Munton, telling her that she accepted blame for the parlous state of their marriage and Tommy's decline; she then came clean with him, by letter, about Puxley, Ellen and Gertrude.* It had a disastrous effect. He never fully recovered from it. Had she filled him in about playing 'boy' and finding in the arms of women the love she hadn't received from Mo? Did she share with him her awakening to what had been going on in her childhood?

All that we know is that Daphne got it into her head that Tommy was seeing things wrong. She wrote to Oriel Malet, 'I do feel very much like Gerda in that fairy tale [*The Snow Queen*], knowing that the ice is not yet out of Kay's eye, and wondering what is the right thing to do about it.' Kay was Tommy; Daphne told Oriel that if she had anything secret to say about Tommy, she could use Kay as his name.

It is likely that when Daphne confessed all to Tommy in 1957 she told him more or less what she told Maureen Baker-Munton in the letter of 4 July the same year, that her affair with Puxley and her 'obsessions – you can only call them that – for poor old Ellen D and Gertrude – were all part of a nervous breakdown going on inside myself, partly to do with my muddled troubles, and writing, and a fear of facing reality'.

Her 'muddled troubles' concerned her relationship with her father, murky with the influence of Uncle Jim. Her 'fear of facing reality' was due to the glimpses she had (in the New York court room) that living and writing within the fantasy realm to which she had been 'introduced' as a child was compulsive, and inimical to her and her life with Tommy.

But did she accuse Uncle Jim? Did she tell Tommy that as a child she, like the Llewelyn Davies boys, had been drawn into this fantasy world by Jim and had ceded control of her mind to him? Was that what Tommy refused to see?

Between 1957 and 1959 Daphne wrote the stories in *The Breaking Point* which are damning of Jim. The suggestion is that, like Peter, she had awakened to the control Jim exercised over her. But how much did Daphne know? Writers deliver truths about their lives *unconsciously* through their fiction. We cannot be sure what Daphne *consciously* knew of the extent of Jim's influence over her at any point.

* Alas, her letter to Tommy is not available.

In *The Snow Queen* the little boy Kay gets a splinter of the hobgoblin's looking-glass in his eye. This has the power to make everything good or beautiful that is reflected in it almost shrink to nothing, while everything worthless and bad is exaggerated and made worse than ever.

Daphne wrote to Oriel that 'the ice is not yet out of Kay's eye'. The implication is that Tommy was seeing things worse than they were, which in turn suggests that, in the summer of 1957, Daphne was still to some extent 'clouded over' about Jim.

Daphne doubted not only Tommy, but also his doctors – 'I am inclined to think [they] have made matters worse.' In her eyes, at this stage, Tommy was the victim, not her.

The mind does everything in its power to avoid a breakdown, to rationalise a situation, to distort 'the facts' to make an impulse seem less threatening. But Daphne, especially in her conversations with Peter Davies, was getting under the mind's defences: she wanted to know what the hypnotist had told her to forget. When she found it, then reality, and anxieties connected with the truth, came rushing in.

By the beginning of 1958, she was in such a state that Oriel became seriously concerned for her sanity.

> Bing became obsessed with some plot which she believed was being hatched against herself, and especially against Tommy. For a time she even persuaded herself that they might try to get at her through me, in Paris. She rang me several times, warning me not to go out at night alone, and to avoid all public places, such as the metro . . . I had either to believe that Bing had gone completely off her head, or that some sort of fearful plot was actually afoot, which might lead, in true Guy Fawkes fashion, to bombs at Buckingham Palace. No-one could shake her out of her delusions.[1]

Daphne suffered the pains of paranoia.

> We must be patient . . . Unless we recognise it in time, accept it, understand it, we are all destroyed, just as the people in 'The Birds' were destroyed . . . For all our sakes, we must know that dark side . . .[2]

Only her son, Kits, could reach her, and did so, just as seven-year-old Jamie Barrie had reached his mother ninety years earlier. Kits encouraged

Daphne to turn her fears into a fantasy game, giving everyone weird tribal names, and he finally made her laugh.

By mid-way through '58, Daphne began to exorcise her fears by pulling together the stories in *The Breaking Point*. Now, she could understand. Now, she knew. 'There comes a moment in the life of every individual,' she wrote, 'when reality must be faced. When this happens, it is as though some link between emotion and reason is stretched to the limit of endurance, and sometimes snaps.'

Every one of the *Breaking Point* stories is about disillusionment and treachery, Barrie's treachery, each one lifting the pressure from her system and perhaps saving her. She wrote to Oriel:

> I have been right down into the depths of horror, but I am coming out now.

'The Chamois' is the subtlest of the stories. It announces Daphne's decision to go on the hunt for the goat-foot god responsible for her family's misery. Writing it was another example of Daphne's astonishing will, her courage and, as ever, her complete faith in the power of texts to change real life.

The chamois is an image of fluency in Daphne's story, its ability to climb to the highest peaks a metaphor for mystical potential. She accords the animal a sixth sense. Stephen persuades his wife to accompany him on a hunting trip. He hunts *only* chamois. He wants them dead because their ability to climb so high terrifies him; while his wife loves them for that very reason and despises 'the communion of flesh' that has bridged her soul and his spiritually barren soul.

The wife in the story is clearly Daphne, and Stephen represents Tommy, who, as Daphne saw it, was out of touch with his spiritual side.

The goatherd who will take them to the chamois has 'the voice of a child' and hypnotic eyes. There is an otherworldly feel, even shades of shamanism, about him: he is called Jesus, or Zus (like Zeus) for short. He and the chamois are identified: they share the same 'whistle' and merge into a half-man, half-goat amalgam, the satyr of myth – Pan.

The wife is 'seized with a kind of horror, for the man's eyes do not go with the gentle, childish voice'. Like Barrie he has 'the sightless gaze of a man without vision', apparently absent from the real world; but if his eyes rested on you, they did so 'with a searching stare impossible to hold'.

That night she has a dream about him, and is shocked that she finds Zus's primitive nature sexually attractive. There is something sensual but repulsive about him. She is afraid of him, but also physically attracted. She realises now that she must turn against him, and join the hunt.

> Stephen was after chamois. I was after Man. Both were symbolic of something abhorrent to our natures. We wanted to destroy the thing that shamed us most.

Imagine how Daphne's thinking at this time fed into the mind of Peter Davies. The mind set of everyone had deteriorated in 1957 – Tommy, Daphne, Peter and Jack. Only Daphne would pull through.

According to Nico, in October '54 Peter had been 'in good form', although in the same year Peter himself referred to 'my innate and circumstantial gloom'. By October '57 Nico wrote to Nanny: 'The business I believe to be thriving, but Peter is not. He hasn't been really well for a year or two. I can't remember how much I've said about this in the past, but I haven't really known what the trouble is until this year.'[3] Unaware of what was really going on, he believed that Peter's fundamental problem was emphysema and indeed Peter was admitted to King Edward VII Sanatorium at Midhurst in West Sussex, a hospital specialising in lung disease, for three or four weeks that autumn. Emphysema was also one of the causes of Jack's death, listed on his death certificate, and he too was in serious depressive decline in 1957.

Breathing affects emotions, and emotions affect breathing. Anxiety and anger are associated with accelerated breathing, and depression with suppressed breathing. It is common for lung disease and depression to go hand in hand. Either can trigger the other. 'The vicious circle can begin with depression,' confirms Dr Rachel Norwood of the National Jewish Medical and Research Centre in Denver. Also, depressed people tend to smoke, and smoking can cause chronic pulmonary disease, which, with emphysema, is what got Jack.

In April 1959, after making only a partial recovery, Tommy announced his retirement from Royal service. On 19 July he returned to live full-time at Menabilly, initially in the care of a nurse. Daphne, seeing how dependent he was going to be – at one stage Tommy had threatened to shoot himself – realised she would have to have a project to take her away from Menabilly. So began *The Infernal World of Branwell Brontë* (1960), with its built-in requirement for research in Yorkshire and London.

In 1954, she had received a serendipitous invitation from the publisher

Macdonald to write an Introduction to *Wuthering Heights*, and Oriel had sent her Fannie Ratchford's *The Brontës' Web of Childhood*. Ratchford, the first to transcribe the Brontë juvenilia, published her complete analysis in 1941. It is amazing, given Daphne's interest in the Brontës, and her empathy with the Brontë siblings' intense involvement with their imaginary worlds, Angria and Gondal, that she hadn't already read it, but its significance in the unravelling of her own secret life should not be underestimated. After a first visit to the Parsonage Museum with Oriel and Flavia in 1955, the idea to write the biography dawned.

However, as it turned out, Daphne's *Branwell* is not really a biography at all. Like almost everything she wrote, it concerns herself. Branwell, the boy who never grew up, the trickster-boy, 'brimful of mischief as a bog pixie', is also the Master, for it is he who first orchestrates the imaginary worlds the Brontë siblings inhabit.

Daphne considered first the physical similarities. Branwell 'was almost insignificantly small – one of life's trials'. Her adult Branwell is a boy 'who had not grown an inch since he turned fourteen', and self-conscious on account of this, brushing his hair 'high off his forehead to help his height'. He also had 'a great, bumpy, intellectual forehead, nearly half the size of the whole facial contour and a downcast look, which never varied'. Nature had maimed him physically and psychologically, and she used Barrie's phrase to characterise Branwell's battle against fate to avoid becoming a 'might-have been'.

The children's imaginary worlds of Gondal and Angria first took shape the day their father brought Branwell a box of lead soldiers. Juliet Barker commented in *The Brontës*[4] that as the stories multiplied, the soldiers changed character. For example, Charlotte's favourite soldier changed from being Arthur Wellesley to the Marquis of Douro and the Duke of Zamorna. But in Daphne's hands this rapidly becomes a Barrie-inspired alchemic ritual, so that it is Charlotte herself who is transformed by the soldiers: 'The plain, intensely shy, seventeen-year-old ex-schoolgirl was none other than Arthur Wellesley, Marquis of Douro, soon to be Duke of Zamorna.' Daphne observes transmutations for Emily and Anne, too, and great pains are taken to depict the transmutation and empowerment of Branwell, 'Chief Genius Brannii', the boyish controller of their infernal world. His whole life is transformed as Alexander Percy, future Viscount Ellrington and Earl of Northangerland, who is everything Branwell longed to be – a mountain of a man, a success with the ladies, heroic, but demonic too. He 'looked like Lucifer, Star of the Morning. And the sneer was here before me too. . .It was a sneer of calm contempt at himself and nature.' It is the sneer in the portrait of Dorian Gray, it is Peter Pan's cynical, 'frightful sneer at the laws of nature'.

So, here we have Daphne's true vision of Uncle Jim – 'Satan had usurped his body . . . that Satan could seize his right hand and master it, compelling it to write what it had no desire to write. The prospect was too hideous to contemplate.'*

The transformation into Percy took Branwell into a pact with the Devil, as Barrie with Peter Pan –

> O Percy! Percy! where art thou? –
> I've sacrificed my God for thee . . .

Percy becomes Branwell's 'second self', though we are never sure whether the whole thing happens only in his mind.

Margaret Forster criticised Daphne for mixing documentary fact 'in the most awkward fashion with entirely imaginary suppositions, greatly to [the book's] detriment'. Go to *The Infernal World of Branwell Brontë* for a biography of Branwell and you may be disappointed, but go to it knowing that Daphne had just come out of a major breakdown over J. M. Barrie's destruction of her family, and you will be enthralled. No wonder that during the writing of it she suffered 'the kind of paranoid imaginings which had afflicted her after Tommy's breakdown'.[5]

And of course Daphne grasped the thrill of fantasy and the clandestine nature of the Angria and Gondal games, which Charlotte described so well:

> How few would believe that from the sources purely imaginary such happiness could be derived – Pen cannot portray the deep Interest of the scenes, of the continued train of events, I have witnessed in that little room with the low narrow bed & bare white-washed walls . . . What a treasure is thought! What a privilege is reverie – I am thankful that I have the power of solacing myself with the dream of creations whose reality I shall never behold – May I never lose that power may I never feel it grow weaker – If I should

* The reference is clearly to Barrie, although Daphne got it wrong, it was his left hand Satan seized. Due to writer's cramp he had been forced to learn to write with the left hand, and noticed the difference in the material it produced. 'The right has the happier nature, the left is naturally sinister,' he wrote in *The Greenwood Hat*. It was not so much that he wrote things with the left as 'it writes things with me . . . I never, as far as I can remember, wrote uncomfortable tales like *Dear Brutus* and *Mary Rose* till I crossed over to my other hand.'

> how little pleasure will life afford me – its lapses of shade are so wide so gloomy. Its gleams of sunshine so limited & dim – ![6]

Daphne understood that 'secrecy must be maintained. If anyone should ever discover about the play, read the hidden books, identify a living figure in one of their fictitious beings . . . there would be a catastrophe.' Secrecy had been Daphne's mode since childhood, and the Brontë method of preserving secrecy by writing in minuscule lettering was familiar to her, because it was a habit of Kicky's.

Part way through writing, Daphne discovered that Winifred Gerin was writing a biography of Branwell too. Whipped on by her publisher, she wrote flat out from New Year 1960 until the last week of March in a race to finish first, which she won.

While Daphne was exorcising her demons in *Branwell*, Peter was submitting to his. On 21 February 1960, he wrote to Dolly from 20 Cadogan Court:

> I can't forgive myself for not writing sooner to thank you for your letter which I so loved getting. Ill health is the weak excuse – my wife's as well as my own. Writing has become a fearful effort. Even if it wasn't so I couldn't write of my beautiful mother of whom I knew so little and remember so much, and whose bony structure and much of whose temperament I believe I inherited. You gave me treasured glimpses of her and of my splendid father, from your own memories.
>
> Now, 'melancholy has marked me for her own.' No more photographs please. We leave here soon, I don't know where for. Thank you so very much for writing.

The pain of the mind control victim is the hopeless pain of the abused. Peter will have felt 'betrayed, exploited and, worst of all, fooled', just as Forster noted Daphne did. Daphne's response, which I believe kept her going, was anger, for what lesser emotion would have galvanised her into writing the nightmare out of herself? Indeed, she transferred this emotion to Peter, writing to Nico:

> Being myself, constantly and for no earthly reason, a potential suicide, I don't think one does it from despair, but from anger – it's a hit out of THEM – THEM being, to the potential suicide everything ONE is not (for that

> particular minute). The violent feelings rising within can only be assuaged by greater violence, hence the train. The off-balance Self says to the mythical THEM, 'If this is what you're doing to me – Right, Here We Go.' A half-bottle of something would help to blot out responsibility, naturally, if obtainable.

In September 1959, Jack died. By then, Peter was himself a psychological and physical wreck: in a letter to Nico, Daphne alluded to 'the fixed look on his face and the shuffled step' at this time. In October, Peter's wife Peggy suffered a nervous breakdown. The following April, Peter walked off the platform at Sloane Square station to his death under a train – no 'awfully big adventure', no 'unfriendly seeker' required, surely no anger either, only the tearful remembrance of a little boy of four forced to walk the plank against his will by Captain Swarthy.

Peggy never recovered. She was taken in by her sister Alison and diagnosed with Huntington's chorea. She died a few years later in hospital. Because Huntington's chorea (now called Huntington's disease) is hereditary her three sons, Rivvy, George and Peter, decided never to have children in case the disease was passed down the line.

CHAPTER THREE

No escape

On the last day of March 1960, five days before Peter's suicide, Daphne wrote to Oriel,

> My own non-Branwell news is that Ellen is flying over in April, and I have promised to unveil a plaque to my grandfather outside the house in Great Russell Street (Doubleday offices). Ellen insists on representing the firm! I don't know what I do; just pull a string, I suppose. I shan't make a speech!

The house in Great Russell Street had been Kicky and Emma's first home after they married in 1863. The ceremony had originally been scheduled for March, but Daphne had postponed it to put the finishing touches to *Branwell*. Peter died on Tuesday, 5 April. The inquest was held between 8 and 12 April. Daphne had no immediate writing commitments, no reason to remain in Cornwall, but there is no record of her being in London until the unveiling of the London County Council's blue plaque on the 22nd. Nico, his two sons and Trixy's son Gerald Millar also attended.

This was terrifically symbolic, coming so soon after Peter's death. For, as Daphne wrote to Nico on 12 April, 'To me personally [Peter] stood for every thought I had ever had about Grandpapa, or Kicky as we used to call him at Café Royal lunches, sometimes with weeping nostalgia.'

Tommy died five years later, aged 68, after which Daphne moved out of Menabilly to Kilmarth, the dower house on the Menabilly estate, where she lived more or less alone until the end of her life in 1989. In her last few years with Tommy, she had found unexpected unity with him in her research for *Castle Dor*, a novel begun by Q and completed by Daphne after his death, which returns the legend of Tristan to modern Cornwall.

Henceforth she discarded any notion of transmuting lives in her fiction. 'Imagination, yes,' she wrote to Oriel Malet, 'but so that you use it to perceive the past, and re-live it . . .' She had been re-reading *Peter Ibbetson*. She was back to the source, untainted by Jim.

It was then, in her closeness to this ancient part of Cornwall, that she enjoyed her greatest 'unity within'. After *Castle Dor* (1962) came *The House on the Strand* (1969), and the non-fiction *Vanishing Cornwall* (1967), with photographs taken by her son. She was digging in, even became a member of the Nationalist Party of Cornwall, and in her final novel, *Rule Britannia* (1972), as an actress simply called Mad, she became the matriarch of all she surveyed in Cornwall.

Uncle Jim had not, however, been forgotten. *The House on the Strand* sprang from her musings about a professor who once lived at Kilmarth, who, she fancied, had dabbled in alchemy. The novel alludes to Peter Llewelyn Davies's suicide, and confirms that she alone knew the reason for it.

Professor Magnus Lane falls under a passing train as it rattles out of a tunnel. The hero, Dick Young, with whom Daphne identifies, realises how his death will seem –

> It would make sense to no one. Not to the police, or to his many friends, or to anyone but myself. I should be asked why a man of his intelligence had wandered close to a railway line on a summer's evening at dusk, and I should have to say that I did not know. I did know.

In the mid-1970s Oriel Malet woke up to the fact that something was once again deeply wrong with Daphne. It had something to do with 'the world of her imagination' and with 'something very early in her life . . . Daphne was so anxious to conceal her fears,' she wrote.

About this time Daphne built an altar in a tiny room in the basement of Kilmarth, which I saw for myself, and which was as likely to carry 'the horn that echoes from the further hill, discordant, shrill', as a Christian cross. There had been beauty and mystery, but in the end she knew that hers could never be a joyous 'other world'. The transmutation could not be undone.

> Last night the other world came much too near,
> And with it fear.
> I heard their voices whisper me from sleep,
> And could not keep
> My mind upon the dream, for still they came,

Calling my name,
The loathly keepers of the netherland
I understand.
My frozen brain rejects the pulsing beat;
My willing feet,
Cloven like theirs, too swiftly recognise
Without surprise.
The horn that echoes from the further hill,
Discordant, shrill,
Has such a leaping urgency of song,
Too loud, too long,
That prayer is stifled like a single note
In the parched throat.
How fierce the flame! How beautiful and bright
The inner light
Of that great world which lives within our own,
Remote, alone.
Let me not see too soon, let me not know,
And so forgo
All that I cling to here, the safety side
Where I would hide.
Old Evil, loose my chains and let me rest
Where I am best.
Here is muted shade of my own dust.
But if I must
Go wandering in Time and seek the source
Of my life force,
Lend me your sable wings, that as I fall
Beyond recall,
The sober stars may tumble in my wake,
For Jesus' sake.[1]

Oriel watched aghast as her friend degenerated during the last years of her life. Daphne began to complain of pains like drug withdrawal, of fears, panic. 'What is happening, I ask myself?' she pleaded in a letter to Oriel in 1981. Not long afterwards she made an attempt on her life, a failed overdose of sleeping pills.

I met Daphne two years before she died. I had approached her with an idea for an illustrated memoir,[2] an ensemble of autobiographical writings and extracts from her Cornish fiction. Meeting her at home on the Menabilly estate, studying her life and visiting the places in Cornwall in which so many of her stories are set, I could not help but be spellbound by her imagination.

I was warned that I might find her frail. In fact, she was delightful. After lunch she took her regular walk down 'Thrombosis Hill', while I took some photographs of the house and garden, exquisite views over the sea. On her return she surprised me in the garden, and mistook me for someone else. What struck me was the look of blind panic on her face. I thought, how appropriate for the author of 'Don't Look Now'. Later I read Oriel Malet's *Letters*, where Oriel wrote: 'On my last visit I had been struck by her look of panic, almost of fear, as she came to the door to greet me. Clutching my arms, she whispered, "Oh, Oriel, Oriel . . ."'

Is this the nightmare vision to take away from *Captivated*, or do we remember the sudden feelings of absolute bliss – Daphne's peak experience, her 'vision of Life and Death, and everything in harmony' one summer's afternoon at Kilmarth, or earlier on a summer's night when she slept out in the Menabilly garden and sensed all around her another time, another world, and immersed herself in the memory of it in 'The Pool'? The 'relief' of that vision had been so tremendous 'that something seemed to burst inside her heart and everything that had ever been fell into place'. Again, a sense of harmony had been key, as it had been for her grandfather. The joy was indescribable, and the *surge* of feeling, almost like a drug, 'like wings about her in the air, lifted her and she had all knowledge. That was it – *the invasion of knowledge*.'

Uncle Jim had promised the boys knowledge. 'One by one as you swung monkey-wise from branch to branch in the wood of make-believe you reached the tree of knowledge,' he told them. But he was never clear what that knowledge was. Michael 'half knew it', Jim told the students at St Andrews in 1922 – 'He half knows something of which they know nothing – the secret that is hidden in the face of the Mona Lisa. As I see him, life is so beautiful to him that its proportions are monstrous.'

But it was all words, no truth. His 'knowledge' was just another cultist piece of nonsense that would extend his control. Even the secret behind the Mona Lisa's smile wasn't his. It was taken from *Peter Ibbetson*. Mary, Duchess of Towers gazes at the picture in the Louvre when Peter sees her for the last time.

Jim's problem was that while Kicky knew, and George and Michael, and certainly Daphne knew, he never could know, he never won Kicky's secret, he never experienced the 'other-world intimacy' that Kicky described in his novel. Nor could he, because his dislocation from the world of reality was born not of innocence and a longing desire to know, like Kicky's dreaming 'boy', but of psychosis.

One piece of very important knowledge did come out of all his trickery, however, and it was the truth that empowered him, namely that ultimate power rests on the boundary between two worlds – the world of reality and the world of illusion. If you can make people believe something of your dream, it will cleave to their perception of reality and they will cede control to you. Every magician, every religious leader, every politician knows this to be true. Barrie proved it.

It is the nature of the poet and the writer of fiction that he or she stands on this boundary between two worlds. Daphne's optimism and faith in the power of texts, to reveal a sense of what both she and her grandfather believed exists just beyond the bounds of human perception, remained undimmed to the end, even as she made her own preparations for death.

The day before she died, she telephoned Oriel, herself a writer. It was a short call.

'Are you writing?' she asked.

As Oriel hesitated, Daphne insisted: 'You must, it's the only way!'

Appendix

On *Women in Love*

Before he met Mary Cannan, D. H. Lawrence had an interest in J. M. Barrie. Barrie's Tommy novels had a profound effect on him. Equally, Barrie regarded *Sons and Lovers* (1913) as 'the best novel that he had read by any of the younger men'.[1] Lawrence must have been fascinated to get the low-down on Barrie from his ex-wife. And he might also have questioned her on Captain Scott. For *Women in Love*,* so significant in the movement of ideas in the twentieth century, denounced the heroic values that Scott embodied, and Mary knew at first hand all about Barrie's relationship with the explorer.

I discovered Lawrence's interest in Scott from Lawrence scholar Peter Fjågesund, whom I happened to meet in 2005 while he was writing an article about *Women in Love*. When I realised that Mary had been close to Lawrence from the time he was writing this novel, it got me reading it again and marvelling at certain parallels with the story of Barrie which I was researching.

Women in Love analyses Britain at a pivotal point in its history, and Lawrence was no different from any writer in being on the lookout for real characters and relationships and images that would stimulate the expression of his ideas. Immediately I was struck by the similarity between the central relationship between Gerald Crick and Rupert Birkin, described by Lawrence as a 'blood brotherhood', and that of Gerald du Maurier and Jim Barrie – both relationships oddly inimical. There is a 'strange enmity between the two men, that was very near to love . . . They burned with each other, inwardly. This they would never admit. They intended to keep their relationship a casual free-and-easy friendship, they were not going to be so unmanly and unnatural as to allow any heart-

* Completed in 1916 but not published until 1920.

burning between them. They had not the faintest belief in deep relationship between men and men, and their disbelief prevented any development of their powerful but suppressed friendliness.'

I am not saying that Lawrence 'pegged' the fictional relationship on the real one, only that something like the same strange balance attended both, which Lawrence expresses beautifully.

At the same time, Gerald Crick bears a physical resemblance to Captain Scott – his beauty is 'a northern kind . . . like light refracted from snow', his hair 'was a glisten like sunshine refracted through crystals of ice'. The polar imagery, as Fjågesund pointed out to me, suggested a link with Scott rather than Gerald du Maurier. But that was as it should be. For any reference to a real relationship was unimportant to Lawrence, except as a stimulus. No exactness was required, as it was by Barrie in his psycho-fiction and alchemic texts. There is a discussion in *Women in Love* about whether art can have a relation to anything outside, and Lawrence, I am sure, went with the character who says: 'You *must not* confuse the relative work of action with the absolute world of art. That you *must not do*.' Lawrence's italics, and one in the eye for Jim. If Lawrence and Frieda, and Mary and Cannan, ever spoke about Barrie, which they must have, such themes were bound to have been a point of discussion, for Barrie's art was soon to fall to that of the new post-war writers, led by Lawrence, Virginia Woolf, Joyce, Pound and Eliot.

Nevertheless, much that was of deep interest to Barrie appears in *Women in Love*. The central 'otherworldly' image of Willey Water in *Women in Love* has the same function as the mermaids' lagoon in *Peter Pan*. There is also a significant death in Lawrence's novel, and there is the same idea that death is an awfully big adventure – 'To die is . . . a joy, a joy of submitting to that which is greater than the known; namely, the pure unknown,' writes Lawrence.

More broadly, Barrie's longing for sensual knowledge is Lawrence's notion of 'knowledge . . . not in your head but in the blood . . . when the mind and the known world is drowned in darkness – everything must go . . . Then you find yourself in a palpable body of darkness, a demon.' Rupert Birkin, who is held by many critics to be speaking largely for Lawrence in the novel, is called 'a dreadful Satanist' for believing this. His is the sensuous, hypnoid absenteeism from conscious life, which so characterised Barrie's relationship with the boys when they were very young. 'You've got to learn not-to-be, before you can come into being,' says Birkin. 'You've got to lapse out before you can know what sensual reality is, lapse into unknowingness, and give up your volition.' This was what Jim 'achieved' with young George, or vice versa. For Birkin, 'the will, the ego, is what is between us and the otherworld', and hypnosis is of course the best way to remove the will in order to facilitate the transition to 'the otherworld'. The fictional ideas are not borrowed, but they are sympathetic.

Again, in line with these ideas and the du Maurier myth, Birkin wants sex 'to revert to the level of the other appetites, to be regarded as a functional process, not as fulfilment. He wanted a further conjunction, where man had being and woman had being, two pure beings, each constituting the freedom of the other, balancing each other like two poles of one force, like two angels, or two demons.'

But there is one character who enters towards the end of the novel, and who puts all these parallels in the shade, because he is so obviously 'pegged' on Barrie. Crick and his girlfriend Gudrun, and Birkin and Gudrun's sister, Ursula, go on holiday together to a hotel at Innsbruck and meet 'a short, energetic-looking man with large moustaches', Herr Loerke, the very image of Barrie, a kind of Austrian version of him attired in loden suit with knee breeches (a nice comical twist – what *would* he have looked like!) –

> The little man with the boyish figure and the round, full, sensitive-looking head, and the quick, full eyes, like a mouse's [who] held himself aloof . . . His body was slight and unformed, like a boy's, but his voice was mature, sardonic, its movement had the flexibility of essential energy, and of a mocking penetrating understanding . . .

Loerke, like Barrie, keeps to himself, but can also be irrepressibly playful, as Barrie was in games with the boys. He is a mischievous trickster, 'a maker of disturbing jokes, with the blank look of inorganic misery behind his buffoonery', as Joyce Carol Oates described him (exactly like Barrie), then suddenly silent again.[2]

When we first see him, he is reciting something in the Cologne dialect, and Gudrun (the Sylvia figure), though she cannot understand a word of it, is 'spellbound watching him'; from the moment he sees her, Loerke wants to make a connection with her.

The holiday is a nightmare of dissolution and dirty disloyalties, just like the holiday Mary and Cannan shared with Barrie and Sylvia during Christmas 1908, at another fashionable Alpine resort, Caux. It was the year after Arthur died, the same year Jim discovered that Scott was having an affair with Cannan's girlfriend, Kathleen Bruce, and it was during the Caux holiday that Gilbert's affair with Mary, facilitated by Sylvia, took flight. If Mary and Cannan had discussed anything about Barrie, they would have discussed Caux.

We know that people are going to be horribly hurt emotionally on the holiday in Lawrence's novel, as indeed they were at Caux. Mackail caught the atmosphere well:

> Pity all this gay extravaganza at the Grand Hotel at Caux. There is something dreadfully ominous about. Something, behind the laughter, as cold and relentless as the Alps.

So, there were negative energies flying around in Caux just as there are at Innsbruck in Lawrence's novel.

Loerke likes men (he has a companion upstairs in his room, a man called Leitner), and has an affair with a beautiful woman. He finds his way menacingly into Gudrun's soul as Barrie found his way into Sylvia's, introducing her to his relentlessly nihilistic interpretation of 'the world as illusion', lifting her up above the masses with his social hatred, discovering the cruel and the cynical at her core, making her feel apart and above the pitiful world. It is the same philosophy as Tommy's, a fictional character who fascinated Lawrence.

Readers of *Women in Love* will already have recognised that my text of Barrie's subjugation of Sylvia is virtually interchangeable with Loerke's of Gudrun, though again there are interesting departures. Gudrun's partner Crick, who is completely destroyed emotionally by Gudrun's apparent infidelity with Loerke, as Arthur Davies was by Sylvia's, does not die like Arthur, but like Captain Oates, the man on Scott's expedition: he goes out into the blizzard and is not seen again. Lawrence jumbles things up, because replicating life in his fiction is definitely not his purpose.

But if one's interest is not principally in Lawrence's novel, but in Barrie, his choosing to jumble up the lives of his characters with the Scott story makes one feel even more convinced that the emotional tapestry was woven out of thread spun by Mary and Cannan in their conversations with the author. Mary Ansell knew the truth about Jim, and Lawrence's fictional picture of Barrie is uniquely authentic.

How interesting, therefore, that Lawrence discusses fratricide in the novel, which, I have argued, was the root cause of Barrie's compulsive personality. Gerald Crick as a boy accidentally killed his brother, and it ruined his life –

> 'They were quite boys,' said Ursula. 'I think it is one of the most horrible stories I know . . .'
>
> 'And isn't it horrible too to think of such a thing happening to one when one was a child, and having to carry the responsibility of it all through one's life. Imagine it, two boys playing together – then this comes upon them, for no reason whatever – out of the air . . .'
>
> 'Perhaps there was an unconscious will behind it,' said Ursula.

In the context of Lawrence's novel, this is almost a gratuitous piece of emotional baggage for Crick to bear, yet it is discussed in great detail. Lawrence cannot let it go, and in the end he attaches it to one of his most important themes: Lawrence 'did not believe that there was any such thing as accident. It all hung together, in the deepest sense.'

If her influence on *Women in Love* was Mary Ansell's one attempt to put the truth across about 'the tragedy in Barrie's life . . .tragedy not to be treated humorously or lightly', which, she wrote to Peter Davies, 'Mr Mackail has ignored', then Lawrence is unforgiving of Barrie. The destruction of the du Mauriers was no accident; blame rested with Barrie. Which is, of course, precisely the line Lawrence took with Mary after hearing of Michael's death.

> J. M. Barrie has a fatal touch for those he loves. They die.

Bibliography

George du Maurier: novels

Peter Ibbetson, 1891.
Trilby, 1894.
The Martian, 1897.

J. M. Barrie: selected works

Better Dead, 1888.
When a Man's Single, 1888.
A Window in the Thrums, 1889.
An Edinburgh Eleven, 1889.
My Lady Nicotine, 1890.
The Little Minister, 1891.
Ibsen's Ghost, 1891 (play, prod. 1891, privately printed 1931).
Richard Savage, 1891 (play, with H. B. Marriot-Watson).
Walker, London, 1892 (play, prod. 1892).
Professor's Love Story, 1892 (play, prod. 1892).
Jane Annie, 1893 (play with A. Conan Doyle).
Margaret Ogilvy, 1896.
Sentimental Tommy, 1896.
Tommy and Grizel, 1900.
Quality Street, 1902 (play).
The Little White Bird, 1902.
The Admirable Crichton, 1902 (play).
Peter Pan: Or The Boy Who Would Not Grow Up, 1904 (play).
Alice Sit-By-The-Fire, 1905 (play, prod. in London and New York 1905).
Peter Pan in Kensington Gardens, 1906.

What Every Woman Knows, 1908 (play).
The Twelve-Pound Look, 1910 (play).
Peter and Wendy, 1911.
The Will, 1913 (play).
A Kiss For Cinderella, 1916 (play).
Dear Brutus, 1917 (play).
A Well-Remembered Voice, 1918 (play).
Mary Rose, 1920 (play).
Shall We Join The Ladies? 1921 (play).
Courage, 1922.
Neil and Tintinnabulum, 1925.
Representative Plays, 1926.
The Plays of J. M. Barrie (including first publication of *Peter Pan*), 1928.
The Greenwood Hat, 1930.
The Boy David, 1936 (play).
Uniform Edition of the Works and Plays, 1913–1937.

Daphne du Maurier: works

The Loving Spirit, 1931.
I'll Never Be Young Again, 1932.
The Progress of Julius, 1933.
Gerald: A Portrait, 1934.
Jamaica Inn, 1936.
The Du Mauriers, 1937.
Rebecca, 1938.
Come Wind, Come Weather, 1940.
Frenchman's Creek, 1941.
Hungry Hill, 1943.
The Years Between, 1945.
The King's General, 1946.
September Tide (play, prod. in London 1948) 1949.
The Parasites, 1949.
The Young George du Maurier: A Selection of his Letters, 1860–1867 (ed.), 1951.
My Cousin Rachel, 1951.
The Apple Tree, 1952.
Happy Christmas, 1953.
Mary Anne, 1954.

Early Stories, 1955.
The Scapegoat, 1957.
The Breaking Point, 1959.
The Infernal World of Branwell Brontë, 1960.
Castle Dor, 1962.
The Glass Blowers, 1963.
The Flight of the Falcon, 1965
Vanishing Cornwall, 1967 and 2007.
The House on the Strand, 1969.
Not After Midnight, 1971.
Rule Britannia, 1972.
Golden Lads: Anthony Bacon, Francis and their Friends, 1975.
The Winding Stair: Francis Bacon, his Rise and Fall, 1976.
Echoes from the Macabre, 1976.
Myself When Young, 1977.
The Rendezvous and Other Stories, 1980.
The Rebecca Notebook and Other Memories, 1981.
Classics from the Macabre, 1987.
Enchanted Cornwall, 1989.

Note: many years ago *The Breaking Point* collection was broken up and some of the stories distributed among other of Daphne's short story collections. A new edition is, however, now planned.

Notes

Part I

Chapter 1

Peter's suicide: a case to answer

1 Interview with Andrew Birkin.
2 Pamela Maude, *World's Away* (1964).
3 *The Story of J.M.B.* (1941).
4 Interview in *The Times*.
5 Letter from Barrie to Ella Terriss (Hicks), 11 December 1905.
6 *The Morgue*. Unpublished history of the du Maurier and Llewelyn Davies family, compiled in six volumes by Peter Llewelyn Davies between 1945 and 1951. The history is to be found at The Walter Beinecke Jnr Collection at Yale University as part of the Beinecke Rare Book and Manuscript Library.
7 David Edwards, *Express Newspapers*, 28 October 2004.
8 Interview with Andrew Birkin, 5 December 1975.
9 Peter Llewelyn Davies, among loose papers found by Andrew Birkin.
10 In Daphne du Maurier, *Myself When Young* (1977).
11 Letter from Jack Llewelyn Davies to his brother Peter, January 1950.
12 Ibid.
13 Letter from Mary Ansell to Peter Llewelyn Davies, 14 April 1941.
14 Letter from Nico Llewelyn Davies to Andrew Birkin, 29 December 1975.
15 Ibid.
16 James Harding, *Gerald du Maurier* (1989).

Chapter 2
What is the secret?

1 Judith Cook, *Daphne* (1991).
2 Letter from Nico Llewelyn Davies to Andrew Birkin, 29 January 1976.
3 Flavia Leng, *Daphne du Maurier* (1994).
4 Oriel Malet, *Letters from Menabilly* (1993).
5 Letter from Daphne du Maurier to Nico Llewelyn Davies, 12 April 1960.
6 Malet, *Letters.*
7 Letter from Daphne du Maurier to her publisher, Victor Gollancz in 1955.
8 Margaret Forster, *Daphne du Maurier* (1993).
9 Letter from Daphne du Maurier to Maureen Baker-Munton, 4 July 1957, the full text of which is published in *Daphne du Maurier* by Margaret Forster (1993).
10 Judith Cook, *Daphne* (1991).
11 Interview with Andrew Birkin.
12 Letter from Nico Llewelyn Davies to Andrew Birkin, 5 January 1976.
13 Daphne du Maurier, ed., *The Young George du Maurier: a selection of his letters* (1951).
14 Letter from Roger Senhouse to Nico Llewelyn Davies.

Part II
Chapter 1
Du Maurier dreamers

1 Introduction by Daphne du Maurier to George du Maurier, *Peter Ibbetson*, Gollancz 1969 edition.
2 Leonée Ormond, *George du Maurier* (1969).
3 George du Maurier, *Peter Ibbetson* (1891).
4 Daphne du Maurier's Introduction to her grandfather's first novel, *Peter Ibbetson* (1891).

Chapter 2
Peak experience

1 George du Maurier, *Trilby* (1894).
2 Article by Val Prinsep in *The Magazine of Art*.
3 Thomas Armstrong in L. M. Lamont's *A Memoir* (1912).
4 Albert Vandam, *The Trail of Trilby* (1895).
5 After first publication, the threat by Whistler of a libel case led to the removal of his character from the story.
6 George du Maurier, *Trilby* (1894).
7 Vandam, *The Trail of Trilby* (1895).
8 Interview with Robert Sherard in *McClure's Magazine*, in 1895.
9 Daphne du Maurier, *The Du Mauriers* (1937).
10 Papers in the du Maurier Archive, Exeter University.
11 Tatar, *Spellbound*.
12 Colin Wilson, *New Pathways in Psychology: Maslow and the Post-Freudian Revolution* (1972).
13 Felix Moscheles, *In Bohemia with du Maurier* (1896).

Chapter 3
The boy who hated mothers

1 W. A. Darlington, *J. M. Barrie* (1938).
2 Preface by J. M. Barrie to R. M. Ballantyne, *The Coral Island* (1913 edn).
3 Darlington, *J. M. Barrie*.
4 Letter from J. M. Barrie to Mrs Oliver, 21 December 1931.
5 J. M. Barrie, *The Greenwood Hat* (1930).
6 J. M. Barrie, *Courage* (1922).
7 J. M. Barrie, *The Greenwood Hat*.
8 J. A. Hammerton, *Barrie: The Story of a Genius* (1929).
9 The notebooks of J. M. Barrie (housed in The Walter Beinecke Jnr Collection at Yale University).
10 J. M. Barrie's Preface to *The Coral Island*.
11 Ibid.
12 Denise Winn, *The Manipulated Mind* (1983).
13 J. M. Barrie, *Tommy and Grizel* (1900).
14 Darlington, *Barrie*.

15 Ibid.
16 Denis Mackail, *The Story of J.M.B.* (1941).
17 J. M. Barrie, *Auld Licht Idylls* (1888).
18 Barrie, *Margaret Ogilvy*.
19 Barrie, *The Greenwood Hat*.
20 Barrie, *Margaret Ogilvy*.

Chapter 4
Nervous breakdown

1 Luke Ionides, *Memories* (1925).
2 Daphne du Maurier (ed.), *The Young George du Maurier: A Selection of his Letters* (1951).
3 Thomas Armstrong in L. M. Lamont, *A Memoir* (1912).
4 Daphne du Maurier in the Preface to *The Young George du Maurier* (1951).
5 From a poem written by George du Maurier for Tom Armstrong in 1859.

Part III
Chapter One
Impotent and ambitious

1 Barrie, *The Greenwood Hat*.
2 Ibid.
3 Jerome K. Jerome, *My Life and Times* (1925).
4 Barrie, *The Greenwood Hat*.
5 Jerome, *My Life and Times* (1925).
6 Ibid.
7 Barrie, *The Greenwood Hat* (1930).
8 Jerome, *My Life and Times* (1925).
9 Barrie, *The Greenwood Hat*.
10 J. M. Barrie, *Tommy and Grizel* (1900).

Chapter Two
Gateway to Neverland

1 Philip V. Allingham, Lakehead University, Ontario, Canada. Article in 'The Victorian Web'.

2 Introduction by Daphne du Maurier to George du Maurier, *Peter Ibbetson* (1969 edn).

3 David Lodge, *Author, Author* (2004).

4 C. C. Hoyer Millar, *George du Maurier and Others* (1937).

5 Introduction to George du Maurier, *Peter Ibbetson* and *Trilby* (1947 edn).

6 *Journal de l'Anatomie et de la Physiologie* and *Revue Philosophique*.

7 *The Recreations of the Rabelais.*

8 Jerome Schneck, 'Henry James, George du Maurier, and Mesmerism', *International Journal of Clinical and Experimental Hypnosis*, vol. 26, no. 2 (1978), pp. 76–80.

9 Lodge, *Author, Author*.

10 *The Complete Notebooks of Henry James*, edited by Leon Edel and Lyall H. Powers (1987).

11 Henry James, 'The Middle Years' (1893), in *Terminations* (1895).

12 Leonée Ormond, *George du Maurier* (1969).

13 J. B. and J. L. Gilder, *Trilbyana* (1895).

14 Daphne du Maurier, *Enchanted Cornwall* (1989).

15 John Masefield, introduction to an omnibus edition of three novels by George du Maurier, published in 1947.

16 M. H. Spielmann and L. S. Layard, *Kate Greenaway* (1905).

17 F. L. Marcuse, *Hypnosis: Fact and Fiction* (1963).

18 Denise Winn, *The Manipulated Mind* (1983, 2000).

19 F. L. Marcuse, *Hypnosis: Fact and Fiction* (1959).

20 Letters from Daphne du Maurier to Oriel Malet, 3 January 1962 and 5 August 1963.

21 Letter to Oriel Malet, 6 August 1969.

22 'The Archduchess', in *The Breaking Point* (1960).

23 Ibid.

Chapter Three
Purloining the key

1 J. M. Barrie, *The Little Minister* (1891).
2 Luke Ionides, *Memories* (1925).
3 Notebook of J. M. Barrie.
4 Introduction to *Jane Annie* by Clifton Coles. Gilbert and Sullivan Archive.
5 Arthur Conan Doyle, *Memories and Adventures* (1924).
6 Andrew Birkin, *J. M. Barrie and the Lost Boys* (1979).
7 Mary Ansell, *Dogs and Men* (1924).

Chapter Four
The corruption of Neverland

1 C. C. Hoyer Millar, *George du Maurier and Others* (1937).
2 Leonée Ormond, *George du Maurier* (1969).
3 Colin Wilson, *Dreaming to Some Purpose: The Autobiography of Colin Wilson* (2004).
4 Daphne du Maurier archive, Exeter University.
5 'The Historical Context of Analytical Psychology', in *The Cambridge Companion to Jung*, Cambridge University Press, edited by Polly Young-Eisendrath and Terence Dawson (1997). Other writers listed are Hugo, Balzac, Dickens, Poe, Dostoevsky, Maupassant, Nietzsche, Wilde, R. L. Stevenson and Proust.

Part IV
Chapter One
Slipping into madness

1 Philip V. Allingham, Lakehead University, Ontario, Canada.
2 Elaine Showalter, Introduction to *Trilby* (1995 edn).
3 Jon Savage, *Teenage: the Creation of Youth 1875–1945* (2007).
4 John Masefield, Introduction to the George du Maurier omnibus (1947).
5 Jacqueline Rose, *The Case of Peter Pan* (1984).
6 Maria M. Tatar, *Spellbound: Studies on Mesmerism and Literature* (1978).

7 Felix Moscheles, *In Bohemia with Kicky* (1896).
8 C. C. Hoyer Millar, *George du Maurier and Others* (1937).

Chapter Two
Predator and victim

1 J. M. Barrie, *The Little White Bird* (1902).
2 Letter to Tom Armstrong.

Chapter Three
Philanderings in the park

1 *The Morgue*.

Chapter Four
The boy in the box

1 Letter from Nico Llewelyn Davies to Andrew Birkin, 29 January 1976.
2 Letter from Nico Llewelyn Davies to Andrew Birkin, 24 March 1976.
3 J. M. Barrie, *Peter and Wendy* (1911).
4 Ibid.
5 'The Alibi', in Daphne du Maurier, *The Breaking Point* (1959).
6 Ibid.
7 'The Little Photographer', in Daphne du Maurier, *The Breaking Point*.
8 J. M. Barrie, *The Little White Bird* (1902).
9 Jacqueline Rose, *The Case of Peter Pan* (1984).

Chapter Five
Flying Uncle Jim to Neverland

1 'The Lordly Ones', in *The Breaking Point*.
2 Mary Ansell, *Dogs and Men* (1924).
3 Barrie, *The Little White Bird*.

4 Robert Todd Carroll, *The Skeptic's Dictionary* (2003).
5 *Peter and Wendy* (1911).
6 Nicholas Spanos in Carroll, *The Skeptic's Dictionary*.
7 Rose, *The Case of Peter Pan*.
8 C. G. Jung, *Memories, Dreams, Reflections*.
9 F. L. Marcuse, *Hypnosis: Fact and Fiction* (1959).
10 Interview by Andrew Birkin with Norma Douglas Henry, March 1978.

Chapter Six
Peter Pan, a demon boy

1 Denis Mackail, *The Story of J.M.B.*
2 David Crane, *Scott of the Antarctic: A Life of Courage and Tragedy in the Extreme South* (2005).
3 J. M. Barrie, Introduction to *The Personal Journals of Captain R. F. Scott, RN, CVO* (1912).
4 Crane, *Scott of the Antarctic*.
5 *The Morgue* and Nico's letters to Andrew Birkin.

Chapter Seven
Sylvia's Will

1 Diana Farr, *Gilbert Cannan: A Georgian Prodigy* (1978).
2 Mackail, *The Story of J.M.B.*
3 Letter from Jack Llewelyn Davies to his brother Peter, 1952.
4 Letter from Nico Llewelyn Davies to Andrew Birkin, 1975.
5 Letter from Nico Llewelyn Davies to Andrew Birkin, 1970.
6 Mackail, *The Story of J.M.B.*
7 Letter from J. M. Barrie to Turley Smith, 10 July 1911.

Part V
Chapter One
Looking for Michael

1 Interview with Andrew Birkin.
2 Dedication to *Peter Pan* (1928).

3 Daphne du Maurier, 'Neil and Tintinnabulum', published in *The Flying Carpet*, edited by Cynthia Asquith (1925).
4 Letter from J. M. Barrie to Turley Smith, 10 May 1911.
5 Letter from Nico Llewelyn Davies to Andrew Birkin, 24 November 1975.
6 *The Morgue*.
7 J. M. Barrie, Dedication to *Peter Pan* (edn 1928).
8 Interview with Andrew Birkin, March 1978.
9 J. M. Barrie, *Peter and Wendy* (1911).
10 Neville Cardus, *Autobiography* (1947).

Chapter Two
Daphne's Initiation

1 Daphne du Maurier, *Gerald: A Portrait* (1934).
2 BBC Radio interview, 1973.
3 Daphne du Maurier, *Gerald: A Portrait* (1934).
4 BBC Radio interview, 1973.
5 Forster, *Daphne du Maurier*.
6 Interview in the *Hampstead and Highgate Express* (1973).
7 Daphne du Maurier, *Gerald: A Portrait* (1934).
8 Interview in the *Hampstead and Highgate Express* (1973).
9 Flavia Leng, *Daphne du Maurier*.
10 Daphne du Maurier, *Myself When Young* (1970).
11 Angela du Maurier, *It's Only the Sister*.
12 *Daily Mail*, 20 May, 2007.
13 Daphne du Maurier, 'A Borderline Case', *Not After Midnight* (1971).
14 Daphne du Maurier, *Myself When Young* (1970).
15 Nina Auerbach, *Daphne du Maurier: Haunted Heiress* (2000).

Chapter Three
Michael's suicide

1 Alison Lurie, *New York Review of Books*, 6 February 1975.
2 'Neil and Tintinnabulum', in *The Flying Carpet*, edited by Cynthia Asquith (1925).
3 Nico's letter to Andrew Birkin, 11 December 1975.

Part VI
Chapter One
Rebecca, a demon boy

1 Andrew Birkin, *J. M. Barrie and the Lost Boys* (1979).
2 Letter from Lawrence to Mary Ansell, 4 July 1921.
3 Charlie Chaplin, *My Trip Abroad* (1922).
4 Janet Dunbar, *J. M. Barrie: The Man behind the Image* (1970).
5 Daphne du Maurier, *Enchanted Cornwall* (1989).
6 Daphne du Maurier, *Gerald: A Portrait* (1934).
7 Daphne du Maurier, *Enchanted Cornwall*.
8 Daphne du Maurier, *The Du Mauriers* (1937).
9 Daphne du Maurier, *Enchanted Cornwall*.
10 Ibid.
11 Letter from Daphne du Maurier to Ellen Doubleday, 10 December 1947.
12 Letter from Daphne du Maurier to Oriel Malet, 31 January 1962.
13 Letter from Daphne du Maurier to Oriel Malet, 6 June 1955.
14 Flavia Leng, *Daphne du Maurier* (1994).
15 Ibid.
16 Ibid.
17 Letter from Daphne du Maurier to Maureen Baker-Munton, 4 July 1957.
18 Forster, *Daphne du Maurier*.
19 Letter from Daphne du Maurier to Maureen Baker-Munton, 4 July 1957.
20 Forster, *Daphne du Maurier*.

Chapter Two
Breakdown and suicide

1 Oriel Malet, *Letters from Menabilly* (1993).
2 Letter from Daphne du Maurier to Maureen Baker-Munton, 4 July 1957.
3 Nico Llewelyn Davies to Nanny Hodgson, 13 October 1957.
4 Published by Weidenfeld in 1994.
5 Margaret Forster, *Daphne du Maurier* (1993).

6 Quoted in Daphne du Maurier, *The Infernal World of Branwell Brontë* (1960).

Chapter Three
No escape

1 'Another World', in Daphne du Maurier *Enchanted Cornwall*.
2 Daphne du Maurier, *Enchanted Cornwall*.

Appendix

1 Letters 11, 225n.
2 Joyce Carol Oates, 'Lawrence's Götterdammerung: the Apocalyptic Vision of *Women in Love*', in Harold Broom (ed.), *D. H. Lawrence* (1986).

Acknowledgements and Sources

My special thanks to Kits Browning, Daphne du Maurier's son and literary executor, and his wife, Hacker, for their support in the research and writing of this book, and for reading and commenting on the text. The work Kits and his sisters, Tessa (Lady Montgomery) and Flavia (Lady Leng), have done since their mother died in 1989 is largely responsible for the vigorous interest in the writings of Daphne du Maurier among a new generation of readers today, as well as among scholars throughout the world.

My sincere gratitude to the writer and film maker Andrew Birkin, without whose permission to quote, from interviews he undertook in the 1970s with people who knew J. M. Barrie, this book would have been immeasurably poorer. Andrew Birkin generously shares his own archive of research through the web site jmbarrie.co.uk.

Unexpected pearls are the diaries and letters of Dorothea Parry, later Lady Ponsonby of Shulbrede, and those of Arthur, Lord Ponsonby, her husband, which provide a fascinating glimpse of life from the late-nineteenth century to the mid-twentieth century, and a special insight into the lives of both the du Maurier and Llewelyn Davies families. I am truly grateful to Laura Ponsonby and Kate Russell for their kind permission to consult this material and quote from it.

Among the many libraries and archives consulted I would in particular like to thank the following for their assistance: Timothy Young, Associate Curator of Modern Books and Manuscripts, Beinecke Rare Book and Manuscript Library, Yale University; Geraldine Gardner and Christine Faunch, the du Maurier Archive, Special Collections, University of Exeter; Colin Harris, Special Collections, New Bodleian Library, University of Oxford; Scott Polar Research Institute, University of Cambridge; Special Collections, Edinburgh Library; and the Institute of Psychiatry, London.

Thanks to Tessa Montgomery and Flavia Leng for reading the manuscript and to Laura Duguid for her permission to quote from the letters of the Llewelyn Davies family.

Thanks to the following for the wisdom of their advice on a wide range of topics: Colin Wilson, David Lodge, Hans Kuyper, Peter Fjagesund, Rupert Tower, Sally Beauman, Margaret Forster, Anthony Sheil, Penelope Hoare, Parisa Ebrahimi and Beth Humphries.

It is with gratitude that I refer readers to the sections entitled 'Notes and References', 'Works of George du Maurier, J.M. Barrie and Daphne du Maurier' and 'Sources', which serve as a guide to the many books and articles I consulted in the course of my research. I would like to thank the publishers and authors of works quoted.

I am grateful to the following for supplying photographs: Andrew Birkin; Kits Browning; Samuel French Ltd; Christine De Poortere, Peter Pan Project Director Great Ormond Street Hospital Children's Charity; Christine Faunch, the du Maurier archive; and Laura Ponsonby and Kate Russell of Shulbrede Priory.

Finally I would like to thank my wife, Dee, for her help and encouragement.

Sources

Ansell, Mary *Dogs and Men* (Duckworth, 1923).

Asquith, Cynthia (Ed.) *The Flying Carpet* (Partridge, 1926).

Auerbach, Nina *Daphne du Maurier: Haunted Heiress* (University of Pennsylvania Press, 2000).

Barker, Juliet *The Brontes* (Weidenfeld, 1994).

Barrie, J M: the Works. These are now mostly out of print, but may be purchased via abebooks.co.uk. Hodder and Stoughton was his principal UK publisher.

Birkin, Andrew *J M Barrie and the Lost Boys* (Constable, 1979; Yale UP, 2003).

Blake, George *Barrie and the Kailyard School* (Barker, 1951).

Cardus, Neville *Autobiography* (Collins, 1947).

Carrington, Dora *Letters and Diaries*, edited by David Garnett (Cape, 1975).

Chaplin, Charlie *My Trip Abroad* (Hurst & Blackett, 1922).

Connolly, Joseph *Jerome K. Jerome* (Orbis, 1982).

Cook, Judith *Daphne* (Bantam Press, 1991).

Crane, David *Scott of the Antarctic: A Life of Courage and Tragedy in the Extreme South* (HarperCollins, 2005).

Darlington, William Aubrey *J M Barrie* (Blackie, 1938).

du Maurier, Angela *It's Only the Sister* (Peter Davies, 1950).

du Maurier, Daphne: the Works. These are published in the UK by Gollancz (Orion) in hardcover and by Virago in paperback.

du Maurier, George: the Works. These are now mostly out of print, but may be purchased via abebooks.co.uk.

Dunbar, Janet *The Man and the Image* (Collins, 1970).

Farr, Diana *Gilbert Cannan: A Georgian Prodigy* (Chatto & Windus, 1978).

Forster, Margaret *Daphne du Maurier* (Chatto & Windus, 1993).

Frazer, James *The Golden Bough* (Macmillan, 1949).

Gilder, Jeanette *Trilbyana* (Critic, 1895).

Goethe, Johann Wolfgang Von *Faust* (Dent, 1908).

Green, Roger Lancelyn *Fifty Years of Peter Pan* (Peter Davies, 1954).

— *J.M. Barrie* (Bodley Head, 1960).

Guillain, Georges *Jean-Martin Charcot, 1825–1893* (Pitman, 1959).

Hammerton, John Alexander *Barrie: The Story of a Genius* (Sampson Low, 1929).

Harding, James *Gerald du Maurier* (Hodder & Stoughton, 1989).

Holroyd, Michael *Lytton Strachey: A Biography* (Penguin, 1971).

Ionides, Alexander Constantine. *Ion: A Grandfather's Tale* (Cuala Press, 1927).

Ionides, Luke *Memories* (Herbert Clarke,1925).

James, Henry *Terminations* (Heinemann, 1893)..

Jerome K. Jerome, *My Life and Times* (Hodder and Stoughton, 1925).

Jung, C.G. *Memories, Dreams, Reflections* (Vintage, 1960).

— *The Archetypes of the Unconscious* (Routledge, 1959).

— *Two Essays on Analytical Psychology* (Princeton/Bollinger, 1966).

— *Psychology and Alchemy* (Routledge, 1953).

Lamont, L.M. (Ed.) *Thomas Armstrong, C.B.: A Memoir* (Martin Secker, 1912).

Lawrence, D.H. *Women in Love* (Martin Secker, 1920).

Leng, Flavia *Daphne du Maurier* (Mainstream, 1994).

Lodge, David *Author, Author* (Secker & Warburg, 2004).

Mackail, Denis *The Story of J.M.B.* (Peter Davies, 1941).

Malet, Oriel *Letters from Menabilly: Portrait of a Friendship* (Orion, 1993).

Marcuse, F.L. *Hypnosis, Fact and Fiction* (Penguin, 1959).

Maude, Pamela *Worlds Away* (Heinemann, 1964).

Millar, C.C. Hoyer *George du Maurier and Others* (Cassell, 1937).

Moore, Harry T *The Priest of Love: A Life of D.H. Lawrence* (Penguin, 1976).

Moscheles, Felix *In Bohemia with George du Maurier* (T.F. Unwin, 1896).

Ormond, Leonee *George du Maurier* (Routledge, 1969).

Otto, Walter *Dionysus, Myth and Cult* (Spring, 1991).

Pearsall, Ronald *Conan Doyle* (Weidenfeld, 1977).

Pearson, Hesketh *Conan Doyle* (Methuen, 1943).

Rabelais, Francois *Gargantua and Pantagruel* (Penguin, 1955).

Rabelais Club, *The Recreations of the Rabelais* (Members only limited editions – 3 vols, 1881–1888).

Raine, Kathleen *Blake and Tradition* (Routledge, 1969).

Rose, Jacqueline *The Case of Peter Pan* (Macmillan, 1984).

Schneck , James 'Henry James, George du Maurier, and *Mesmerism: The International Journal of Clinical and Experimental Hypnosis* (1978, Vol. XXVI, No.2, 76-80).

Scott, Robert Falcon *The Personal Journals of Captain R F Scott, RN, CVO, on his Journey to the South Pole* (John Murray, 1923).

Showalter, Elaine *Introduction to: Trilby* (Oxford UP, 1995).

Spielmann, M.H. and Layard, L.S. *Kate Greenaway* (Black, 1905).

Stevenson, R.L. *Dr Jekyll and Mr Hyde* (Penguin, 1979).

Tatar, Maria M *Spellbound: Studies on Mesmerism and Literature* (New Jersey: Princeton UP, 1978).

Savage, Jon *Teenage: the Creation of Youth 1875–1945* (Chatto & Windus, 2007).

Van Druten, John *Behold, we Live* (Gollancz, 1932).

Vandam, Albert *The Trail of Trilby* (1895).

Wilson, Colin *New Pathways in Psychology: Maslow and the Post-Freudian Revolution* (Gollancz 1972).

— *The Occult* (Hodder & Stoughton, 1971).

— *Dreaming to some Purpose* (Century, 2004).

Winn, Denise *The Manipulated Mind, Brainwashing, Conditioning and Indoctrination* (Malor, 2000).

Young-Eisendrath, Polly and Dawson, Terence (Ed.) *The Historical Context of Analytical Psychology* (Cambridge UP, 1997).

Index